ANDROID™ 6 FOR PRO
AN APP-DRIVEN APPRO
DEITEL® DEVELOPER SERIES

PAUL DEITEL • HARVEY DEITEL • ALEXANDER WALD
DEITEL & ASSOCIATES, INC.

PRENTICE HALL

Boston • Columbus • Indianapolis • New York • San Francisco
Amsterdam • Capetown • Dubai • London • Madrid • Milan • Munich
Paris • Montreal • Toronto • Deli • Mexico City • São Paulo • Sydney
Hong Kong • Seoul • Singapore • Taipei • Tokyo

Deitel® Series Page

Deitel® Developer Series

Android™ 6 for Programmers: An App-Driven Approach, 3/E
C for Programmers with an Introduction to C11
C++11 for Programmers
C# 2015 for Programmers
iOS® 8 for Programmers: An App-Driven Approach with Swift™
Java™ for Programmers, 3/E
JavaScript for Programmers
Swift™ for Programmers

How To Program Series

Android™ How to Program, 3/E
C++ How to Program, 9/E
C How to Program, 7/E
Java™ How to Program, Early Objects Version, 10/E
Java™ How to Program, Late Objects Version, 10/E
Internet & World Wide Web How to Program, 5/E
Visual Basic® 2015 How to Program, 7/E
Visual C#® 2015 How to Program, 6/E

Simply Series

Simply C++: An App-Driven Tutorial Approach
Simply Java™ Programming: An App-Driven Tutorial Approach
(continued in next column)

(continued from previous column)
Simply C#: An App-Driven Tutorial Approach
Simply Visual Basic® 2010: An App-Driven Approach, 4/E

CourseSmart Web Books

`www.deitel.com/books/CourseSmart/`

C++ How to Program, 8/E and 9/E
Simply C++: An App-Driven Tutorial Approach
Java™ How to Program, 9/E and 10/E
Simply Visual Basic® 2010: An App-Driven Approach, 4/E
Visual Basic® 2015 How to Program, 6/E
Visual Basic® 2012 How to Program, 5/E
Visual C#® 2015 How to Program, 5/E
Visual C#® 2012 How to Program, 4/E

LiveLessons Video Learning Products

`www.deitel.com/books/LiveLessons/`

Android™ 6 App Development Fundamentals, 3/e
C++ Fundamentals
Java™ Fundamentals, 2/e
C# 2015 Fundamentals
C# 2012 Fundamentals
iOS® 8 App Development Fundamentals, 3/e
JavaScript Fundamentals
Swift™ Fundamentals

To receive updates on Deitel publications, Resource Centers, training courses, partner offers and more, please join the Deitel communities on

- Facebook®—`facebook.com/DeitelFan`
- Twitter®—`@deitel`
- Google+™—`google.com/+DeitelFan`
- YouTube™—`youtube.com/DeitelTV`
- LinkedIn®—`linkedin.com/company/deitel-&-associates`

and register for the free *Deitel® Buzz Online* e-mail newsletter at:

`www.deitel.com/newsletter/subscribe.html`

To communicate with the authors, send e-mail to:

`deitel@deitel.com`

For information on *Dive-Into® Series* on-site seminars offered by Deitel & Associates, Inc. worldwide, write to us at `deitel@deitel.com` or visit:

`www.deitel.com/training/`

For continuing updates on Pearson/Deitel publications visit:

`www.deitel.com`
`www.pearsonhighered.com/deitel/`

Visit the Deitel Resource Centers that will help you master programming languages, software development, Android and iOS app development, and Internet- and web-related topics:

`www.deitel.com/ResourceCenters.html`

To the Android software-engineering community:

For creating and evolving a platform that challenges app developers to test the limits of their imagination

Paul and Harvey Deitel

Trademarks

Contents

2   Welcome App   35

3   Tip Calculator App   73

Introducing `GridLayout`, `EditText`, `SeekBar`, *Event Handling,* `NumberFormat`,
Customizing the App's Theme and Defining App Functionality with Java

4   Flag Quiz App   105

Fragments, Menus, Preferences, Explicit Intents, Handler, AssetManager, Tweened
Animations, Animators, Toasts, Color State Lists, Layouts for Multiple Device
Orientations, Logging Error Messages for Debugging

5   Doodlz App   165

2D Graphics, Canvas, Bitmap, Accelerometer, SensorManager, Multitouch Events,
MediaStore, Printing, Android 6.0 Permissions, Gradle

6   Cannon Game App   217

Manual Frame-By-Frame Animation, Graphics, Sound, Threading,
SurfaceView and SurfaceHolder, Immersive Mode and Full-Screen

7   WeatherViewer App   256

REST Web Services, AsyncTask, HttpUrlConnection, *Processing JSON Responses,*
JSONObject, JSONArray, ListView, ArrayAdapter, ViewHolder *Pattern,*
TextInputLayout, FloatingActionButton

8   Twitter® Searches App   286

*SharedPreferences, SharedPreferences.Editor, Implicit Intents, Intent
Choosers, RecyclerView, RecyclerView.Adapter, RecyclerView.ViewHolder,
RecyclerView.ItemDecoration*

9 Address Book App   322

FragmentTransactions and the Fragment Back Stack, SQLite, `SQLiteDatabase`,
`SQLiteOpenHelper`, `ContentProvider`, `ContentResolver`, `Loader`, `LoaderManager`,
Cursor and GUI Styles

10   Google Play and App Business Issues   384

Preface

Welcome to the dynamic world of Android *smartphone* and *tablet* app development with the Android Software Development Kit (SDK), the Java™ programming language and the rapidly evolving Android Studio Integrated Development Environment (IDE). Many of the Android techniques we present also apply to Android Wear and Android TV app development, so after reading this book, you'll be well prepared to investigate developing apps for these platforms.

Android 6 for Programmers: An App-Driven Approach presents leading-edge mobile computing technologies for professional software developers. In our *app-driven approach*, we present concepts in *complete working Android apps*, rather than using code snippets. Chapters 2–9 each present one app. Each chapter begins with an introduction to the app, an app test-drive showing one or more sample executions and an overview of the technologies we used to build the app. Then we present a detailed source-code walkthrough. All of the source code is available at

```
http://www.deitel.com/books/AndroidFP3
```

We recommend that you view each app's source code in the IDE as you read the chapter.

The opportunities for Android app developers are enormous. Sales of Android devices and app downloads have been growing exponentially. The first-generation Android phones were released in October 2008. According to IDC, after the first three months of 2015, Android had 78% of the global smartphone market share, compared to 18.3% for Apple, 2.7% for Microsoft and 0.3% for Blackberry.[1] Over one billion Android devices shipped in 2014 alone.[2] At the 2015 Google I/O conference, Google announced that in the prior 12 months there had been 50 billion app installs from Google Play™—Google's marketplace for Android apps.[3] Fierce competition among popular mobile platforms and carriers is leading to rapid innovation and falling prices. In addition, competition among the hundreds of Android device manufacturers is driving hardware and software innovation within the Android community.

Copyright Notice and Code License

---

1. http://www.idc.com/prodserv/smartphone-os-market-share.jsp.
2. http://www.businessinsider.com/android-1-billion-shipments-2014-strategy-analytics-2015-2.
3. http://bit.ly/2015GoogleIOKeynote.

expressed or implied, with regard to these programs or to the documentation contained in this book. The authors and publisher shall not be liable in any event for incidental or consequential damages in connection with, or arising out of, the furnishing, performance, or use of these programs. You're welcome to use the apps in the book as shells for your own apps, building on their existing functionality (within the terms of the preceding license). If you have any questions, contact us at `deitel@deitel.com`.

Intended Audience

We assume that you're a Java programmer with object-oriented programming experience. We also assume that you're familiar with XML—as you'll see, Android projects contain many XML files, though you'll often interact with them through editors that hide much or all of the XML from you. We use only complete, working apps, so if you don't know Java but have object-oriented programming experience in a C-based language such as C++, C#, Swift or Objective-C you should be able to master the material quickly, learning a good amount of Java and Java-style object-oriented programming along the way.

This book is *not* a Java tutorial. If you're interested in learning Java, you may want to check out our publications:

- *Java for Programmers, 3/e* (`http://www.deitel.com/books/javafp3`)
- *Java Fundamentals, 2/e* LiveLessons videos. These videos are available to `Safari-BooksOnline.com` subscribers and may be purchased from `Informit.com` and `Udemy.com`. Visit `http://www.deitel.com/LiveLessons` for subscription and purchase links.
- *Java How to Program, 10/e* (`http://www.deitel.com/books/jhtp10`; ISBN# 0-13-380780-0)

If you're not familiar with XML, many free online tutorials are available, including:

- `http://www.ibm.com/developerworks/xml/newto`
- `http://www.w3schools.com/xml/default.asp`
- `http://bit.ly/DeitelXMLBasics`
- `http://bit.ly/StructureXMLData`

Features

Here are some of this book's key features:

App-Driven Approach. Chapters 2–9 each present one completely coded app—we discuss what the app does, show screenshots of the app in action, test-drive it and overview the technologies and architecture we used to build it. Then we build the app's GUI and resource files, present the complete code and do a detailed code walkthrough. We discuss the programming concepts and demonstrate the functionality of the Android APIs used in the app.

Android 6 SDK. We cover various new Android 6 Software Development Kit (SDK) features.

Android Studio IDE. The free Android Studio (based on IntelliJ IDEA Community Edition) is now Google's preferred IDE for Android app development (the original Android development tools were based on the Eclipse IDE). Android Studio, combined with the free Android Software Development Kit (SDK) and the free Java Development Kit (JDK), provide all the software you'll need to create, run and debug Android apps, export them for distribution (e.g., upload them to Google Play™) and more. See the Before You Begin section after this Preface for download and installation instructions for all this software.

Material Design. With Android 5, Google introduced its new Android look-and-feel, based on their material design specification:

```
http://www.google.com/design/spec/material-design/introduction.html
```

In the specification, Google overviews the goals and principles of material design, then provides details on animation techniques, styling on-screen elements, positioning elements, uses of specific user-interface components, user-interaction patterns, accessibility, internationalization and more. Google now uses material-design principles in its mobile and browser-based apps.

Material design is a massive topic. In this book, we focus on the following aspects of material design:

- Using Android's built-in `Material` *themes*—these give Android's built-in user-interface components a look-and-feel that's consistent with material design principles.

- Using built-in Android Studio *app templates*—these are designed by Google to adhere to material design principles.

- Using *user-interface components*, as appropriate, that are recommended by the material design guidelines for specific purposes, such as `FloatingActionButtons`, `TextInputLayouts` and `RecyclerViews`.

In addition to Google's material design specification, you may want to read the book *Android User Interface Design: Implementing Material Design for Developers, 2nd Edition*:

```
http://bit.ly/IanCliftonMaterialDesign
```

by our professional colleague and past *Android for Programmers* reviewer Ian Clifton. From Ian: "Google announced the material design guidelines in 2014, creating a design system that suggested how an app should look as well as behave. The goal was to provide a design framework that would improve the visual appearance of all apps and create a behavioral consistency that did not exist previously across apps. *Android User Interface Design: Implementing Material Design for Developers, 2nd Edition* covers material design in detail, making user-centered design, color theory, typography, interaction patterns and other aspects of design accessible to all developers."

Support and App Compatibility Libraries. A big challenge developers face when using new Android features is backward compatibility with earlier Android platforms. Many new Android features are now introduced via support libraries. These enable you to use new features in apps targeting current and past Android platforms. One such library is the App-Compat library. Android Studio's app templates have been updated to use the AppCompat library and its themes, enabling the new apps you create to run on most Android devices. By creating apps with the AppCompat library from the start, you avoid having to reimplement your code if you decide to support older Android versions to target a wider audience.

In addition, at the 2015 Google I/O developer conference, Google introduced the Android Design Support Library

```
http://android-developers.blogspot.com/2015/05/android-design-
      support-library.html
```

for using material design in Android 2.1 and higher. Material design support also is built into most of Android Studio's app templates.

REST Web Services and JSON. Chapter 7 presents the **Weather Viewer** app, which demonstrates how to invoke Representational State Transfer (REST) web services—in this case, the 16-day weather-forecast service from OpenWeatherMap.org. This web service returns the weather forecast in JavaScript Object Notation (JSON)—a popular text-based data-interchange format used to represent objects as key–value pairs of data. The app also use classes from the org.json package to process the web service's JSON response.

Android 6.0 Permissions. Android 6.0 has a new permissions model that's designed for a better user experience. Before Android 6.0, a user was required at installation time to grant in advance all permissions that an app would ever need, which often discouraged users from installing apps. With the new model, the app is installed without asking for any permissions. Instead, the user is asked to grant a permission only the first time the corresponding feature is used. Chapter 5 introduces the new permissions model and uses it to request permission from the user to store an image on the device's external storage.

Fragments. Starting with Chapter 4, we use Fragments to create and manage portions of each app's GUI. You can combine several fragments to create user interfaces that take advantage of tablet screen sizes. You also can easily interchange fragments to make your GUIs more dynamic, as you'll do in Chapter 9.

View-Holder Pattern, ListView and RecyclerView. The apps in Chapters 7–9 each display scrollable lists of data. Chapter 7 presents the data in a ListView and introduces the view-holder pattern, which improves scrolling performance by reusing GUI components that scroll off-screen. With ListViews, using the view-holder pattern is recommended. Chapters 8 and 9 each present a list of data in the more flexible and more efficient RecyclerView for which the view-holder pattern is required.

Printing. We demonstrate class PrintHelper (Chapter 5) from Android's printing framework for printing from an app. Class PrintHelper provides a user interface for selecting a printer, has a method for determining whether a given device supports printing and provides a method for printing a Bitmap. PrintHelper is part of the Android Support Library.

Immersive Mode. The status bar at the top of the screen and the menu buttons at the bottom can be hidden, allowing your apps to fill more of the screen. Users can access the status bar by swiping down from the top of the screen, and the system bar (with the back button, home button and recent apps button) by swiping up from the bottom.

Testing on Android Smartphones, Tablets and the Android Emulator. For the best app-development experience and results, you should test your apps on actual Android smartphones and tablets. You can still have a meaningful experience using just the Android emulator (see the Before You Begin section); however, it's processor intensive and can be slow, particularly with games that have a lot of moving parts. In Chapter 1, we mention some Android features that are not supported on the emulator.

Cloud Test Lab. Google is working on a new *Cloud Test Lab*—an online site for testing your apps across a wide range of devices, device orientations, locales, spoken languages and network conditions. You'll be able to run automated tests and receive detailed reports containing screenshots and videos of your app in action, as well as error logs to help you find problems and improve your apps. For more information and to sign up to be notified when Cloud Test Lab becomes available, visit:

```
http://developers.google.com/cloud-test-lab/
```

Android Wear and Android TV. Android Wear runs on smart watches. Android TV runs directly on some smart TVs and media players that you can connect to your TV (typically via HDMI cables). Many Android techniques we present also apply to Android Wear and Android TV app development. The Android SDK provides Android Wear and Android TV emulators, so you can test your apps for these platforms, even if you don't have devices. To learn more about these technologies from the developer perspective, visit:

```
http://developer.android.com/wear/index.html
```

for Android Wear and

```
http://developer.android.com/tv/index.html
```

for Android TV.

Multimedia. The apps use a range of Android multimedia capabilities, including graphics, images, frame-by-frame animation and audio.

Uploading Apps to Google Play. Chapter 10, Google Play and App Business Issues, discusses Google Play and setting up a merchant account so you can sell your apps. You'll learn how to prepare apps for submission to Google Play, find tips for pricing your apps, and find resources for monetizing them with in-app advertising and in-app sales of virtual goods. You'll also find resources for marketing your apps. Chapter 10 can be read after Chapter 1.

Pedagogic Features

Syntax Shading. For readability, we syntax shade the code, similar to Android Studio's use of syntax coloring. Our syntax-shading conventions are as follows:

```
comments appear like this
keywords appear like this
constants and literal values appear like this
all other code appears like this
```

Code Highlighting. We emphasize the key code segments in each program by enclosing them in light blue rectangles.

Using Fonts for Emphasis. We use various font conventions:

- The defining occurrences of key terms appear bold blue for easy reference.
- On-screen IDE components appear in **bold Helvetica** (e.g., the **File** menu).
- Program source code appears in Lucida (e.g., int x = 5;).

In this book you'll create GUIs using a combination of visual programming (point-and-click, drag-and-drop) and writing code. We use different fonts when we refer to GUI elements in program code versus GUI elements displayed in the IDE:

- When we refer to a GUI component that we create in a program, we place its class name and object name in a Lucida font—e.g., Button saveContactButton.

- When we refer to a GUI component that's part of the IDE, we place the component's text in a **bold Helvetica** font and use a plain text font for the component's type—e.g., "the **File** menu" or "the **Run** button."

Using the > Character. We use the > character to indicate selecting a menu item from a menu. For example, we use the notation **File > New** to indicate that you should select the **New** menu item from the **File** menu.

Source Code. All of the book's source code is available for download from

```
http://www.deitel.com/books/AndroidFP3
```

Documentation. All the Android documentation you'll need to develop Android apps is available at

```
http://developer.android.com
```

An overview of Android Studio is available at

```
http://developer.android.com/tools/studio/index.html
```

Chapter Objectives. Each chapter begins with a list of learning objectives.

Figures. Numerous tables, source-code listings and screenshots are included.

Software Engineering. We stress program clarity and performance, and we concentrate on building well-engineered, object-oriented software.

Index. We include an extensive index for reference. The page number of the defining occurrence of each key term is highlighted in bold blue.

Working with Open-Source Apps

The numerous free, open-source Android apps available online are excellent resources for learning Android app development. We encourage you to download open-source apps and read their source code to understand how they work.

Caution: The terms of open-source licenses vary considerably. Some allow you to use the app's source code freely for any purpose, while others stipulate that the code is available for personal use only—not for creating for-sale or publicly available apps. **Be sure to read the licensing agreements carefully. If you wish to create a commercial app based on an open-source app, you should consider having an intellectual-property attorney read the license; be aware that these attorneys charge significant fees.**

Android 6 App-Development Fundamentals LiveLessons Video Training Products

Our *Android 6 App-Development Fundamentals* LiveLessons videos show you what you need to know to start building robust, powerful Android apps with Android 6, the Java™ programming language and Android Studio. Included are approximately 16–20 hours of expert training synchronized with *Android 6 for Programmers: An App-Driven Approach*. For additional information about Deitel LiveLessons video products, visit

```
http://www.deitel.com/livelessons
```

or contact us at deitel@deitel.com. You also can access our LiveLessons videos if you have a subscription to SafariBooksOnline.com. For a free 10-day trial, register at

```
http://www.safaribooksonline.com/register
```

Join the Deitel & Associates, Inc. Social Networking Communities

To receive updates on this and our other publications, new and updated apps, online Resource Centers, instructor-led on-site training courses and more, join the Deitel social networking communities on

- Facebook®—http://facebook.com/DeitelFan
- LinkedIn®—http://bit.ly/DeitelLinkedIn
- Twitter®—http://twitter.com/deitel
- Google+™—http://google.com/+DeitelFan
- YouTube®—http://youtube.com/DeitelTV

and subscribe to the *Deitel® Buzz Online* newsletter

```
http://www.deitel.com/newsletter/subscribe.html
```

Contacting the Authors

We'd sincerely appreciate your comments, criticisms, corrections and suggestions for improvement. Please address all questions and other correspondence to

```
deitel@deitel.com
```

We'll respond promptly and post corrections and clarifications as Android evolves at:

```
http://www.deitel.com/books/AndroidFP3
```

and on Facebook, LinkedIn, Twitter, Google+ and the *Deitel® Buzz Online*.
    Visit http://www.deitel.com to

- download code examples
- check out the growing list of online programming Resource Centers
- receive updates for this book, subscribe to the free *Deitel® Buzz Online* e-mail newsletter at http://www.deitel.com/newsletter/subscribe.html
- receive information on our *Dive Into® Series* instructor-led programming-language training courses offered at customer sites worldwide.

Acknowledgments

Thanks to Barbara Deitel for long hours devoted to this project—she created all of our Android Resource Centers and patiently researched hundreds of technical details.

We appreciate the efforts and 20-year mentorship of our friend and professional colleague Mark L. Taub, Editor-in-Chief of the Pearson Technology Group. Mark and his team publish all of our professional books and LiveLessons video products. Michelle Housley recruited distinguished members of the Android community to review the manuscript. We selected the cover art and Chuti Prasertsith designed the cover. John Fuller manages the production of all of our Deitel Developer Series books.

We thank Michael Morgano, a former colleague of ours at Deitel & Associates, Inc., now an Android developer at PHHHOTO, who co-authored the first editions of this book and our book, *iPhone for Programmers: An App-Driven Approach*. Michael is an extraordinarily talented software developer.

Finally, we thank Abbey Deitel, former President of Deitel & Associates, Inc., and a graduate of Carnegie Mellon University's Tepper School of Management where she received a B.S. in Industrial Management. Abbey managed the business operations of Deitel & Associates, Inc. for 17 years, along the way co-authoring a number of our publications, including the previous editions' versions of Chapters 1 and 10.

Reviewers of the Content from Android 6 for Programmers: An App-Driven Approach *and* Android How to Program *Recent Editions*

We'd like to thank the following professionals and academics who reviewed this book and/or its previous editions. They scrutinized the text and the code and provided countless suggestions for improving the presentation: Paul Beusterien (Principal, Mobile Developer Solutions), Eric J. Bowden, COO (Safe Driving Systems, LLC), Tony Cantrell (Georgia Northwestern Technical College), Ian G. Clifton (Independent Contractor, Android App Developer and author of *Android User Interface Design: Implementing Material Design for Developers, 2nd Edition*), Daniel Galpin (Android Advocate and author of *Intro to Android Application Development*), Jim Hathaway (Application Developer, Kellogg Company), Douglas Jones (Senior Software Engineer, Fullpower Technologies), Charles Lasky (Nagautuck Community College), Enrique Lopez-Manas (Lead Android Architect, Sixt, and Computer Science Teacher at the University of Alcalá in Madrid), Sebastian Nykopp (Chief Architect, Reaktor), Michael Pardo (Android Developer, Mobiata), Luis Ramirez (Lead Android Engineer at Reverb), Ronan "Zero" Schwarz (CIO, OpenIntents), Arijit Sengupta (Wright State University), Donald Smith (Columbia College), Jesus Ubaldo Quevedo-Torrero (University of Wisconsin, Parkside), Dawn Wick (Southwestern Community College) and Frank Xu (Gannon University).

Well, there you have it! *Android 6 for Programmers: An App-Driven Approach* will quickly get you started developing Android apps with Android 6 and Android Studio. We hope you enjoy reading the book as much as we enjoyed writing it!

Paul Deitel
Harvey Deitel

About the Authors

Paul Deitel, CEO and Chief Technical Officer of Deitel & Associates, Inc., is a graduate of MIT, where he studied Information Technology. He holds the Java Certified Programmer and Java Certified Developer designations and is an Oracle Java Champion. Paul was also named as a Microsoft® Most Valuable Professional (MVP) for C# in 2012–2014.

Through Deitel & Associates, Inc., he has delivered hundreds of programming courses worldwide to clients, including Cisco, IBM, Siemens, Sun Microsystems, Dell, Fidelity, NASA at the Kennedy Space Center, the National Severe Storm Laboratory, White Sands Missile Range, Rogue Wave Software, Boeing, SunGard, Nortel Networks, Puma, iRobot, Invensys and many more. He and his co-author, Dr. Harvey Deitel, are the world's best-selling programming-language textbook/professional book/video authors.

Dr. Harvey Deitel, Chairman and Chief Strategy Officer of Deitel & Associates, Inc., has over 50 years of experience in the computer field. Dr. Deitel earned B.S. and M.S. degrees in Electrical Engineering from MIT and a Ph.D. in Mathematics from Boston University—he studied computing in each of these programs before they spun off Computer Science departments. He has extensive college teaching experience, including earning tenure and serving as the Chairman of the Computer Science Department at Boston College before founding Deitel & Associates, Inc., in 1991 with his son, Paul. The Deitels' publications have earned international recognition, with translations published in Japanese, German, Russian, Spanish, French, Polish, Italian, Simplified Chinese, Traditional Chinese, Korean, Portuguese, Greek, Urdu and Turkish. Dr. Deitel has delivered hundreds of programming courses to corporate, academic, government and military clients.

Alexander Wald, a Deitel summer intern, helped us convert the book and our Android apps from Android 4.3 and 4.4 using Eclipse to Android 6 using Android Studio. Alexander is currently pursuing a B.S. in Computer Science at Worcester Polytechnic Institute with a minor in Electrical Engineering. He became interested in mathematics and the sciences at an early age and has been writing code for approximately 9 years. He's motivated by his passion to be creative and innovative and his interest in sharing his knowledge with others.

About Deitel & Associates, Inc.

Deitel & Associates, Inc., founded by Paul Deitel and Harvey Deitel, is an internationally recognized authoring and corporate training organization, specializing in Android and iOS app development, computer programming languages, object technology and Internet and web software technology. The company's clients include many of the world's largest corporations, government agencies, branches of the military, and academic institutions. The company offers instructor-led training courses delivered at client sites worldwide on major programming languages and platforms, including Android app development, iOS app development, Swift™, Java™, C++, C, Visual C#®, Visual Basic®, Internet and web programming and a growing list of additional programming and software-development courses.

Through its 40-year publishing partnership with Prentice Hall/Pearson, Deitel & Associates, Inc., publishes leading-edge programming professional books, college textbooks and *LiveLessons* video courses. Deitel & Associates, Inc. and the authors can be reached at:

```
deitel@deitel.com
```

To learn more about Deitel's *Dive-Into*® *Series* Corporate Training curriculum, visit

```
http://www.deitel.com/training
```

To request a proposal for worldwide on-site, instructor-led training at your organization, send an e-mail to deitel@deitel.com.

   Individuals wishing to purchase Deitel books and *LiveLessons* video training can do so via links posted at http://www.deitel.com. Bulk orders by corporations, the government, the military and academic institutions should be placed directly with Pearson. For more information, visit

   http://www.informit.com/store/sales.aspx

Before You Begin

In this section, you'll set up your computer for use with this book. Google frequently updates the Android™ development tools, so before reading this section, check the book's website

        http://www.deitel.com/books/AndroidFP3

to see if we've posted an updated version of this Before You Begin section.

Software and Hardware System Requirements

To develop Android apps, you need a Windows®, Linux® or Mac® OS X® system. To view the latest operating-system requirements visit

        http://developer.android.com/sdk/index.html#Requirements

and scroll down to the **System Requirements** heading. We developed the apps in this book using the following software:

- Java SE 7 Software Development Kit

- Android Studio 1.4 Integrated Development Environment (IDE)

- Android 6 SDK (API 23)

You'll see how to obtain each of these in the following sections.

Installing the Java Development Kit (JDK)

Android requires the Java Development Kit version 7 (JDK 7). All Java language features in JDK 7 are supported in Android Studio, but the try-with-resources statement is supported only for Android platform versions with API levels 19 and higher. To download JDK 7 for Windows, OS X or Linux, go to

        http://www.oracle.com/technetwork/java/javase/downloads/java-
            archive-downloads-javase7-521261.html

Choose the appropriate 32-bit or 64-bit version for your computer hardware and operating system. Be sure to follow the installation instructions at

        http://docs.oracle.com/javase/7/docs/webnotes/install/index.html

Android does not yet support Java 8 language features, such as lambda expressions, new interface features and the stream APIs. You can use JDK 8 (as we did when developing this book's apps), provided that you use no Java 8 language features in your code.

Installing Android Studio

Google's Android Studio comes with the latest Android Software Development Kit (SDK) and is based on the popular Java IDE from JetBrains called IntelliJ® IDEA. To download Android Studio, go to

```
http://developer.android.com/sdk/index.html
```

and click the **Download Android Studio** button. When the download completes, run the installer and follow the on-screen instructions to complete the installation. If you previously installed an earlier Android Studio version, a **Complete Installation** window will appear at the end of the install process and give you the option to import your previous settings. At the time of this writing, Android Studio 1.4 is the current released version and Android Studio 1.5 is available as an early access release.

Using Early Access Releases

When building apps for release to Google Play or other app stores, it's best to use the currently released version of Android Studio. If you'd like to work with new features in Android Studio early access and beta releases, Google releases these versions in the so-called **Canary Channel** and **Beta Channel**. You can configure Android Studio to obtain updates from these channels. To update Android Studio to the latest early access or beta release:

1. Open Android Studio.
2. In the **Welcome to Android Studio** window, click **Configure**.
3. Click **Check for Update**.
4. In the **Platform and Plugin Updates** dialog, click the **Updates** link.
5. In the **Updates** dialog, select **Canary Channel** or **Beta Channel** from the drop-down to the right of the **Automatically check updates for** checkbox.
6. Click **OK**, then click **Close**.
7. Click **Check for Update** again.
8. The IDE will check for updates and tell you whether there are updates to apply.
9. Click **Update and Restart** to install the latest Android Studio version.

If you've previously opened a project in Android Studio and did not close the project, the IDE skips the **Welcome to Android Studio** window and opens the last project. In this case, you can access the **Updates** dialog on a Mac via **Android Studio > Check for Updates…** or on Windows/Linux via **Help > Check for Update…**. Then continue from *Step 4* above. For a Google's list of Android Studio Tips and Tricks, visit:

```
http://developer.android.com/sdk/installing/studio-tips.html
```

Configure Android Studio to Show Line Numbers

By default, Android Studio does not show line numbers next to the code that you write. To turn on line numbers to make it easier to follow our line-numbered code examples:

1. Open Android Studio ().

2. When the **Welcome to Android Studio** window appears, click **Configure**, then click **Settings** to open the **Default Settings** window. If the **Welcome to Android Studio** window does not appear, use the menus on Mac to select **Android Studio > Preferences…** or on Windows/Linux to select **File > Other Settings > Default Settings….**

3. Expand the **Editor > General** node and select **Appearance**, then ensure that **Show line numbers** is selected and click **OK**.

Configure Android Studio to Disallow Code Folding

By default, Android Studio's code-folding feature is enabled. This feature collapses multiple lines of code into a single line so you can focus on other aspects of the code. For example, all the `import` statements in a Java source-code file can be collapsed into a single line to hide them, or an entire method can be collapsed into a single line. You can expand these lines if you need to look at the code in detail. We disabled this feature in our IDE. If you wish to do so, follow the steps in the preceding section, then under **Editor > General > Code Folding** uncheck **Show code folding outline**.

Android 6 SDK

This book's code examples were written using Android 6. At the time of this writing, the Android 6 SDK was bundled with Android Studio. As new Android versions are released, the latest version will be bundled, which may prevent our apps from compiling properly. When you work with this book, we recommend using Android 6. You can install prior Android platform versions as follows:

1. Open Android Studio ( ).

2. When the **Welcome to Android Studio** window appears, click **Configure**, then click **SDK Manager** to display the **Android SDK** manager. If a project window appears rather than the **Welcome to Android Studio** window, you can access the **Android SDK** manager via **Tools > Android > SDK Manager**.

3. In the SDK Platforms tab, check the versions of Android you wish to install, then click **Apply** and **OK**. The IDE then downloads and installs the additional platform versions. The IDE also will help you keep your installed versions up-to-date.

Creating Android Virtual Devices (AVDs)

The Android SDK's Android emulator allows you to test apps on your computer rather than on an Android device—this is essential, of course, if you do not have Android devices. To do so, you create Android Virtual Devices (AVDs) that run in the emulator. The emulator can be slow, so most Android developers prefer testing on actual devices. Also, the emulator does not support various features, including phone calls, USB connections, headphones and Bluetooth. For the latest emulator capabilities and limitations, visit

```
http://developer.android.com/tools/devices/emulator.html
```

That page's **Using Hardware Acceleration** section discusses features that can improve emulator performance, such as using the computer's graphics processing unit (GPU) to increase graphics performance, and using the Intel HAXM (hardware accelerated execution manager) emulator to increase overall AVD performance. There are also faster third-party emulators, such as Genymotion.

After you've installed the Android Studio and before you run an app in the emulator, you must create at least one Android Virtual Device (AVD) for Android 6. Each AVD defines the characteristics of the device you wish to emulate, including

- its screen size in pixels

- its pixel density

- its screen's physical size

- the size of the SD card for data storage

- and more.

To test your apps for multiple Android devices, you can create AVDs that emulate each unique device. You also can use Google's new Cloud Test Lab

```
https://developers.google.com/cloud-test-lab/
```

a website that will enable you to upload your app and test it on many of today's popular Android devices. By default, Android Studio creates for you one AVD that's configured to use the version of Android bundled with the IDE. For this book, we use AVDs for two of Google's Android reference devices—the Nexus 6 phone and the Nexus 9 tablet—which run standard Android without the modifications made by many device manufacturers. It's easiest to create AVDs in Android Studio once you already have a project open in the IDE. For this reason, we'll show how to create the Android 6 AVDs in Section 1.9.

Setting Up an Android Device for Testing Apps

Testing apps on Android devices tends to be quicker than using AVDs. In addition, recall that there are some features you can test only on actual devices. To execute your apps on Android devices, follow the instructions at

```
http://developer.android.com/tools/device.html
```

If you're developing on Microsoft Windows, you'll also need the Windows USB driver for Android devices that you installed earlier in this Before You Begin section. In some cases on Windows, you may also need the manufacturer's device-specific USB drivers. For a list of USB driver sites for various device brands, visit

```
http://developer.android.com/tools/extras/oem-usb.html
```

Downloading the Book's Code Examples

The source code for *Android 6 for Programmers: An App-Driven Approach* is available for download at

```
http://www.deitel.com/books/AndroidFP3/
```

Click the **Download Code Examples** link to download a ZIP archive file containing the examples to your computer. Depending on your operating system, double click the ZIP file to unzip the archive or right click and select the option to extract the archive's contents. Remember where the extracted files are located on your system so you can access them later.

A Note Regarding Android Studio and the Android SDK

If you import one of our apps into Android Studio and it does not compile, this could be the result of updates to Android Studio or the Android platform tools. For such issues, please check Android questions and answers on StackOverflow at:

```
http://stackoverflow.com/questions/tagged/android
```

and the Google+ Android Development community at:

```
http://bit.ly/GoogleAndroidDevelopment
```

or write to us at

```
deitel@deitel.com
```

You've now installed all the software and downloaded the code examples you'll need to study Android app development with *Android 6 for Programmers: An App-Driven Approach* and to begin developing your own apps. Enjoy!

Introduction to Android

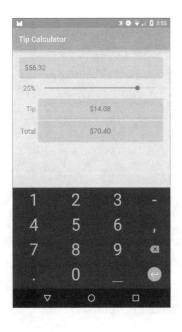

Objectives

In this chapter you'll be introduced to:

- The history of Android and the Android SDK.
- Google Play Store for downloading apps.
- The Android packages used in this book to help you create Android apps.
- A quick refresher of object-technology concepts.
- Key software for Android app development, including the Android SDK, the Java SDK and the Android Studio Integrated Development Environment (IDE).
- Important Android documentation.
- Test-driving an Android tip-calculator app in Android Studio.
- Characteristics of great Android apps.

1.1 Introduction

Welcome to Android app development! We hope that working with *Android 6 for Programmers: An App-Driven Approach* will be an informative, challenging, entertaining and rewarding experience for you.

This book is geared toward *Java programmers*. We use only complete working apps, so if you don't know Java but have object-oriented programming experience in another language, such as C#, Objective-C/Cocoa or C++ (with class libraries), you should be able to master the material quickly, learning a good amount of Java and Java-style object-oriented programming as you learn Android app development.

App-Driven Approach

We use an app-driven approach—new features are discussed in the context of complete working Android apps, with one app per chapter. For each app, we first describe it, then have you *test-drive* it. Next, we briefly overview the key Android Studio IDE (Integrated Development Environment), Java and Android SDK (Software Development Kit) technologies we use to implement the app. For apps that require it, we walk through designing the GUI using Android Studio. Then we provide the complete source-code listing, using line numbers, *syntax coloring* and *code highlighting* to emphasize the key portions of the code. We also show one or more screenshots of the running app. Then we do a detailed code walkthrough, emphasizing the new programming concepts introduced in the app. You can download the source code for all of the book's apps from

http://www.deitel.com/books/AndroidFP3/

1.2 Android—The World's Leading Mobile Operating System

Android device sales are growing quickly, creating enormous opportunities for Android app developers.

- The first-generation Android phones were released in October 2008. As of June 2015, Android had 82.8% of the global smartphone market share, compared to 13.9% for Apple and 2.6% for Microsoft.[1]

- Billions of apps have been downloaded from Google Play and more than one billion Android devices were shipped worldwide in 2014.[2]

- According to *PC World*, approximately 230 million tablets shipped in 2014 of which 67.3% were Android tablets, compared to 27.6% for iOS and 5.1% for Microsoft Windows.[3]

- Android devices now include smartphones, tablets, e-readers, robots, jet engines, NASA satellites, game consoles, refrigerators, televisions, cameras, health-care devices, smartwatches, automobile in-vehicle "infotainment" systems (for controlling the radio, GPS, phone calls, thermostat, etc.) and more.[4]

- A recent report says that mobile app revenue (across all mobile platforms) is expected to reach reach $99 billion by 2019.[5]

1.3 Android Features

Openness and Open Source

One benefit of developing Android apps is the openness of the platform. The operating system is *open source* and free. This allows you to view Android's source code and see how its features are implemented. You can contribute to Android by reporting bugs:

```
http://source.android.com/source/report-bugs.html
```

or by participating in the Open Source Project discussion groups

```
http://source.android.com/community/index.html
```

Numerous open-source Android apps from Google and others are available on the Internet (Fig. 1.1). Figure 1.2 shows you where you can get the Android source code, learn about the philosophy behind the open-source operating system and get licensing information.

---

1. http://www.idc.com/prodserv/smartphone-os-market-share.jsp.
2. http://www.cnet.com/news/android-shipments-exceed-1-billion-for-first-time-in-2014/.
3. http://www.pcworld.com/article/2896196/windows-forecast-to-gradually-grab-tablet-market-share-from-ios-and-android.html.
4. http://www.businessweek.com/articles/2013-05-29/behind-the-internet-of-things-is-android-and-its-everywhere.
5. http://www.telecompetitor.com/mobile-app-forecast-calls-for-revenue-of-99-billion-by-2019/.

URL	Description

`http://en.wikipedia.org/wiki/`
`   List_of_open_source_Android`
`   _applications`
	Extensive list of open-source apps, organized by category (e.g., games, communication, emulators, multimedia, security).

`http://developer.android.com/` `   tools/samples/index.html`	Instructions for accessing Google's sample apps for the Android platform; includes approximately 100 apps and games demonstrating various Android capabilities.
`http://github.com`	GitHub allows you to share your apps and source code and contribute to others' open-source projects.
`http://f-droid.org`	Hundreds of free and open-source Android apps.
`http://www.openintents.org`	Open-source libraries that can be used to enhance app capabilities.
`http://www.stackoverflow.com`	Stack Overflow is a question-and-answer website for programmers. Users can vote on each answer, and the best responses rise to the top.

Fig. 1.1 | Open-source Android app and library resource sites.

Title	URL
Get Android Source Code	`http://source.android.com/source/downloading.html`
Licenses	`http://source.android.com/source/licenses.html`
FAQs	`http://source.android.com/source/faqs.html`

Fig. 1.2 | Resources and source code for the open-source Android operating system.

The openness of the platform spurs rapid innovation. Unlike Apple's *proprietary* iOS, which is available only on Apple devices, Android is available on devices from dozens of original equipment manufacturers (OEMs) and through numerous telecommunications carriers worldwide. The intense competition among OEMs and carriers benefits customers.

Java

Android apps are developed with Java—one of the world's most widely used programming languages. Java was a logical choice for the Android platform, because it's powerful, free, open source and used by millions of developers. Experienced Java programmers can quickly dive into Android development, using Google's Android APIs (Application Programming Interfaces) and others available from third parties.

Java is object oriented and has access to extensive class libraries that help you quickly develop powerful apps. GUI programming in Java is *event driven*—in this book, you'll write apps that respond to various user-initiated *events* such as *screen touches*. In addition to directly programming portions of your apps, you'll also use the Android Studio IDE to conveniently drag and drop predefined objects such as buttons and textboxes into place on your screen, and label and resize them. Using Android Studio, you can create, run, test and debug Android apps quickly and conveniently.

Multitouch Screen

Android smartphones wrap the functionality of a mobile phone, Internet client, MP3 player, gaming console, digital camera and more into a handheld device with full-color *multitouch screens*. With the touch of your fingers, you can navigate easily between using your phone, running apps, playing music, web browsing and more. The screen can display a keyboard for typing e-mails and text messages and entering data in apps (some Android devices also have physical keyboards).

Gestures

The multitouch screens allow you to control the device with *gestures* involving one touch or multiple simultaneous touches (Fig. 1.3).

Gesture name	Physical action	Used to
Touch	Tap the screen once.	Open an app, "press" a button or a menu item.
Double touch	Tap the screen twice.	Zoom in on pictures, Google Maps and web pages. Tap the screen twice again to zoom back out.
Long press	Touch the screen and hold your finger in position.	Select items in a view—for example, checking an item in a list.
Swipe	Touch the screen, then move your finger in the swipe direction and release.	Flip item-by-item through a series, such as photos. A swipe automatically stops at the next item.
Drag	Touch and drag your finger across the screen.	Move objects or icons, or scroll through a web page or list.
Pinch zoom	Pinch two fingers together, or spread them apart.	Zoom in and out on the screen (e.g., resizing text and pictures).

Fig. 1.3 | Some common Android gestures.

Built-in Apps

Android devices come with several default apps, which may vary, depending on the device, the manufacturer or the mobile service carrier. Some apps commonly included are **Phone, Contacts, Messenger, Browser, Calculator, Calendar, Clock** and **Photos**.

Web Services

Web services are software components stored on one computer that can be accessed by an app (or other software component) on another computer over the Internet. With web services, you can create mashups, which enable you to rapidly develop apps by quickly *combining* complementary web services, often from different organizations and possibly other forms of information feeds. For example, 100 Destinations

```
http://www.100destinations.co.uk
```

combines the photos and tweets from Twitter with the mapping capabilities of Google Maps to allow you to explore countries around the world through the photos of others.

Programmableweb

```
http://www.programmableweb.com/
```

provides a directory of over 14,000 APIs and mashups, plus how-to guides and sample code for creating your own mashups. Figure 1.4 lists some popular web services. We use `OpenWeatherMap.org`'s weather web services in Chapter 7.

Web services source	How it's used
Google Maps	Mapping services
Twitter	Microblogging
YouTube	Video search
Facebook	Social networking
Instagram	Photo sharing
Foursquare	Mobile check-in
LinkedIn	Social networking for business
Netflix	Movie rentals
eBay	Internet auctions
Wikipedia	Collaborative encyclopedia
PayPal	Payments
Amazon eCommerce	Shopping for books and lots of other products
Salesforce.com	Customer Relationship Management (CRM)
Skype	Internet telephony
Microsoft Bing	Search
Flickr	Photo sharing
Zillow	Real-estate pricing
Yahoo Search	Search
WeatherBug	Weather

Fig. 1.4 | Some popular web services (`http://www.programmableweb.com/category/all/apis`).

1.4 Android Operating System

The Android operating system was developed by Android, Inc., which was acquired by Google in 2005. In 2007, the Open Handset Alliance™

```
http://www.openhandsetalliance.com/oha_members.html
```

was formed to develop, maintain and evolve Android, driving innovation in mobile technology and improving the user experience while reducing costs.

In this section, we walk through the evolution of the Android operating system, showing its versions and their key functionality. The Android marketplace is fragmented—many devices still use older Android versions—so as a developer it's helpful for you to be aware of the features introduced in each version.

Android Version Naming Convention

Each new version of Android is named after a dessert, going in alphabetical order (Fig. 1.5).

Android version	Name	Android version	Name
Android 1.5	Cupcake	Android 4.0	Ice Cream Sandwich
Android 1.6	Donut	Android 4.1–4.3	Jelly Bean
Android 2.0–2.1	Eclair	Android 4.4	KitKat
Android 2.2	Froyo	Android 5.0–5.1	Lollipop
Android 2.3	Gingerbread	Android 6.0	Marshmallow
Android 3.0–3.2	Honeycomb		

Fig. 1.5 | Android version numbers and the corresponding names.

1.4.1 Android 2.2 (Froyo)

Android 2.2 (also called Froyo, released in May 2010) introduced external storage, allowing you to store apps on an external memory device rather than just in the Android device's internal memory. It also introduced the Android Cloud to Device Messaging (C2DM) service. Cloud computing allows you to use software and data stored in the "cloud"—i.e., accessed on remote computers (or servers) via the Internet and available on demand—rather than having it stored on your desktop, notebook computer or mobile device. Cloud computing gives you the flexibility to increase or decrease computing resources to meet your resource needs at any given time, making it more cost effective than purchasing expensive hardware to ensure that you have enough storage and processing power for occasional peak levels. Android C2DM allows app developers to send data from their servers to their apps installed on Android devices, even when the apps are *not* currently running. The server notifies the apps to contact it directly to receive updated app or user data.[6] C2DM is now deprecated in favor of Google Cloud Messaging, which was introduced in 2012.

For information about additional Android 2.2 features—OpenGL ES 2.0 graphics capabilities, the media framework and more—visit

```
http://developer.android.com/about/versions/android-2.2-
    highlights.html
```

1.4.2 Android 2.3 (Gingerbread)

Android 2.3 (Gingerbread), released later in 2010, added more user refinements, such as a redesigned keyboard, improved navigation capabilities, increased power efficiency and more. It also added several developer features for communications (e.g., technologies that make it easier to make and receive calls from within an app), multimedia (e.g., new audio and graphics APIs) and gaming (e.g., improved performance and new sensors, such as a gyroscope for better motion processing).

---

6. http://code.google.com/android/c2dm/.

One of the most significant new features in Android 2.3 was support for near-field communication (NFC)—a short-range wireless connectivity standard that enables communication between two devices within a few centimeters. NFC support and features vary by Android device. NFC can be used for payments (for example, touching your NFC-enabled Android device to a payment device on a soda machine), exchanging data such as contacts and pictures, pairing devices and accessories and more. For more Android 2.3 developer features, see

```
http://developer.android.com/about/versions/android-2.3-
    highlights.html
```

1.4.3 Android 3.0 through 3.2 (Honeycomb)

Android 3.0 (Honeycomb) included user-interface improvements specifically for large-screen devices (e.g., tablets), such as a redesigned keyboard for more efficient typing, a visually appealing 3D user interface, easier navigation between screens within an app and more. New Android 3.0 developer features included:

- fragments, which describe portions of an app's user interface and can be combined into one screen or used across multiple screens

- a persistent Action Bar at the top of the screen providing users with options for interacting with apps

- the ability to add large-screen layouts to existing apps designed for small screens to optimize your app for use on different screen sizes

- a visually attractive and more functional user interface, known as "Holo" for its holographic look and feel

- a new animation framework

- improved graphics and multimedia capabilities

- ability to use multicore processor architectures for enhanced performance

- increased Bluetooth support (e.g., enabling an app to determine if there are any connected devices such as headphones or a keyboard)

- and an animation framework for animating user-interface or graphics objects.

For a list of Android 3.0 user and developer features and platform technologies, go to

```
http://developer.android.com/about/versions/android-3.0-
    highlights.html
```

1.4.4 Android 4.0 through 4.0.4 (Ice Cream Sandwich)

Android 4.0 (Ice Cream Sandwich), released in 2011, merged Android 2.3 (Gingerbread) and Android 3.0 (Honeycomb) into one operating system for use on all Android devices. This allowed you to incorporate into your smartphone apps Honeycomb's features that previously were available only on tablets—the "Holo" user interface, a new launcher (used to customize the device's home screen and launch apps) and more—and easily scale your apps to work on different devices. Ice Cream Sandwich also added several APIs for improved communication between devices, accessibility for users with disabilities (e.g., vision impairments), social networking and more (Fig. 1.6). For a complete list of Android 4.0 APIs, see

```
http://developer.android.com/about/versions/android-4.0.html
```

Feature	Description
Face detection	Using the camera, compatible devices can determine the positioning of the user's eyes, nose and mouth. The camera also can track the user's eye movement, allowing you to create apps that change perspective, based on where the user is looking.
Virtual camera operator	When filming video of multiple people, the camera will automatically focus on the person who is speaking.
Android Beam	Using NFC, Android Beam allows you to touch two Android devices to share content (e.g., contacts, pictures, videos).
Wi-Fi Direct	Wi-Fi P2P (peer-to-peer) APIs allow you to connect multiple Android devices using Wi-Fi. The devices can communicate wirelessly at a greater distance than when using Bluetooth.
Social API	Access and share contact information across social networks and apps (with the user's permission).
Calendar API	Add and share events across multiple apps, manage alerts and attendees and more.
Accessibility APIs	Use the new Accessibility Text-to-Speech APIs to enhance the user experience of your apps for people with disabilities such as vision impairments and more. The explore-by-touch mode allows users with vision impairments to touch anywhere on the screen and hear a voice description of the touched content.
Android@Home framework	Use the Android@Home framework to create apps that control appliances in users' homes, such as, thermostats, irrigation systems, networked light bulbs and more.
Bluetooth health devices	Create apps that communicate with Bluetooth health devices such as scales, heart-rate monitors and more.

Fig. 1.6 | Some Android Ice Cream Sandwich developer features (`http://developer.android.com/about/versions/android-4.0.html`).

1.4.5 Android 4.1–4.3 (Jelly Bean)

Android Jelly Bean, released in 2012, focused on many behind-the-scenes platform improvements, such as better performance, accessibility, support for international users and more. Other new features included support for enhanced Bluetooth connectivity (Bluetooth LE was introduced in Android 4.3), external displays, support for multiple users on one tablet, restricted user profiles, improved security, appearance enhancements (e.g., resizable app widgets, lock screen widgets, and expandable notifications), optimized location and sensor capabilities, better media capabilities (audio/video), and more seamless switching between apps and screens (Fig. 1.7). In addition, Google introduced new APIs that are developed separately from Android platform versions:

- Google Cloud Messaging—a cross-platform solution that enables developers to deliver messages to devices
- Google Play Services—a set of APIs for incorporating Google functionality into your apps.

For the Jelly Bean features list, see

```
http://developer.android.com/about/versions/jelly-bean.html
```

Feature	Description
Android Beam	Enhanced to enable communication via Bluetooth in addition to NFC.
Lock screen widgets	Create widgets that appear on the user's screen when the device is locked, or modify your existing home-screen widgets so that they're also visible when the device is locked.
Photo Sphere	APIs for working with the new panoramic photo features that enable users to take 360-degree photos, similar to those used for Google Maps Street View.
Daydreams	Daydreams are interactive screensavers that are activated when a device is docked or charging. Daydreams can play audio and video and respond to user interactions.
Language support	New features help your apps reach international users, such as bidirectional text (left-to-right or right-to-left), international keyboards, additional keyboard layouts and more.
Developer options	Several new tracking and debugging features help you improve your apps, such as bug reports that include a screenshot and device state information.

Fig. 1.7 | Some Android Jelly Bean features (`http://developer.android.com/about/versions/jelly-bean.html`).

1.4.6 Android 4.4 (KitKat)

Android 4.4 KitKat, released in October 2013, includes several performance improvements that make it possible to run the operating system on all Android devices, including older, memory-constrained devices, which are particularly popular in developing countries.[7]

Enabling more users to update to KitKat reduced the "fragmentation" of Android versions in the market, which has been a challenge for developers who previously had to design apps to run across multiple versions of the operating system, or limit their potential market by targeting their apps to a specific version of the operating system.

Android KitKat also includes security and accessibility enhancements, improved graphics and multimedia capabilities, memory-use analysis tools and more. Figure 1.8 lists some of the key KitKat features. For a complete list, see

```
http://developer.android.com/about/versions/kitkat.html
```

---

7. `http://techcrunch.com/2013/10/31/android-4-4-kitkat-google/`.

Feature	Description
Immersive mode	The status bar at the top of the screen and the menu buttons at the bottom can be hidden, allowing your apps to fill more of the screen. Users can access the status bar by swiping down from the top of the screen, and the system bar (with the back button, home button and recent apps button) by swiping up from the bottom.
Printing framework	Build printing functionality into your apps, including locating available printers over Wi-Fi or the cloud, selecting the paper size and specifying which pages to print.
Storage access framework	Create document storage providers that allow users to browse, create and edit files (e.g., documents and images) across multiple apps.
SMS provider	Create SMS (Short Message Service) or MMS (Multimedia Messaging Service) apps using the new SMS provider and APIs. Users can now select their default messaging app.
Transitions framework	The new framework makes it easier to create transition animations.
Screen recording	Record video of your app to create tutorials and marketing materials.
Enhanced accessibility	The captioning manager API allows apps to check the user's captioning preferences (e.g., language, text styles and more).
Chromium WebView	Supports the latest standards for displaying web content including HTML5, CSS3 and a faster version of JavaScript.
Step detector and step counter	Create apps that detect whether the user is running, walking or climbing stairs and count the number of steps.
Host Card Emulator (HCE)	HCE enables any app to perform secure NFC transactions (e.g., mobile payments) without the need for a secure element on the SIM card controlled by the wireless carrier.

Fig. 1.8 | Some Android KitKat features (`http://developer.android.com/about/versions/kitkat.html`).

1.4.7 Android 5.0 and 5.1 (Lollipop)

Android Lollipop—released in November 2014—was a major update with thousands of API enhancements for phones and tablets, and new capabilities that enable developers to create apps for wearables (e.g., smart watches), TVs and cars. One of the biggest changes was material design—a complete user-interface redesign (also used in Google's web apps). Other features included: a new Android runtime, notification enhancements (enabling users to interact with a notification without leaving the current app), networking enhancements (Bluetooth, Wi-Fi, cellular and NFC), high-performance graphics (OpenGL ES 3.1 and the Android Extension Pack), better audio capabilities (capture, multichannel mixing, playback and support for USB peripherals), enhanced camera capabilities, screen sharing, new sensor support, enhanced accessibility features, multiple SIM card support and more. Figure 1.9 lists some of the key Lollipop features. For a complete list, see

```
http://developer.android.com/about/versions/lollipop.html
http://developer.android.com/about/versions/android-5.0.html
http://developer.android.com/about/versions/android-5.1.html
```

Feature	Description
Material design	Google's new look-and-feel for Android and web applications was the key new feature in Lollipop. Material design helps you create apps with nice transition effects, shadows that add depth to the user interface and emphasize actionable components, customization capabilities and more. For details, visit `https://www.google.com/design/spec/material-design/introduction.html`.
ART runtime	Google replaced the original Android runtime with the new 64-bit compatible ART runtime, which uses a combination of interpretation, ahead-of-time (AOT) compilation and just-in-time (JIT) compilation to improve performance.
Concurrent documents and activities in the recent apps screen	Apps can now specify that multiple activities and documents should appear on the recent apps screen. For example, if the user has multiple tabs open in a web browser or multiple documents open in a text-editing app, when the user touches the recent apps button (■), each browser tab or document can appear as a separate item that the user can select.
Screen capturing and sharing	Apps can now capture the device's screen and share the contents with other users across a network.
Project Volta	Features that help preserve battery life, including the new `JobScheduler` that can execute asynchronous tasks when the device is charging, connected to an unmetered network (i.e., use Wi-Fi vs. cellular data) or idle.

Fig. 1.9 | Some Android Lollipop features (`http://developer.android.com/about/versions/lollipop.html`).

1.4.8 Android 6 (Marshmallow)

Android Marshmallow, released in September 2015, is the current version of Android at the time of this writing. Some new features include Now on Tap (for getting Google Now information in the context of an app), Doze and App Standby (for saving battery), a new permissions model to make apps easier to install, fingerprint authentication, better data protection, better text-selection support, 4K display support, new audio and video capabilities, new camera capabilities (flashlight and image-reprocessing APIs) and more. Figure 1.10 lists some of the key Lollipop features. For a complete list, see

```
http://developer.android.com/about/versions/marshmallow/android-
    6.0-changes.html
```

Feature	Description
Doze	Using software and sensors, Android determines when a device is stationary for a period of time—such as when you place it on a table overnight—and defers background processes that drain the battery.

Fig. 1.10 | Some Android Marshmallow features (`http://developer.android.com/about/versions/marshmallow/android-6.0-changes.html`). (Part I of 2.)

Feature	Description
App Standby	For apps that a user has open but has not interacted with recently, Android defers background network activity.
Now on Tap	Tap and hold the home button while inside any app and Google Now inspects what's on the screen and presents relevant information in the form of cards. For example, in a text message discussing a movie, a card containing information about that movie is displayed. Similarly, in a text message mentioning a restaurant name, a card with the ratings, location and phone number appears.
New permissions model	Before Android 6.0, a user was required at installation time to grant in advance all permissions that an app would ever need—this caused many people not to install certain apps. With the new model, the app is installed without asking for any permissions. Instead, the user is asked to grant a permission only the first time the corresponding feature is used.
Fingerprint authentication	For devices with fingerprint readers, apps can now authenticate users via their fingerprints.
App linking	Enables developers to associate apps with their own web domains and craft web links that launch specific apps from the same developer.
Automatic backup	Android can automatically backup and restore an app's data.
Direct Share	You can define direct share targets in your app that enable users to share data via other apps, directly from your app.
Voice Interaction API	Enables apps to respond to voice interactions.
Bluetooth stylus support	Apps can respond to pressure-sensitive interactions from a Bluetooth stylus—for example, in a drawing app, pressing the stylus against the screen harder could result in a thicker line.

Fig. 1.10 | Some Android Marshmallow features (`http://developer.android.com/about/versions/marshmallow/android-6.0-changes.html`). (Part 2 of 2.)

1.5 Downloading Apps from Google Play

At the time of this writing, there were over 1.6 million apps in Google Play, and the number is growing quickly.[8] Figure 1.11 lists some popular free and fee-based apps in various categories. You can download apps through the **Play Store** app installed on your Android device. You also can log into your Google Play account at

> `http://play.google.com`

then specify the Android device on which to install the app. It will then download via the device's Wi-Fi or 3G/4G connection. In Chapter 10, Google Play and App Business Issues, we discuss additional app stores, offering your apps for free or charging a fee, app pricing and more.

---

8. `http://www.statista.com/statistics/266210/number-of-available-applications-in-the-google-play-store/`.

Google Play category	Some popular apps in the category
Books and Reference	WolframAlpha, Dictionary.com, Audible for Android, Kindle
Business	Polaris Office, OfficeSuite 8, QuickBooks Online, PayPal Here
Communication	Snapchat, LinkedIn, Pinterest, Instagram, WeChat, Line
Education	Google Classroom, Star Tracker, Sight Words, Math Tricks
Entertainment	Showtime Anytime, History Channel, Discovery Channel
Finance	PayPal, Credit Karma, Google Wallet, Chase Mobile
Games	Pac-Man 256, Angry Birds 2, Fruit Ninja, Tetris, Solitaire
Health & Fitness	RunKeeper, ViewRanger GPS, Calorie Counter
Lifestyle	Assistant, Horoscope, Food Network, Starbucks
Live Wallpaper	Facebook, Next Launcher 3D Shell, Weather Live
Media & Video	VHS Camera Recorder, VivaVideo Pro, musical.ly, GIF Keyboard
Medical	Feed Baby Pro, CareZone, FollowMyHealth, Essential Anatomy
Music & Audio	SoundCloud, Spotify, Beats Music, Pandora, iHeartRadio
News & Magazines	BBC News, CBS News, NPR News, Reuters, NBC News
Photography	Google Camera, Instagram, Retrica, GoPro App, Pencil Sketch
Productivity	Pocket, Wunderlist, Microsoft Word, Google Docs, SwiftKey
Shopping	Zappos, Groupon, JackThreads, Fancy, Etsy, Home Depot
Social	Snapchat, Instagram, Meetup, textPlus, Pinterest, Tumblr
Sports	Fox Sports, theScore, NBA 2015–16, ESPN, CBS Sports
Tools	CM Security Antivirus, Clean Master, Google Translate
Transportation	Uber, Lyft, MarrineTraffic, BringGo, DigiHUD Speedometer
Travel & Local	Priceline, Google Earth, Eat24, GasBuddy, Hotels.com
Weather	AccuWeather, Weather Underground, Yahoo Weather
Widgets	Facebook, Pandora, Pocket Casts, Tasker, Weather Timeline

Fig. 1.11 | Some popular Android apps in Google Play.

1.6 Packages

Android uses a collection of *packages*, which are named groups of related, predefined classes. Some of the packages are Android specific, some are Java specific and some are Google specific. These packages allow you to conveniently access Android OS features and incorporate them into your apps. The Android packages help you create apps that adhere to Android's unique look-and-feel conventions and style guidelines,

```
http://developer.android.com/design/index.html
```

Figure 1.12 lists many of the packages we discuss in this book. For a complete list of Android packages, see

```
http://developer.android.com/reference/packages.html
```

Several of the packages we use are from the Android Support libraries, which enable you to use newer Android features in apps that run on current and older platforms. For an overview of the key features in the Android Support libraries, visit:

```
https://developer.android.com/tools/support-library/features.html
```

Package	Description
android.animation	Classes for property animation. (Chapter 4's **Flag Quiz** app and Chapter 5's **Doodlz** app.)
android.app	Includes high-level classes in the Android app model. (Chapter 4's **Flag Quiz** app and Chapter 5's **Doodlz** app.)
android.content	Access and publish data on a device. (Chapter 6's **Cannon Game** app.)
android.content.res	Classes for accessing app resources (e.g., media, colors, drawables, etc.), and device-configuration information affecting app behavior. (Chapter 4's **Flag Quiz** app.)
android.database	Handling data returned by the content provider. (Chapter 9's **Address Book** app.)
android.database.sqlite	SQLite database management for private databases. (Chapter 9's **Address Book** app.)
android.graphics	Graphics tools used for drawing to the screen. (Chapter 4's **Flag Quiz** app and Chapter 5's **Doodlz** app.)
android.graphics. drawable	Classes for display-only elements (e.g., gradients, etc.). (Chapter 4's **Flag Quiz** app.)
android.hardware	Device hardware support. (Chapter 5's **Doodlz** app.)
android.media	Classes for handling audio and video media interfaces. (Chapter 6's **Cannon Game** app.)
android.net	Network access classes. (Chapter 8's **Twitter® Searches** app.)
android.os	Operating-systems services. (Chapter 3's **Tip Calculator** app.)
android.preference	Working with an app's user preferences. (Chapter 4's **Flag Quiz** app.)
android.provider	Access to Android content providers. (Chapter 5's **Doodlz** app.)
android.support. design.widget	Android Design Support Library classes that enable recent GUI enhancements to run on current and older Android platforms. (Chapter 7's **Weather Viewer** app.)
android.support.v4. print	Part of the v4 Android Support Library for use in platform API levels 4 and higher. Includes features for using the Android 4.4 printing framework. (Chapter 5's **Doodlz** app.)
android.support.v7.app	Part of the v7 Android Support Library for use in platform API levels 7 and higher. Includes application-compatibility library components, such as app bars (formerly action bars). (Chapter 7's **Weather Viewer** app.)

Fig. 1.12 | Android and Java packages used in this book, listed with the chapter in which they *first* appear. We discuss additional packages in Volume 2. (Part 1 of 2.)

Package	Description
`android.support.v7. widget`	Part of the v7 Android Support Library for use in platform API levels 7 and higher. Includes GUI components and layouts. (Chapter 7's **Weather Viewer** app.)
`android.text`	Rendering and tracking text changes. (Chapter 3's **Tip Calculator** app.)
`android.util`	Utility methods and XML utilities. (Chapter 4's **Flag Quiz** app.)
`android.widget`	User-interface classes for widgets. (Chapter 3's **Tip Calculator** app.)
`android.view`	User interface classes for layout and user interactions. (Chapter 4's **Flag Quiz** app.)

Fig. 1.12 | Android and Java packages used in this book, listed with the chapter in which they *first* appear. We discuss additional packages in Volume 2. (Part 2 of 2.)

1.7 Android Software Development Kit (SDK)

The Android SDK provides the tools you'll need to build Android apps. It gets installed with Android Studio. See the Before You Begin section (after the Preface) for details on downloading the software you'll need to develop Android apps, including Java SE 7 and Android Studio.

Android Studio

Android Studio[9] was announced at the Google I/O developer conference in 2013 and is now Google's preferred Android IDE. The IDE includes:

- GUI designer

- code editor with support for syntax coloring and line numbering

- auto-indenting and auto-complete (i.e., type hinting)

- debugger

- version control system

- refactoring support

and more.

The Android Emulator

The Android emulator, included in the Android SDK, allows you to run Android apps in a simulated environment within Windows, Mac OS X or Linux, without using an actual Android device. The emulator displays a realistic Android user-interface window. It's particularly useful if you do not have access to Android devices for testing. You should certainly test your apps on a variety of Android devices before uploading them to Google Play.

Before running an app in the emulator, you'll need to create an Android Virtual Device (AVD), which defines the characteristics of the device on which you want to test, including the hardware, system image, screen size, data storage and more. If you want to

---

9. Android Studio is based on the JetBrains IntelliJ IDEA Java IDE (http://www.jetbrains.com/idea/)

test your apps for multiple Android devices, you'll need to create separate AVDs to emulate each unique device, or use Google's Cloud Test Lab

```
https://developers.google.com/cloud-test-lab
```

which enables you to test on many different devices.

You can reproduce on the emulator most of the Android gestures (Fig. 1.13) and controls (Fig. 1.14) using your computer's keyboard and mouse. The gestures on the emulator are a bit limited, since your computer probably cannot simulate all the Android hardware features. For example, to test GPS apps in the emulator, you'll need to create files that simulate GPS readings. Also, although you can simulate orientation changes (to *portrait* or *landscape* mode), simulating particular accelerometer readings (the accelerometer allows the device to respond to up/down, left/right and forward/backward acceleration) requires features that are not built into the emulator. The emulator can, however, use sensor data from an actual Android device connected to the computer, as described at

```
http://tools.android.com/tips/hardware-emulation
```

Figure 1.15 lists Android functionality that's *not* available on the emulator. You can install your app on an Android device to test these features. You'll start creating AVDs and using the emulator to develop Android apps in Chapter 2's **Welcome** app.

Gesture	Emulator action
Touch	Click the mouse once. Introduced in Chapter 3's **Tip Calculator** app.
Double touch	Double click the mouse.
Long press	Click and hold the mouse. Introduced in Chapter 8's **Twitter® Searches** app.
Drag	Click, hold and drag the mouse. Introduced in Chapter 6's **Cannon Game** app.
Swipe	Click and hold the mouse, move the pointer in the swipe direction and release the mouse. Introduced in Chapter 7's **Weather Viewer** app.
Pinch zoom	Press and hold the *Ctrl* (*Control*) key. Two circles that simulate the two touches will appear. Move the circles to the start position, click and hold the mouse and drag the circles to the end position.

Fig. 1.13 | Android gestures on the emulator.

Control	Emulator action
Back	*Esc*
Call/dial button	*F3*
Camera	*Ctrl-KEYPAD_5*, *Ctrl-F3*
End call button	*F4*
Home	*Home* button
Menu (left softkey)	*F2* or *Page Up* button

Fig. 1.14 | Android hardware controls in the emulator (for additional controls, go to `http://developer.android.com/tools/help/emulator.html`). (Part 1 of 2.)

Control	Emulator action
Power button	*F7*
Search	*F5*
* (right softkey)	*Shift-F2* or *Page Down* button
Rotate to previous orientation	*KEYPAD_7, Ctrl-F11*
Rotate to next orientation	*KEYPAD_9, Ctrl-F12*
Toggle cell networking on/off	*F8*
Volume up button	*KEYPAD_PLUS, Ctrl-F5*
Volume down button	*KEYPAD_MINUS, Ctrl-F6*

Fig. 1.14 | Android hardware controls in the emulator (for additional controls, go to `http://developer.android.com/tools/help/emulator.html`). (Part 2 of 2.)

Android functionality not available on the emulator

- Making or receiving real phone calls (the emulator allows simulated calls only)
- Bluetooth
- USB connections
- Device-attached headphones
- Determining network connected state
- Determining battery charge or power charging state
- Determining SD card insert/eject
- Direct support for sensors (accelerometer, barometer, compass, light sensor, proximity sensor)—it is possible, however, to use sensor data from a USB-connected device

Fig. 1.15 | Android functionality not available in the emulator (`http://developer.android.com/tools/devices/emulator.html#limitations`).

1.8 Object-Oriented Programming: A Quick Refresher

Android uses object-oriented programming techniques, so in this section we review the basics of object technology. We use all of these concepts in this book.

Building software quickly, correctly and economically remains an elusive goal at a time when demands for new and more powerful software are soaring. *Objects*, or more precisely—as we'll see in Chapter 3—the *classes* objects come from, are essentially *reusable* software components. There are date objects, time objects, audio objects, video objects, automobile objects, people objects, etc. Almost any *noun* can be reasonably represented as a software object in terms of *attributes* (e.g., name, color and size) and *behaviors* (e.g., calculating, moving and communicating). Software developers are discovering that using a modular, object-oriented design-and-implementation approach can make software development groups much more productive than they could be with earlier popular techniques like "structured programming"—object-oriented programs are often easier to understand, correct and modify.

1.8.1 The Automobile as an Object

To help you understand objects and their contents, let's begin with a simple analogy. Suppose you want to *drive a car and make it go faster by pressing its accelerator pedal*. What must happen before you can do this? Well, before you can drive a car, someone has to *design* it. A car typically begins as engineering drawings, similar to the *blueprints* that describe the design of a house. These drawings include the design for an accelerator pedal. The pedal *hides* from the driver the complex mechanisms that actually make the car go faster, just as the brake pedal *hides* the mechanisms that slow the car, and the steering wheel *hides* the mechanisms that turn the car. This enables people with little or no knowledge of how engines, braking and steering mechanisms work to drive a car easily.

   Just as you cannot cook meals in the kitchen of a blueprint, you cannot drive a car's engineering drawings. Before you can drive a car, it must be *built* from the engineering drawings that describe it. A completed car has an *actual* accelerator pedal to make it go faster, but even that's not enough—the car won't accelerate on its own (hopefully!), so the driver must *press* the pedal to accelerate the car.

1.8.2 Methods and Classes

Let's use our car example to introduce some key object-oriented programming concepts. Performing a task in a program requires a method. The method houses the program statements that actually perform its tasks. The method hides these statements from its user, just as the accelerator pedal of a car hides from the driver the mechanisms of making the car go faster. A class houses the methods that perform the class's tasks. For example, a class that represents a bank account might contain one method to *deposit* money to an account, another to *withdraw* money from an account and a third to *inquire* what the account's current balance is. A class is similar in concept to a car's engineering drawings, which house the design of an accelerator pedal, steering wheel, and so on.

1.8.3 Instantiation

Just as someone has to *build a car* from its engineering drawings before you can actually drive a car, you must *build an object* of a class before a program can perform the tasks that the class's methods define. The process of doing this is called *instantiation*. An object is then referred to as an instance of its class.

1.8.4 Reuse

Just as a car's engineering drawings can be *reused* many times to build many cars, you can *reuse* a class many times to build many objects. Reuse of existing classes when building new classes and programs saves time and effort. Reuse also helps you build more reliable and effective systems, because existing classes and components often have gone through extensive testing, debugging and performance tuning. Just as the notion of *interchangeable parts* was crucial to the Industrial Revolution, reusable classes are crucial to the software revolution that has been spurred by object technology.

1.8.5 Messages and Method Calls

When you drive a car, pressing its gas pedal sends a *message* to the car to perform a task—that is, to go faster. Similarly, you *send messages to an object*. Each message is a method call that tells a method of the object to perform its task. For example, a program might call a particular bank-account object's *deposit* method to increase the account's balance.

I.8.6 Attributes and Instance Variables

A car, besides having capabilities to accomplish tasks, also has *attributes*, such as its color, its number of doors, the amount of gas in its tank, its current speed and its record of total miles driven (i.e., its odometer reading). Like its capabilities, the car's attributes are represented as part of its design in its engineering diagrams (which, for example, include an odometer and a fuel gauge). As you drive an actual car, these attributes are carried along with the car. Every car maintains its *own* attributes. For example, each car knows how much gas is in its own gas tank, but *not* how much is in the tanks of *other* cars.

An object, similarly, has attributes that it carries along as it's used in a program. These attributes are specified as part of the object's class. For example, a bank-account object has a *balance attribute* that represents the amount of money in the account. Each bank-account object knows the balance in the account it represents, but *not* the balances of the *other* accounts in the bank. Attributes are specified by the class's instance variables.

I.8.7 Encapsulation

Classes encapsulate (i.e., wrap) attributes and methods into objects—an object's attributes and methods are intimately related. Objects may communicate with one another, but they're normally not allowed to know how other objects are implemented—implementation details are *hidden* within the objects themselves. This information hiding is crucial to good software engineering.

I.8.8 Inheritance

A new class of objects can be created quickly and conveniently by inheritance—the new class absorbs the characteristics of an existing one, possibly customizing them and adding unique characteristics of its own. In our car analogy, a "convertible" certainly *is an* object of the more *general* class "automobile," but more *specifically*, the roof can be raised or lowered.

I.8.9 Object-Oriented Analysis and Design (OOAD)

How will you create the code for your programs? Perhaps, like many programmers, you'll simply turn on your computer and start typing. This approach may work for small programs, but what if you were asked to create a software system to control thousands of automated teller machines for a major bank? Or suppose you were asked to work on a team of 1,000 software developers building the next U.S. air traffic control system? For projects so large and complex, you should not simply sit down and start writing programs.

To create the best solutions, you should follow a detailed analysis process for determining your project's requirements (i.e., defining *what* the system is supposed to do) and developing a design that satisfies them (i.e., deciding *how* the system should do it). Ideally, you'd go through this process and carefully review the design (and have your design reviewed by other software professionals) before writing any code. If this process involves analyzing and designing your system from an object-oriented point of view, it's called an object-oriented analysis and design (OOAD) process. Languages like Java are object oriented. Programming in such a language, called object-oriented programming (OOP), allows you to implement an object-oriented design as a working system.

1.9 Test-Driving the Tip Calculator App in an Android Virtual Device (AVD)

In this section, you'll run and interact with your first Android app using an Android Virtual Device and, if you have one, an actual Android device. The **Tip Calculator** (Fig. 1.16(a))—which you'll build in Chapter 3—calculates and displays for a restaurant bill the tip amount and the total bill amount. As you enter each digit of the bill amount by touching the numeric keypad, the app calculates and displays the tip and total bill for a tip percentage that you specify with the app's **SeekBar**—we use 15% by default (Fig. 1.16(a)). You can select a tip percentage in the range 0–30% by moving the **Seek-Bar**'s thumb—this updates the tip percentage **TextView** and displays the updated tip and bill total in the **TextView**s below the **SeekBar** (Fig. 1.16(b)).

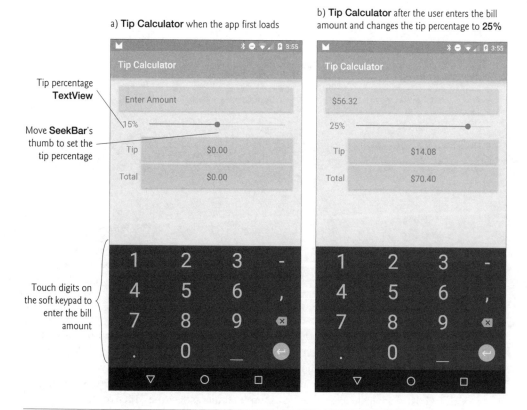

a) **Tip Calculator** when the app first loads

b) **Tip Calculator** after the user enters the bill amount and changes the tip percentage to **25%**

Tip percentage **TextView**

Move **SeekBar**'s thumb to set the tip percentage

Touch digits on the soft keypad to enter the bill amount

Fig. 1.16 | **Tip Calculator** when the app first loads, then after the user enters the bill amount and changes the tip percentage.

1.9.1 Opening the Tip Calculator App's Project in Android Studio

To open the **Tip Calculator** app's project, perform the following steps:

1. *Checking your setup.* If you have not done so already, perform the steps specified in the Before You Begin section.

2. *Opening Android Studio.* Use the Android Studio shortcut

to open the IDE. On Windows, the shortcut will appear in your **Start** menu or **Start** screen. On OS X, the shortcut is located in your `Applications` folder. On Linux, the shortcut's location depends on where you extract the ZIP file containing the Android Studio files. Once you open Android Studio for the first time, the **Welcome to Android Studio** window appears (Fig. 1.17).

Fig. 1.17 | Welcome to Android Studio window.

3. *Opening the **Tip Calculator** app's project.* In Android Studio, when another project is already open, you can select **File > Open...** to navigate to that project's location and open it, or in the **Welcome to Android Studio Window** (Fig. 1.17), you can click **Open an existing Android Studio Project** to open the **Open File or Project** dialog (Fig. 1.18). Navigate to the book's examples folder, select the `TipCalculator` folder and click **Choose** (Mac) or **OK** (Windows/Linux). Android Studio stores the Android SDK's path in the project settings for each project you create. When you open our projects on your system, you'll receive an error message if the SDK on your system is in a different location from ours. Simply click the **OK** button in the

error dialog that appears, and Android Studio will update the project settings to use the SDK on your system. At this point, the IDE opens the project and displays its contents in the **Project** window (Fig. 1.19) at the IDE's left side. If the **Project** window is not visible, you can view it by selecting **View > Tool Windows > Project**.

Fig. 1.18 | Open File or Project dialog.

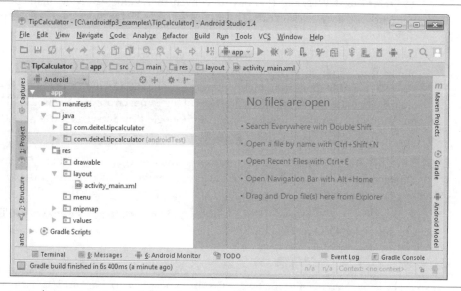

Fig. 1.19 | Project window for the **Tip Calculator** project.

1.9.2 Creating Android Virtual Devices (AVDs)

As we discussed in the Before You Begin section, you can test apps for multiple Android devices by creating Android Virtual Devices (AVDs) that emulate each unique device.[10] In this section you'll create Android 6 AVDs for the devices we used to test this book's apps—the Google's Nexus 6 phone and the Nexus 9 tablet. To create these AVDs, perform the following steps:

1. In Android Studio, select **Tools > Android > AVD Manager** to display the **Android Virtual Device Manager** window (Fig. 1.20).

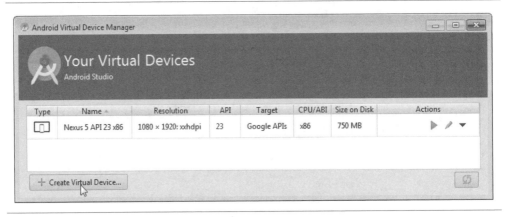

Fig. 1.20 | Android Virtual Device Manager window.

2. Click **Create Virtual Device...** to open the **Virtual Device Configuration** window (Fig. 1.21). By default the **Category** "Phone" is selected, but you may also create AVDs for **Tablet, Wear** and **TV**. For your convenience, Google provides many preconfigured devices that you can use to quickly create AVDs. Select **Nexus 6**, then click **Next**.

3. Select the system image for the virtual device you wish to create—in this case, the one with the Android platform **Release Name** value **Marshmallow**, the **API Level** value **23**, the **ABI** (application binary interface) value **x86** and the **Target** value **Android 6.0 (with Google APIs)**, then click **Next**. This **Target** creates an Android AVD for Android 6 that also includes support for Google Play Services APIs.

4. For the **AVD Name**, specify **Nexus 6 API 23**.

5. Click the **Show Advanced Settings** button in the lower-left of the **Virtual Device Configuration** window, then scroll to the bottom of the advanced settings and *uncheck* the **Enable Keyboard Input** option and click **Finish** to create the AVD.

6. Repeat Steps 1–6 to create a Nexus 9 tablet AVD named **Nexus 9 API 23**—you'll use this tablet AVD in Chapter 2.

---

10. At the time of this writing, when you set up Android Studio, it configures an AVD that emulates a Google Nexus 5 phone running Android 6.0 (Marshmallow). You'll still need to perform Section 1.9.2's steps to create the additional AVDs you need for testing.

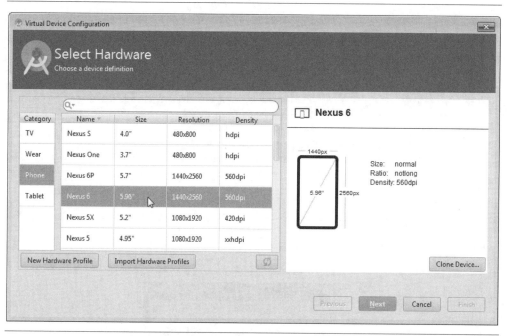

Fig. 1.21 | Virtual Device Configuration window.

If you leave the **Enable Keyboard Input** option checked in Step 5 above, you can use your computer's keyboard to enter data into apps running in the AVD. However, this prevents the soft keyboard shown in the screen captures from displaying.

Each AVD you create has many other options specified in its `config.ini` file. To more precisely match a particular device's hardware configuration, you can modify `config.ini` as described at:

```
http://developer.android.com/tools/devices/managing-avds.html
```

1.9.3 Running the Tip Calculator App on the Nexus 6 Smartphone AVD

To test-drive the **Tip Calculator** app, perform the following steps:

1. *Checking your setup.* If you have not done so already, perform the steps specified in the Before You Begin section.

2. *Launching the Nexus 6 AVD.* For this test-drive, we'll use the Nexus 6 smartphone AVD that you configured in Section 1.9.2. To launch the Nexus 6 AVD, select **Tools > Android > AVD Manager** to display the **Android Virtual Device Manager** dialog (Fig. 1.22). Click the **Launch this AVD in the emulator button** (▶) in the row for the **Nexus 6 API 23** AVD. An AVD can take some time to load—do not attempt to execute the app until the AVD finishes loading. When it's done loading, the AVD will display the lock screen. On an actual device, you unlock it by swiping up with your finger. You perform the swipe gesture on an AVD by placing the mouse over the AVD's "screen" and dragging up with the mouse. Figure 1.23 shows the AVD after you unlock it.

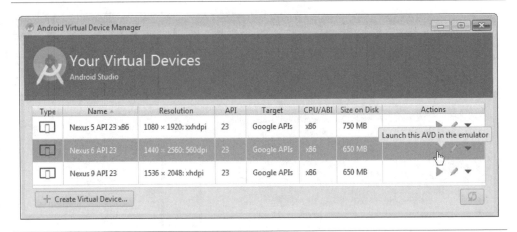

Fig. 1.22 | Android Virtual Device Manager dialog.

Fig. 1.23 | Nexus 6 AVD home screen after you unlock the AVD.

3. *Launching the Tip Calculator app.* In Android Studio, select **Run > Run 'app'** or click the **Run 'app'** button (▶) on the Android Studio toolbar. This will display a **Device Chooser** dialog (Fig. 1.24) with the currently running AVD already selected. Click **OK** to run the **Tip Calculator** in the AVD (Fig. 1.25) that you

launched in Step 2.[11] As an alternative to opening the **Android Virtual Device** Manager dialog in Step 2, you can click the **Run 'app'** button (▶) on the Android Studio toolbar and the **Device Chooser** dialog will appear. You can then use the **Launch emulator** option at the bottom of the dialog to select an AVD to launch, and in which to run the app.

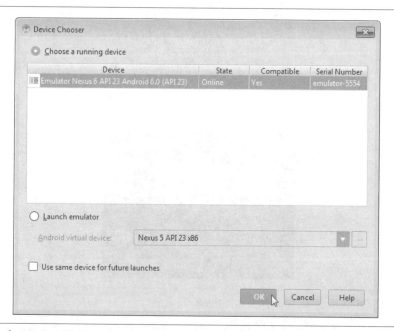

Fig. 1.24 | Device Chooser for selecting AVD or device on which to test an app.

4. *Exploring the AVD.* At the AVD screen's bottom are various *soft buttons* that appear on the device's touch screen. You touch these to interact with apps and the Android OS. In an AVD touches are performed by clicking with the mouse. The down button (▼) dismisses the keypad. When there is no keypad on the screen the back button (◀) appears instead. Touching this button takes you back to an app's prior screen, or back to a prior app if you're in the current app's initial screen. The home button (◉) returns you to the device's home screen. The recent apps button (■) allows you to view the recently used apps list, so that you can switch back to recent apps quickly. At the screen's top is the app's app bar, which displays the app's name and may contain other app-specific soft buttons— some may appear on the app bar and the rest in the app's options menu, which

---

11. The keypad in Fig. 1.25 may differ, based on your AVD's or device's Android version or whether you've installed and selected a custom keyboard. We configured our AVD to display the dark keyboard for better contrast in our screen captures. To do so: Touch the home (◉) icon on your AVD or device. On the home screen, touch the launcher (⊞) icon, then open the **Settings** app. In the **Personal** section, touch **Language and Input**. On an AVD, touch **Android Keyboard (AOSP)**. On a device touch **Google Keyboard** (the standard Android keyboard). Touch **Appearance & layouts**, then touch **Theme. Touch Material Dark** to change to the keyboard with the dark background.

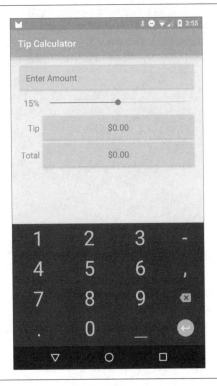

Fig. 1.25 | Tip Calculator app running in the AVD.

appears in the app bar at the top of the screen as ⋮. The number of options on the app bar depends on the size of the device—we discuss this in Chapter 5.

5. *Entering a Bill Total.* Enter the bill total 56.32 by touching numbers on the numeric keypad. If you make a mistake, press the delete button (⌫) in the bottom-right corner of the keypad to erase the last digit you entered. Even though the keypad contains a decimal point, the app is configured so that you may enter only the digits 0–9. Each time you touch a digit or delete one, the app reads what you've entered so far and converts it to a number—if you delete all the digits the app redisplays **Enter Amount** in the **TextView** at the top of the app. The app divides the value by 100 and displays the result in the blue **TextView**. The app then calculates and updates the tip and total amounts that are displayed. We use Android's locale-specific currency-formatting capabilities to display monetary values formatted for the device's current locale. For the U.S. locale, as you enter the four digits 5, 6, 3 and 2, the bill total is displayed successively as $0.05, $0.56, $5.63 and $56.32, respectively.

6. *Selecting a Custom Tip Percentage.* The **SeekBar** allows you to select a custom percentage, and the **TextView**s in the right column below the **SeekBar** display the corresponding tip and the total bill. Drag the **SeekBar** thumb to the right until the custom percentage reads **25%**. As you drag the thumb, the **SeekBar** value continuously changes. The app updates the tip percentage, the tip amount and the

bill total accordingly for each **SeekBar** value until you release the thumb. Figure 1.26 shows the app after you've entered the bill amount and selected the tip percentage.

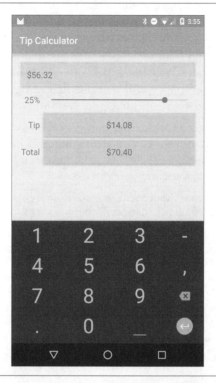

Fig. 1.26 | Tip Calculator after entering the bill amount and selecting a 25% tip.

7. *Returning to the home screen.* You can return to the AVD's home screen by tapping the home (⊙) button on the AVD.

Troubleshooting AVD Startup

If you have trouble executing an Android Virtual Device, it might be that too much of your computer's memory is allocated to the AVD. To reduce AVD's memory size:

1. In Android Studio, select **Tools > Android > AVD Manager** to open the **Android Virtual Device Manager** window.

2. You'll see a list of existing AVDs. For the AVD you'd like to reconfigure, click the pencil icon (✎) in the **Actions** column.

3. In the **Virtual Device Configuration** window, click **Show Advanced Settings**, and scroll to the **Memory and Storage** section.

4. Decrease value for **RAM** from the default 1536 MB (1.5 GB) down to 1 GB.

5. Click **Finish** and close the **Android Virtual Device Manager** window.

If you still cannot run the AVD, repeat these steps and reduce the memory to 768 MB.

1.9.4 Running the Tip Calculator App on an Android Device

If you have an Android device, you can easily execute an app on it for testing purposes.

1. *Enabling the developer options on the device.* First, you must enable debugging on the device. To do so, go to the device's **Settings** app, then select **About phone** (or **About tablet**), locate the **Build number** (at the bottom of the list) and tap it seven times until you see **You are now a developer** on the screen. This will enable an entry named **Developer options** in the **Settings** app.

2. *Enabling debugging on the device.* Return to the **Settings** app's main screen, select **Developer options** and ensure that **USB debugging** is checked—this is the default when you first enable the developer options on the device.

3. *Connecting your device.* Next, use the USB cable that came with your device to connect the device to your computer. If you're a Windows user, recall from the Before You Begin section that you might need to install a USB driver for your device. See the following web pages for details:

```
http://developer.android.com/tools/device.html
http://developer.android.com/tools/extras/oem-usb.html
```

4. *Running Tip Calculator on the Android device.* In Android Studio, select **Run > Run 'app'** or click the **Run 'app'** button (▶) on the Android Studio toolbar. This will display the **Device Chooser** dialog that you saw in Fig. 1.24. Select your device from the list of running AVDs and devices. Click **OK** to run the **Tip Calculator** on the AVD or device you selected.

Test-Drives for the Book's Apps

To get a broad sense of the capabilities that you'll learn in this book, check out the test-drives of the book's apps in Chapters 2–9.

Preparing to Distribute Apps

When you build apps for distribution via app stores like Google Play, you should test the apps on as many actual devices as you can. Remember that some features can be tested *only* on actual devices. If you don't have Android devices available to you, create AVDs that simulate the various devices on which you'd like your app to execute—the AVD Manager provides many preconfigured AVD templates. When you configure each AVD to simulate a particular device, look up the device's specifications online and configure the AVD accordingly. In addition, you can modify the AVD's config.ini file as described in the section **Setting hardware emulation options** at

```
http://developer.android.com/tools/devices/managing-avds-
    cmdline.html#hardwareopts
```

This file contains options that are not configurable via the **Android Virtual Device Manager**. Modifying these options allows you to more precisely match the hardware configuration of an actual device.

1.10 Building Great Android Apps

With over 1.6 million apps in Google Play,[12] how do you create an Android app that people will find, download, use and recommend to others? Consider what makes an app fun, useful, interesting, appealing and enduring. A clever app name, an attractive icon and an engaging description might lure people to your app on Google Play or one of the many other Android app marketplaces. But once users download the app, what will make them use it regularly and recommend it to others? Figure 1.27 shows some characteristics of great apps.

Characteristics of great apps

Great Games
- Entertaining and fun.
- Challenging.
- Progressive levels of difficulty.
- Show your scores and use leaderboards to record high scores.
- Provide audio and visual feedback.
- Offer single-player, multiplayer and networked versions.
- Have high-quality animations.
- Offloading input/output and compute-intensive code to separate threads of execution to improve interface responsiveness and app performance.
- Innovate with augmented reality technology—enhancing a real-world environment with virtual components; this is particularly popular with video-based apps.

Useful Utilities
- Provide useful functionality and accurate information.
- Increase personal and business productivity.
- Make tasks more convenient (e.g., maintaining a to-do list, managing expenses).
- Make the user better informed.
- Provide topical information (e.g., the latest stock prices, news, severe-storm warnings, traffic updates).
- Use location-based services to provide local services (e.g., coupons for local businesses, best gas prices, food delivery).

General Characteristics
- Up-to-date with the latest Android features, but compatible with multiple Android versions to support the widest possible audience.
- Work properly.
- Bugs are fixed promptly.
- Follow standard Android app GUI conventions.
- Launch quickly.
- Are responsive.

Fig. 1.27 | Characteristics of great apps. (Part 1 of 2.)

---

12. http://www.statista.com/statistics/266210/number-of-available-applications-in-the-google-play-store/.

Characteristics of great apps

General Characteristics (cont.)

- Don't require excessive memory, bandwidth or battery power.
- Are novel and creative.
- Enduring—something that your users will use regularly.
- Use professional-quality icons that will appear in Google Play and on the user's device.
- Use quality graphics, images, animations, audio and video.
- Are intuitive and easy to use (don't require extensive help documentation).
- Accessible to people with disabilities (`http://developer.android.com/guide/topics/ui/accessibility/index.html`).
- Give users reasons and a means to tell others about your app (e.g., you can give users the option to post their game scores to Facebook or Twitter).
- Provide additional content for content-driven apps (e.g., game levels, articles, puzzles).
- Localized (Chapter 2) for each country in which the app is offered (e.g., translate the app's text and audio files, use different graphics based on the locale, etc.).
- Offer better performance, capabilities and ease-of-use than competitive apps.
- Take advantage of the device's built-in capabilities.
- Do not request excessive permissions.
- Are designed to run optimally across a broad variety of Android devices.
- Future-proofed for new hardware devices—specify the exact hardware features your app uses so Google Play can filter and display it in the store for only compatible devices (`http://android-developers.blogspot.com/2010/06/future-proofing-your-app.html`).

Fig. 1.27 | Characteristics of great apps. (Part 2 of 2.)

1.11 Android Development Resources

Figure 1.28 lists some of the key documentation from the Android Developer site. As you dive into Android app development, you may have questions about the tools, design issues, security and more. There are several Android developer newsgroups and forums where you can get the latest announcements or ask questions (Fig. 1.29). Figure 1.30 lists several websites where you'll find Android development tips, videos and resources.

Title	URL
App Components	`http://developer.android.com/guide/components/index.html`
Using the Android Emulator	`http://developer.android.com/tools/devices/emulator.html`
Package Index	`http://developer.android.com/reference/packages.html`
Class Index	`http://developer.android.com/reference/classes.html`

Fig. 1.28 | Key online documentation for Android developers. (Part 1 of 2.)

Title	URL
Android Design	`http://developer.android.com/design/index.html`
Data Backup	`http://developer.android.com/guide/topics/data/backup.html`
Security Tips	`http://developer.android.com/training/articles/security-tips.html`
Android Studio	`http://developer.android.com/sdk/index.html`
Debugging	`http://developer.android.com/tools/debugging/index.html`
Tools Help	`http://developer.android.com/tools/help/index.html`
Performance Tips	`http://developer.android.com/training/articles/perf-tips.html`
Keeping Your App Responsive	`http://developer.android.com/training/articles/perf-anr.html`
Launch Checklist (for Google Play)	`http://developer.android.com/distribute/tools/launch-checklist.html`
Getting Started with Publishing	`http://developer.android.com/distribute/googleplay/start.html`
Managing Your App's Memory	`http://developer.android.com/training/articles/memory.html`
Google Play Developer Distribution Agreement	`http://play.google.com/about/developer-distribution-agreement.html`

Fig. 1.28 | Key online documentation for Android developers. (Part 2 of 2.)

Title	Subscribe	Description
Android Discuss	*Subscribe using Google Groups:* `android-discuss` *Subscribe via e-mail:* `android-discuss-subscribe@googlegroups.com`	A general Android discussion group where you can get answers to your app-development questions.
Stack Overflow	`http://stackoverflow.com/questions/tagged/android`	Use this for Android app-development questions and questions about best practices.
Android Developers	`http://groups.google.com/forum/?fromgroups#!forum/android-developers`	Experienced Android developers use this list for troubleshooting apps, GUI design issues, performance issues and more.
Android Forums	`http://www.androidforums.com`	Ask questions, share tips with other developers and find forums targeting specific Android devices.

Fig. 1.29 | Android newsgroups and forums.

Android development tips, videos and resources	URL
Android Sample Code and Utilities from Google	`https://github.com/google` (use the filter `"android"`)
Bright Hub™ website for Android programming tips and how-to guides	`http://www.brighthub.com/mobile/google-android.aspx`
The Android Developers Blog	`http://android-developers.blogspot.com/`
HTC's Developer Center for Android	`http://www.htcdev.com/`
The Motorola Android development site	`http://developer.motorola.com/`
Top Android Users on Stack Overflow	`http://stackoverflow.com/tags/android/topusers`
Android Weekly Newsletter	`http://androidweekly.net/`
Chet Haase's Codependent blog	`http://graphics-geek.blogspot.com/`
Romain Guy's Android blog	`http://www.curious-creature.org/category/android/`
Android Developers Channel on YouTube®	`http://www.youtube.com/user/androiddevelopers`
Google I/O 2015 Developer Conference session videos	`https://events.google.com/io2015/videos`

Fig. 1.30 | Android development tips, videos and resources.

1.12 Wrap-Up

This chapter presented a brief history of Android and discussed its functionality. We provided links to some of the key online documentation and to the newsgroups and forums you can use to connect with the developer community and get your questions answered. We discussed features of the Android operating system. We introduced the Java, Android and Google packages that enable you to use the hardware and software functionality you'll need to build a variety of Android apps. You'll use many of these packages in this book. We also discussed Java programming and the Android SDK. You learned the Android gestures and how to perform each on an Android device and on the emulator. We provided a quick refresher on basic object-technology concepts, including classes, objects, attributes, behaviors, encapsulation, information hiding, inheritance and more. You test-drove the **Tip Calculator** app on the Android emulator for both smartphone and tablet AVDs.

In Chapter 2, you'll build your first Android app in Android Studio. The app will display text and an image. You'll also learn about Android accessibility and internationalization.

Welcome App

Dive-Into® Android Studio: Introducing Visual GUI Design, Layouts, Accessibility and Internationalization

Objectives

In this chapter you'll:

- Understand the basics of the Android Studio IDE, which you'll use to write, test and debug your Android apps.

- Use the IDE to create a new app project.

- Design a graphical user interface (GUI) visually (without programming) using the IDE's layout editor.

- Display text and an image in a GUI.

- Edit the properties of views (GUI components).

- Build and launch an app in the Android emulator.

- Make the app more accessible to visually impaired people by specifying strings for use with Android's TalkBack and Explore-by-Touch features.

- Support internationalization so your app can display strings localized in different languages.

2.1 Introduction

In this chapter, you'll build the **Welcome** app that displays a welcome message and an image. You'll use Android Studio to create a simple app (Fig. 2.1) that runs on Android phones and tablets in both portrait and landscape orientations:

- In portrait the device's height is greater than its width.
- In landscape the width is greater than the height.

You'll use Android Studio's layout editor to build the GUI using *drag-and-drop* techniques. You'll also edit the GUI's XML directly. You'll execute your app in the Android *emulator* and on an Android device, if you have one.

You'll provide descriptive text for the app's image to make the app more *accessible* for people with visual impairments. As you'll see, Android's *Explore by Touch* enables users to touch items on the screen and hear *TalkBack* speak the corresponding descriptive text. We'll discuss how to test these features, which are available only on Android devices.

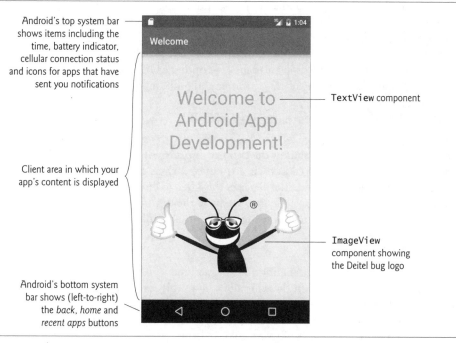

Android's top system bar shows items including the time, battery indicator, cellular connection status and icons for apps that have sent you notifications

Client area in which your app's content is displayed

Android's bottom system bar shows (left-to-right) the *back, home* and *recent apps* buttons

`TextView` component

`ImageView` component showing the Deitel bug logo

Fig. 2.1 | **Welcome** app running in the Android emulator.

Finally, you'll *internationalize* the app so that you can provide *localized* strings in different languages. You'll then change the locale setting on the Android emulator so that you can test the app in Spanish. When your app executes, Android chooses the correct strings based on the device's locale. We show how to change the locale on a device. We assume that you've read the Preface, Before You Begin and Section 1.9.

2.2 Technologies Overview

This section introduces the technologies you'll use to build the **Welcome** app.

2.2.1 Android Studio

In Section 2.3, you'll use the Android Studio integrated development environment (IDE) to create a new app. As you'll see, the IDE creates a default GUI that contains the text `"Hello world!"` You'll then use the layout editor's **Design** and **Text** views and the **Properties** window to visually build a simple graphical user interface (GUI) consisting of text and an image (Section 2.5).

2.2.2 `LinearLayout`, `TextView` and `ImageView`

GUI components in Android are called views. Layouts are views that contain and arrange other views. You'll use a vertical `LinearLayout` to arrange the app's text and image with each occupying half the `LinearLayout`'s vertical space. A `LinearLayout` also can arrange views horizontally.

This app's text is displayed in a `TextView` and its image is displayed in an `ImageView`. The default GUI created by Android Studio already contains a `TextView`. You'll modify its properties, including its text, font size and font color and its size relative to the `ImageView` within the `LinearLayout` (Section 2.5.5). You'll use the layout editor's **Palette** of views (Fig. 2.11) to drag and drop an `ImageView` onto the GUI (Section 2.5.11), then configure its properties, including its image source and positioning within the `LinearLayout`.

2.2.3 Extensible Markup Language (XML)

Extensible Markup Language (XML) is a natural way to express GUIs. XML is human- and computer-readable text and, in the context of Android, helps you specify the layouts and components to use, as well as their attributes, such as size, position, color, text size, margins and padding. Android Studio parses the XML to display your design in the layout editor and to generate the Java code that produces the runtime GUI. You'll also use XML files to store app resources, such as strings, numbers and colors (Section 2.2.4).

2.2.4 App Resources

It's considered good practice to define all strings, numeric values and other values in XML resource files that are placed in the subfolders of a project's `res` folder. In Section 2.5.5, you'll create resources for strings (such as the text on a `TextView`) and measurements (such as a font's size). For the `TextView`'s font color, you'll create a color resource using a color selected from Google's Material Design color palette:

```
http://www.google.com/design/spec/style/color.html
```

2.2.5 Accessibility

Android provides *accessibility* features to help people with certain disabilities use their devices. People with visual impairments can use Android's TalkBack to allow a device to speak screen text or text that you provide to help them understand the purpose and contents of a view. Android's Explore by Touch enables the user to touch the screen to hear TalkBack speak what's on the screen near the touch. Section 2.7 shows how to enable these features and configure your app's views for accessibility.

2.2.6 Internationalization

Android devices are used worldwide. To reach the most users with your apps, you should consider customizing them for various *locales* and spoken languages. Configuring your app so that it can be customized for various locales is known as internationalization. Customizing your app for a specific locale is known as localization. Section 2.8 shows how to provide Spanish text for the **Welcome** app's `TextView` and the `ImageView`'s accessibility string, and how to test the app on an AVD or device configured for Spanish.

2.3 Creating an App

This book's examples were developed using the Android 6 SDK that was current at the time of this writing. This section shows you how to use Android Studio to create a new project. We introduce additional features of the IDE throughout the book.

2.3.1 Launching Android Studio

As you did in Section 1.9, open Android Studio via its shortcut:

The IDE displays either the **Welcome** window (Fig. 1.17) or the last project you had open.

2.3.2 Creating a New Project

A *project* is a group of related files, such as code files, resource files and images that make up an app. To create an app, you must first create its project. To do so, click **Start a new Android Studio project** in the **Welcome** window or, if a project is open, select **File > New > New Project...**. This displays the **Create New Project** dialog (Fig. 2.2).

Current step being performed in the **Create New Project** dialog

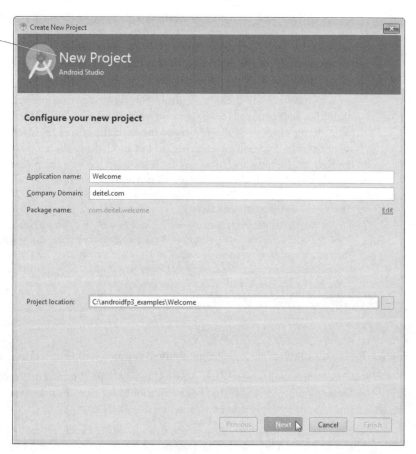

Fig. 2.2 | Create New Project dialog—New Project step.

2.3.3 Create New Project Dialog

In the **Create New Project** dialog's **Configure your new project** step (Fig. 2.2), specify the following information, then click **Next**:

1. **Application name:** field—Your app's name. Enter `Welcome` in this field.

2. **Company Domain:** field—Your company website's domain name. We used our `deitel.com` website domain. For learning purposes you can use `example.com`, but this must be changed if you intend to distribute your app.

3. **Package name:** field—The Java package name for your app's source code. Android and the Google Play store use this as the app's *unique identifier*, which must remain the same in all versions of your app that you upload to the Google Play store. The package name normally begins with your company's or institution's **Company Domain** *in reverse*—our **Company Domain** is `deitel.com`, so our Java package names begin with `com.deitel`. This is followed by a dot (.) and the app's name in all lowercase letters with any spaces removed. By convention, package names use only lowercase letters. The IDE sets the package name using the text you enter for **Application Name** and **Company Domain**. You can click the **Edit** link to the right of the generated package name to customize the **Package name**.

4. **Project location:** field—The path of the location on your computer in which to store the project. By default, Android Studio places new project folders in the subfolder `AndroidStudioProjects` in your user account directory. A project's folder name consists of the project name with the spaces removed. You also can customize the location by entering a path or clicking the ellipsis (...) button to the right of the field and browsing for a location to store the project. After selecting a location, click **OK**. Click **Next** to move to the next step.

> **Error-Prevention Tip 2.1**
>
> *If the path to the folder in which you wish to save a project contains spaces, the* **Create New Project** *dialog displays the message* "Your project location contains whitespace. This can cause problems on some platforms and is not recommended." *To resolve this, click the ellipsis (...) button to the right of the* **Create New Project** *dialog's* **Project location** *field and select a location that does not contain spaces; otherwise, your project might not compile or execute correctly.*

2.3.4 Target Android Devices Step

In the **Create New Project** dialog's **Target Android Devices** step (Fig. 2.3):

1. Check the checkbox for each Android device type (**Phone and Tablet**, **TV**, **Wear**, **Android Auto** and **Glass**) that your app should support. For the **Welcome** app, ensure that only the **Phone and Tablet** type is checked.

2. Next, select a **Minimum SDK** in the drop-down for each type of device that you selected, then click **Next**. The **Minimum SDK** is the minimum Android API level that's required to run your app. This allows your app to execute on devices supporting that API level and higher. Select **API23: Android 6.0 (Marshmallow)** for this

book's apps and click **Next**. Figure 2.4 shows the Android SDK versions and their API levels—versions not shown here are deprecated and should not be used. The percentage of Android devices running each platform version is shown at

```
http://developer.android.com/about/dashboards/index.html
```

 Software Engineering Observation 2.1
*Lower **Minimum SDK** values enable your app to run on more devices—e.g., at the time of this writing, you could reach 94% of devices with API 15. Generally you should target the lowest API level on which your app can run. You must disable newer features that are not available on older platforms when your app is installed on those platforms.*

Create New Project

Target Android Devices

Select the form factors your app will run on

Different platforms may require separate SDKs

☑ Phone and Tablet

    Minimum SDK   API 23: Android 6.0 (Marshmallow)

    Lower API levels target more devices, but have fewer features available. By targeting API 23 and later, your app will run on < 1% of the devices that are active on the Google Play Store.

    Help me choose

☐ Wear

    Minimum SDK   API 21: Android 5.0 (Lollipop)

☐ TV

    Minimum SDK   API 21: Android 5.0 (Lollipop)

☐ Android Auto

☐ Glass (Not Installed)   Download

    Minimum SDK

Previous   Next   Cancel   Finish

Fig. 2.3 | Create New Project dialog—Target Android Devices step.

SDK version	API level	SDK version	API level	SDK version	API level
6.0	23	4.3	18	2.3.3–2.3.7	10
5.1	22	4.2.x	17	2.2	8
5.0	21	4.1.x	16		
4.4	19	4.0.3–4.0.4	15		

Fig. 2.4 | Android SDK versions and API levels. (`http://developer.android.com/about/dashboards/index.html`)

2.3.5 Add an Activity to Mobile Step

In the **Add an Activity to Mobile** step (Fig. 2.5), you'll select an app template. Templates provide preconfigured starting points for common app designs and app logic.

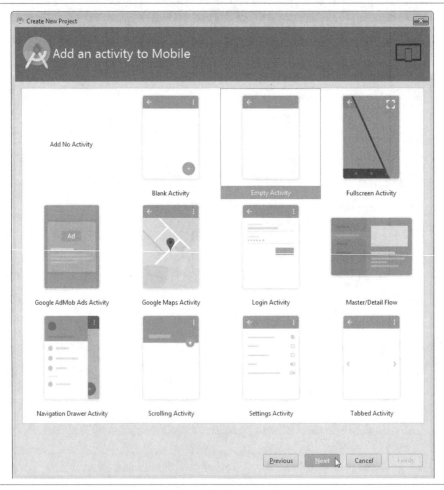

Fig. 2.5 | Create New Project dialog—Add an activity to Mobile step.

Figure 2.6 briefly describes four commonly used templates from Fig. 2.5. For this app, select **Empty Activity**, then click **Next**. This template defines a one-screen app that displays **Hello World!**. We'll use other templates in later chapters. For multiscreen apps, you also can define a new screen by adding one of the Fig. 2.5 activities to an existing app. For example, in Chapter 4's **Flag Quiz** app, we'll add a **Settings Activity** that provides a screen in which the user can specify the quizzes settings.

Template	Description
Blank Activity	Used for a *single-screen app* in which you build most of the GUI yourself. Provides an *app bar* at the top of the app that displays the app's name and can display controls that enable a user to interact with the app. Also includes a material design `FloatingActionButton`.
Fullscreen Activity	Used for a *single-screen app* (similar to **Blank Activity**) that occupies the entire screen, but can toggle visibility of the device's status bar and the app's app bar.
Master/Detail Flow	Used for an app that displays a *master list* of items from which a user can choose one item to see its *details*—similar to the built-in **Email** and **Contacts** apps. Includes basic logic for enabling a user to select an item from the master list and display that item in the detail view. For tablets, the master list and details are shown side-by-side on the same screen. For phones, the master list is shown on one screen, and selecting an item displays the item's details in a separate screen.

Fig. 2.6 | Activity templates.

2.3.6 Customize the Activity Step

This step (Fig. 2.7) depends on the template selected in the previous step. For the **Empty Activity** template, this step allows you to specify:

- **Activity Name**—`MainActivity` is the default name provided by the IDE. This is the name of an `Activity` subclass that controls the app's execution. Starting in Chapter 3, we'll modify this class to implement the app's functionality.

- **Layout Name**—`activity_main` is the default name provided by the IDE. This file (which has the `.xml` extension) stores an XML representation of the app's GUI that you'll build in Section 2.5 using visual techniques.

For this app, keep the default settings, then click **Finish** to create the project.

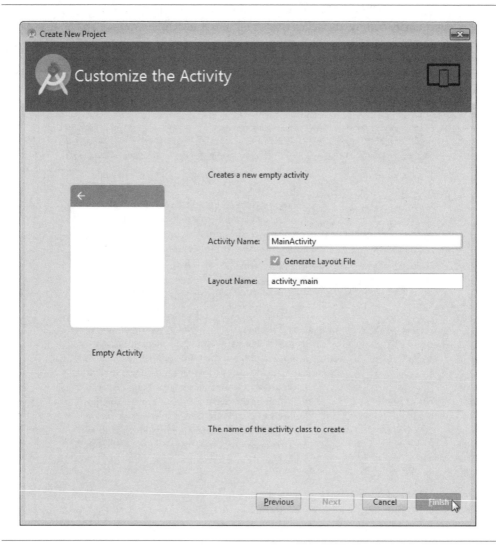

Fig. 2.7 | Create New Project dialog—**Customize the Activity** step.

2.4 Android Studio Window

When you finish creating the project, the IDE opens both MainActivity.java and activity_main.xml. Close MainActivity.java so that the IDE appears as shown in Fig. 2.8. The IDE shows the layout editor, so you can begin designing your app's GUI. In this chapter, we discuss only the IDE features we need to build the **Welcome** app. We'll introduce more IDE features throughout the book.

Project window displays the project's files in the **app** node

Editor windows—like the layout and code editors—appear here

Component Tree with the currently selected item properties displayed in the **Properties** window

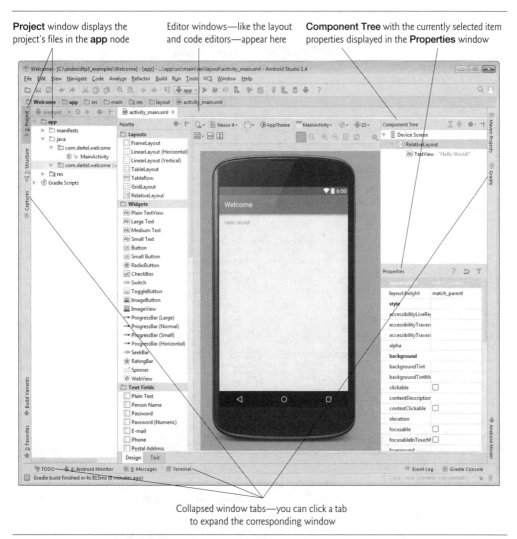

Collapsed window tabs—you can click a tab
to expand the corresponding window

Fig. 2.8 | Welcome project open in the Android Studio.

2.4.1 Project Window

The **Project** window provides access to all of the project's files. You can have many projects open in the IDE at once—each in its own window. Figure 2.9 shows the **Welcome** app project's contents in the **Project** window—we expanded the res folder and it's nested layout folder. The app folder contains the files you'll edit to create your apps' GUIs and logic. The app folder's contents are organized into nested folders containing files. In this chapter, you'll use only files located in the res folder, which we discuss in Section 2.4.4—we'll discuss the other folders and files as we use them in later chapters.

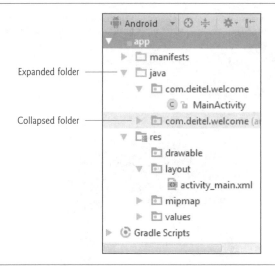

Expanded folder ————

Collapsed folder ————

Fig. 2.9 | Project window.

2.4.2 Editor Windows

To the right of the **Project** window in Fig. 2.8 is the layout editor window. When you double click a file in the **Project** window, its contents are displayed in an appropriate editor window, depending on the file's type. For a Java file, the Java source-code editor is displayed. For an XML file that represents a GUI (such as `activity_main.xml`), the layout editor's **Design** tab is displayed by default and you can click the **Text** tab to view the corresponding XML side-by-side with a design preview—if the preview does not appear, you can view it by selecting **View > Tool Windows > Preview**. For other XML files, a custom XML editor or text-based XML editor is displayed, depending on the XML files' purposes. The code editors for Java and XML help you write code quickly and correctly via *code-completion*—as you type, you can press *Enter* (or *Return*) to auto-complete a Java code element or an XML element name, attribute name or value that is currently highlighted in the code-completion window.

2.4.3 Component Tree Window

When the layout editor is open in **Design** view, the **Component Tree** appears at the right side of the IDE (Fig. 2.8). This window shows the *layouts* and *views* (GUI components) that comprise the GUI and their parent-child relationships—for example, a layout (the parent) might contain many nested views (the children), including other layouts.

2.4.4 App Resource Files

Layout files like `activity_main.xml` are app resources and are stored in subfolders of the project's `res` folder. The subfolders contain different resource types. The ones we use in this app are shown in Fig. 2.10, and the others (`menu`, `animator`, `anim`, `color`, `mipmap`, `raw` and `xml`) are discussed as we need them later in the book.

Resource subfolder	Description
drawable	Folder names that begin with drawable typically contain images. These folders may also contain XML files representing shapes and other types of drawables (such as the images that represent a button's *unpressed* and *pressed* states).
layout	Folder names that begin with layout contain XML files that describe GUIs, such as the activity_main.xml file.
values	Folder names that begin with values contain XML files that specify values for *arrays* (arrays.xml), *colors* (colors.xml), *dimensions* (dimens.xml—values such as widths, heights and font sizes), *strings* (strings.xml) and *styles* (styles.xml). These file names are used by convention but are *not* required—actually, you can place all resources of these types in *one* file. It's considered good practice to define the data from hard-coded arrays, colors, sizes, strings and styles as *resources* so they can be modified easily without changing the app's Java code. For example, if a *dimension resource* is referenced from many locations in your code, you can change the dimension's value in the resource file, rather than search for every occurrence of a hard-coded dimension value in your app's Java source files.

Fig. 2.10 | Subfolders of the project's res folder that are used in this chapter.

2.4.5 Layout Editor

When you first create a project, the IDE opens the app's activity_main.xml file in the layout editor (Fig. 2.11). You also can double click activity_main.xml in the res/layout folder to open the file in the layout editor.

Selecting the Screen Type for GUI Design

Android devices can run on many types of devices. In this chapter, you'll design an Android phone GUI. As we mentioned in the Before You Begin section, we use an AVD that emulates the Google Nexus 6 phone for this purpose. The layout editor comes with many device configurations that represent various screen sizes and resolutions that you can use to design your GUI. For this chapter, we use the predefined **Nexus 6**, which you can select in the virtual-device drop-down at the top of the layout editor in Fig. 2.11—**Nexus 4** is selected by default. This does not mean that the app can execute only on a Nexus 6 device—it simply means that the design is for devices similar in screen size and resolution to the Nexus 6. In later chapters, you'll see how to design your GUIs to scale appropriately for a wide range of devices.

The **Palette** contains **Widgets** (views),
Layouts and other items that can be dragged
and dropped onto the canvas

The virtual device drop-down lists devices you
can use to design your GUI—select **Nexus 6** for
this chapter

Layout editor's **Design** tab

Canvas (the GUI design area)

Fig. 2.11 | Layout editor view of the app's default GUI.

2.4.6 Default GUI

The default GUI for a **Blank Page** app (Fig. 2.11) consists of a RelativeLayout with a
white background and a TextView containing "Hello World!". A RelativeLayout arrang-
es views *relative to one another* or *relative to the layout itself*—for example, you can specify
that one view should appear *below* another and be *centered horizontally* within the RelativeLayout. For the **Welcome** app, you'll change the RelativeLayout to a vertical
LinearLayout in which text and an image will be arranged top-to-bottom on the screen

and each will occupy half the layout's height. A TextView displays text. You'll add an ImageView to display the image. We'll say more about each of these in Section 2.5.

2.4.7 XML for the Default GUI

As we mentioned previously, the file activity_main.xml contains the GUI's XML representation. Figure 2.12 shows the initial XML. We reduced the amount of indentation in the default XML for book-publication purposes. You'll edit this XML directly to change the RelativeLayout to a LinearLayout.

```
 1   <?xml version="1.0" encoding="utf-8"?>
 2   <RelativeLayout xmlns:android="http://schemas.android.com/apk/res/android"
 3       xmlns:tools="http://schemas.android.com/tools"
 4       android:layout_width="match_parent"
 5       android:layout_height="match_parent"
 6       android:paddingBottom="@dimen/activity_vertical_margin"
 7       android:paddingLeft="@dimen/activity_horizontal_margin"
 8       android:paddingRight="@dimen/activity_horizontal_margin"
 9       android:paddingTop="@dimen/activity_vertical_margin"
10       tools:context=".MainActivity">
11
12       <TextView
13           android:layout_width="wrap_content"
14           android:layout_height="wrap_content"
15           android:text="@string/hello_world" />
16
17   </RelativeLayout>
```

Fig. 2.12 | Initial contents of the project's activity_main.xml file.

The attribute values that begin with @, such as

```
@dimen/activity_vertical_margin
```

in line 6, are *resources* with values defined in other files. By default, the XML editor displays a resource's literal value (16dp for the resource in line 6) and highlights the value with a light green background (or light gray, if you're using the dark Android Studio theme). This enables you to see the resource's actual value that's used in a particular context. If you click the literal value (16dp for @dimen/activity_vertical_margin), the editor instead displays the corresponding resource name.

2.5 Building the App's GUI with the Layout Editor

You'll now create the **Welcome** app's GUI. The IDE's layout editor allows you to build your GUI by dragging and dropping views—such as TextViews, ImageViews and Buttons—onto the layout editor. By default, the GUI layout for an app based on the **Empty Activity** template is stored in an XML file called activity_main.xml, located in the project's res folder in the layout subfolder. In this chapter, we'll use the layout editor and the **Component Tree** window to build the GUI. You'll edit the XML in activity_main.xml only to change the layout used to arrange this app's TextView and ImageView.

2.5.1 Adding an Image to the Project

For this app, you'll need to add an image to the project. We'll use the Deitel bug logo[1] image (bug.png), which is located with the book's examples in the images folder's Welcome subfolder. File names for image resources—and all the other resources you'll use in later chapters—must be in all *lowercase* letters.

drawable *Folders*

Android devices have various *screen sizes*, *resolutions* and *pixel densities* (that is, dots per inch or DPI), so you typically provide images in various resolutions that the operating system chooses based on a device's pixel density. These are placed in drawable folders (in a project's res folder) that store images with different pixel densities (Fig. 2.13). For example, images for devices that are similar in pixel density to the Google Nexus 6 phone (560 dpi) we use in our phone AVD would be placed in the folder drawable-xxxhdpi. Images for devices with lower pixel densities are placed in the other drawable folders—normally the folder that represents the closest pixel density to the actual device.

Density	Description
drawable-ldpi	*Low density*—approximately 120 dots-per-inch.
drawable-mdpi	*Medium density*—approximately 160 dots-per-inch.
drawable-hdpi	*High density*—approximately 240 dots-per-inch.
drawable-xhdpi	*Extra-high density*—approximately 320 dots-per-inch.
drawable-xxhdpi	*Extra-Extra-high density*—approximately 480 dots-per-inch.
drawable-xxxhdpi	*Extra-Extra-Extra-high density*—approximately 640 dots-per-inch.

Fig. 2.13 | Android pixel densities.

Android Studio displays only one drawable folder containing the app's drawable resources, even if your project contains resources for multiple densities. For a resource stored in the project's folder drawable-xxxhdpi on disk, Android Studio displays

    filename.xml (xxxhdpi)

in the project's drawable folder.

For this app, we provide only one version of the image. If Android cannot find an image in the drawable folder that most closely matches the device's pixel density, Android will scale the version from another drawable folder up or down as necessary. By default, Android Studio creates only a drawable folder without a DPI qualifier, which we'll use for this initial app. For detailed information on supporting multiple screens and screen sizes in Android, visit:

    http://developer.android.com/guide/practices/screens_support.html

---

1. Before you use any image in an app, you should ensure that you've properly licensed the image. Some image licenses require you to pay for the right to use an image and others provide free open-source or Creative Commons (creativecommons.org) licenses.

Look-and-Feel Observation 2.1

Low-resolution images do not scale well. For images to render nicely, a high-pixel-density device needs highe-resolution images than a low-pixel-density device.

Adding **bug.png** to the Project

Perform the following steps to add the images to this project:

1. In the **Project** window, expand the project's res folder.

2. In the book's examples folder on your file system, open the images folder, then the Welcome subfolder.

3. Copy the bug.png file, then in Android Studio's **Project** window select res folder's drawable subfolder and paste the file into that subfolder.

4. In the **Copy** dialog that appears, click **OK**.

The image can now be used in the app.

2.5.2 Adding an App Icon

When your app is installed on a device, its icon and name appear with all other installed apps in the launcher, which you can access via the 🔡 icon on your device's home screen. To add the app's launcher icon, right click the res folder, then select **New > Image Asset**. This will open the **Asset Studio** window (Fig. 2.14), which enables you to configure the app's icon from an existing image, a piece of clip art or text.

For this app, we chose the DeitelOrange.png image located in the images folder with the book's examples. To use this image:

1. Click the ellipsis button to the right of the **Image file:** field.

2. Navigate to the images folder in the book's examples folder.

3. Select DeitelOrange.png and click **OK**. Previews of the scaled images are shown in the dialog's **Preview** area.

4. Click **Next**, then click **Finish**.

The IDE creates several scaled versions of the image, each named ic_launcher.png, and places them in the project's mipmap[2] subfolders of the res folder. The mipmap subfolders are similar to the drawable subfolders, but are specifically for the app's icon. When you upload an app to Google Play, you can upload multiple versions of the app for various device sizes and screen resolutions. All images in the mipmap folders are uploaded with every versions of your app, whereas you can remove extra drawable folders for specific pixel densities from a given app version to minimize the total installation size for a particular device.

Look-and-Feel Observation 2.2

Images do not always scale well. For apps that you intend to place in the Google Play store, you might want to have an artist design icons for the appropriate resolutions. In Chapter 10, we discuss submitting apps to the Google Play store and list several companies that offer free and fee-based icon-design services.

---

2. For the origin of the term *mipmap*, see https://en.wikipedia.org/wiki/Mipmap.

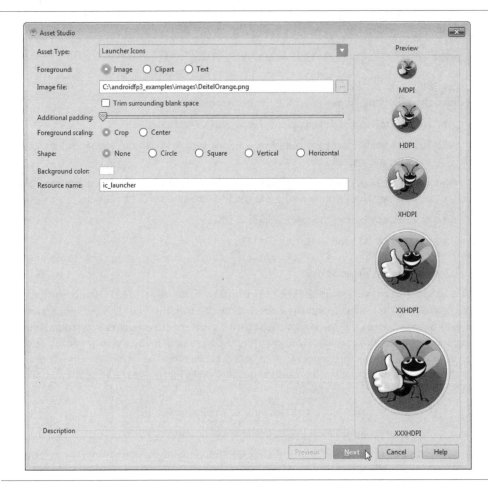

Fig. 2.14 | Configuring the launcher icon in the **Asset Studio** window.

2.5.3 Changing RelativeLayout to a LinearLayout

When you open a layout XML file, the layout's design appears in the layout editor and the layout's views and their hierarchical relationships appear in the **Component Tree** window (Fig. 2.15). To configure a layout or view, you can select it in the layout editor or in the **Component Tree**, then use the **Properties** window below the **Component Tree** to specify the view's property values without editing the XML directly. When designing and modifying more complex layouts, it's often easier to work directly in the **Component Tree**.

Fig. 2.15 | Hierarchical GUI view in the **Component Tree** window.

For some GUI modifications—such as changing the default RelativeLayout to a LinearLayout—you must edit the layout's XML directly. (This might change as Google improves the layout editor's capabilities.) To do so:

1. Click the **Text** tab at the bottom of the layout editor to switch from the **Design** view to the layout's XML text.

2. At the top of the XML (line 2 in Fig. 2.12), double click the XML element name RelativeLayout to select it, then start typing LinearLayout.

3. As you type in line 2, the IDE edits the corresponding ending XML tag (line 17 in Fig. 2.12) simultaneously to keep them in sync, and a code-completion window appears containing element names that begin with the letters you've typed so far. Once LinearLayout appears in the code-completion window and is highlighted, press *Enter* (or *Return*) to select LinearLayout and enable Android Studio to auto-complete the edit.

4. Save the changes and switch back to the layout editor's **Design** tab.

The **Component Tree** should now appear as in Fig. 2.16.

Fig. 2.16 | Component Tree after changing from a RelativeLayout to a LinearLayout.

2.5.4 Changing the LinearLayout's id and orientation

In this section, you'll customize the LinearLayout's properties. In general, give each layout and component a relevant name. This helps you easily identify each view in the **Component Tree** and enables you to manipulate the views programmatically, as we'll do in subsequent apps.

When a GUI is displayed in the layout editor, you can use the **Properties** window below the **Component Tree** (Fig. 2.8) to configure the selected view's properties. You also can edit a view's most commonly used properties (as you'll do in this section) by double clicking the view in the canvas. The layout editor then displays a small dialog in which you can set the view's id property and other properties that depend on the specific view:

- For a LinearLayout, you can set the orientation to specify whether the layout's children are arranged in horizontal or vertical orientation.

- For a TextView, you can set the text that's displayed.

- For an ImageView, you can set the src (source) of the image to display.

Setting the **LinearLayout***'s* **orientation** *and* **id** *Properties*
To change the LinearLayout's orientation, double click the virtual phone screen's white background in the layout editor to display the dialog of common LinearLayout properties, then select **vertical** from the **orientation:** drop-down as shown in Fig. 2.17. This sets the property's value and dismisses the dialog. A view's name is defined by setting its **id**

property, which is specified in the layout's XML with the attribute `android:id`. Double click the virtual phone screen's white background, enter the name `welcomeLinearLayout` in the **id:** field, then press *Enter* (or *Return*) to set the value and dismiss the dialog.

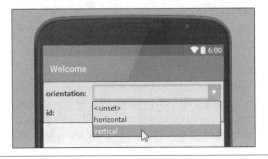

Fig. 2.17 | Setting the `LinearLayout`'s orientation.

The `id` Property's XML Representation
In the layout's XML representation—viewable via the **Text** tab at the bottom of the layout editor—the `LinearLayout`'s `android:id` has the value:

```
@+id/welcomeLinearLayout
```

The + in the syntax `@+id` indicates that a *new* id should be created with the identifier to the right of the forward slash (/). In some cases, the XML contains the same syntax without the + to refer to an existing view—for example, to specify the relationships between views in a `RelativeLayout`.

2.5.5 Configuring the `TextView`'s `id` and `text` Properties
The **Welcome** app's default GUI already contains a `TextView`, so you'll simply modify its properties.

Setting the `TextView`'s `id` Property
Double click the `TextView` in the layout editor, then in the dialog that appears set the **id:** to `welcomeTextView` and press *Enter* (or *Return*).

Configuring the `TextView`'s `text` Property Using a String Resource
According to the Android documentation for application resources

```
http://developer.android.com/guide/topics/resources/index.html
```

it's considered good practice to place strings, string arrays, images, colors, font sizes, dimensions and other app resources in XML files within the subfolders of the project's `res` folder, so these resources can be managed separately from your app's Java code. This is known as *externalizing* the resources. For example, if you externalize color values, all components that use the same color can be updated to a new color simply by changing the color value in a central resource file.

  If you wish to *localize* your app in several languages, storing the strings *separately* from the app's code allows you to change them easily. In your project's `res` folder, the subfolder values contains a `strings.xml` file that's used to store the app's default language strings—English for our apps. To provide localized strings for other languages, you can create separate `values` folders for each language, as we'll demonstrate in Section 2.8.

To set the `TextView`'s `text` property, create a new string resource in the `strings.xml` file as follows:

1. Either double click the `welcomeTextView` in the layout editor or select `welcome-TextView` and locate its `text` property in the **Properties** window

2. Click the ellipsis (...) button to the right of the property's value to display the **Resources** dialog.

3. In the **Resources** dialog, click **New Resource**, then select **New String Value...** to display the **New String Value Resource** dialog and fill the **Resource name:** and **Resource value:** fields as shown in Fig. 2.18. Leave the other settings (we'll discuss these in later sections and apps) and click **OK** to create the new string resource named `welcome` and set it as the value of the `TextView`'s `text` property.

Fig. 2.18 | New String Value Resource dialog.

In the **Properties** window, the `text` property should now appear as in Fig. 2.19. The `@string/` prefix indicates that a string resource will be used to obtain the value for the `text` property and `welcome` indicates the specific string resource to use. By default, the resource is placed in the `strings.xml` file (located in the project's `res/values` folder).

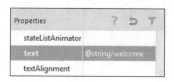

Fig. 2.19 | **Properties** window after changing the `TextView`'s `text` property.

2.5.6 Configuring the `TextView`'s `textSize` Property—Scaled Pixels and Density-Independent Pixels

Sizes can be specified in various measurement units (Fig. 2.20). The documentation for supporting multiple screen sizes recommends that you use *density-independent pixels* for dimensions of views and other screen elements, and *scale-independent pixels* for font sizes:

```
http://developer.android.com/guide/practices/screens_support.html
```

Unit	Description	Unit	Description
px	pixel	in	inches
dp or dip	density-independent pixel	mm	millimeters
sp	scale-independent pixel		

Fig. 2.20 | Measurement units.

Defining your GUIs with density-independent pixels enables the Android platform to *scale* the GUI, based on the pixel density of a given device's screen. One *density-independent pixel* is equivalent to one pixel on a 160-dpi screen. On a 240-dpi screen, each density-independent pixel will be scaled by a factor of 240/160 (i.e., 1.5). So, a component that's 100 *density-independent pixels* wide will be scaled to 150 *actual pixels* wide. On a screen with 120 dpi, each density-independent pixel is scaled by a factor of 120/160 (i.e., 0.75). So, the same component that's 100 density-independent pixels wide will be 75 actual pixels wide. Scale-independent pixels are scaled like density-independent pixels, but they're also scaled by the user's *preferred font size* (as specified in the device's settings).

Creating a Dimension Resource for the Font Size on a Phone Device
You'll now increase the `TextView`'s font size. To change the font size:

1. Select the `welcomeTextView` in the layout editor.

2. Locate the `textSize` property, then click in the right column to reveal the ellipsis (...) button and click the button to display the **Resources** dialog.

3. In the **Resources** dialog, click **New Resource**, then select **New Dimension Value...** to display the **New Dimension Value Resource** dialog.

4. In the dialog that appears, specify `welcome_textsize` for the **Resource name** and `40sp` for the **Resource value**, then click **OK** to dismiss the dialog and return to the **Resources** dialog. The letters `sp` in the value `40sp` indicate that this is a scale-independent pixel measurement. The letters `dp` in a dimension value (e.g., `10dp`) indicate a density-independent pixel measurement. We used the value `40sp` for displaying text on a phone.

In the **Properties** window, the `textSize` property now contains the value:

```
@dimen/welcome_textsize
```

The `@dimen/` prefix indicates that the `textSize` property's value is a dimension resource and `welcome_textsize` indicates the specific dimension resource to use. By default, the resource is placed in the `dimens.xml` file—located in the project's `res/values` folder.

Creating a Dimension Resource for the Font Size on a Large Tablet Device

The 40sp font size works well for phone-sized devices, but is small for tablets. Android can automatically choose different resource values based on device sizes, orientations, pixel densities, spoken languages, locales and more. To specify a separate font size for larger devices such as tablets:

1. Reopen the **New Dimension Value Resource** dialog as described above.

2. Enter welcome_textsize for the **Resource name** (the resource names must match for Android to select different resource values automatically) and enter 80sp for the **Resource value.**

3. Next, you'll create a new values resource folder that's specific to larger devices such as tablets that have widths and heights that are each *at least* 600dp. In the **New Dimension Value Resource** dialog, uncheck the **values** checkbox, and click the **Add** button (➕) to open the **New Resource Directory** dialog. In this dialog's **Available qualifiers** list, select **Screen Width**, then click the **>>** button to add the screen **Screen Width** qualifier to the **Chosen qualifiers** list. Next, enter 600 in the **Screen width** field.

4. Next, add the **Screen Height** qualifier to the **Chosen qualifiers** list and enter 600 for the **Screen height.**

5. Click **OK** to create a new resource folder named values-xlarge.

6. In the **New Dimension Value Resource** dialog, check the values-w600dp-h600dp checkbox, then click **OK.** This creates another welcome_textsize dimension resource in a dimens.xml file that's stored on disk in the project's res/values-w600dp-h600dp folder. Android will use that resource for devices with extra-large screen widths and heights that are at least 600dp, typical of most Android tablets. The new dimens.xml resource file appears in Android Studio in the project's res/values/dimens.xml node as

```
dimens.xml (w600dp-h600dp)
```

2.5.7 Setting the TextView's textColor Property

When you need custom colors in your apps, Google's Material Design guidelines recommend using colors from the Material Design color palette at:

```
http://www.google.com/design/spec/style/color.html
```

Colors are specified as RGB (red-green-blue) or ARGB (alpha-red-green-blue) values. An RGB value consists of integer values in the range 0–255 that define the amounts of red, green and blue in the color, respectively. Custom colors are defined in *hexadecimal* format, so the RGB components are values in the range 00 (the hexadecimal value for 0) to FF (the hexadecimal value for 255).

Android also supports alpha (transparency) values in the range 00 (completely transparent) to FF (completely opaque). To use alpha, you specify the color as #AARRGGBB, where the first two hexadecimal digits represent the alpha value.

If both digits of each color component are the same, you can use the abbreviated value formats #RGB or #ARGB. For example, the RGB value #9AC is equivalent to #99AACC and the ARGB value #F9AC is equivalent to #FF99AACC.

To set the TextView's **textColor** property to a new color resource:

1. In the **Properties** window click the ellipsis (...) button to display the **Resources** dialog, then click **New Resource** and select **New Color Value...**.

2. In the **New Color Value Resource** dialog, enter welcome_text_color for the **Resource name** and #2196F3 for the **Resource value** (Fig. 2.21), then click **OK**.

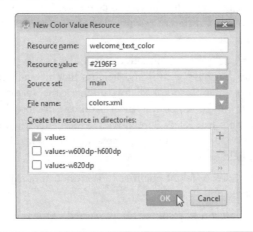

Fig. 2.21 | Creating a **New Color Value Resource** for the TextView's textColor property.

2.5.8 Setting the TextView's gravity Property

To center the text in the TextView if it wraps to multiple lines, you can set its **gravity** property to center. To do so, expand the node for this property, then check the **center** checkbox (Fig. 2.22).

Fig. 2.22 | Options for the **Gravity** property of a TextView.

2.5.9 Setting the `TextView`'s `layout:gravity` Property

Each view you place in a layout has various `layout` properties that enable you to customize the view's size and positioning within the layout. When you select a view in the layout editor or **Component Tree**, the **Properties** window lists the `layout` and `style` properties at the top, followed by the view-specific properties in alphabetical order (Fig. 2.23).

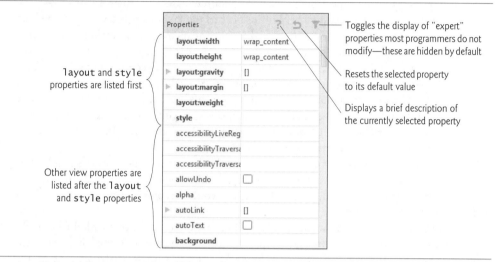

Fig. 2.23 | **Properties** window showing `layout` and `style` properties at the top.

In this app, we'd like to center the `TextView` horizontally within the `LinearLayout`. To do this, you'll set its `layout:gravity` property to center horizontally as follows:

1. With the `TextView` selected, expand the `layout:gravity` property's node in the **Properties** window.

2. Click the value field to the right of the `center` option that appears, then select the `horizontal` option (Fig. 2.24).

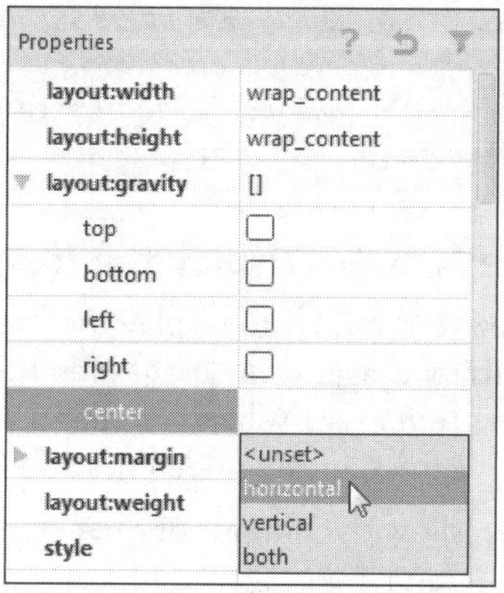

Fig. 2.24 | Setting the `layout:gravity` for the `TextView`.

In the layout XML file, layout properties have attribute names that begin with `layout_`. The preceding `layout:gravity` property setting is represented in XML as:

```
android:layout_gravity="center_horizontal"
```

2.5.10 Setting the `TextView`'s `layout:weight` Property

A `LinearLayout` can proportionally size its children based on their `layout:weight`s, which specify the view's relative size with respect to the layout's other views. By default, the `layout:weight` is 0 for each view you add to a `LinearLayout`, indicating that the view should not be proportionally sized.

In this app, we'd like the `TextView` and `ImageView` to each occupy half of the `LinearLayout`'s vertical space. You accomplish this by setting each view's `layout:weight` to the same value. The `LinearLayout` uses the ratio of each view's `layout:weight` to the total `layout:weight` to allocate space to the views. In this app, you'll set the `layout:weight` to 1 for both the `TextView` and `ImageView` (Section 2.5.11)—the total `layout:weight` will be 2 and each view will occupy 1/2 the layout's height.

If you wanted the `TextView` to occupy one-third of the `LinearLayout`'s height, you could set its `layout:weight` to 1 and the `ImageView`'s `layout:weight` to 2. In this case, the total `layout:weight` is 3, so the `TextView` would occupy 1/3 the height and the `ImageView` 2/3 the height.

Set the `TextView`'s `layout:weight` to 1. The layout editor displays a light bulb (💡) icon to the left of the `layout:height` property—if it does not do so immediately, click the `layout:height` property in the **Properties** window. These icons—generated by a tool in the IDE known as *Android Lint*—warn you of potential problems and help you fix them. When you click the light bulb, the IDE displays the message, "Use a `layout_height` of 0dp instead of `wrap_content` for better performance." Click the message to apply the recommendation. This change enables the `LinearLayout` to calculate its children's sizes more efficiently. The layout editor window should now appear as shown in Fig. 2.25.

Error-Prevention Tip 2.2

*Android Lint checks your project for common errors, and makes suggestions for better security, enhanced performance, improved accessibility, internationalization and more. Some checks occur as you build your apps and write code. You also can select **Analyze > Inspect Code...** to perform additional checks on specific files or your entire project. For more information, visit http://developer.android.com/tools/help/lint.html. For Android Lint's configuration options and output, see http://developer.android.com/tools/debugging/improving-w-lint.html.*

2.5.11 Adding an `ImageView` to Display the Image

Next, you'll add an `ImageView` to the GUI to display the image you added to the project in Section 2.5.1. You'll do this by dragging an `ImageView` from the **Palette**'s **Widgets** section onto the canvas below the `TextView`. When you drag a view onto the canvas, the layout editor displays orange guide lines, green guide lines and a tooltip:

- The *orange guide lines* show the bounds of each existing view in the layout.
- The *green guide lines* indicate where the new view will be placed with respect to the existing views—by default, new views are added at the bottom of a vertical

Fig. 2.25 | Layout editor window after configuring the `TextView`.

LinearLayout, unless you position the mouse above the orange box that bounds the layout's topmost view.

- The *tooltip* displays how the view will be configured if you drop it at the current position.

To add and configure the `ImageView`:

1. From the **Palette**'s **Widgets** section, drag an `ImageView` onto the canvas as shown in Fig. 2.26. *Before releasing the mouse*, ensure that **center** appears in the tooltip at the top of the design—this indicates that the layout editor will set the Image-View's `layout:gravity` property to center the `ImageView` horizontally in the LinearLayout. When you drop the `ImageView` by releasing the mouse, the layout editor assumes that the `ImageView`'s `layout:weight` should be the same as the `TextView`'s and sets the `layout:weight` to 1. It also sets the `layout_height` to 0dp as we did for the `TextView`. The new `ImageView` appears below the `TextView` in the design and below `welcomeTextView` in the **Component Tree**. The Image-View's properties are displayed in the **Properties** window.

Tooltip indicating that the layout editor will set the new `ImageView`'s `layout:gravity` property to center the `ImageView` horizontally in the `LinearLayout`

Orange guide lines showing the `TextView`'s bounds

When you drag the `ImageView` onto the design, the layout editor displays a green line indicating where the `ImageView` (or any other view you drag) will be placed

Fig. 2.26 | Dragging and dropping an `ImageView` onto the GUI.

2. In the **Properties** window, locate the `ImageView`'s `src` property (which specifies the image to display), then click its value field's ellipsis button to display the **Resources** dialog (Fig. 2.27). When the dialog opens, type `bug` to search the list of resources for the image you added in Section 2.5.1, then click **OK**. For every image you place in a `drawable` folder, the IDE generates a unique resource ID (i.e., a resource name) that you can use to reference that image. An image's resource ID is the image's file name without the file-name extension—`bug` for the `bug.png` file.

3. Double-click the `ImageView` in the layout editor and set its `id:` to `bugImageView`.

The GUI should now appear as in Fig. 2.28. If you select the `ImageView` in the layout editor, Android Lint displays a light bulb (💡) next to the `ImageView`—clicking this displays a message indicating that a property is missing for visually impaired users. You'll correct this in Section 2.7.

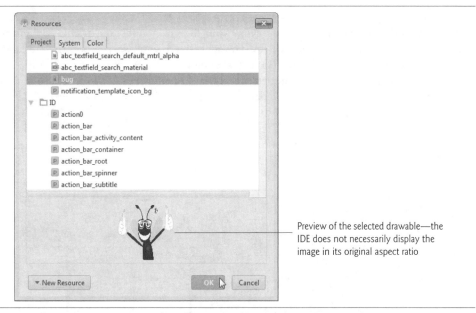

Preview of the selected drawable—the
IDE does not necessarily display the
image in its original aspect ratio

Fig. 2.27 | Selecting the bug image resource from the **Resources** dialog.

Android Lint indicating
that the **ImageView** is
missing a property for
visually impaired users

Fig. 2.28 | Preview of the completed design.

2.5.12 Previewing the Design

Android Studio also enables you to preview your design in landscape orientation and to preview your design for multiple devices. To toggle the design between portrait and landscape orientations, simply click the **Go to next state** button (🔲) in the toolbar at the top of the layout editor. This helps you determine whether your design adjusts appropriately for each orientation. To preview the design for multiple devices, click the virtual device drop-down (Fig. 2.11) at the top of the layout editor, then select **Preview All Screen Sizes**.This displays miniature screens (Fig. 2.29) for many devices listed in the virtual device drop-down—some in portrait and some in landscape. These help you quickly determine whether your design works appropriately on various devices.

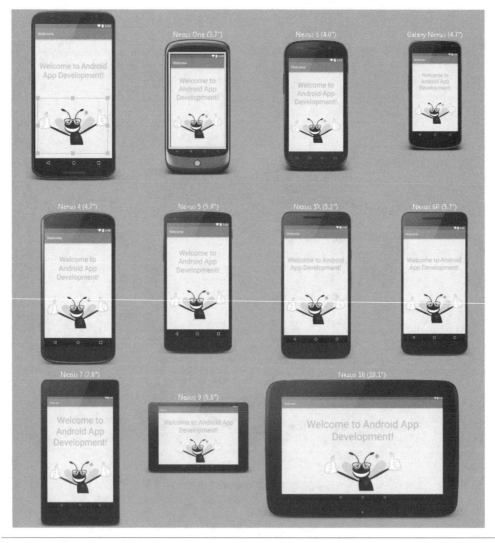

Fig. 2.29 | Previewing various devices for the **Welcome** app's design.

You can return to displaying one device by clicking the virtual device drop-down and selecting **Remove Previews**. You also can preview your design for a particular device be selecting that device in the virtual device drop-down.

2.6 Running the Welcome App

You're now ready to run the **Welcome** app. Perform the steps shown in Section 1.9.3 to run the app on the AVDs you configured previously for both the Nexus 6 phone and Nexus 9 tablet. Figures 2.30–2.31 show the app running in the Nexus 6 AVD (in portrait and landscape) and the Nexus 9 AVD (in landscape), respectively. You can toggle an AVD between portrait and landscape orientations by typing *Ctrl + F11* or *control + F11*. Typically, for apps that run on both phones and tablets, you'll also provide a tablet layout that makes better use of the screen's available space, as we'll demonstrate in later chapters. If you have an Android device, you can follow the steps in Section 1.9.4 to run the app on your device.

Fig. 2.30 | **Welcome** app running in the Nexus 6 AVD.

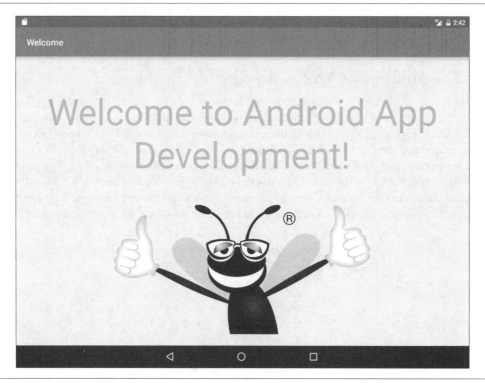

Fig. 2.31 | **Welcome** app running in the Nexus 9 AVD.

2.7 Making Your App Accessible

Android contains *accessibility* features to help people with certain disabilities use their devices. For people with visual disabilities, Android's TalkBack can speak screen text or text that you provide (when designing your GUI or programmatically) to help the user understand the purpose of a view. Android also provides *Explore by Touch*, which enables the user to hear TalkBack speak what's on the screen where the user touches.

When TalkBack is enabled and the user touches a view for which accessibility text is specified, the device vibrates to indicate that the user touched a significant view and TalkBack speaks the views's accessibility text. All standard Android views support accessibility. For those that display text, TalkBack speaks that text by default—e.g., when the user touches a TextView, TalkBack speaks the TextView's text. You enable TalkBack in the **Settings** app under **Accessibility**. From that page, you also can enable other Android accessibility features such as a *larger default text size* and the ability to use *gestures that magnify areas of the screen*. TalkBack is *not* currently supported on AVDs, so you must run this app on a device to hear TalkBack speak the text. When you enable TalkBack, Android walks you through a tutorial on using TalkBack with Explore by Touch.

Enabling TalkBack for the ImageViews

In the **Welcome** app, we don't need more descriptive text for the TextView, because TalkBack will read the TextView's content. For an ImageView, however, there is no text for

TalkBack to speak unless you provide it. It's considered good practice in Android to ensure that *every* view can be used with TalkBack by providing text for the `contentDescription` property of any view that does not display text. For that reason, the IDE warned us that something was wrong by displaying a light-bulb icon (🔆—as you saw in Fig. 2.28) in the layout editor next to the `ImageView`. If you click the light bulb, you'll see the message, "[Accessibility] Missing `contentDescription` attribute on image." The text you provide should help the user understand the purpose of the component. For an `ImageView`, the text should describe the image.

To add the `ImageView`'s `contentDescription` (and eliminate the warning):

1. Select the `bugImageView` in the layout editor.

2. In the **Properties** window, click the ellipsis button to the right of the `contentDescription` property to open the **Resources** dialog.

3. Click **New Resource**, then select **New String Value...** to display the **New String Value Resource** dialog.

4. In the **Resource name** field specify `deitel_logo` and in the **Resource value** field specify `"Deitel double-thumbs-up bug logo"`, then press **OK**. The new string resource is chosen automatically as the `contentDescription` value.

After you set the `ImageView`'s `contentDescription`, the layout editor removes the warning light bulb.

Testing the App with TalkBack Enabled
Run this app on a device with TalkBack enabled, then touch the `TextView` and `ImageView` to hear TalkBack speak the corresponding text.

Dynamically Created Views
Some apps dynamically create views in response to user interactions. For such views, you can programmatically set the accessibility text. For more information on this and Android's other accessibility features, and for a checklist to follow when developing accessible apps, visit:

```
http://developer.android.com/design/patterns/accessibility.html
http://developer.android.com/guide/topics/ui/accessibility
```

2.8 Internationalizing Your App

To reach the largest possible audience, you should consider designing your apps so that they can be customized for various locales and spoken languages. Then, if you intend to offer your app, for example, in France, you would translate its resources (text, audio files, etc.) into French. You might also choose to use different colors, graphics and sounds based on the *locale*. For each locale, you'll have a separate, customized set of resources. When the user launches the app, Android automatically finds and loads the resources that match the device's locale settings. Designing an app so it can be customized is known as *internationalization*. Customizing an app's resources for each locale is known as *localization*.

2.8.1 Localization

A key benefit of defining your string values as string resources (as we did in this app) is that you can easily *localize* your app by creating additional XML resource files for those string resources in other languages. In each file, you use the same string-resource names, but provide the *translated* string. Android can then choose the appropriate resource file based on the device user's preferred language.

2.8.2 Naming the Folders for Localized Resources

The XML resource files containing localized strings are placed on disk in subfolders of the project's `res` folder. Android uses a special folder-naming scheme to automatically choose the correct localized resources—for example, the folder `values-fr` would contain a `strings.xml` file for French and the folder `values-es` would contain a `strings.xml` file for Spanish. You also can name these folders with region information—`values-en-rUS` would contain a `strings.xml` file for United States English and `values-en-rGB` would contain a `strings.xml` file for United Kingdom English. If localized resources are not provided for a given locale, Android uses the app's *default* resources—that is, those in the `res` folder's `values` subfolder. We discuss these alternative-resource naming conventions in more detail in later chapters.

2.8.3 Adding String Translations to the App's Project

Android Studio provides a **Translations Editor** for quickly and easily adding translations for existing strings in your app. Follow these steps to add translated strings to the project:

1. In the **Project** window, expand the `values` node, then open the `strings.xml` file.

2. In the editor's upper-right corner, click the **Open editor** link to open the **Translations Editor.**

3. In the upper-left corner of the **Translations Editor,** click the **Add Locale** button (🌐), then select **Spanish (es)**—you can search for this entry by typing part of the language name or its abbreviation (es). After you select the locale in the list, a new `strings.xml (es)` file will be created and be placed in the `strings.xml` node in the **Project** window (the file is stored in a `values-es` folder on disk). The **Translations Editor** also displays a new column for the Spanish translations.

4. To add a Spanish translation for a given `String` resource, click the cell for the resource's **Spanish (es)** translation, then in the **Translation:** field at the bottom of the window enter the Spanish text. If a string should not be translated (for example, a string that's never displayed to the user), check the **Untranslatable** checkbox for that `String` resource. For the **Welcome** app, use the translations in Section 2.8.4.

Repeat the preceding steps for each language you wish to support.

2.8.4 Localizing Strings

In this app, the GUI contains one `TextView` that displays a string and one content-description string for the `ImageView`. These strings were defined as string resources in the `strings.xml` file. You can now provide the translated strings that will be stored in the new version of the `strings.xml` file. For this app, you'll replace the strings

```
"Welcome to Android App Development!"
"Deitel double-thumbs-up bug logo"
```

with the Spanish strings

```
"¡Bienvenido al Desarrollo de App Android!"
"El logo de Deitel que tiene el insecto con dedos pulgares
    hacia arriba"
```

In the **Translation Editor** window:

1. Click the cell for the `welcome` resource **Spanish (es)** translation, then in the **Translation:** field at the bottom of the window enter the Spanish string "`¡Bienvenido al Desarrollo de App Android!`". If you cannot type special Spanish characters and symbols on your keyboard, you can copy the Spanish strings from our `res/values-es/strings.xml` file in the final version of the **Welcome** app (located in the `WelcomeInternationalized` folder with the chapter's examples), then paste the Spanish string into the **Translation:** field.

2. Next, click the cell for the `deitel_logo` resource's value and enter in the **Translation:** field "`El logo de Deitel que tiene el insecto con dedos pulgares hacia arriba`".

3. We chose not to translate the resource `app_name`, though we could have. The window should appear as in Fig. 2.32.

4. Save the Spanish `strings.xml` file by selecting **File > Save All** or clicking the **Save All** toolbar button (⊟).

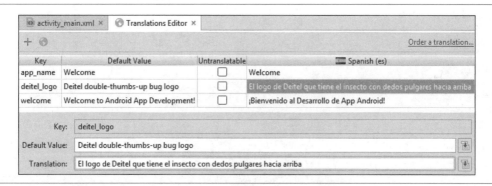

Fig. 2.32 | Translations Editor window with the Spanish strings.

2.8.5 Testing the App in Spanish on an AVD

To test the app in Spanish on an AVD, you can use the **Custom Locale** app that's installed on the AVD.

1. Click the home (⬤) icon on your AVD.

2. Click the launcher (⊕) icon, then locate and click the **Custom Locale** app's icon to open it.

3. Drag the mouse to scroll to the **es - español** option, then click it and click the **SELECT 'ES'** button to change the AVD's locale.

The emulator or device changes its language setting to Spanish.

Next, run the **Welcome** app, which installs and launches the localized app (Fig. 2.33). When the app begins executing, Android checks the AVD's (or device's) language settings, determines that the AVD (or device) is set to Spanish and uses the Spanish `welcome` and `deitel_logo` string resources defined in `res/values-es/strings.xml`. Notice, however, that the app's name still appears in *English* in the app bar at the top of the app. This is because we did *not* provide a localized version of the `app_name` string resource in the `res/values-es/strings.xml` file. If Android cannot find a localized version of a string resource, it uses the default version in the `res/values/strings.xml` file.

Returning the AVD to English
To return your AVD to English:

1. Click the home (⦿) icon on your AVD.

2. Click the launcher (⊕) icon, then locate and click the **Custom Locale** app's icon to open it.

3. Drag the mouse to scroll to the **en-US - en-us** option, then click it and click the **SELECT 'EN-US'** button to change the AVD's locale.

Fig. 2.33 | **Welcome** app running in Spanish in the Nexus 6 AVD.

2.8.6 Testing the App in Spanish on a Device
To test on a device you must change the language settings for your device. To do so:

1. Touch the home (⦿) icon on your device.

2. Touch the launcher (⊕) icon, then locate and touch the **Settings** app (⚙) icon.

3. In the **Settings** app, scroll to the **Personal** section, then touch **Language & input**.

4. Touch **Language** (the first item in the list), then select **Español (España)** from the list of languages.

The device changes its language setting to Spanish and returns to the **Language & input** settings, which are now displayed in Spanish. Run the app from the IDE to install and run the localized version on your device.

Returning Your Device to English
To return your AVD (or Device) to English:

1. Touch the home (⊙) icon on the emulator or on your device.

2. Touch the launcher (⊕) icon, then locate and touch the **Settings** app (⚙) icon—the app is now called **Ajustes** in Spanish.

3. Touch the item **Idioma e introduccion de texto** to access the language settings.

4. Touch the item **Idioma**, then in the list of languages select **English (United States)**.

2.8.7 TalkBack and Localization

TalkBack currently supports English, Spanish, Italian, French and German. If you run the **Welcome** app on a device with Spanish specified as the device's language and TalkBack enabled, TalkBack will speak the app's Spanish strings as you touch each view.

When you first switch your device to Spanish and enable TalkBack, Android will automatically download the Spanish text-to-speech engine. If TalkBack does *not* speak the Spanish strings, then the Spanish text-to-speech engine has not finished downloading and installing yet. In this case, you should try executing the app again later.

2.8.8 Localization Checklist

For more information on localizing your app's resources, be sure to check out the Android *Localization Checklist* at:

```
http://developer.android.com/distribute/tools/localization-
   checklist.html
```

2.8.9 Professional Translation

App-development companies often have translators on staff or hire other companies to perform translations. In fact, in the Google Play Developer Console—which you use to publish your apps in the Google Play store—you can find translation-services companies, and in the **Translations Editor** window there is an **Order translations...** link. For more information on the Google Play Developer Console, see Chapter 10 and

```
http://developer.android.com/distribute/googleplay/developer-
   console.html
```

For more information regarding translation, see

```
https://support.google.com/l10n/answer/6227218
```

2.9 Wrap-Up

In this chapter, you used Android Studio to build the **Welcome** app that displays a welcome message and an image without writing any code. You created a simple GUI using the IDE's layout editor and configured view properties using the **Properties** window.

In the layout XML file, you changed the default RelativeLayout to a LinearLayout, which you then configured to arrange views vertically. The app displayed text in a TextView and a picture in an ImageView. You modified the TextView from the default GUI to display the app's text centered in the GUI, with a larger font size and in one of the standard theme colors. You also used the layout editor's **Palette** of GUI controls to drag and drop the ImageView onto the GUI. Following good practice, you defined all strings and numeric values in resource files in the project's res folder.

You learned that Android has accessibility features to help people with certain disabilities use their devices. We showed how to enable Android's TalkBack to allow a device to speak screen text or speak text that you provide to help the visually impaired user understand the purpose and contents of a view. We discussed Android's Explore by Touch feature, which enables the user to touch the screen to hear TalkBack speak what's on the screen near the touch. For the app's ImageViews, you provided content descriptions that could be used with TalkBack and Explore by Touch.

Finally, you learned how to use Android's internationalization features to reach the largest possible audience for your apps. You localized the **Welcome** app with Spanish strings for the TextView's text and the ImageViews' accessibility strings, then tested the app on an AVD configured for Spanish.

Android development is a combination of GUI design and Java coding. In the next chapter, you'll develop a simple **Tip Calculator** app by using the layout editor to develop the GUI visually and Java programming to specify the app's behavior.

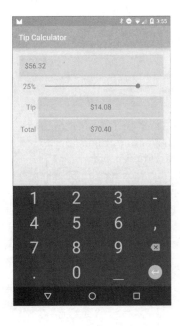

3

Tip Calculator App

Introducing GridLayout, EditText, SeekBar, Event Handling, NumberFormat, Customizing the App's Theme and Defining App Functionality with Java

Objectives
In this chapter you'll:

- Change the default GUI theme.
- Customize the GUI theme's colors.
- Design a GUI using a GridLayout.
- Use the IDE's **Component Tree** window to add views to a GridLayout.
- Use TextViews, an EditText and a SeekBar.
- Use Java object-oriented programming capabilities, including classes, objects, interfaces, anonymous inner classes and inheritance to add functionality to an app.
- Programmatically change the text in a TextView.
- Use event handling to respond to user interactions with an EditText and a SeekBar.
- Specify that the keypad should display by default when the app executes.
- Specify that the app supports only portrait orientation.

Outline

3.1 Introduction

The **Tip Calculator** app (Fig. 3.1(a)) calculates and displays the tip and total for a restaurant bill amount. As you touch the numeric keypad to enter the bill amount's digits, the app calculates and displays the tip and total bill amounts for the current tip percentage (15% by default). You specify a tip percentage from 0% to 30% by moving the `SeekBar` *thumb*—this updates the displayed tip percentage and recalculates the tip and total. All numeric values are displayed using *locale-specific* formatting. Figure 3.1(b) shows the app after the user enters the amount 56.32 and changes the tip percentage to 25%.

You'll begin by test-driving the app. Then we'll overview the technologies you'll use to create the app. You'll build the app's GUI using Android Studio's layout editor and the **Component Tree** window. Finally, we'll present the complete Java code for the app and do a detailed code walkthrough.

Note Regarding the Keyboard in Our Screen Captures

The keypad in Fig. 3.1 may differ, based on your AVD's or device's Android version or whether you've installed and selected a custom keyboard on your device. We configured our AVD to display the *dark keyboard* for better contrast in our screen captures. To do so:

   1. Touch the home (⊙) icon on your AVD or device.

a) Initial GUI

b) GUI after user enters the amount 56.32 and changes the tip percentage to 25%

Move the SeekBar thumb to change the tip percentage

Selected tip percentage is displayed here

Touch the keypad's numbers to enter the bill amount as a whole number of pennies—the app divides your input by 100.0 to calculate the bill amount

Touch ⊗ to delete digits from right to left

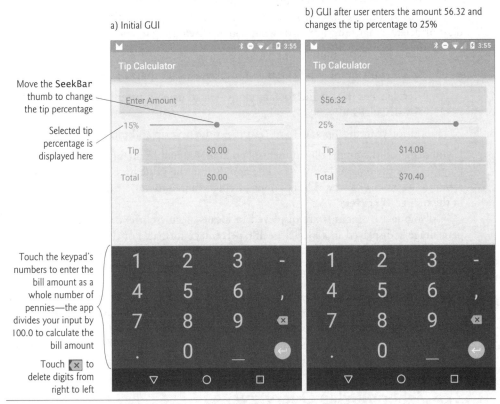

Fig. 3.1 | Entering the bill total and calculating the tip.

2. On the home screen, touch the launcher (⊞) icon, then open the **Settings** app.

3. In the **Personal** section, touch **Language and Input**.

4. On an AVD, touch **Android Keyboard (AOSP)**. On a device touch **Google Keyboard**—we assume you're using the standard Android keyboard.

5. Touch **Appearance & layouts**, then touch **Theme**.

6. Touch **Material Dark** to change to the keyboard with the dark background.

3.2 Test-Driving the Tip Calculator App

Opening and Running the App

Perform the steps in Sections 1.9.1– and 1.9.3 to open the **Tip Calculator** app project in Android Studio and run the app on the Nexus 6 AVD. If you prefer, perform the steps in Section 1.9.4 to run the app on an Android phone.

Entering a Bill Total

Enter the bill total 56.32 by touching numbers on the numeric keypad. If you make a mistake, press the keypad's delete button (⊗) to erase the last digit you entered. Even though the keypad contains a decimal point, the app is configured so that you may enter only the digits 0 through 9—other input buttons on the keypad are ignored and an Android device will vibrate to indicate when you touch an invalid input button. Each time you touch a digit or delete a digit, the app reads what you've entered so far, and

- converts it to a number

- divides the number by 100.0 and displays the new bill amount

- recalculates the tip and total amounts, based on the current tip percentage (**15%** by default) and

- displays in the **Tip** and **Total** TextViews the new tip and total amounts.

If you delete all the digits, the app redisplays **Enter Amount** in the blue TextView and displays 0.00 in the orange TextViews. The app divides the value by 100.0 and displays the result in the blue TextView. The app then calculates and updates the tip and total amounts in the orange TextViews.

All monetary amounts are displayed in locale-specific currency formats and the tip percentage is displayed in a locale-specific percentage format. For the U.S. locale, as you enter the four digits 5, 6, 3 and 2, the bill total is displayed successively as **$0.05**, **$0.56**, **$5.63** and **$56.32**, respectively.

Selecting a Tip Percentage

Use the Seekbar—often called a *slider* in other GUI technologies—to specify the tip percentage. Drag the Seekbar's *thumb* until the percentage reads **25%** (Fig. 3.1(b)). As you drag the thumb, the tip and total update continuously. By default, the Seekbar allows you to select values from 0 to 100, but we specified a maximum value of 30 for this app.

3.3 Technologies Overview

This section introduces the IDE and Android features you'll use to build the **Tip Calculator** app. We assume that you're already familiar with Java object-oriented programming—we present Java in our book *Java SE 8 for Programmers* (http://bit.ly/JavaSE8FP). You'll

- use various Android classes to create objects

- call methods on classes and objects

- define and call your own methods

- use inheritance to create a class that defines the **Tip Calculator**'s functionality and

- use event handling, anonymous inner classes and interfaces to process the user's GUI interactions.

3.3.1 Class Activity

Android apps have four types of executable components—*activities, services, content providers* and *broadcast receivers*. In this chapter, we'll discuss activities, which are defined as subclasses of Activity (package android.app). An app can have many activities, one of which is the first you see after launching the app. You interact with an Activity through views—GUI components that inherit from class View (package android.view).

Before Android 3.0, a separate Activity was typically associated with each screen of an app. As you'll see, starting in Chapter 4, an Activity can manage multiple Fragments.

On a phone, each `Fragment` typically occupies the entire screen and the `Activity` switches between the `Fragments`, based on user interactions. On a tablet, activities typically display multiple `Fragments` per screen to take advantage of the larger screen size.

3.3.2 `Activity` Lifecycle Methods

Throughout its life, an `Activity` can be in one of several *states—active* (i.e., *running*), *paused* or *stopped*. The `Activity` transitions between these states in response to various *events*:

- An *active* `Activity` is *visible* on the screen and "has the focus"—that is, it's in the *foreground*. You can interact with the `Activity` currently in the foreground.

- A *paused* `Activity` is *visible* on the screen but *does not* have the focus—such as when an alert dialog is displayed. You cannot interact with the *paused* activity until it becomes active—for example, after the user dismisses an alert dialog.

- A *stopped* activity is *not visible* on the screen—it's in the *background* and is likely to be killed by the system when its memory is needed. An `Activity` is *stopped* when another `Activity` enters the *foreground* and becomes *active*. For example, when you answer a phone call, the phone app becomes *active* and the app you previously were using is *stopped*.

As an `Activity` transitions among these states, the Android runtime calls various `Activity` *lifecycle methods*—all of which are defined by the `Activity` class in package `android.app`. You'll override the `onCreate` method in *every* activity. This method is called by the Android runtime when an `Activity` is *starting*—that is, when its GUI is about to be displayed so you can interact with the `Activity`. Other lifecycle methods include `onStart`, `onPause`, `onRestart`, `onResume`, `onStop` and `onDestroy`. We'll discuss most of these in later chapters. Each activity lifecycle method you override *must* call the superclass's version; otherwise, an *exception* will occur. This is required because each lifecycle method in superclass `Activity` contains code that must execute in addition to the code you define in your overridden lifecycle methods. For more on the `Activity` lifecycle see

```
http://developer.android.com/reference/android/app/Activity.html
```

3.3.3 AppCompat Library and Class `AppCompatActivity`

A big challenge developers face when using new Android features is backward compatibility with earlier Android platforms. Google now introduces many new Android features via the *Android Support Library*—a set of libraries that enable you to use newer Android features in apps targeting current and past Android platforms.

One such library is the `AppCompat` library, which enables apps to provide an app bar (formerly called an action bar) and more on devices running Android 2.1 (API 7) and higher—app bars were originally introduced in Android 3.0 (API 11). Android Studio's app templates have been updated to use the `AppCompat` library, enabling the new apps you create to run on almost all Android devices.

Android Studio's **Empty Activity** app template defines the app's `MainActivity` class as a subclass of `AppCompatActivity` (package `android.support.v7.app`)—an indirect subclass of `Activity` that supports using newer Android features in apps running on current and older Android platforms.

Software Engineering Observation 3.1

By creating apps with the AppCompat *library from the start, you avoid having to reimplement your code if you decide to support older Android versions to target a wider potential audience for your app.*

Software Engineering Observation 3.2

Some Android features are not available in earlier Android versions, even if you use the AppCompat *libraries. For example, Android's printing capabilities are available only in Android 4.4 and higher. If you use such features in your app, you must either restrict the app to the supported platforms or disable those features on Android versions that do not support them.*

For more details on Android Support Libraries, including when to use them and how to set them up, visit:

```
http://developer.android.com/tools/support-library
```

3.3.4 Arranging Views with a GridLayout

Recall that you arrange a GUI's views in layouts. We'll use a GridLayout (package android.widget) to arrange views into cells in a rectangular grid. Cells can occupy *multiple* rows and columns, allowing for complex layouts. Normally, GridLayout requires API level 14 or higher. However, the *Android Support Library* provides alternate versions of GridLayout and many other views and layouts so that you can use them in older Android versions. For more information on this library and how to use it in your apps, visit

```
http://developer.android.com/tools/support-library/index.html
```

We'll cover more layouts and views in later chapters—for a complete list, visit

```
http://developer.android.com/reference/android/widget/package-
    summary.html
```

3.3.5 Creating and Customizing the GUI with the Layout Editor and the Component Tree and Properties Windows

You'll create TextViews, an EditText and a SeekBar using the layout editor (that you used in Chapter 2) and **Component Tree** window, then customize them with the IDE's **Properties** window.

An EditText—often called a *text box* or *text field* in other GUI technologies—is a *subclass* of TextView (presented in Chapter 2) that can display text *and* accept text input from the user. You'll specify an EditText for numeric input, allow users to enter only digits and restrict the maximum number of digits that can be entered.

A SeekBar represents an integer in the range 0–100 by default and allows the user to select a number in that range by moving the SeekBar's thumb. You'll customize the SeekBar so the user can choose a tip percentage from the more limited range 0 to 30.

3.3.6 Formatting Numbers as Locale-Specific Currency and Percentage Strings

You'll use class NumberFormat (package java.text) to create *locale-specific* currency and percentage strings—an important part of *internationalizing* your apps. You also can add *accessibility* strings and internationalize the app's other text using the techniques you learned in Sections 2.7—2.8.

3.3.7 Implementing Interface `TextWatcher` for Handling `EditText` Text Changes

To respond to events when the user changes the text in this app's `EditText`, you'll use an *anonymous inner class* to implement the `TextWatcher` *interface* (from package `android.text`). In particular, you'll use method `onTextChanged` to display the currency-formatted bill amount and to calculate the tip and total as the user enters each digit. If you're not familiar with *anonymous inner classes*, visit

```
http://bit.ly/AnonymousInnerClasses
```

3.3.8 Implementing Interface `OnSeekBarChangeListener` for Handling `SeekBar` Thumb Position Changes

You'll use another anonymous inner class to implement the `SeekBar.OnSeekBarChange-Listener` interface (from package `android.widget`) to respond to the user moving the `SeekBar`'s *thumb*. In particular, you'll use method `onProgressChanged` to display the selected tip percentage and to calculate the tip and total as the user moves the `SeekBar`'s thumb.

3.3.9 Material Themes

A theme gives an app a look-and-feel that's consistent with Android. Projects that you create for Android 5 and higher use themes that adhere to Google's material design guidelines. There are several predefined material design themes:

- The "light" theme has a white app bar, a white app background and text that is black or shades of dark gray.

- The "light" theme with a dark app bar is the same as above, but the app bar is black with white text by default.

- The "dark" has a black app bar, a dark gray app background and text that is white or shades of light gray.

For each of these themes, there is

- a `Theme.Material` version (e.g., `Theme.Material.Light`) for apps that do not use any `AppCompat` libraries and run on Android 5 and higher, and

- a `Theme.AppCompat` version (e.g., `Theme.AppCompat.Light`) for apps that use `AppCompat` libraries and run on Android 2.1 and higher.

When designing a GUI, you can choose from the predefined themes, or even create your own new ones. For this chapter, we'll use `Theme.AppCompat.Light.DarkActionBar`, which is the default theme in Android Studio's app templates. Apps that use the `App-Compat` libraries must use one of the `AppCompat` themes; otherwise, some views will not render correctly. For more information about each theme and to see sample screen captures, visit

```
http://www.google.com/design/spec/style/color.html#color-themes
http://developer.android.com/training/material/theme.html
```

Performance Tip 3.1

Many of today's Android phones use AMOLED displays. On such displays, a black pixel is turned off and does not consume power. Apps that use mostly black themes can reduce power consumption by approximately 40% (http://bit.ly/AndroidAMOLEDDisplay).

3.3.10 Material Design: Elevation and Shadows

Google's material design guidelines recommend that objects in your user interfaces cast shadows just as real-world objects do. When you set a view's `elevation` property, Android automatically casts a shadow for that view. Larger `elevation` values result in more pronounced shadows. For this app, we'll set the `elevation` of the blue and orange `TextViews` that display monetary amounts.

The material design guidelines contain elevation recommendations for various on-screen components—for example, a dialog's recommended elevation is `24dp` and a menu's is `8dp`. For other recommended elevations, see:

```
http://www.google.com/design/spec/what-is-material/elevation-
    shadows.html
```

3.3.11 Material Design: Colors

App developers often customize a theme's colors to match a company's branding. If you need to customize theme colors, Google's material design guidelines for color[1] recommend that you choose a color palette consisting of a primary color—with no more than three hues (shades)—and an accent color. The primary colors typically are used to color the status bar and the app bar at the top of the screen and also can be used in your GUI. The accent color is used to tint various views in your GUI, such as `SeekBars`, `CheckBoxes` and `RadioButtons`. Once you choose a palette, you can use Android Studio's **Theme Editor** (Section 3.5.2) to modify a theme's colors.

You can find recommended sample color swatches from the material design color palette at

```
http://www.google.com/design/spec/style/color.html#color-color-
    palette
```

For palette color recommendations, visit

```
http://www.materialpalette.com/
```

This site enables you to click two colors from Google's material design color palette, then it recommends three shades of the primary color, one secondary color and colors for your app's text and icons.

In this app, we'll use color swatches displayed in the Android Studio **Theme Editor** to select

- a blue *primary color* for app bar's background color
- a darker blue *dark primary color* for the status bar that appears above the app bar, and
- an orange *accent color* used to tint the `SeekBar`.

---

1. http://www.google.com/design/spec/style/color.html.

For the amount TextView's light blue color and the tip and total TextViews' light orange color, we used Google's material design color palette to choose lighter shades of the primary and accent colors.

3.3.12 AndroidManifest.xml

The `AndroidManifest.xml` file is created by the IDE when you create a new app project. This file contains many of the settings that you specify in the **Create New Project** dialog—the app's name, package name and `Activity` name(s) and more. You'll edit this file's XML to add a new setting that forces the *soft keyboard* to be displayed when the app begins executing. You'll also specify that the app supports only *portrait orientation*—that is, the device's longer dimension is vertical.

3.3.13 Searching in the Properties Window

The **Properties** window allows you to search for properties by their names or portions of their names, which can help you find and set properties faster. To do so, click the **Properties** window's title bar and begin typing. At the top of the property list, a **Search for** tooltip appears showing what you've typed so far, and Android Studio highlights parts of every property name in the list that matches all or part of what you've typed. Then you can scroll through the list looking at the property names containing highlights.

The window will also scroll to the specific property that best matches what you type. For example, when searching a TextView's properties, if you type "text co" or "textco", the **Properties** window will highlight portions of many properties, but it specifically scrolls to and highlights the `textColor` property.

3.4 Building the GUI

In this section, we'll show the precise steps for building the **Tip Calculator**'s GUI, including how to customize the Material theme's primary and accent colors.

3.4.1 GridLayout Introduction

This app uses a `GridLayout` (package `android.widget`) to arrange views into four *rows* and two *columns*, each indexed from 0 like the elements in an array. You can specify a Grid-Layout's number of rows and columns in the **Properties** window. Each cell can be *empty* or can hold one or more *views*, including layouts *containing* other views. A row's *height* is determined by the row's *tallest* view. Similarly, a column's *width* is defined by the column's *widest* view. Figure 3.2 shows the **Tip Calculator**'s GridLayout labeled by its rows and columns—we drew horizontal lines to delineate the rows and a vertical line to delineate the columns. Views can span *multiple* rows and/or columns—for example, the **Enter Amount** TextView in Fig. 3.2 spans both columns in row 0.

When you drag a view onto a GridLayout in the **Component Tree**, the view occupies the next available grid cell—cells populate the GridLayout left-to-right until a given row is full, then the next view appears in the first column of the next row. As you'll see, you also can specify the exact row and column in which to place a view. We'll discuss other GridLayout features as we present the GUI-building steps.

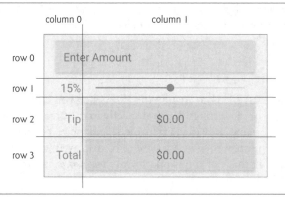

Fig. 3.2 | Tip Calculator GUI's GridLayout labeled by its rows and columns.

id *Property Values for This App's Views*

Figure 3.3 shows the views' id property values. For clarity, our naming convention is to use the view's class name in the id property and the corresponding Java variable name. In the first row, there are actually *two* components in the *same* grid cell—the amountTextView (which initially displays **Enter Amount**) *hides* the amountEditText that receives the user input. As you'll soon see, we restrict the user's input to whole-number values entered as integer digits, so the user enters the bill amount $34.56 as 3456. This ensures the user *cannot* enter invalid input. However, this amount should be displayed as *currency*. As the user enters each digit, we divide the amount by 100.0 and display in the amountTextView the locale-specific, currency-formatted amount.

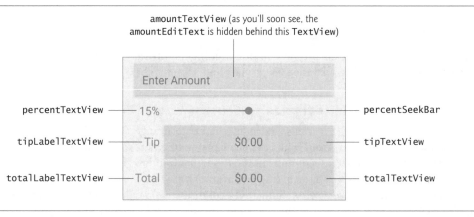

Fig. 3.3 | Tip Calculator views labeled with their id property values.

3.4.2 Creating the TipCalculator Project

Follow the steps in Section 2.3 to create a new project using the **Empty Activity** template. Specify the following values in the **Create New Project** dialog's **New Project** step:

- **Application name:** Tip Calculator
- **Company Domain:** deitel.com (or specify your own domain name)

For the remaining steps in the **Create New Project** dialog, use the same settings as in Section 2.3. Also, follow the steps in Section 2.5.2 to add an app icon to your project.

Once the project is open in Android Studio, in the layout editor, select **Nexus 6** from the virtual-device drop-down list (Fig. 2.11). Once again, we'll use this device as the basis for our design. Also, delete the **Hello world!** TextView.

3.4.3 Changing to a GridLayout

Recall that the default layout for an **Empty Activity** is a RelativeLayout. Here, you'll change that to a GridLayout:

1. Click the **Text** tab at the bottom of the layout editor to switch from the **Design** view to the layout's XML text.

2. At the top of the XML, change RelativeLayout to GridLayout.

3. Switch back to the layout editor's **Design** tab.

Specifying Two Columns and Default Margins for the **GridLayout**
Recall that the GUI in Fig. 3.2 consists of two columns. To specify this, select GridLayout in the **Component Tree** window, then change its columnCount property to 2—this property appears near the top of the **Properties** window with the other layout properties. You do not need to set the rowCount—it will be increased as we build the GUI.

By default, there are *no margins*—spacing that separates views—around a GridLayout's cells. The material design guidelines recommend 8dp minimum spacing between views:

http://developer.android.com/design/style/metrics-grids.html.

GridLayout can enforce this recommended spacing. With the GridLayout selected in the **Component Tree**, in the **Properties** window, check the GridLayout's useDefaultMargins property (which sets it to true) to use the recommended margins around the layout's cells.

3.4.4 Adding the TextViews, EditText and SeekBar

You'll now build the GUI in Fig. 3.2. You'll start with the basic layout and views in this section. In Section 3.4.5, you'll customize the views' properties to complete the design. Then, in Section 3.5, you'll change the default theme and customize two of its colors. As you add each view to the GUI, immediately set its id property using the names in Fig. 3.3. You'll add views to the GridLayout using the **Component Tree** window. If you drop a view in the wrong location in the **Component Tree**, you can drag it to the correct location.

You may also drag views directly onto the layout editor. For a GridLayout, the layout editor displays a grid of green guidelines to help you position the view. As you drag a view over the grid, the layout editor displays a tooltip indicating the row and column in which the view will be placed if you drop the view at that location.

Error-Prevention Tip 3.1

The cells in the layout editor's grid of green guidelines are small. If you drop a view in the wrong location, the layout editor might change the GridLayout's rowCount and columnCount property values and incorrectly set the view's layout:row and layout:column property values, causing your GUI to lay out incorrectly. If so, reset the GridLayout's rowCount and columnCount, based on your design, and change the view's layout:row and layout:column property values to the correct row and column for your design.

Step 1: Adding Views to the First Row

The first row consists of the amountTextView and the amountEditText—both occupy the same cell and span two columns. Each time you drop a view onto the GridLayout in the **Component Tree** window, the view is placed in the layout's *next open cell*, unless you specify otherwise by setting the view's layout:row and layout:column properties. You'll do that in this step so that the amountEditText and amountTextView appear in the same cell with the amountTextView in the foreground.

This app's TextViews use the *medium*-sized font from the app's theme. The layout editor's **Palette** provides preconfigured TextViews named **Plain Text**, **Large Text**, **Medium Text** and **Small Text** (in the **Widgets** section) for various text sizes. The **Plain Text** TextView uses the theme's default font size. For the others, the IDE configures the TextView's text-Appearance property using the Material theme's styles for the corresponding font sizes.

Perform the following steps to add to the GridLayout an EditText and a TextView for receiving and displaying the bill amount:

1. This app allows you to enter only *nonnegative integers*, which the app divides by 100.0 to display the bill amount. The **Palette's Text Fields** section provides *preconfigured* EditTexts for various forms of input, including person names, passwords, e-mail addresses, phone numbers, times, dates and numbers. When the user interacts with an EditText, an appropriate keyboard is displayed, based on the EditText's *input type*. From the **Palette's Text Fields** section, drag and drop a **Number** EditText onto the GridLayout node in the **Component Tree** window—this creates an EditText with the id editText in the GridLayout. Change the id to amountEditText. The EditText is placed in the *first* column of the GridLayout's *first* row. Set the EditText's layout:column to 0 and the layout:columnSpan to 2—these settings ensure that the TextView spans both columns of row 0.

2. Drag a **Medium Text** TextView from the **Palette's Widgets** section over the amountEditText in the **Component Tree** window—a horizontal black line appears below amountEditText, indicating that the TextView will be placed after amountEditText. The IDE creates a new TextView named textView and nests it in the GridLayout node. The default text "Medium Text" appears in the layout editor. You'll change this in *Step 5* (Section 3.4.5). Change the TextView's id to amountTextView, then set the layout:row to 0, the layout:column to 0 and the layout:columnSpan to 2—these settings ensure that the TextView spans both columns of row 0, as you'll see once we change the TextView's background color.

Step 2: Adding Views to the Second Row

Next, add the percentTextView and percentSeekBar to the GridLayout for displaying and selecting the tip percentage (be sure to set each view's id to the name we specify):

1. Drag a **Medium** TextView (percentTextView) from the **Palette's Widgets** section over the amountTextView in the GridLayout node in the **Component Tree** window. The new view becomes the first view in row 1 (the second row).

2. Drag a SeekBar (percentSeekBar) from the **Palette's Widgets** section over the percentTextView in the GridLayout node in the **Component Tree** window. The new view becomes the second view in row 1.

Step 3: Adding Views to the Third Row

Next, add the `tipLabelTextView` and the `tipTextView` to the `GridLayout` for displaying the tip amount:

1. Drag a **Medium** `TextView` (`tipLabelTextView`) over the `percentSeekBar` in the `GridLayout` node. The new view becomes the first view in row 2 (the third row).

2. Drag a **Medium** `TextView` (`tipTextView`) over the `tipLabelTextView` in the `GridLayout` node. The new view becomes the second view in row 2.

Step 4: Adding Views to the Fourth Row

Next, add the `totalLabelTextView` and the `totalTextView` to the `GridLayout` for displaying the tip amount:

1. Drag a **Medium** `TextView` (`totalLabelTextView`) over the `tipTextView` in the `GridLayout` node. This becomes the first view in row 3 (the fourth row).

2. Drag a **Medium** `TextView` (`totalTextView`) over the `totalLabelTextView` in the `GridLayout` node. This becomes the second view in row 3.

Reviewing the Layout So Far

The GUI and **Component Tree** window should now appear as shown in Fig. 3.4. The warning symbols shown in the layout editor and the **Component Tree** window will go away as you complete the GUI design in Section 3.4.5.

a) GUI design so far

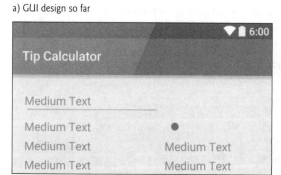

b) **Component Tree** window showing the **Tip Calculator**'s layout and views

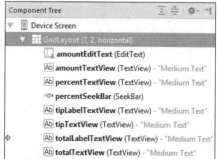

Fig. 3.4 | GUI and the **Component Tree** window after adding the views to the `GridLayout`.

A Note Regarding the **EditText**'s *Virtual Keyboard*

When the virtual keyboard is displayed, the device's back button (◀) changes to a down button (▼) that enables you to dismiss the keyboard. If you do so, the down button (▼) changes to a back button (◀) that you can touch to return to the previous `Activity`—possibly a prior app or the device's home screen.

Normally, you'd touch the `EditText` to redisplay the virtual keyboard. In this app, however, the `EditText` is hidden behind a `TextView`. If you were to dismiss this app's keyboard, you'd have to leave the app and return to it to redisplay the keyboard. We could programmatically force the keyboard to stay on the screen, but this would prevent the back button from ever being displayed in this app. This, in turn, would prevent you from returning to the previous Activity—a basic Android feature that every user expects.

We used an Android virtual keyboard to demonstrate how to choose the keyboard displayed for a given EditText. Another approach would be to provide Buttons representing the digits 0–9 that always remain on the screen. We could handle their click events and use String manipulation rather than an EditText to keep track of the user input.

3.4.5 Customizing the Views

You'll now customize additional view properties. As you did in Section 2.5, you'll also create several String, dimension and color resources.

Step 5: Specifying Literal Text

Next, you'll specify the literal text for the amountTextView, percentTextView, tipLabel-TextView and totalLabelTextView. When a TextView's text property is empty, its **hint property**'s value (if you specify one) is displayed—this property is commonly used with an EditText (a subclass of TextView) to help the user understand the EditText's purpose. We're using it similarly in the amountTextView to tell the user to enter a bill amount:

1. In the **Component Tree**, select amountTextView and locate its hint property in the **Properties** window.

2. Click the ellipsis (...) button to the right of the property's value to display the **Resources** dialog.

3. In the dialog, click **New Resource**, then select **New String Value...** to display the **New String Value Resource** dialog and set the **Resource name** to enter_amount and **Resource value** to "Enter Amount". Leave the other settings and click **OK** to create the new String resource and set it as amountTextView's hint.

Repeat these steps to set the text property for the percentTextView, tipLabelTextView and totalLabelTextView using the values shown in Fig. 3.5.

View	Resource name	Resource Value
percentTextView	tip_percentage	15%
tipLabelTextView	tip	Tip
totalLabelTextView	total	Total

Fig. 3.5 | String resource values and names.

Step 6: Right Aligning the TextViews in the Left Column

In Fig. 3.2, the percentTextView, tipLabelTextView and totalLabelTextView are right aligned. You can accomplish this for all three TextViews at once as follows:

1. Select the percentTextView.

2. Hold *Ctrl* on Windows/Linux or *Command* on Mac and click the tipLabelText-View and totalLabelTextView. Now all three TextViews are selected.

3. Expand the layout:gravity property's node and check the right checkbox.

Step 7: Configuring the `amountEditText`

In the final app, the `amountEditText` is *hidden* behind the `amountTextView` and is configured to allow only *digits* to be entered by the user. Select the `amountEditText` and set the following properties:

1. Set the `digits` property to 0123456789—this allows *only* digits to be entered, even though the numeric keypad contains other characters, such as minus (-), comma (,) and period (.).

2. Set the `maxLength` property to 6. This restricts the bill amount to a maximum of *six* digits—so the largest supported bill amount is 9999.99.

Step 8: Configuring the `amountTextView`

To complete the `amountTextView`'s formatting, select it and set the following properties:

1. Delete the default value of the `text` property ("Medium Text")—we'll programmatically display text here, based on the user's input.

2. Expand the `layout:gravity` property's node and set the `fill` to `horizontal`. This indicates that the `TextView` should occupy all remaining horizontal space in this `GridLayout` row.

3. Set the `background` property (which specifies the view's background color) to a new color resource named `amount_background` with the value #BBDEFB—a light blue color chosen from Google's material design color palette.

4. Add padding around the `TextView`. A view's `padding` specifies extra space around a view's content. The `all` property specifies that the padding amount should be applied to the top, right, bottom and left of the view's contents. You may also set the padding for each of these individually. Expand the `padding` property's node, click the `all` property, then click the ellipsis button. Create a new dimension resource named `textview_padding` with the value 12dp. You'll use this resource again shortly.

5. Finally, add a shadow to the view by setting the `elevation` property to a new dimension resource named `elevation` with the value 4dp. We chose this value for demonstration purposes to emphasize the shadow effect.

Step 9: Configuring the `percentTextView`

Notice that the `percentTextView` is aligned higher than the `percentSeekBar`. This looks better if it's *vertically centered*. To do this, expand the `layout:gravity` property's node, then set the `center` value to `vertical`. Recall that you previously set the `layout:gravity` to `right`. The combination of these settings appears in the layout XML as

```
android:layout_gravity="center_vertical|right"
```

A *vertical bar* (|) is used to separate multiple `layout:gravity` values—in this case indicating that the `TextView` should be *centered vertically* and *right aligned* within the grid cell.

Step 10: Configuring the `percentSeekBar`

Select `percentSeekBar` and configure the following properties:

1. By default, a `SeekBar`'s range is 0 to 100 and its current value is indicated by its `progress` property. This app allows tip percentages from 0 to 30 and specifies a

default of 15 percent. Set the SeekBar's max property to 30 and the progress property to 15.

2. Expand the layout:gravity property's node and set the fill to horizontal so the SeekBar occupies all horizontal space in the SeekBar's GridLayout column.

3. Set the layout:height property to a new dimension resource (seekbar_height) with the value 40dp to increase vertical space in which the SeekBar is displayed.

Step 11: Configuring the *tipTextView and totalTextView*
To complete the formatting of the tipTextView and totalTextView, select both and set the following properties:

1. Delete the default value of the text property ("Medium Text")—we'll programmatically display the calculated tip and total.

2. Expand the layout:gravity property's node and set the fill to horizontal so each TextView occupies all horizontal space in the TextViews' GridLayout column.

3. Set the background property to a new color resource named result_background with the value #FFE0B2—a light orange color chosen from Google's material design color palette.

4. Set the gravity property to center so the calculated tip and total amounts will be centered within these TextViews.

5. Expand the padding property's node, click the ellipsis button for the all value, then select the dimension resource named textview_padding that you created previously for the amountTextView.

6. Finally, add a shadow to each view by setting the elevation property to the elevation dimension resource you created earlier.

3.5 Default Theme and Customizing Theme Colors

Each app has a theme that defines the default look-and-feel of the standard views you use. The theme is specified in the app's AndroidManifest.xml file (Section 3.7). You can customize aspects of the theme, such those that define an app's color scheme, by defining style resources in the styles.xml file located in the in the app's res/values folder.

3.5.1 parent Themes

The style.xml resource file contains a style with the name "AppTheme" that's referenced from the app's AndroidManifest.xml file to specify the app's theme. This style also specifies a parent theme, which is similar to a superclass in Java—the new style inherits its parent theme's attributes and their default values. Just as in a Java subclass, a style can override parent theme attributes with values customized for specific apps. A company might do this, for example, to use the company's branding colors. We'll use this concept in Section 3.5.2 to customize three colors used in the app's theme.

As we mentioned previously, Android Studio's app templates now include support for the AppCompat libraries that enable you to use newer Android features in older Android versions. By default, Android Studio sets the parent theme to

```
Theme.AppCompat.Light.DarkActionBar
```

one of several predefined themes from the `AppCompat` library—apps that use this theme have a light background, except for the dark app bar at the top of the app. Each `AppCompat` theme uses Google's material design recommendations to style your apps' GUIs.

3.5.2 Customizing Theme Colors

Section 3.3.11 discussed where a theme's primary, dark primary and accent colors are applied in an app's on-screen elements. In this section, you'll use the new Android Studio **Theme Editor** to change the app's primary, dark primary and accent colors, thus overriding the values of the `android:colorPrimary`, `android:colorPrimaryDark` and `android:colorAccent` theme attributes shown in Fig. 3.6. These are three of many theme attributes you can override. For the complete list, visit:

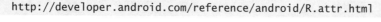

```
http://developer.android.com/reference/android/R.attr.html
```

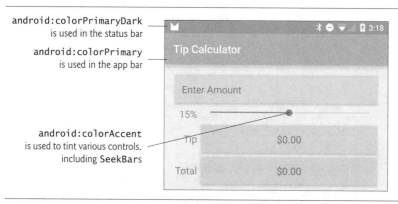

Fig. 3.6 | Theme attributes for the primary, primary dark and accent colors.

Modifying the Theme's Primary, Dark Primary and Accent Colors
To customize the colors:

1. Open `styles.xml`. In the editor's upper-right corner, click the **Open editor** link to display the **Theme Editor** (Fig. 3.7) showing the current colors for `colorPrimary` (dark blue), `colorPrimaryDark` (a darker shade of `colorPrimary`) and `colorAccent` (bright pink)—these are the default colors specified in Android Studio's **Empty Activity** app template. For this app, we'll change `colorPrimary` and `colorPrimaryDark` to lighter blues and change `colorAccent` to orange.

2. Customize the app's `colorPrimary` value by clicking its color swatch (Fig. 3.7) to display the **Resources** dialog (Fig. 3.8). In the dialog, click the **Material Blue 500** color swatch, then click **OK** to change `colorPrimary`'s value—hovering the mouse cursor over a color swatch displays its color name in a tooltip. The number **500** represents a particular shade of the **Material Blue** color. Shades of each color range from 50 (a light shade) to 900 (a dark shade)—you can view samples of each color's shades at

```
https://www.google.com/design/spec/style/color.html#color-
    color-palette
```

Color swatches for the theme's `colorPrimary`, `colorPrimaryDark` and `colorAccent` attributes

Fig. 3.7 | Theme Editor shows styled view previews on the left and theme attributes on the right.

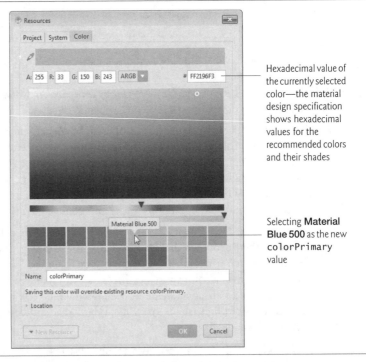

Hexadecimal value of the currently selected color—the material design specification shows hexadecimal values for the recommended colors and their shades

Selecting **Material Blue 500** as the new `colorPrimary` value

Fig. 3.8 | Selecting the **Material Blue 500** color swatch for `colorPrimary`.

3. Next, click the `colorPrimaryDark` color swatch in the **Theme Editor** to display the **Resources** dialog. The **Theme Editor** recognizes the new `colorPrimary` value and automatically displays a color swatch containing the recommended darker `colorPrimary` shade you should use for `colorPrimaryDark`—in this case, **Material Blue 700**. Click that color swatch (Fig. 3.9), then click **OK**.

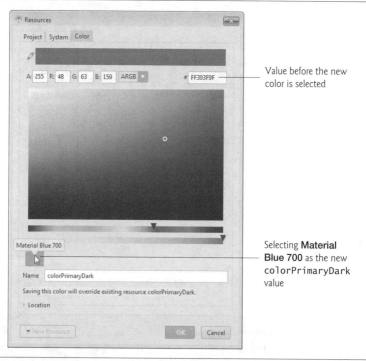

Fig. 3.9 | Selecting the **Material Blue 700** color swatch for `colorPrimaryDark`.

4. Next, click the `colorAccent` color swatch in the **Theme Editor** to display the **Resources** dialog. Again, the **Theme Editor** recognizes that you changed the `color-Primary` value and displays swatches for various complementary accent colors. In the dialog, click the **Orange accent 400** color swatch, then click **OK** to change `colorAccent`'s value (Fig. 3.10), then click **OK**.

You've now completed the app's design, which should appear as shown in Fig. 3.11.

3.5.3 Common `View` Property Values as Styles

As you'll see in later apps, `style` resources can define common property values that should be applied to multiple views. You apply a `style` resource to a given view by setting its `style` property. Any subsequent changes you make to a `style` are automatically applied to all views using the `style`. For example, consider the `tipTextView` and `totalTextView` that we configured identically in Step 11 of Section 3.4.5. We could have defined a `style` resource specifying the `layout:gravity`, `background`, `gravity`, `padding` and `elevation` properties' values, then set both `TextView`s' `style` properties to the same `style` resource.

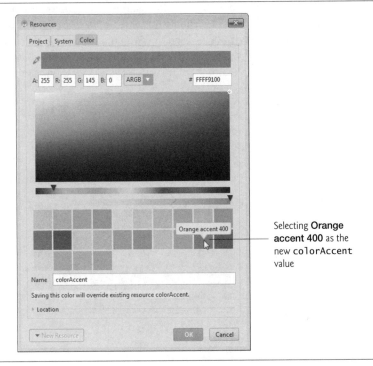

Selecting **Orange accent 400** as the new colorAccent value

Fig. 3.10 | Selecting the **Orange accent 400** color swatch for colorAccent.

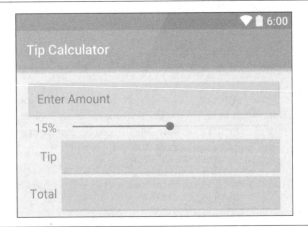

Fig. 3.11 | Completed design.

3.6 Adding the App's Logic

Class MainActivity (Figs. 3.12–3.18) implements the **Tip Calculator** app's logic. It calculates the tip and total bill amounts, then displays them in locale-specific currency format. To view the file, in the Project window, expand the app/Java/com.deitel.tipcalculator node and double click `MainActivity.java`. You'll need to enter most of the code in Figs. 3.12–3.18.

3.6.1 `package` and `import` Statements

Figure 3.12 shows the `package` statement and `import` statements in `MainActivity.java`. The `package` statement in line 3 was inserted when you created the project. When you open a Java file in the IDE, the `import` statements are collapsed—one is displayed with a ⊕ to its left. You can click the ⊕ to see the complete list of `import` statements.

```
 1   // MainActivity.java
 2   // Calculates a bill total based on a tip percentage
 3   package com.deitel.tipcalculator;
 4
 5   import android.os.Bundle; // for saving state information
 6   import android.support.v7.app.AppCompatActivity; // base class
 7   import android.text.Editable; // for EditText event handling
 8   import android.text.TextWatcher; // EditText listener
 9   import android.widget.EditText; // for bill amount input
10   import android.widget.SeekBar; // for changing the tip percentage
11   import android.widget.SeekBar.OnSeekBarChangeListener; // SeekBar listener
12   import android.widget.TextView; // for displaying text
13
14   import java.text.NumberFormat; // for currency formatting
15
```

Fig. 3.12 | `MainActivity`'s `package` and `import` statements.

Lines 5–14 `import` the classes and interfaces the app uses:

- Class `Bundle` of package `android.os` (line 5) stores key–value pairs of information—typically representing an app's state or data that needs to be passed between activities. When another app is about to appear on the screen—e.g., when the user *receives a phone call* or *launches another app*—Android gives the currently executing app the opportunity to *save its state* in a `Bundle`. The Android runtime might subsequently kill the app—e.g., to reclaim its memory. When the app returns to the screen, the Android runtime passes the `Bundle` of the previously saved state to `Activity` method `onCreate` (Section 3.6.4). Then, the app can use the saved state to return the app to the state it was in when another app became active. We'll use `Bundle`s in Chapter 8 to pass data between activities.

- Class `AppCompatActivity` of package `android.support.v7.app` (line 6) provides the basic *lifecycle methods* of an app—we'll discuss these shortly. `AppCompatActivity` is an indirect subclass of `Activity` (package `android.app`) that supports using newer Android features apps running on current and older Android platforms.

- Interface `Editable` of package `android.text` (line 7) allows you to modify the content and markup of text in a GUI.

- You implement interface `TextWatcher` of package `android.text` (line 8) to respond to events when the user changes the text in an `EditText`.

- Package `android.widget` (lines 9, 10 and 12) contains the *widgets* (i.e., views) and layouts that are used in Android GUIs. This app uses `EditText` (line 9), `SeekBar` (line 10) and `TextView` (line 12) widgets.

- You implement interface `SeekBar.OnSeekBarChangeListener` of package `android.widget` (line 11) to respond to the user moving the `SeekBar`'s *thumb*.

- Class `NumberFormat` of package `java.text` (line 14) provides numeric formatting capabilities, such as *locale-specific* currency and percentage formats.

3.6.2 `MainActivity` Subclass of `AppCompatActivity`

Class `MainActivity` (Figs. 3.13–3.18) is the **Tip Calculator** app's `Activity` subclass. When you created the `TipCalculator` project, the IDE generated this class as a subclass of `AppCompatActivity` (an indirect subclass of `Activity`) and provided an override of class `Activity`'s inherited `onCreate` method (Fig. 3.15). Every `Activity` subclass *must* override this method. We'll discuss `onCreate` shortly.

```
16   // MainActivity class for the Tip Calculator app
17   public class MainActivity extends Activity {
18
```

Fig. 3.13 | Class `MainActivity` is a subclass of `Activity`.

3.6.3 Class Variables and Instance Variables

Figure 3.14 declares class `MainActivity`'s variables. The `NumberFormat` objects (lines 20–23) are used to format currency values and percentages, respectively. `NumberFormat`'s `static` method `getCurrencyInstance` returns a `NumberFormat` object that formats values as currency using the device's locale. Similarly, `static` method `getPercentInstance` formats values as percentages using the device's locale.

```
19       // currency and percent formatter objects
20       private static final NumberFormat currencyFormat =
21          NumberFormat.getCurrencyInstance();
22       private static final NumberFormat percentFormat =
23          NumberFormat.getPercentInstance();
24
25       private double billAmount = 0.0; // bill amount entered by the user
26       private double percent = 0.15; // initial tip percentage
27       private TextView amountTextView; // shows formatted bill amount
28       private TextView percentTextView; // shows tip percentage
29       private TextView tipTextView; // shows calculated tip amount
30       private TextView totalTextView; // shows calculated total bill amount
31
```

Fig. 3.14 | `MainActivity` class's instance variables.

The bill amount entered by the user into `amountEditText` will be read and stored as a `double` in `billAmount` (line 25). The tip percentage (an integer in the range 0–30) that the user sets by moving the `Seekbar` *thumb* will be divided by 100.0 to create a `double` for use in calculations, then stored in `percent` (line 26). For example, if you select 25 with the SeekBar, `percent` will store 0.25, so the app will multiply the bill amount by 0.25 to calculate the 25% tip.

Software Engineering Observation 3.3

For precise monetary calculations, use class `BigDecimal` (package `java.math`)—rather than type `double`—to represent the monetary amounts and perform calculations.

Line 27 declares the `TextView` that displays the currency-formatted bill amount. Line 28 declares the `TextView` that displays the tip percentage, based on the `SeekBar` *thumb's* position (see the **15%** in Fig. 3.1(a)). The variables in line 29–30 will refer to the `TextViews` in which the app displays the calculated tip and total.

3.6.4 Overriding `Activity` Method `onCreate`

The `onCreate` method (Fig. 3.15)—which is *autogenerated* with lines 33–36 when you create the app's project—is called by the system when an `Activity` is *started*. Method `onCreate` typically initializes the `Activity`'s instance variables and views. This method should be as simple as possible so that the app *loads quickly*. In fact, if the app takes longer than five seconds to load, the operating system will display an **ANR (Application Not Responding) dialog**—giving the user the option to *forcibly terminate the app*. You'll learn how to prevent this problem in Chapter 9.

```
32    // called when the activity is first created
33    @Override
34    protected void onCreate(Bundle savedInstanceState) {
35       super.onCreate(savedInstanceState); // call superclass's version
36       setContentView(R.layout.activity_main); // inflate the GUI
37
38       // get references to programmatically manipulated TextViews
39       amountTextView = (TextView) findViewById(R.id.amountTextView);
40       percentTextView = (TextView) findViewById(R.id.percentTextView);
41       tipTextView = (TextView) findViewById(R.id.tipTextView);
42       totalTextView = (TextView) findViewById(R.id.totalTextView);
43       tipTextView.setText(currencyFormat.format(0)); // set text to 0
44       totalTextView.setText(currencyFormat.format(0)); // set text to 0
45
46       // set amountEditText's TextWatcher
47       EditText amountEditText =
48          (EditText) findViewById(R.id.amountEditText);
49       amountEditText.addTextChangedListener(amountEditTextWatcher);
50
51       // set percentSeekBar's OnSeekBarChangeListener
52       SeekBar percentSeekBar =
53          (SeekBar) findViewById(R.id.percentSeekBar);
54       percentSeekBar.setOnSeekBarChangeListener(seekBarListener);
55    }
56
```

Fig. 3.15 | Overriding `Activity` method onCreate.

onCreate's Bundle *Parameter*

During the app's execution, the user could change the device's configuration—for example, by *rotating the device, connecting to a Bluetooth keyboard* or *sliding out a hard keyboard*. For a good user experience, the app should continue operating smoothly through such configuration changes. When the system calls onCreate, it passes a Bundle argument containing the Activity's saved state, if any. Typically, you save state in Activity methods onPause or onSaveInstanceState (demonstrated in later apps). Line 35 calls the superclass's onCreate method, which is *required* when overriding onCreate.

Generated *R Class Contains Resource IDs*

As you build your app's GUI and add *resources* (such as strings in the strings.xml file or views in the activity_main.xml file) to your app, the IDE generates a class named R that contains *nested classes* representing each type of resource in your project's res folder. The nested classes are declared static, so that you can access them in your code with R.*ClassName*. Within class R's nested classes, the IDE creates static final int constants that enable you to refer to your app's resources programmatically (as we'll discuss momentarily). Some of the nested classes in class R include

- class R.drawable—contains constants for any drawable items, such as *images*, that you put in the various drawable folders in your app's res folder
- class R.id—contains constants for the *views* in your *XML layout files*
- class R.layout—contains constants that represent each *layout file* in your project (such as, activity_main.xml), and
- class R.string—contains constants for each String in the strings.xml file.

Inflating the GUI

The call to setContentView (line 36) receives the constant R.layout.activity_main which indicates the XML file that represents MainActivity's GUI—in this case, the constant represents the activity_main.xml file. Method setContentView uses this constant to load the corresponding XML document, which Android parses and converts into the app's GUI. This process is known as inflating the GUI.

Getting References to the Widgets

Once the layout is *inflated*, you can *get references to the individual widgets* so that you can interact with them programmatically. To do so, you use class Activity's findViewById method. This method takes an int constant representing a specific view's **Id** and returns a reference to the view. The name of each view's R.id constant is determined by the component's **Id** property that you specified when designing the GUI. For example, amount-EditText's constant is R.id.amountEditText.

Lines 39–42 obtain references to the TextViews that we change programmatically in the app. Line 39 obtains a reference to the amountTextView that's updated when the user enters the bill amount. Line 40 obtains a reference to the percentTextView that's updated when the user changes the tip percentage. Lines 41–42 obtain references to the TextViews where the calculated tip and total are displayed.

Displaying Initial Values in the `TextViews`

Lines 43–44 set `tipTextView`'s and `totalTextView`'s text to 0 in a *locale-specific* currency format by calling the `currencyFormat` object's `format method`. The text in each of these `TextViews` will change as the user enters the bill amount.

Registering the Event Listeners

Lines 47–49 get the `amountEditText` and call its `addTextChangedListener` method to register the `TextWatcher` object that responds to events generated when the user changes the `EditText`'s contents. We define this listener (Fig. 3.18) as an anonymous-inner-class object and assign it to the `amountEditTextWatcher` instance variable. Though we could have defined the anonymous inner class in place of `amountEditTextWatcher` in line 49, we chose to define it later in the class so that the code is easier to read.

 Software Engineering Observation 3.4
Rather than defining anonymous inner classes in large methods, define them as `private` `final` *instance variables to make your code easier to debug, modify and maintain.*

Lines 52–53 get a reference to the `percentSeekBar`. Line 54 calls the `SeekBar`'s `setOnSeekBarChangeListener` method to register the `OnSeekBarChangeListener` object that responds to *events* generated when the user moves the `SeekBar`'s thumb. Figure 3.17 defines this listener as an anonymous-inner-class object that's assigned to the instance variable `seekBarListener`.

Note Regarding Android 6 Data Binding

Android now has a Data Binding support library that you can use with Android apps targeting Android 2.1 (API level 7) and higher. You now can include in your layout XML files data-binding expressions that manipulate Java objects and dynamically update data in your apps' user interfaces.

In addition, each layout XML file that contains views with `id`s has a corresponding autogenerated class. For each view with an `id`, the class has a `public final` instance variable referencing that view. You can create an instance of this "`Binding`" class to replace all calls to `findViewById`, which can greatly simplify your `onCreate` methods in `Activity` and `Fragment` classes with complex user interfaces. Each instance variable's name is the `id` specified in the layout for the corresponding view. The "`Binding`" class's name is based on the layout's name—for `activity_main.xml`, the class name is `ActivityMainBinding`.

At the time of this writing, the Data Binding library is an early beta release that's subject to substantial changes, both in the syntax of data-binding expressions and in the Android Studio tool support. You can learn more about Android data binding at

```
https://developer.android.com/tools/data-binding/guide.html
```

3.6.5 `MainActivity` Method `calculate`

Method `calculate` (Fig. 3.16) is called by the `EditText`'s and `SeekBar`'s listeners to update the tip and total `TextViews` each time the user *changes* the bill amount. Line 60 displays the tip percentage in the `percentTextView`. Lines 63–64 calculate the tip and total, based on the `billAmount`. Lines 67–68 display the amounts in currency format.

```
57    // calculate and display tip and total amounts
58    private void calculate() {
59       // format percent and display in percentTextView
60       percentTextView.setText(percentFormat.format(percent));
61
62       // calculate the tip and total
63       double tip = billAmount * percent;
64       double total = billAmount + tip;
65
66       // display tip and total formatted as currency
67       tipTextView.setText(currencyFormat.format(tip));
68       totalTextView.setText(currencyFormat.format(total));
69    }
70
```

Fig. 3.16 | MainActivity Method calculate.

3.6.6 Anonymous Inner Class That Implements Interface OnSeekBarChangeListener

Lines 72–87 (Fig. 3.17) create the *anonymous-inner-class* object that responds to percent-SeekBar's *events*. The object is assigned to the instance variable seekBarListener. Line 54 (Fig. 3.15) registered seekBarListener as percentSeekBar's OnSeekBarChangeListener *event-handling* object. For clarity, we define all but the simplest event-handling objects in this manner so that we do not clutter the onCreate method with this code.

```
71    // listener object for the SeekBar's progress changed events
72    private final OnSeekBarChangeListener seekBarListener =
73       new OnSeekBarChangeListener() {
74          // update percent, then call calculate
75          @Override
76          public void onProgressChanged(SeekBar seekBar, int progress,
77             boolean fromUser) {
78             percent = progress / 100.0; // set percent based on progress
79             calculate(); // calculate and display tip and total
80          }
81
82          @Override
83          public void onStartTrackingTouch(SeekBar seekBar) { }
84
85          @Override
86          public void onStopTrackingTouch(SeekBar seekBar) { }
87       };
88
```

Fig. 3.17 | Anonymous inner class that implements interface OnSeekBarChangeListener.

Overriding Method onProgressChanged of Interface OnSeekBarChangeListener
Lines 75–86 (Fig. 3.17) implement interface OnSeekBarChangeListener's methods. Method onProgressChanged is called whenever the SeekBar's thumb position changes. Line 78 calculates the percent value using the method's progress parameter—an int rep-

resenting the SeekBar's *thumb* position. We divide this by 100.0 to get the percentage. Line 79 calls method `calculate` to recalculate and display the tip and total.

Overriding Methods *onStartTrackingTouch* and *onStopTrackingTouch* of Interface *OnSeekBarChangeListener*

Java requires that you override *every* method in an interface that you implement. This app does not need to know when the user starts moving the SeekBar's thumb (`onStartTrackingTouch`) or stops moving it (`onStopTrackingTouch`), so we simply provide an empty body for each (lines 82–86) to fulfill the interface contract.

Android Studio Tools for Overriding Methods

Android Studio can create for you empty methods that override inherited methods from the class's superclasses or that implement interface methods. When you place the cursor in a class's body, then select the **Code > Override Methods...** menu option, the IDE displays a **Select Methods to Override/Implement** dialog that lists every method you can override in the current class. This list includes all the inherited methods in the class's hierarchy and the methods of any interfaces implemented throughout the class's hierarchy.

Error-Prevention Tip 3.2

Using Android Studio's **Code > Override Methods...** *menu option helps you write code faster and with fewer errors.*

3.6.7 Anonymous Inner Class That Implements Interface `TextWatcher`

Lines 90–114 of Fig. 3.18 create an *anonymous-inner-class* object that responds to amount-EditText's *events* and assign it to the instance variable `amountEditTextWatcher`. Line 49 (Fig. 3.15) registered this object to *listen* for amountEditText's events that occur when the text changes.

```
89      // listener object for the EditText's text-changed events
90      private final TextWatcher amountEditTextWatcher = new TextWatcher() {
91         // called when the user modifies the bill amount
92         @Override
93         public void onTextChanged(CharSequence s, int start,
94            int before, int count) {
95
96            try { // get bill amount and display currency formatted value
97               billAmount = Double.parseDouble(s.toString()) / 100.0;
98               amountTextView.setText(currencyFormat.format(billAmount));
99            }
100           catch (NumberFormatException e) { // if s is empty or non-numeric
101              amountTextView.setText("");
102              billAmount = 0.0;
103           }
104
105           calculate(); // update the tip and total TextViews
106        }
107
```

Fig. 3.18 | Anonymous inner class that implements interface `TextWatcher`. (Part 1 of 2.)

```
108        @Override
109        public void afterTextChanged(Editable s) { }
110
111        @Override
112        public void beforeTextChanged(
113            CharSequence s, int start, int count, int after) { }
114    };
115 }
```

Fig. 3.18 | Anonymous inner class that implements interface TextWatcher. (Part 2 of 2.)

*Overriding Method **onTextChanged** of Interface **TextWatcher***
The onTextChanged method (lines 92–106) is called whenever the text in the amount-
EditText is *modified*. The method receives four parameters. In this example, we use only
CharSequence s, which contains a copy of amountEditText's text. The other parameters
indicate that the count characters starting at start *replaced* previous text of length before.

Line 97 converts the user input from amountEditText to a double. We allow users to
enter only whole numbers in pennies, so we divide the converted value by 100.0 to get the
actual bill amount—e.g., if the user enters 2495, the bill amount is 24.95. Line 98 displays
the updated bill amount. If an exception occurs, lines 101–102 clear the amountTextView
and set the billAmount to 0.0. Lines 105 calls calculate to recalculate and display the
tip and total, based on the current bill amount.

*Other Methods of the **amountEditTextWatcher** TextWatcher*
This app does *not* need to know what changes are about to be made to the text (before-
TextChanged) or that the text has already been changed (afterTextChanged), so we simply
override each of these TextWatcher interface methods with an *empty* body (lines 108–113)
to fulfill the interface contract.

3.7 AndroidManifest.xml

In this section, you'll modify the AndroidManifest.xml file to specify that this app's
Activity supports only a device's portrait orientation and that the virtual keyboard
should always be displayed when the Activity first appears on the screen or navigates back
to the Activity. To open the manifest, double click AndroidManifest.xml in the **Project**
window's manifests folder. Figure 3.19 shows the completed manifest with our changes
highlighted—the rest of the file was autogenerated by Android Studio when we created
the app's project. We'll discuss some aspects of the manifest here. For a list of all the elements a manifest may contain, their attributes and their values, visit

```
http://developer.android.com/guide/topics/manifest/manifest-
    intro.html
```

```
1  <?xml version="1.0" encoding="utf-8"?>
2  <manifest xmlns:android="http://schemas.android.com/apk/res/android"
3      package="com.deitel.tipcalculator" >
4
```

Fig. 3.19 | AndroidManifest.xml contents. (Part 1 of 2.)

```
 5      <application
 6          android:allowBackup="true"
 7          android:icon="@mipmap/ic_launcher"
 8          android:label="@string/app_name"
 9          android:supportsRtl="true"
10          android:theme="@style/AppTheme" >
11          <activity
12              android:name=".MainActivity"
13              android:label="@string/app_name"
14              android:screenOrientation="portrait"
15              android:windowSoftInputMode="stateAlwaysVisible">
16              <intent-filter>
17                  <action android:name="android.intent.action.MAIN" />
18
19                  <category android:name="android.intent.category.LAUNCHER" />
20              </intent-filter>
21          </activity>
22      </application>
23
24  </manifest>
```

Fig. 3.19 | AndroidManifest.xml contents. (Part 2 of 2.)

3.7.1 manifest Element

The manifest element (lines 2–24) indicates that this XML file's contents represent the app's manifest. This element's package attribute specifies the app's Java package name that was configured when you created the app's project (Section 3.4.2). Recall that for apps you submit to the Google Play store, the package name is used as the app's unique identifier.

3.7.2 application Element

The manifest element's nested application element (lines 5–21) specifies attributes of the application, including

- android:allowBackup—Whether or not the app's data should be backed up automatically by Android so that the data can be restored to the device or a new device at a later time.

- android:icon—The app icon that you touch in the launcher to execute the app.

- android:label—The app's name that's typically displayed below the icon in the launcher and often displayed in the app bar when the app is executing.

- android:supportsRtl—Whether or not the app's interface can be flipped horizontally to support right-to-left languages like Arabic and Hebrew.

- android:theme—The theme that determines the default look-and-feel of the app's views.

Elements nested in the application element define the app's components, such as its activities.

3.7.3 activity Element

The application element's nested activity element (lines 10–20) describes an Activity. An app can have many activities, one of which is designated as the Activity that's displayed when the user touches the app's icon in the launcher to execute the app. Each activity element specifies at least the following attributes:

- android:name—The Activity's class name. The notation ".MainActivity" is shorthand for "com.deitel.MainActivity" (where com.deitel is the reverse of the domain name you specified when creating the app's project).

- android:label—The Activity's name. This is often displayed in the app bar when the Activity is on the screen. For single Activity apps, this name is typically the same as the app's name.

For MainActivity, we added the following attributes:

- android:screenOrientation—In general, most apps should support *both* portrait and landscape orientations. In *portrait* orientation, the device's longer dimension is vertical. In *landscape orientation*, the device's longer dimension is horizontal. In the **Tip Calculator** app, rotating the device to landscape orientation on a typical phone would cause the numeric keypad to obscure most of the **Tip Calculator**'s GUI. For this reason, we set this property to "portrait" to support *only* portrait orientation.

- android:windowSoftInputMode—In the **Tip Calculator** app, the soft keypad should be displayed immediately when the app executes and should reappear each time the user returns to the **Tip Calculator** app. For this reason we set this property to "stateAlwaysVisible". This will *not* display the soft keyboard if a hard keyboard is present.

3.7.4 intent-filter Element

Intents are Android's mechanism for communicating between executable components—such as activities, background services and the operating system. You *state your intent*, then Android uses intent messaging to coordinate the executable components to accomplish what you intend to do. This *loose coupling* makes it easy to mix and match parts of different applications. You tell Android what you want to accomplish, then let Android find the installed applications with activities that can handle the task.

Inter-App Communication
One example of how Intents are used is *coordinating efforts between separate apps*. Consider how photo sharing can be handled in Android:

- Most social-networking Android apps provide their own photo-sharing capabilities. Each app can advertise in its manifest its specific Activity that uploads a photo to the user's account.

- Other apps can use these photo-sharing capabilities, rather than implementing their own. For example, a photo-editing app can provide a **Share Photo** option. The app can respond to a user's photo-sharing request by *stating its intent* to share a photo—that is, creating a photo-sharing Intent and passing it to Android.

- Android looks at the Intent to determine which installed applications provide activities that can share photos.

- If there's only *one* such app, Android executes that app's photo-sharing Activity.

- If there are *many* such apps, Android displays a list of apps and asks the *user to decide* which app's photo-sharing Activity should execute.

A key benefit of this loosely coupled approach is that the photo-editing app's developer does not need to incorporate support for every possible social-networking site. By issuing a photo-sharing Intent, the app automatically supports *any* app that declares a photo-sharing Activity in its manifest, including those apps the user has already installed and any the user chooses to install in the future. For a list of the items that can be used with Intents, visit

```
http://developer.android.com/reference/android/content/
    Intent.html#constants
```

Executing Apps

Another example of how Intents are used is in *launching activities*. When you touch an app's icon in the device's launcher app, your intent is to execute the app. In this case, the launcher issues an Intent to execute that app's main Activity (discussed momentarily). Android responds to this Intent by launching the app and executing the specific Activity designated in the app's manifest as the main Activity.

Determining Which Activity to Execute

Android uses information in the manifest to determine the activities that can respond to Intents and which Intents each Activity can handle. In the manifest, the activity element's nested `intent-filter` element (Fig. 3.19, lines 16–20) determines which Intent types can launch an Activity. If an Intent matches only one Activity's intent-filter, Android executes that Activity. If there are multiple matches, Android presents a list from which the user can choose an app, then executes the appropriate Activity in that app.

Android also passes the Intent to the Activity, because an Intent often contains data the Activity can use to perform its task. For example, a photo-editing app can include in a share-photo Intent the specific photo to share.

The intent-filter element must contain one or more `action` elements. The action "android.intent.action.MAIN" in line 17 of Fig. 3.19 indicates that MainActivity is the Activity to execute when the app launches. The optional `category` element in line 19 specifies what initiates the Intent—for "android.intent.category.LAUNCHER", it's the device's launcher. This category also indicates that the Activity should appear as an icon in the device's launcher with the icons for the user's other installed apps.

We'll discuss and program with Intents in the next chapter. For more information on Intents and Intent filters, visit

```
http://developer.android.com/guide/components/intents-filters.html
```

3.8 Wrap-Up

In this chapter, you created the interactive **Tip Calculator** app. We discussed the app's capabilities, then you test-drove it to calculate the tip and total, based on the bill amount.

You built the app's GUI using Android Studio's layout editor, **Component Tree** window and **Properties** window. You also edited the layout's XML and used the **Theme Editor** to customize the Theme.AppCompat.Light.DarkActionBar theme's primary, dark primary and accent colors that were set by the IDE when you created the project. We presented the code for class MainActivity, a subclass of AppCompatActivity (and an indirect subclass of Activity) that defined the app's logic.

In the app's GUI, you used a GridLayout to arrange the views into rows and columns. You displayed text in TextViews and received input from an EditText and a SeekBar.

The MainActivity class required many Java object-oriented programming capabilities, including classes, objects, methods, interfaces, anonymous inner classes and inheritance. We explained the notion of inflating the GUI from its XML file into its screen representation. You learned about Android's Activity class and part of the Activity lifecycle. In particular, you overrode the onCreate method to initialize the app when it's launched. In the onCreate method, you used Activity method findViewById to get references to each of the views the app interacts with programmatically. You defined an anonymous inner class that implements the TextWatcher interface so the app can calculate new tips and totals as the user enters the bill amount in the EditText. You also defined an anonymous inner class that implements the OnSeekBarChangeListener interface so the app can calculate a new tip and total as the user changes the tip percentage by moving the SeekBar's thumb.

Finally, you edited the AndroidManifest.xml file to specify that the MainActivity supports only portrait orientation and that the MainActivity should always display the keypad. We also discussed the other elements that Android Studio placed in the manifest when you created the project.

In Chapter 4, you'll build the **Flag Quiz** app in which the user is shown a graphic of a country's flag and must guess the country from 2, 4, 6 or 8 choices. You'll use a menu and checkboxes to customize the quiz, specifying the number of guess options and limiting the flags to specific regions of the world.

Flag Quiz App

Fragments, Menus, Preferences, Explicit Intents, Handler, AssetManager, Tweened Animations, Animators, Toasts, Color State Lists, Layouts for Multiple Device Orientations, Logging Error Messages for Debugging

Objectives

In this chapter you'll:

- Use Fragments to make better use of available screen real estate in an Activity's GUI on phones and tablets.
- Display a settings icon on the app bar to enable users to access the app's user preferences.
- Use a PreferenceFragment to automatically manage and persist an app's user preferences.
- Use a SharedPreferences.Editor to modify key-value pairs of data associated with an app.
- Use an app's assets subfolders to organize image resources and manipulate them with an AssetManager.
- Define an animation and apply it to a View.
- Use a Handler to schedule a future task to perform on the GUI thread.
- Use Toasts to display messages briefly to the user.
- Launch a specific Activity with an explicit Intent.
- Use collections from the java.util package.
- Define layouts for multiple device orientations.
- Use Android's logging mechanism to log error messages.

4.1 Introduction

The **Flag Quiz** app tests your ability to correctly identify 10 flags from various countries and territories (Fig. 4.1). By default, the app presents a flag image and four country-name **But-**tons that you click to guess the answer—one is correct and the others are randomly selected, *nonduplicated* incorrect answers. The app displays the user's progress throughout the quiz, showing the question number (out of 10) in a TextView above the current flag image.

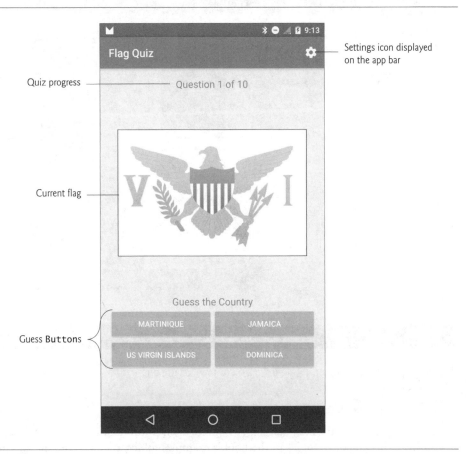

Fig. 4.1 | Flag Quiz app running on a smartphone in portrait orientation.

As you'll see, the app also allows you to control the quiz difficulty by specifying whether to display two, four, six or eight guess Buttons, and by choosing the world regions that should be included in the quiz. These options are displayed differently, based on the device that's running the app and the orientation of the device—the app supports portrait orientation on *any* device, but landscape orientation only on tablets.

In portrait orientation, the app displays on the app bar a settings icon (⚙). When the user touches this icon, the app displays a separate screen (another Activity) for setting the number of guess Buttons, and the world regions to use in the quiz. On a tablet in landscape orientation (Fig. 4.2), the app uses a different layout that always displays the app's settings and the quiz at the same time.

First you'll test-drive the app. Then we'll overview the technologies we used to build it. Next, you'll design the app's GUI. Finally, we'll present and walk through the app's complete source code, discussing the app's new features in more detail.

Fig. 4.2 | Flag Quiz app running on a tablet in landscape orientation.

4.2 Test-Driving the Flag Quiz App

You'll now test-drive the **Flag Quiz** app. To do so, open Android Studio, open the **Flag Quiz** app from the FlagQuiz folder in the book's examples folder, then execute the app in the AVD or on a device. This builds the project and runs the app (Fig. 4.1 or Fig. 4.2).

4.2.1 Configuring the Quiz's Settings

When you first install and run the app, the quiz is configured to display four guess Buttons and to select flags from *all* of the world's regions. For this test-drive, you'll change the app's options to select flags only from North America and you'll keep the app's default setting of four guess Buttons per flag.

On a phone, a tablet or an AVD in portrait orientation, touch the settings icon (⚙) on the app bar (Fig. 4.1) to view the **Settings** screen (Fig. 4.3(a)). On a tablet device or tablet AVD in *landscape* orientation, the app's settings appear at the left side of the screen (Fig. 4.2). Touch **Number of Choices** to display the dialog for selecting the number of Buttons that should be displayed with each flag (Fig. 4.3(b)). (On a tablet device or tablet AVD in landscape orientation, the entire app is grayed out and the dialog is centered on the screen.) By default, **4** is selected—we used this default setting. To make the quiz easier, you could select 2, or to make the quiz more challenging, you could select **6** or **8**. Touch **CANCEL** (or touch the screen outside the dialog) to return to the **Settings** screen.

a) Menu with the user touching **Number of Choices**   b) Dialog showing options for number of choices

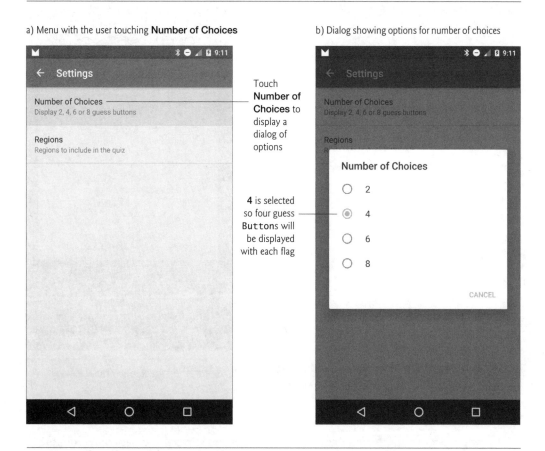

Touch **Number of Choices** to display a dialog of options

4 is selected so four guess **Button**s will be displayed with each flag

Fig. 4.3 | Flag Quiz settings screen and the **Number of Choices** dialog.

Next, touch **Regions** (Fig. 4.4(a)) to display the checkboxes representing the world regions (Fig. 4.4(b)). By default, all regions are enabled when the app first executes, so every flag we provide with the app can be selected randomly for a quiz. Touch the checkboxes next to **Africa**, **Asia**, **Europe**, **Oceania** (Australia, New Zealand and the islands in that vicinity) and **South America** to uncheck them—this excludes those regions' countries from the quiz. Touch **OK** to save your settings. On a phone, a tablet or an AVD in portrait orientation, touch the back button (◁) to return to the quiz screen and start a new quiz with your updated settings. On a tablet device or tablet AVD in landscape orientation, a new quiz with the updated settings is immediately displayed at the right side of the screen.

a) Menu with the user touching **Regions**

b) Dialog showing regions

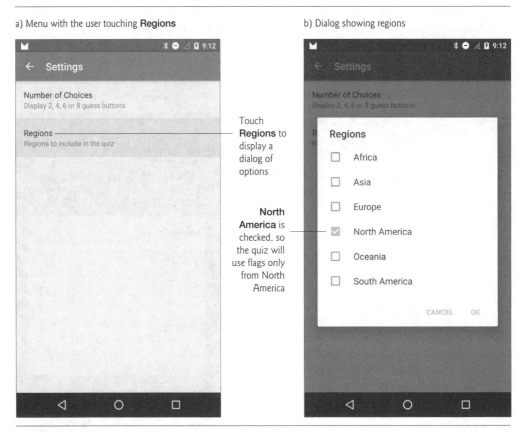

Touch **Regions** to display a dialog of options

North America is checked, so the quiz will use flags only from North America

Fig. 4.4 | Flag Quiz settings screen and the **Regions** dialog (after unchecking **Africa**, **Asia**, **Europe**, **Oceania** and **South America**).

4.2.2 Taking the Quiz

A new quiz starts with the number of answer choices you selected and flags only from the region(s) you selected. Work through the quiz by touching the guess Button for the country that you think matches each flag.

Making a Correct Selection

If the choice is correct (Fig. 4.5(a)), the app disables all the answer Buttons and displays the country name in green, followed by an exclamation point at the bottom of the screen (Fig. 4.5(b)). After a short delay, the app loads the next flag and animates the flag and a new set of answer Buttons onto the screen. The app transitions from the current quiz question to the next with a *circular reveal* animation:

- First, a large-diameter circle shrinks onto the screen until its diameter is zero, thus hiding the current quiz question's flag and guess Buttons.

- Then, the circle's diameter grows from zero until the new question's flag and guess Buttons are fully visible on the screen.

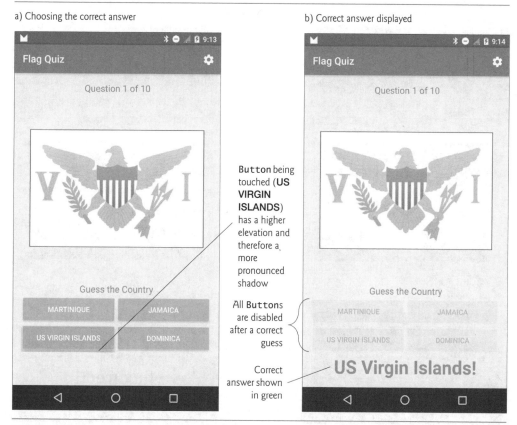

Fig. 4.5 | User choosing the correct answer and the correct answer displayed.

Making an Incorrect Selection

For each incorrect country-name Button you touch (Fig. 4.6(a)), the app

- disables the corresponding country name Button
- uses an animation to *shake* the flag horizontally and
- displays **Incorrect!** in red at the bottom of the screen (Fig. 4.6(b)).

Continue guessing until you get the correct answer for that flag.

Completing the Quiz

After you select the 10 correct country names, a popup AlertDialog displays over the app, showing your total number of guesses and the percentage of correct answers (Fig. 4.7). This is a modal dialog, so you must interact with it to dismiss it—for a non-modal dialog, touching the AVD's or device's back button (◁) will dismiss the dialog. When you touch the dialog's **RESET QUIZ** Button, Android dismisses the dialog and a new quiz begins, using the same number of guess options and region(s) as the quiz you just completed.

a) Choosing an incorrect answer

b) **Incorrect!** displayed

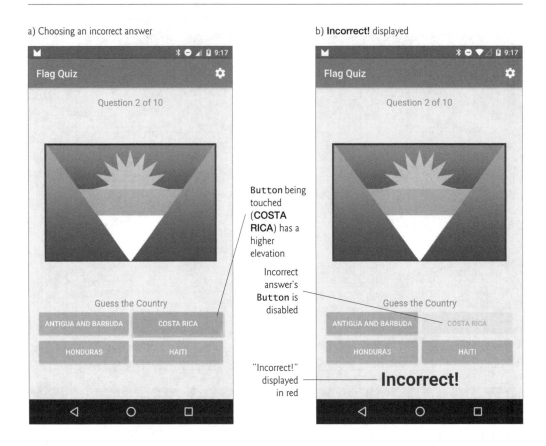

Button being touched (**COSTA RICA**) has a higher elevation

Incorrect answer's **Button** is disabled

"Incorrect!" displayed in red

Fig. 4.6 | Disabled incorrect answer in the **Flag Quiz** app.

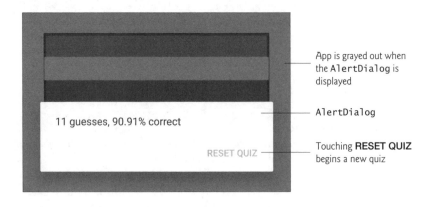

App is grayed out when the **AlertDialog** is displayed

AlertDialog

Touching **RESET QUIZ** begins a new quiz

Fig. 4.7 | Results displayed after quiz completion.

4.3 Technologies Overview

This section introduces the features you'll use to build the **Flag Quiz** app.

4.3.1 Menus

When you create an app's project in the IDE, the MainActivity is configured to display an options menu (⋮) at the right side of the action bar. In this app, you'll display the options menu only when the app is in portrait orientation. Touching the ⋮ icon expands a menu that, by default, contains only a **Settings** menu item—this typically is used to display an app's settings to the user. For this app, we'll modify the menu's XML file by providing an icon (⚙) for the **Settings** menu item and specifying that the icon should be displayed directly on the app bar. This will enable the user to touch once to view the app's settings, rather than having to first open the options menu, then touch **Settings**. You'll use Android Studio's **Vector Asset Studio** to add the material design settings icon to the project. In later apps, you'll see how to create additional menu items.

The options menu is an object of class Menu (package android.view). You override Activity method onCreateOptionsMenu (Section 4.6.5) and use the method's Menu argument to add the menu items—either programmatically or by inflating an XML document that describes the menu items. When the user selects a menu item, Activity method onOptionsItemSelected (Section 4.6.6) responds to the selection.

4.3.2 Fragments

A fragment typically represents a reusable portion of an Activity's user interface, but may also represent reusable program logic. This app uses fragments to create and manage portions of the app's GUI. You can combine several fragments to create user interfaces that make better use of tablet screen sizes. You also can easily interchange fragments to make your GUIs more dynamic—you'll do this in Chapter 9.

Class Fragment (package android.app) is the base class of all fragments. When using subclasses of AppCompatActivity with Fragments you must use the Android Support Library's version of this class from package android.support.v4.app. The **Flag Quiz** app defines the following direct and indirect Fragment subclasses:

- Class MainActivityFragment (Section 4.7)—a direct subclass of Fragment—displays the quiz's GUI and defines the quiz's logic. Like an Activity, each Fragment has its own layout that's typically defined as an XML layout resource file (GUIs also can be created dynamically). In Section 4.5.2, you'll build MainActivityFragment's GUI. You'll create *two* layouts for MainActivity—one for devices in portrait orientation and one only for tablets in landscape orientation. You'll then reuse the MainActivityFragment in both layouts.

- Class SettingsActivityFragment (Section 4.9) is a subclass of PreferenceFragment (package android.preference), which automatically maintains an app's user preferences in a file associated with the app. As you'll see, you create an XML file describing the user preferences, then class PreferenceFragment uses that file to build an appropriate preferences GUI (Figs. 4.3–4.4). We discuss preferences more in Section 4.3.5.

- When you finish a quiz, the app creates an anonymous subclass of `DialogFragment` (package `android.support.v4.app`) and displays an `AlertDialog` (introduced in Section 4.3.15) containing the quiz results (Section 4.7.10).

Fragments *must* be hosted by an `Activity`—they cannot execute independently. When this app runs in landscape orientation on a tablet, the `MainActivity` hosts all of the Fragments. In portrait orientation (on any device), the `SettingsActivity` (Section 4.8) hosts the `SettingsActivityFragment` and the `MainActivity` hosts the others.

4.3.3 Fragment Lifecycle Methods

Like an `Activity`, each `Fragment` has a *lifecycle* and provides methods that you can override to respond to *lifecycle events*. In this app, you'll override

- `onCreate`—This method (which you'll override in class `SettingsActivityFragment`) is called when a `Fragment` is created. The `MainActivityFragment` and `SettingsActivityFragment` are created when the app inflates their parent activities' layouts. The `DialogFragment` that displays the quiz results is created and displayed dynamically when the user completes a quiz.

- `onCreateView`—This method (which you'll override in class `MainActivityFragment`) is called after `onCreate` to build and return a `View` containing the Fragment's GUI. As you'll see, this method receives a `LayoutInflater`, which you'll use to programmatically inflate a Fragment's GUI from the components specified in a predefined XML layout.

Fragments can add their own menu items to a host `Activity`'s menu. Like class `Activity`, Fragments also have lifecycle method `onCreateOptionsMenu` and event-handling method `onOptionsItemSelected`.

We'll discuss other `Fragment` lifecycle methods as we encounter them throughout the book. For the complete lifecycle details, visit

```
http://developer.android.com/guide/components/fragments.html
```

4.3.4 Managing Fragments

An Activity manages its Fragments via a `FragmentManager` (package `android.app`)—accessible via Activity's `getFragmentManager` method. If the Activity needs to interact with a Fragment that's declared in the Activity's layout and has an **id**, the Activity can call FragmentManager method `findFragmentById` to obtain a reference to the specified Fragment. As you'll see in Chapter 9, a FragmentManager can use `FragmentTransactions` to dynamically *add*, *remove* and *transition* between Fragments.

For backward compatibility, subclasses of `AppCompatActivity` must use the Android Support Library's version of FragmentManager from package `android.support.v4.app`, rather than the one in package `android.app`. Class `AppCompatActivity` inherits method `getSupportFragmentManager` from the Android Support Library's `FragmentActivity` class to obtain the correct `FragmentManager`.

4.3.5 Preferences

In Section 4.2.1, you customized the quiz by changing the app's settings. These settings are stored persistently in a file as *key–value* pairs—each *key* enables you to quickly look up a corresponding *value*. The keys in the file must be Strings, and the values can be Strings or primitive-type values. Such a file is manipulated via an object of class SharedPreferences (package android.content) and the file is accessible only to the app that creates the file.

A PreferenceFragment uses Preference objects (package android.preference) to manage app settings and stores those settings in a file via a SharedPreferences object. This app uses Preference subclass ListPreference to manage the number of guess Buttons displayed for each flag and Preference subclass MultiSelectListPreference to manage the world regions to include in the quiz. A ListPreference creates *mutually exclusive* radio buttons in which only one can be selected (Fig. 4.3(b)). A MultiSelectListPreference creates a GUI containing checkboxes, any number of which can be selected (Fig. 4.4(b)). You'll use a PreferenceManager object (package android.preference) to access and interact with the app's default SharedPreferences file.

You'll also interact directly with the app's default SharedPreferences file:

- When starting a quiz, you'll query the app's preferences to determine the number of guess Buttons to display and the region(s) from which to select flags.

- When the user changes the regions preference, the app will ensure that at least one region is selected; otherwise, there would be no flags to include in the quiz. If none is selected, the app edits the regions preference to select North America.

To modify a SharedPreferences file's contents, you'll use a SharedPreferences.Editor object (Section 4.6.7).

4.3.6 assets Folder

This app's flag images are loaded into the app only when needed and are located in the app's **assets folder**.[1] To add the images to the project, we copied each region's folder from our file system into the assets folder in the **Project** window (Section 4.4.4). The images are located in the images/FlagQuizImages folder with the book's examples.

Unlike an app's drawable folders, which require their image contents to be at the root level in each folder, the assets folder may contain files of any type and they can be organized in subfolders—we maintain the flag images for each region in a separate subfolder. Files in the assets subfolders are accessed via an **AssetManager** (package android.content.res), which can provide a list of all of the file names in a specified subfolder and can be used to access each asset.

4.3.7 Resource Folders

In Section 2.4.4, you learned about the drawable, layout and values subfolders of an app's res folder. In this app, you'll also use the menu, anim, color and xml resource folders. Figure 4.8 overviews these folders as well as the animator and raw folders.

---

1. We obtained the images from http://www.free-country-flags.com.

Resource subfolder	Description
anim	Folder names that begin with anim contain XML files that define *tweened animations*, which can change an object's *transparency, size, position* and *rotation* over time. You'll define such an animation in Section 4.4.10, then in Section 4.7.10 you'll play it to create a *shake effect* to provide the user with visual feedback for an incorrect guess.
animator	Folder names that begin with animator contain XML files that define *property animations*, which change the value of an object's property over time. In Java, a property is typically implemented in a class as an instance variable with both *set* and *get* accessors.
color	Folder names that begin with color contain XML files that define color state lists—lists of colors for various states, such as the states of a Button (*unpressed, pressed, enabled, disabled,* and so on). We'll use a color state list to define separate colors for when the guess Buttons are *enabled* or *disabled* in Section 4.4.8.
raw	Folder names that begin with raw contain resource files (such as audio clips) that are read into an app as streams of bytes. We'll use such resources in Chapter 6 to play sounds.
menu	Folder names that begin with menu contain XML files that describe the contents of menus. When you create a project, the IDE automatically defines a menu with a **Settings** option.
xml	Folder names that begin with xml contain XML files that do not fit into the other resource categories—often XML data files used by the app. In Section 4.4.11, you'll create an XML file that represents the preferences displayed by this app's SettingsActivityFragment.

Fig. 4.8 | Other subfolders within a project's res folder.

4.3.8 Supporting Different Screen Sizes and Resolutions

In Section 2.5.1 you learned that Android devices have various *screen sizes, resolutions* and *pixel densities* (dots per inch or DPI). You also learned that you typically provide images and other visual resources in multiple resolutions so Android can choose the best resource for a device's pixel density. Similarly, in Section 2.8, you learned how to provide String resources for different languages and regions. Android uses resource folders with *qualified names* to choose the appropriate images, based on a device's pixel density, and the correct language strings, based on a device's locale and region settings. This mechanism also can be used to select resources from any of the resource folders discussed in Section 4.3.7.

For this app's MainActivity, you'll use minimum screen width and orientation qualifiers to determine which layout to use—one for portrait orientation on phones and tablets and another only for tablets in landscape orientation. To do this, you'll define two layouts that present MainActivity's contents:

- content_main.xml is the default layout that displays only the MainActivity-Fragment.

- content_main.xml (sw700dp-land) is used *only* on devices (i.e., tablets) when the app is in landscape (land) orientation.

Qualified resource folder names (on disk) have the format:

name-qualifiers

where *qualifiers* consists of one or more qualifiers separated by dashes (-). There are currently 19 qualifier types that you can use to designate when Android should choose specific resource files. We'll explain other qualifiers as we use them throughout the book. For a complete description of all the `res` subfolder qualifiers and the rules for the order in which they must be defined in a fully qualified folder's name, visit

```
http://developer.android.com/guide/topics/resources/providing-
    resources.html#AlternativeResources
```

4.3.9 Determining the Device Orientation

In this app, we display the Menu only when the app is running on a phone-sized device or when it's running on a tablet in portrait orientation (Section 4.6.5). To determine this, we'll obtain an object of class `Configuration` (package `android.content.res`), which contains `public` instance variable `orientation` containing either `ORIENTATION_PORTRAIT` or `ORIENTATION_LANDSCAPE` for the device's current orientation.

4.3.10 Toasts for Displaying Messages

A `Toast` (package `android.widget`) briefly displays a message, then disappears from the screen. `Toast`s are often used to display minor error messages or informational messages. We use `Toast`s as follows:

- To indicate that the quiz will be reset after the user changes the app's settings.
- To indicate that at least one region must be selected if the user deselects all regions—in this case, the app sets North America as the quiz's default region.

4.3.11 Using a `Handler` to Execute a `Runnable` in the Future

When the user makes a correct guess, the app displays the correct answer for two seconds before displaying the next flag. To do this, we use a `Handler` (package `android.os`). `Handler` method `postDelayed` receives as arguments a `Runnable` to execute and a delay in milliseconds. After the delay has passed, the `Handler`'s `Runnable` executes in the *same thread* that created the `Handler`.

Error-Prevention Tip 4.1

Operations that interact with or modify the GUI must be performed in the GUI thread (also called the UI thread or main thread), because GUI components are not thread safe.

4.3.12 Applying an Animation to a `View`

When the user makes an incorrect choice, the app shakes the flag by applying an `Animation` (package `android.view.animation`) to the `ImageView`. We use `AnimationUtils` `static` method `loadAnimation` to load the animation from an XML file that describes the animation's options. We also specify the number of times the animation should repeat with `Animation` method `setRepeatCount` and perform the animation by calling `View` method `startAnimation` (with the `Animation` as an argument) on the `ImageView`.

4.3.13 Using `ViewAnimationUtils` to Create a Circular Reveal Animator

Animations can make an app more visually appealing. In this app, shortly after the user makes a correct choice, the app animates the flag and answer `Buttons` off the screen and the next flag and answer `Buttons` onto the screen. To do this, in Section 4.7.9, you'll use the `ViewAnimationUtils` class to create a *circular reveal* `Animator` object by calling the `createCircularReveal` method. You'll then set the animation's duration and start the animation by calling `Animator` methods `setDuration` and `start`, respectively. The animation appears as a shrinking or expanding circular window that displays part of a UI element.

4.3.14 Specifying Colors Based on a `View`'s State Via a Color State List

A color state list resource file defines a color resource that changes colors based on a `View`'s state. For example, you could define a color state list for a `Button`'s background color that specifies different colors for the `Button`'s *pressed*, *unpressed*, *enabled* and *disabled* states. Similarly, for a `CheckBox`, you could specify different colors for its *checked* or *unchecked* states.

In this app, when the user makes an incorrect guess, the app disables that guess `Button`, and when the user makes a correct guess, the app disables all the guess `Buttons`. In a disabled `Button`, the white text is difficult to read. To solve this issue you'll define a color state list that specifies a `Button`'s text color, based on the `Button`'s enabled or disabled state (Section 4.4.8). For more information on color state lists, visit

```
http://developer.android.com/guide/topics/resources/color-list-
    resource.html
```

4.3.15 `AlertDialog`

You can display messages, options and confirmations to app users via `AlertDialogs` (package `android.app`). An `AlertDialog` is a modal dialog—when it's displayed, the user cannot interact with the app until the dialog is dismissed (closed). As you'll see, you create and configure the `AlertDialog` with an `AlertDialog.Builder` object, then use it to create the `AlertDialog`.

`AlertDialogs` can display buttons, checkboxes, radio buttons and lists of items that the user can touch to respond to the dialog's message. They can also display custom GUIs. A standard `AlertDialog` may have up to three buttons that represent:

- A *negative action*—Cancels the dialog's specified action, often labeled with **CANCEL** or **NO**. This is the leftmost button when there are multiple buttons in the dialog.

- A *positive action*—Accepts the dialog's specified action, often labeled with **OK** or **YES**. This is the rightmost button when there are multiple buttons in the dialog.

- A *neutral action*—This button indicates that the user does not want to cancel or accept the action specified by the dialog. For example, an app that asks the user to register to gain access to additional features might provide a **REMIND ME LATER** neutral button.

We use an `AlertDialog` at the end of a quiz to display the quiz results to the user (Section 4.7.10) and enable the user to touch a button to reset the quiz. You'll implement the interface `DialogInterface.OnClickListener` (package `android.content`) to handle the button's event. You can learn more about Android dialogs at

```
http://developer.android.com/guide/topics/ui/dialogs.html
```

4.3.16 Logging Exception Messages

When exceptions occur or when you want to track important aspects of your code's execution, you can *log* messages for debugging purposes with Android's built-in logging mechanism. Android provides class `Log` (package `android.util`) with several `static` methods that represent messages of varying detail. Logged messages can be viewed in the bottom of the Android Device Monitor's **LogCat** tab or with the Android `logcat` tool. You can open the Android Device Monitor window from Android Studio by selecting **View > Tool Windows > Android Monitor**. For more details on logging messages, visit

```
http://developer.android.com/tools/debugging/debugging-log.html
```

4.3.17 Launching Another `Activity` Via an Explicit `Intent`

As you learned in Section 3.7.4, Android uses a technique known as *intent messaging* to communicate information between activities within one app or activities in separate apps. Each `Activity` declared in the `AndroidManifest.xml` file can specify *intent filters* indicating *actions* the `Activity` is capable of handling. In each app so far, the IDE created an intent filter for the app's only `Activity` indicating that it could respond to the predefined action named `android.intent.action.MAIN`, which specifies that the `Activity` can be used to *launch* the app to begin its execution. An `Activity` is launched by using an `Intent` that indicates an *action* to be performed and the *data* on which to perform that action.

Implicit and Explicit *Intents*

This app uses an explicit `Intent`. When this app runs in portrait orientation, its preferences are displayed *explicitly* in the `SettingsActivity` (Section 4.8)—the specific `Activity` that understands how to manage this app's preferences. Section 4.6.6 shows how to use an explicit `Intent` to launch a specific `Activity` in the same app.

Android also supports implicit `Intent`s for which you do *not* specify explicitly which component should handle the `Intent`. For example, you can create an `Intent` to display the contents of a URL and allow Android to launch the most appropriate activity (a web browser), based on the type of data. If *multiple* activities can handle the action and data passed to `startActivity`, the system will display a *dialog* in which the user can select the activity to use (possibly one of several browsers the user has installed). If the system cannot find an activity to handle the action, then method `startActivity` throws an `Activity-NotFoundException`. In general, it's a good practice to handle this exception to prevent your app from crashing. You can also prevent this exception from happening by first using `Intent` method `resolveActivity` to determine whether there is an `Activity` to handle the `Intent`. For a more information on `Intent`s, visit

```
http://developer.android.com/guide/components/intents-filters.html
```

4.3.18 Java Data Structures

This app uses various data structures from the `java.util` package. The app dynamically loads the image file names for the enabled regions and stores them in an Array-List<String>. We use `Collections` method `shuffle` to randomize the order of the image file names for each new game (Section 4.7.7). We use a second `ArrayList<String>` to hold the image file names for the countries eligible to be used in the current quiz. We also use a `Set<String>` to store the world regions included in a quiz. We refer to the Array-List<String> object with a variable of interface type `List<String>`.

Software Engineering Observation 4.1

Refer to collection objects using variables of the corresponding generic interface type, so you can change data structures easily without affecting the rest of your app's code.

4.3.19 Java SE 7 Features

Android fully supports Java SE 7. For a complete list of the features introduced in Java SE 7, visit

```
http://www.oracle.com/technetwork/java/javase/jdk7-relnotes-
   418459.html
```

This app uses the following Java SE 7 features:

- Type inference for generic instance creation—If the compiler can infer a generic object's type from the context, you can replace *<type>* with <> when creating the object. For example, in the **Flag Quiz**'s `MainActivityFragment` code, the instance variable `quizCountriesList` is declared to be of type `List<String>`, so the compiler knows the collection must contain `Strings`. Thus, when we create the corresponding `ArrayList` object, we can use Java SE 7's *diamond operator* <> as in the following statement, and the compiler infers that <> should be `<String>`, based on `quizCountriesList`'s declaration:

  ```
  quizCountriesList = new ArrayList<>();
  ```

- The `try`-*with-resources* statement—Rather than declaring a resource, using it in a try block and closing it in a `finally` block, you can use the `try`-*with-resources* statement to declare the resource in the `try` block's parentheses and use the resource in the `try` block. The resource is *implicitly* closed when program control leaves the `try` block. For example, in the **Flag Quiz**'s `MainActivityFragment` code, we use an `InputStream` to read the bytes of the app's flag images and use them to create `Drawables` (Section 4.7.7):

  ```
  try (InputStream stream =
      assets.open(region + "/" + nextImage + ".png")) {
      // code that might throw an exception
  }
  ```

4.3.20 `AndroidManifest.xml`

As you learned in Chapter 3, the `AndroidManifest.xml` file is created for you when you create an app. All activities in an Android app must be listed in the app's manifest file. We'll show you how to add additional activities to the project. When you add the SettingsActivity to the project (Section 4.4.12), the IDE will also add it to the manifest file. For the complete details of AndroidManifest.xml, visit

```
http://developer.android.com/guide/topics/manifest/manifest-
    intro.html
```

We'll cover various other aspects of the AndroidManifest.xml file in subsequent apps.

4.4 Creating the Project, Resource Files and Additional Classes

In this section, you'll create the project and configure the String, array, color and animation resources used by the **Flag Quiz** app. You'll also create additional classes for a second Activity that enables the user to change the app's settings.

4.4.1 Creating the Project

Follow the steps in Section 2.3 to create a new project. Specify the following values in the **Create New Project** dialog's **New Project** step:

- **Application name:** Flag Quiz
- **Company Domain:** deitel.com (or specify your own domain name)

For the remaining steps in the **Create New Project** dialog, use the same settings as in Section 2.3, but this time in the **Add an activity to Mobile** step, select **Blank Activity** rather than **Empty Activity** and check the **Use a Fragment** checkbox. Keep the default names provided for the **Activity Name, Layout Name, Title** and **Menu Resource Name**, then click **Finish** to create the project. The IDE will create various Java and resource files, including

- a MainActivity class
- a Fragment subclass called MainActivityFragment that's displayed by the MainActivity
- layout files for the MainActivity and MainActivityFragment, and
- a menu_main.xml file that defines MainActivity's options menu.

Also, follow the steps in Section 2.5.2 to add an app icon to your project.

When the project opens in Android Studio, the IDE displays content_main.xml in the layout editor. Select **Nexus 6** from the virtual-device drop-down list (Fig. 2.11)—once again, we'll use this device as the basis for our design.

4.4.2 Blank Activity Template Layouts

The **Blank Activity** template is a backward-compatible app template (for Android 2.1 and higher) that uses features of the Android Design Support Library. This template can be used with or without a Fragment. When you choose to use the Fragment option, the IDE creates layouts named activity_main.xml, content_main.xml and fragment_main.xml.

activity_main.xml

The layout in activity_main.xml contains a CoordinatorLayout (from the package android.support.design.widget in the Android Design Support Library). The CoordinatorLayout layouts defined Android Studio's app templates typically contain an app bar, defined as a `Toolbar` (package `android.support.v7.widget`). The templates define the app bar explicitly for backward compatibility with early Android versions that did not support app bars. `CoordinatorLayouts` also help manage material-design-based interactions with nested views—such as moving a portion of a GUI out of the way when a view animates onto the screen and restoring the GUI to its original location when a view animates off the screen.

The default `activity_main.xml` layout embeds (via an `<include>` element in the XML) the GUI defined in `content_main.xml`. The default layout also contains a `FloatingActionButton`—a round image button from the Android Design Support Library that has a higher elevation than the GUI's other components, so it "floats" over the GUI. A `FloatingActionButton` typically emphasizes an important action that the user can perform by touching the button. Each app based on the **Blank Activity** template includes a `FloatingActionButton` and other material design features. You'll use `FloatingAction-Buttons` starting in Chapter 7.

content_main.xml

The `content_main.xml` layout defines the portion of `MainActivity`'s GUI that appears below the app bar and above the system bar. When you choose the **Blank Activity** template's Fragment option, this file contains only a `<fragment>` element that displays the `MainActivityFragment`'s GUI defined in `fragment_main.xml`. If you do not choose the template's Fragment option, this file defines a `RelativeLayout` containing a `TextView`, and you'd define `MainActivity`'s GUI here.

fragment_main.xml

The `fragment_main.xml` layout is defined only when you choose the **Blank Activity** template's Fragment option. When using a `Fragment`, this is where you define the main GUI.

Preparing to Design the GUI

We don't need the `FloatingActionButton` for this app, so open the `activity_main.xml` layout and delete the bright pink button in the layout's bottom-right corner. Also, select the `CoordinatorLayout` in the **Component Tree** and set the layout's **id** to `coordinatorLay-out`. Open the `fragment_main.xml` layout and remove the **Hello World!** `TextView` defined by the app template.

4.4.3 Configuring Java SE 7 Support

We use Java SE 7 programming features in this app. By default, a new Android Studio project uses Java SE 6. To use Java SE 7:

1. Right click the project's **app** folder and select **Open Module Settings** to open the **Project Structure** window.

2. Ensure that the **Properties** tab is selected at the top of the window.

3. In both the **Source Compatibility** and **Target Compatibility** drop-down lists, select `1.7`, then click **OK**.

4.4.4 Adding the Flag Images to the Project

Follow these steps to create an `assets` folder and add the flags to the project:

1. Right click the app folder in the **Project** window and select **New > Folder > Assets Folder**. In the **Customize the Activity** dialog that appears, click **Finish**.

2. Navigate to the folder on disk containing the book's examples and copy all of the folders located in the `images/FlagQuizImages` folder.

3. Click the `assets` folder in the **Project** window, then paste the folders you copied in the preceding step. In the **Copy** dialog that appears, click **OK** to copy the folders and their images into your project.

4.4.5 `strings.xml` and Formatted `String` Resources

In Section 3.4.5, you learned how to create a `String` resource using the **Resources** dialog. For this app, we'll create the `String` (and many other) resources in advance, then use them as we design the GUI and from the program's code. You'll now create new `String` resources using the **Translations Editor** that you first saw in Section 2.8:

1. In the **Project** window, expand the `res/values` node, then open `strings.xml`.

2. In the editor's upper-right corner, click the **Open Editor** link to open the **Translations Editor**.

3. In the upper-left corner of the **Translations Editor**, click the **Add Key** button ( ).

4. In the dialog that appears, enter `number_of_choices` for the **Key** and `Number of Choices` for the **Default Value**, then click **OK** to create the new resource.

5. Repeat *Step 4* for each of the remaining string resources listed in the table (Fig. 4.9).

Look-and-Feel Observation 4.1

The Android design guidelines indicate that text displayed in your GUI should be brief, simple and friendly with the important words first. For details on the recommended writing style, see `http://developer.android.com/design/style/writing.html`.

Key	Default value
number_of_choices_description	Display 2, 4, 6 or 8 guess buttons
world_regions	Regions
world_regions_description	Regions to include in the quiz
guess_country	Guess the Country
results	%1$d guesses, %2$.02f%% correct
incorrect_answer	Incorrect!
default_region_message	One region must be selected. Setting North America as the default region.
restarting_quiz	Quiz will restart with your new settings
question	Question %1$d of %2$d
reset_quiz	Reset Quiz
image_description	Image of the current flag in the quiz
default_region	North_America

Fig. 4.9 | `String` resources used in the **Flag Quiz** app.

*Format **Strings** as **String** Resources*

The results and question resources are *format Strings*. When a String resource contains multiple format specifiers, you must number them for localization purposes. In the results resource

```
%1$d guesses, %2$.02f%% correct
```

the notation 1$ in %1$d indicates that the *first* value to insert in the String should replace the format specifier %1$d. Similarly, 2$ in %2$.02f indicates that the *second* value to insert in the String should replace the format specifier %2$.02f. The d in the first format specifier formats an integer and the f in the second one formats a floating-point number. In localized versions of strings.xml, the format specifiers %1$d and %2$.02f can be reordered as necessary to properly translate the String resource. The *first* value to insert will replace %1$d—*regardless* of where it appears in the format String—and the *second* value will replace %2$.02f *regardless* of where it appears in the format String.

4.4.6 arrays.xml

Technically, all of your app's resources in the res/values folder can be defined in the *same* file. However, to make it easier to manage different types of resources, separate files are typically used for each. For example, by convention array resources are normally defined in arrays.xml, colors in colors.xml, Strings in strings.xml and numeric values in values.xml. This app uses three String array resources that are defined in arrays.xml:

- regions_list specifies the names of the world regions with their words separated by *underscores*—these values are used to load image file names from the appropriate folders and as the selected values for the world regions the user selects in the SettingsActivityFragment.

- regions_list_for_settings specifies the names of the world regions with their words separated by *spaces*—these values are used in the SettingsActivityFragment to display the region-name checkboxes to the user.

- guesses_list specifies the Strings 2, 4, 6 and 8—these values are used in the SettingsActivityFragment to display the radio buttons that enable the user to select the number of guess Buttons to display.

Figure 4.10 shows the names and element values for these three array resources.

Array resource name	Values
regions_list	Africa, Asia, Europe, North_America, Oceania, South_America
regions_list_for_settings	Africa, Asia, Europe, North America, Oceania, South America
guesses_list	2, 4, 6, 8

Fig. 4.10 | String array resources defined in arrays.xml.

To create `arrays.xml` and configure the array resources, perform the following steps:

1. In the project's `res` folder, right click the `values` folder, then select **New > Values resource file** to display the **New Resource File** dialog. Because you right-clicked the `values` folder, the dialog is preconfigured to add a **Values** resource file in the `values` folder.

2. Specify `arrays.xml` in the **File name** field and click **OK** to create the file.

3. Android Studio does not provide a `String` resource editor for `String` arrays, so you'll need to edit the XML to create the `String` array resources.

Each `String`-array resource has the following format:

```
<string-array name="resource_name">
    <item>first element value</item>
    <item>second element value</item>
    ...
</string-array>
```

Figure 4.11 shows the completed XML file.

```
 1    <?xml version="1.0" encoding="utf-8"?>
 2    <resources>
 3
 4        <string-array name="regions_list">
 5            <item>Africa</item>
 6            <item>Asia</item>
 7            <item>Europe</item>
 8            <item>North_America</item>
 9            <item>Oceania</item>
10            <item>South_America</item>
11        </string-array>
12
13        <string-array name="regions_list_for_settings">
14            <item>Africa</item>
15            <item>Asia</item>
16            <item>Europe</item>
17            <item>North America</item>
18            <item>Oceania</item>
19            <item>South America</item>
20        </string-array>
21
22        <string-array name="guesses_list">
23            <item>2</item>
24            <item>4</item>
25            <item>6</item>
26            <item>8</item>
27        </string-array>
28
29    </resources>
```

Fig. 4.11 | `arrays.xml` defines `String` array resources used in the **Flag Quiz** app.

4.4.7 colors.xml

This app displays correct answers in green and incorrect answers in red. As with any other resource, color resources should be defined in XML so you can easily change colors without modifying your app's Java source code and so you can use Android's resource-choosing capabilities to provide colors resources for various scenarios (different locales, night and day colors, and so on). Typically, colors are defined in the file colors.xml, which is created for you by most of Android Studio's app templates or created when you define colors using the technique shown in Section 2.5.7; otherwise, you must create the file.

The **Blank Activity** app template already contains a colors.xml file that defines the theme's primary, primary dark and accent color resources. Here you'll add color resources for the correct and incorrect answers and modify the app's accent color. To do so, you'll edit the XML directly, rather than using the **Theme Editor** to modify theme colors, as you did in Section 3.5.

Open colors.xml (Fig. 4.12) from the project's res/values folder and add lines 6 and 7. Also, change the hexadecimal value for the color named colorAccent (line 5) from #FF4081 (the default bright pink defined by the app template) to #448AFF (a lighter shade of blue than those used for colorPrimary and colorPrimaryDark). Notice in the IDE that the XML editor shows a color swatch to the left of each color.

```
1    <?xml version="1.0" encoding="utf-8"?>
2    <resources>
3        <color name="colorPrimary">#3F51B5</color>
4        <color name="colorPrimaryDark">#303F9F</color>
5        <color name="colorAccent">#448AFF</color>
6        <color name="correct_answer">#00CC00</color>
7        <color name="incorrect_answer">#FF0000</color>
8    </resources>
```

Fig. 4.12 | colors.xml defines the app's color resources.

4.4.8 button_text_color.xml

As we discussed in Section 4.3.14, when a color state list resource is provided for a Button color (either foreground or background), the appropriate color from the list of colors is selected, based on the Button's state. For this app you'll define colors for the answer Buttons' text color in the *enabled* and *disabled* states. To create the color state list resource file:

1. Right click the project's res folder, then select **New > Andorid resource file** to display the **New Resource File** dialog.

2. Specify button_text_color.xml as the **File name**.

3. In the **Resource type** drop-down, select **Color**. The **Root element** will automatically change to selector and the **Directory name** will automatically change to color.

4. Click **OK** to create the file. The button_text_color.xml file will be placed in a res/color folder, which the IDE automatically creates with the file.

5. Add the text shown in Fig. 4.13 to the file.

The `<selector>` element (lines 2–10) contains `<item>` elements that each specify a color for a particular `Button` state. In this color state list, we specify the `android:state_enabled` property in each `<item>`—once for the *enabled* state (`true`; lines 3–5) and once for the *disabled* state (`false`; lines 7–9). The `android:color` property (lines 4 and 8) specifies the color for that state.

```
 1   <?xml version="1.0" encoding="utf-8"?>
 2   <selector xmlns:android="http://schemas.android.com/apk/res/android">
 3      <item
 4         android:color="@android:color/primary_text_dark"
 5         android:state_enabled="true"/>
 6
 7      <item
 8         android:color="@android:color/darker_gray"
 9         android:state_enabled="false"/>
10   </selector>
```

Fig. 4.13 | `button_text_color.xml` defines a button's text color for the *enabled* and *disabled* states.

4.4.9 Editing `menu_main.xml`

In the test-drive, you touched the (⚙) icon to access the app's settings. Here, you'll add this icon to the project, then edit `menu_main.xml` to display this icon on the app bar. To add the icon to the project:

1. Select **File > New > Vector Asset** to display the **Vector Asset Studio**—this tool enables you to add to your project any of Google's recommended *material design icons* (`https://www.google.com/design/icons/`). Each icon is defined as a scalable vector graphic that smoothly scales to any size.

2. Click the **Choose** button, then in the dialog that appears, scroll to locate the (⚙) icon, select it and click **OK**. The IDE updates the **Resource name** automatically to match the selected icon—you can edit this name if you wish. Keep the other settings in the dialog as is.

3. Click **Next**, then **Finish** to add to the `res/drawable` folder the icon's scalable representation—`ic_settings_24dp.xml`.

4. By default, each icon you add to the project in this manner is black, which would be difficult to see against the dark blue app bar background. To change this, open `ic_settings_24dp.xml` and change the `<path>` element's `android:fillColor` attribute to white, as in

    `android:fillColor="@android:color/white"`

Next, you'll add the icon to `menu_main.xml`:

1. Open `menu_main.xml` in the editor—this file is located in the `res/menu` folder.

2. In the `<item>` element, add the following `android:icon` attribute (a preview of the icon appears in the gray margin to the left of the line):

    `android:icon="@drawable/ic_settings_24dp"`

3. You can force a menu item to display on the app bar, in which case it's known as an *action*. By default, the action is displayed as the menu item's icon (if there is one); otherwise, the menu item's text is displayed. To force the menu item to appear as an action on the app bar, change the <item> element's app:showAsAction attribute to

```
app:showAsAction="always"
```

In the next chapter, you'll see how to specify that menu items should be shown on the app bar only if there is room.

4.4.10 Creating the Flag Shake Animation

In this section, you'll create the animation that shakes the flag when the user guesses incorrectly. We'll show how the app uses this animation in Section 4.7.10. To create the animation:

1. Right click the project's res folder, then select **New > Android resource file** to open the **New Resource file** dialog.

2. In the **File name** field, enter incorrect_shake.xml.

3. In the **Resource type** drop-down, select **Animation**. The IDE changes the **Root element** to set and the **Directory name** to anim.

4. Click **OK** to create the file. The XML file opens immediately.

The IDE does not provide an editor for animations, so you must modify the XML contents of the file as shown in Fig. 4.14.

```
 1    <?xml version="1.0" encoding="utf-8"?>
 2
 3    <set xmlns:android="http://schemas.android.com/apk/res/android"
 4       android:interpolator="@android:anim/decelerate_interpolator" >
 5
 6       <translate android:duration="100" android:fromXDelta="0"
 7          android:toXDelta="-5%p" />
 8
 9       <translate android:duration="100" android:fromXDelta="-5%p"
10          android:toXDelta="5%p" android:startOffset="100" />
11
12       <translate android:duration="100" android:fromXDelta="5%p"
13          android:toXDelta="-5%p" android:startOffset="200" />
14    </set>
```

Fig. 4.14 | incorrect_shake.xml defines a flag animation that's played when the user makes an incorrect guess.

In this example, we use View animations to create a *shake effect* that consists of three animations in an animation set (lines 3–14)—a collection of animations that make up a larger animation. Animation sets may contain any combination of tweened animations—alpha (transparency), scale (resize), translate (move) and rotate. Our shake animation consists of a series of three `translate` animations. A `translate` animation moves a `View` within its parent. Android also supports *property animations* in which you can animate any property of any object.

The first `translate` animation (lines 6–7) moves a `View` from a starting location to an ending position over a specified period of time. The `android:fromXDelta` attribute is the `View`'s offset when the animation starts and the `android:toXDelta` attribute is the `View`'s offset when the animation ends. These attributes can have

- absolute values (in pixels)
- a percentage of the animated `View`'s size
- a percentage of the animated `View`'s *parent's* size.

For the `android:fromXDelta` attribute, we specified an absolute value of 0. For the `android:toXDelta` attribute, we specified the value `-5%p`, which indicates that the `View` should move to the *left* (due to the minus sign) by 5% of the parent's width (indicated by the p). To move by 5% of the `View`'s width, simply remove the p. The `android:duration` attribute specifies how long the animation lasts in milliseconds. So the animation in lines 6–7 will move the `View` to the left by 5% of its parent's width in 100 milliseconds.

The second animation (lines 9–10) continues from where the first finished, moving the `View` from the `-5%p` offset to a `%5p` offset in 100 milliseconds. By default, animations in an animation `set` are applied simultaneously (i.e., in parallel), but you can use the `android:startOffset` attribute to specify the number of milliseconds into the future at which an animation should begin. This can be used to sequence the animations in a `set`. In this case, the second animation starts 100 milliseconds after the first. The third animation (lines 12–13) is the same as the second, but in the reverse direction, and it starts 200 milliseconds after the first animation.

4.4.11 `preferences.xml` for Specifying the App's Settings

In this section, you'll create the `preferences.xml` file that the `SettingsActivityFragment` uses to display the app's preferences. To create the file:

1. Right click the project's `res` folder, then select **New > Android resource file** to open the **New Resource File** dialog.

2. In the **File name** field enter the name `preferences.xml`.

3. In the **Resource type** drop-down list, select **XML**. The **Root element** will automatically change to `PreferenceScreen`, which represents a screen in which preferences are displayed. The **Directory name** will automatically change to `xml`.

4. Click **OK** to create the file. The `preferences.xml` file will be placed in the `xml` folder, which is created automatically.

5. If the IDE did not open `res/xml/preferences.xml` automatically, double click the file to open it.

You'll now add two types of preferences to the file, a **ListPreference** and a **MultiSelectList-Preference**. Each preference has properties that we explain in Fig. 4.15 for **ListPreference** and Fig. 4.16 for **MultiSelectListPreference**. To add the preferences and their properties to the file, you'll need to edit the XML. Figure 4.17 shows the completed XML file.

Property	Value	Description
entries	@array/guesses_list	An array of Strings that will be displayed in the list of options.
entryValues	@array/guesses_list	An array of values associated with the options in the **Entries** property. The selected entry's value will be stored in the app's SharedPreferences.
key	pref_numberOfChoices	The name of the preference stored in the app's SharedPreferences.
title	@string/number_of_choices	The title of the preference displayed in the GUI.
summary	@string/number_of_choices_description	A summary description of the preference that's displayed below its title.
persistent	true	Whether the preference should persist after the app terminates—if true, class PreferenceFragment immediately persists the preference value each time it changes.
defaultValue	4	The item in the **Entries** property that's selected by default.

Fig. 4.15 | ListPreference property values.

Property	Value	Description
entries	@array/regions_list_for_settings	An array of Strings that will be displayed in the list of options.
entryValues	@array/regions_list	An array of the values associated with the options in the **Entries** property. The selected entries' values will *all* be stored in the app's SharedPreferences.
key	pref_regionsToInclude	The name of the preference stored in the app's SharedPreferences.
title	@string/world_regions	The title of the preference displayed in the GUI.
summary	@string/world_regions_description	A summary description of the preference that's displayed below its title.
persistent	true	Whether the preference should persist after the app terminates.
defaultValue	@array/regions_list	An array of the default values for this preference—in this case, all of the regions will be selected by default.

Fig. 4.16 | MultiSelectListPreference property values.

```
 1    <?xml version="1.0" encoding="utf-8"?>
 2    <PreferenceScreen
 3       xmlns:android="http://schemas.android.com/apk/res/android">
 4
 5       <ListPreference
 6          android:entries="@array/guesses_list"
 7          android:entryValues="@array/guesses_list"
 8          android:key="pref_numberOfChoices"
 9          android:title="@string/number_of_choices"
10          android:summary="@string/number_of_choices_description"
11          android:persistent="true"
12          android:defaultValue="4" />
13
14       <MultiSelectListPreference
15          android:entries="@array/regions_list_for_settings"
16          android:entryValues="@array/regions_list"
17          android:key="pref_regionsToInclude"
18          android:title="@string/world_regions"
19          android:summary="@string/world_regions_description"
20          android:persistent="true"
21          android:defaultValue="@array/regions_list" />
22
23    </PreferenceScreen>
```

Fig. 4.17 | preferences.xml defines the preferences displayed by the SettingsActivityFragment.

4.4.12 Adding Classes SettingsActivity and SettingsActivityFragment to the Project

In this section, you'll create the SettingsActivity class (discussed in Section 4.8) and the SettingsActivityFragment class (Section 4.9) by adding to the project a new **Blank Acitivity** that uses a Fragment. To add the SettingsActivity and SettingsActivityFragment (and their layouts) to the project, perform the following steps:

1. Right click the app folder and select **New > Activity > Blank Activity** to open the **New Android Activity** dialog.

2. In the **Activity Name** field, enter SettingsActivity. The **Layout Name** and **Title** will automatically update based on what you enter in the **Activity Name** field.

3. Specify Settings in the **Title** field to add a new String resource to strings.xml that will be displayed in the SettingsActivity's app bar.

4. Check **Use a Fragment** which will create the SettingsActivityFragment class and its corresponding layout.

5. Select MainActivity as the **Hierarchical Parent** of the new SettingsActivity (use the ... button to the right of the drop-down list). This tells Android Studio to generate code that places in the activity's app bar a button that the user can touch to return to the parent activity (i.e., MainActivity). This button is known as the *up button*.

6. Click **Finish** to create the new classes and layouts.

The IDE creates the layout files `activity_settings.xml`, `content_settings.xml` and `fragment_settings.xml` in the app's res/layout folder, and the code files `Settings-Activity.java` and `SettingsActivityFragment.java` in the app's Java package folder. Open the `activity_settings.xml` layout and delete the `FloatingActionButton` as you did in Section 4.4.2 for `activity_main.xml`.

4.5 Building the App's GUI

In this section, you'll build the **Flag Quiz** app's user interface. In the two previous chapters, you saw how to create a GUI and configure component properties, so Sections 4.5.1—4.5.4 focus primarily on new features. Many of the component properties you need to set are specified in tables.

4.5.1 `activity_main.xml` Layout for Devices in Portrait Orientation

In the two prior apps, you defined the app's GUI in `activity_main.xml`. When working with Fragments, an Actvity's GUI typically displays one or more Fragments' GUIs. In this app, the layout for `MainActivity`—`activity_main.xml`—uses an `<include>` element in the XML to include in `MainActivity`'s layout the GUI defined in `content_main.xml`. The `content_main.xml` layout, in turn, displays `MainActivityFragment` for which the GUI is defined in `fragment_main.xml`. All three layout files were created by the IDE when you created the project in Section 4.4.1.

The `content_main.xml` file defined by the IDE contains a `<fragment>` element as its root layout. At runtime, the `MainActivityFragment`'s GUI will fill the part of the screen occupied by this `<fragment>` element.

Look-and-Feel Observation 4.2
According to the Android design guidelines, 16dp is the recommended space between the edges of a device's touchable screen area and the app's content; however, many apps (such as games) use the full screen.

We work with multiple Fragments in this app's code. To make the code more readable when obtaining references to these Fragments, we changed this `<fragment>` element's **id** property. To do so:

1. Open `content_main.xml` in the **Design** tab.

2. In the **Component Tree** window select `fragment`—the default **id** created by the IDE.

3. In the **Properties** window, set the **id** to `quizFragment`.

4. Save `content_main.xml`.

4.5.2 Designing `fragment_main.xml` Layout

You'll typically define a layout for each of your Fragments, though you will not need to define one for this app's `SettingsActivityFragment`—its GUI will be auto-generated by the capabilities inherited from its superclass `PreferenceFragment`. This section presents the `MainActivityFragment`'s layout (`fragment_main.xml`). Figure 4.18 shows the Main-ActivityFragment GUI's **id** property values—you should set these **id** values as you add the components to the layout.

Fig. 4.18 | **Flag Quiz** GUI's components labeled with their **id** property values—the components are arranged in a vertical LinearLayout.

Using the techniques you learned in Chapter 3, you'll build the GUI in Fig. 4.18. Recall that it's often easiest to select a particular GUI component in the **Component Tree** window. You'll start with the basic layout and controls, then customize the controls' properties to complete the design.

Step 1: Changing from a RelativeLayout to a LinearLayout
As in the activity_main.xml layouts for the two prior apps, the default layout in fragment_main.xml is a RelativeLayout. Here, you'll change this to a vertical Linear-Layout for this app's design:

1. Open the fragment_main.xml **file**, and switch to the **Text** tab.

2. In the XML, change RelativeLayout to LinearLayout.

3. Switch back to the **Design** tab.

4. In the **Component Tree** select LinearLayout.

5. In the **Properties** window, set the LinearLayout's **orientation** to vertical.

6. Ensure that **layout:width** and **layout:height** are set to match_parent.

7. Set the LinearLayout's **id** to quizLinearLayout for programmatic access.

By default, the IDE set the layout's **Padding Left** and **Padding Right** properties to a predefined dimension resource named `@dimen/activity_horizontal_margin`—located in the `dimens.xml` file of the project's `res/values` folder. This resource's value is 16dp, so there will be 16dp of padding on the layout's left and right sides. The IDE created this resource when you created the app's project. Similarly, the IDE sets the **Padding Top** and **Padding Bottom** properties to `@dimen/activity_vertical_margin`—another predefined dimension resource with the value 16dp. So there will be 16dp of padding above and below the layout. Thus, all of `MainActivityFragment`'s GUI will be inset 16dp from the rest of `MainActivity`'s GUI.

Step 2: Adding the `questionNumberTextView` to the `LinearLayout`

Drag a **Medium Text** component from the **Palette**'s **Widgets** section onto the `quizLinearLayout` in the **Component Tree** window, then set its **id** property to `questionNumberTextView`. Use the **Properties** window to set the following properties:

- **layout:gravity center:** `horizontal`—Centers the component horizontally within the layout.

- **layout:margin:** `@dimen/spacing`—Set this only for the **bottom margin** to add 8dp of space below this component. *Create this dimension resource* using the techniques you learned in Section 2.5.6.

- **text:** `@string/question`—To set this property, click the **text** property's field, then click the ellipsis (...) button. In the **Resources** dialog's **Project** tab (Fig. 4.19), select the `question` resource, then click **OK**.

Step 3: Adding the `flagImageView` to the `LinearLayout`

Drag an **ImageView** component from the **Palette**'s **Widgets** section onto the `quizLinearLayout` in the **Component Tree** window, then set its **id** property to `flagImageView`. Use the **Properties** window to set the following properties:

- **layout:width:** `match_parent`

- **layout:height:** `0dp`—This will let the `View`'s height be determined by the **layout:weight** property.

- **layout:gravity center:** `both`

- **layout:margin bottom:** `@dimen/spacing`—Adds 8dp of space below this component.

- **layout:margin left** and **right:** `@dimen/activity_horizontal_margin`—Adds 16dp of space to the left and right of this component, so the complete flag displays during the flag-shake animation that moves the flag left and right.

- **layout:weight:** `1`—Setting the **layout:weight** of this component to 1 (the default is 0 for all components) makes the `flagImageView` more important than the other components in the `quizLinearLayout`. When Android lays out the components, they'll use *only the vertical space they need* and the `flagImageView` will occupy *all remaining vertical space*. Setting `flagImageView`'s **layout:height** to `0dp` is recommended by the IDE to help Android lay out the GUI faster at runtime.

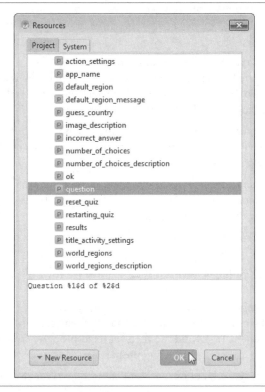

Fig. 4.19 | **Resource Chooser** dialog—selecting the existing String resource question.

- **adjustViewBounds:** true—Setting the ImageView's **Adjust View Bounds** property to true (by checking its checkbox) indicates that the ImageView maintains its image's aspect ratio.

- **contentDescription:** @string/image_description

- **scaleType:** fitCenter—This indicates that the ImageView should scale the image to fill either the ImageView's width or height while maintaining the original image's aspect ratio. If the image's width is less than the ImageView's, the image is centered horizontally. Similarly, if the image's height is less than the ImageView's, the image is centered vertically.

 Look-and-Feel Observation 4.3
Recall that it's considered a best practice in Android to ensure that every GUI component can be used with TalkBack. For components that don't have descriptive text, such as ImageViews, set the component's **contentDescription** *property.*

Step 4: Adding the guessCountryTextView to the LinearLayout
Drag a **Medium Text** component from the **Palette's Widgets** section onto the quizLinear-Layout in the **Component Tree** window, then set its **id** property to guessCountryTextView. Use the **Properties** window to set the following properties:

- **layout:gravity center:** `horizontal`
- **text:** `@string/guess_country`

Step 5: Adding the **Buttons** to the **LinearLayout**

For this app, we add the Buttons to the layout in rows—each row is a horizontal Linear-Layout containing two Buttons. You'll set the properties of the eight Buttons in *Step 7*. Follow these steps to add the eight Buttons to the layout:

1. Drag a **LinearLayout (Horizontal)** from the **Palette's Layouts** section to the qui-zLinearLayout in the **Component Tree** and set its **id** to row1LinearLayout and its **layout:height** to `wrap_content`.

2. Drag a Button from the **Palette's Widgets** section onto the row1LinearLayout in the **Component Tree**. You do not need to set its **id** because the Buttons are not referenced by their **id**s in this app's Java code.

3. Repeat *Step 2* for the other Button in the first row.

4. Repeat *Steps 1–3* for the three remaining LinearLayouts and set their **id**s to the values shown in Fig. 4.18 to create the last three rows of buttons.

Step 6: Adding the **answerTextView** to the **LinearLayout**

Drag a **Medium Text** component from the **Palette's Widgets** section onto the quizLinear-Layout in the **Component Tree** window, then set its **id** property to answerTextView. Use the **Properties** window to set the following properties:

- **layout:gravity:** Check **bottom** and set **center** to `horizontal`.
- **gravity:** `center_horizontal`—This centers the TextView's text when it displays as two or more lines.
- **textSize:** `@dimen/answer_size`—This changes the text's size to `36sp`. Create this dimension resource using the techniques you learned in Section 2.5.6.
- **textStyle:** `bold`

This TextView's **text** property will be set programmatically. At this point, the **Component Tree** window should appear as shown in Fig. 4.20.

Step 7: Setting the Properties of the **Buttons**

Once you've completed *Step 6*, configure the properties of the Buttons with the values shown in Fig. 4.21—you can select all eight Buttons in the **Component Tree**, then set these properties to configure all the Buttons at the same time:

- Setting each Button's **layout:width** to `0dp` and **layout:weight** to `1` enables the Buttons in a given LinearLayout to divide the horizontal space equally.
- Setting each Button's **layout:height** to `match_parent` sets the Button's height to the LinearLayout's height.
- Setting each Button's **lines** property to `2` ensures that all of the Buttons are the same height for country names that take up different numbers of lines—if a Button's text is too long, any text that does not fit in two lines is simply truncated.

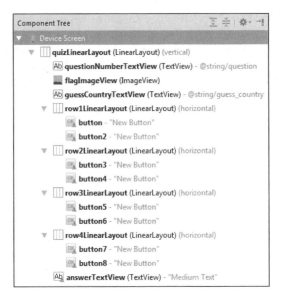

Fig. 4.20 | Component Tree window for `fragment_main.xml`.

- Setting the **style** property to @android:style/Widget.Material.Button.Colored causes the Button to take on a colored appearance, based on the colors of the app's theme. The Buttons' color will be the app's accent color, which you specified in Section 4.4.7. To set this property, click the ellipsis (...) to open the **Resources** dialog, then select Widget.Material.Button.Colored from the **System** tab and click **OK**.

- Setting the textColor property to the @color/button_text_color color state list you defined in Section 4.4.8 ensures that the text changes color based on each Button's enabled/disabled states.

GUI component	Property	Value
Buttons	*Layout Parameters*	
	layout:width	0dp
	layout:height	match_parent
	layout:weight	1
	Other Properties	
	lines	2
	textColor	@color/button_text_color
	style	@android:style/Widget.Material.Button.Colored

Fig. 4.21 | Property values for the Buttons components in `fragment_main.xml`.

4.5.3 Graphical Layout Editor Toolbar

You've now completed the MainActivityFragment's GUI. The layout editor's toolbar (Fig. 4.22) contains various buttons that enable you to preview the design for other screen sizes and orientations. In particular, you can view thumbnail images of many screen sizes and orientations. To do so, first open content_main.xml, then click the virtual device drop-down at the top of the layout editor and select **Preview All Screen Sizes**. Figure 4.23 overviews some of the buttons in the layout editor's toolbar.

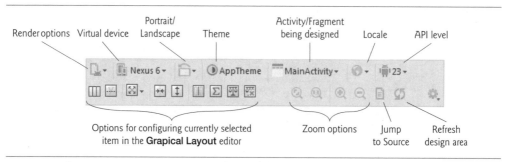

Fig. 4.22 | Canvas configuration options.

Option	Description
Render options	View one design screen at a time or see your design on a variety of screen sizes all at once.
Virtual device	Android runs on a wide variety of devices, so the layout editor comes with many device configurations that represent various screen sizes and resolutions that you can use to design your GUI. In this book, we use the predefined **Nexus 6** and **Nexus 9** screens, depending on the app. In Fig. 4.22, we selected **Nexus 6**.
Portrait/landscape	Toggles the design area between *portrait* and *landscape* orientations.
Theme	Can be used to set the theme for the GUI.
Activity/fragment being designed	Shows the Activity or Fragment class that corresponds to the GUI being designed.
Locale	For *internationalized* apps (Section 2.8), allows you to select a specific localization, so that you can see, for example, what your design looks like with different language strings.
API level	Specifies the target API level for the design. With each new API level, there have typically been new GUI features. The layout editor window shows only features that are available in the selected API level.

Fig. 4.23 | Explanation of the canvas configuration options.

4.5.4 content_main.xml Layout for Tablet Landscape Orientation

As we mentioned previously, MainActivity's default content_main.xml layout displays the MainActivityFragment's GUI. You'll now define MainActivity's layout for tablets in landscape orientation, which will show both the SettingsActivityFragment and the

`MainActivityFragment` side-by-side. To do so, you'll create a second `content_main.xml` layout that Android will use only on appropriate devices.

Creating `content_main.xml` for Tablets in Landscape Orientation

To create the layout, perform the following steps:

1. Right click the project's `res/layout` folder, and select **New > Layout resource file**.

2. Enter `content_main.xml` in the **File name** field of the **New Resource File** dialog.

3. Ensure that `LinearLayout` is specified in the **Root element** field.

4. In the **Available qualifiers** list, select the **Smallest Screen Width** qualifier, then click the **>>** button to add the qualifier to the **Chosen Qualifiers** list and set its value to 700—the layout is meant for screens that are at least 700 pixels wide.

5. In the **Available qualifiers** list, select the **Orientation** qualifier, then click the **>>** button to add the qualifier to the **Chosen Qualifiers** list and set its value to `Landscape`.

6. Click **OK**.

This creates the new `content_main.xml` file, which is stored in a `res` subfolder named

```
layout-sw700dp-land
```

indicating that the layout should be used only on a device with a minumum screen width (`sw`) of 700dp and only when the device is in landscape (`land`) orientation. Android uses the qualifiers `sw` and `land` to select appropriate resources at runtime.

In Android Studio, the **Project** window does not show the separate `layout` and `layout-sw700dp-land` folders that you'll see if you explore the project's folders on disk. Instead, it combines both layouts into a single node `content_main.xml` (2) node in the **Project** window's `res/layout` folder—(2) indicates that there are two layouts in the node. Expanding this node shows

- `content_main.xml` and
- `content_main.xml` (sw700dp-land).

The layout without qualifiers in parentheses is the default layout. The one with qualifiers is used only if appropriate. After creating the file, Android Studio opens the layout in the layout editor. The **Design** view presents the layout in layout orientation.

Creating the Tablet Layout's GUI

Next, you'll build the tablet layout's GUI:

1. Select `LinearLayout` (`vertical`) in the **Component Tree** window and set the **orientation** property to `horizontal`.

2. Click **<fragment>** in the **Palette**'s **Custom** section. In the **Fragments** dialog, select `SettingsActivityFragment`, and click **OK**. Then click the `LinearLayout` node in the **Component Tree** window. This adds the **<fragment>** to the layout. Set the **id** of the **<fragment>** to `settingsActivityFragment`.

3. Repeat the preceding step, but this time select `MainActivityFragment`. Also, set the **id** of this **<fragment>** to `quizFragment`.

4. Select the `settingsActivityFragment` node in the **Component Tree** window. Set **layout:width** to `0dp`, **layout:height** to `match_parent` and **layout:weight** to 1.

5. Select the quizFragment node in the **Component Tree** window. Set **layout:width** to 0dp, **layout:height** to match_parent and **layout:weight** to 2. MainActivity-Fragment's **layout:weight** is 2 and SettingsActivityFragment's is 1, so the total of the weights is 3 and MainActivityFragment will occupy two-thirds of the layout's horizontal space.

6. Switch to the **Text** tab and add the following two lines to the opening Linear-Layout tag to ensure that the top of the layout appears below the app bar, rather than behind it:

```
xmlns:app="http://schemas.android.com/apk/res-auto"
app:layout_behavior="@string/appbar_scrolling_view_behavior"
```

Selecting a Fragment to Preview in the Layout Editor's Design *View*

The layout editor's **Design** view can show a preview of any fragment(s) displayed in a layout. If you do not specify which fragment to preview, the layout editor displays a **"Rendering Problems"** message. To specify the fragment to preview, right click the fragment—either in **Design** view or in the **Component Tree**—and click **Choose Preview Layout....** Then in the **Resources** dialog, select the name of the fragment layout.

4.6 MainActivity Class

Class MainActivity (Sections 4.6.1—4.6.7) hosts the app's MainActivityFragment when the app is running in portrait orientation, and hosts both the SettingsActivityFragment and MainActivityFragment when the app is running on a tablet in landscape orientation.

4.6.1 package Statement and import Statements

Figure 4.24 shows the MainActivity package statement and import statements. Lines 6–19 import the various Android and Java classes and interfaces that the app uses. We've highlighted the new import statements, and we discuss the corresponding classes and interfaces in Section 4.3 and as they're encountered in Sections 4.6.2—4.6.7.

```
1   // MainActivity.java
2   // Hosts the MainActivityFragment on a phone and both the
3   // MainActivityFragment and SettingsActivityFragment on a tablet
4   package com.deitel.flagquiz;
5
6   import android.content.Intent;
7   import android.content.SharedPreferences;
8   import android.content.SharedPreferences.OnSharedPreferenceChangeListener;
9   import android.content.pm.ActivityInfo;
10  import android.content.res.Configuration;
11  import android.os.Bundle;
12  import android.preference.PreferenceManager;
13  import android.support.v7.app.AppCompatActivity;
14  import android.support.v7.widget.Toolbar;
```

Fig. 4.24 | MainActivity package statement and import statements. (Part 1 of 2.)

```
15   import android.view.Menu;
16   import android.view.MenuItem;
17   import android.widget.Toast;
18
19   import java.util.Set;
20
```

Fig. 4.24 | MainActivity package statement and import statements. (Part 2 of 2.)

4.6.2 Fields

Figure 4.25 shows class MainActivity's fields. Lines 23–24 define constants for the preference keys you created in Section 4.4.11. You'll use these to access the preference values. The boolean variable phoneDevice (line 26) specifies whether the app is running on a phone—if so, the app will allow only portrait orientation. The boolean variable preferences-Changed (line 27) specifies whether the app's preferences have changed—if so, the MainActivity's onStart lifecycle method (Section 4.6.4) will call the MainActivityFragment's methods updateGuessRows (Section 4.7.4) and updateRegions (Section 4.7.5) to reconfigure the quiz, based on the new settings. We set this boolean to true initially so that when the app first executes, the quiz is configured using the default preferences.

```
21   public class MainActivity extends Activity {
22      // keys for reading data from SharedPreferences
23      public static final String CHOICES = "pref_numberOfChoices";
24      public static final String REGIONS = "pref_regionsToInclude";
25
26      private boolean phoneDevice = true; // used to force portrait mode
27      private boolean preferencesChanged = true; // did preferences change?
28
```

Fig. 4.25 | MainActivity declaration and fields.

4.6.3 Overridden Activity Method onCreate

Fig. 4.26 shows the overridden Activity method onCreate—we removed the predefined event handler for the FloatingActionButton, which is not used in this app. Line 33 calls setContentView to set MainActivity's GUI. Recall that activity_main.xml embeds in its layout the contents of the file content_main.xml, and that this app has two versions of that file. When inflating activity_main.xml, Android embeds the default content_main.xml file from the app's res/layout folder unless the app is running on a devices that's at least 700 pixels wide in landscape orientation—in that case, Android uses the version in the res/layout-sw700dp-land folder. Lines 34–35 were generated by the IDE to set the Toolbar defined in MainActivity's layout as the app bar (formerly called the action bar)—again, this is the backward-compatible manner in which an app displays an app bar.

Setting the Default Preference Values and Registering a Change Listener
When you install and launch the app for the first time, line 38 sets the app's *default preferences* by calling PreferenceManager method **setDefaultValues**—this creates and initializes the app's SharedPreferences file using the default values that you specified in preferences.xml. The method requires three arguments:

```
29      // configure the MainActivity
30      @Override
31      protected void onCreate(Bundle savedInstanceState) {
32         super.onCreate(savedInstanceState);
33         setContentView(R.layout.activity_main);
34         Toolbar toolbar = (Toolbar) findViewById(R.id.toolbar);
35         setSupportActionBar(toolbar);
36
37         // set default values in the app's SharedPreferences
38         PreferenceManager.setDefaultValues(this, R.xml.preferences, false);
39
40         // register listener for SharedPreferences changes
41         PreferenceManager.getDefaultSharedPreferences(this).
42            registerOnSharedPreferenceChangeListener(
43               preferencesChangeListener);
44
45         // determine screen size
46         int screenSize = getResources().getConfiguration().screenLayout &
47            Configuration.SCREENLAYOUT_SIZE_MASK;
48
49         // if device is a tablet, set phoneDevice to false
50         if (screenSize == Configuration.SCREENLAYOUT_SIZE_LARGE ||
51            screenSize == Configuration.SCREENLAYOUT_SIZE_XLARGE)
52            phoneDevice = false; // not a phone-sized device
53
54         // if running on phone-sized device, allow only portrait orientation
55         if (phoneDevice)
56            setRequestedOrientation(
57               ActivityInfo.SCREEN_ORIENTATION_PORTRAIT);
58      }
59
```

Fig. 4.26 | MainActivity overridden Activity method onCreate.

- The preferences' Context (package android.content), which provides access to information about the environment in which the app is running and allows you to use various Android services—in this case, the Context is the Activity (this) for which you are setting the default preferences.

- The resource ID for the preferences XML file (R.xml.preferences) that you created in Section 4.4.11.

- A boolean indicating whether the default values should be reset each time method setDefaultValues is called—false indicates that the default preference values should be set only the first time this method is called.

Each time the user changes the app's preferences, MainActivity should call MainActivityFragment's methods updateGuessRows or updateRegions to reconfigure the quiz. MainActivity registers an OnSharedPreferenceChangedListener (lines 41–43) so that it will be notified each time a preference changes. PreferenceManager method getDefaultSharedPreferences returns a reference to the SharedPreferences object representing the app's preferences, and SharedPreferences method registerOnSharedPreferenceChangeListener registers the listener (defined in Section 4.6.7).

Configuring a Phone Device for Portrait Orientation
Lines 46–52 determine whether the app is running on a tablet or a phone. Inherited method **getResources** returns the app's **Resources** object (package android.content.res) for accessing an app's resources and determining information about its environment. Method **getConfiguration** returns a **Configuration** object (package android.content.res) containing public instance variable screenLayout, which specifies the device's screen-size category. To do so, first you combine the value of screenLayout with Configuration.SCREENLAYOUT_SIZE_MASK using the bitwise AND (&) operator. Then, you compare the result to the constants SCREENLAYOUT_SIZE_LARGE and SCREENLAYOUT_SIZE_XLARGE (lines 50–51). If either is a match, the app is running on a tablet-sized device. Finally, if the device is a phone, lines 56–57 call inherited Activity method setRequestedOrientation to force the app to display MainActivity in only portrait orientation.

4.6.4 Overridden `Activity` Method `onStart`

Overridden Activity lifecycle method onStart (Fig. 4.27) is called in two scenarios:

- When the app first executes, onStart is called after onCreate. We use onStart in this case to ensure that the quiz is configured correctly based on the app's default preferences when the app is installed and executes for the first time or based on the user's updated preferences when the app is launched subsequently.

- When the app is running in portrait orientation and the user opens the SettingsActivity, the MainActivity is *stopped* while the SettingsActivity is displayed. When the user returns to the MainActivity, onStart is called again. We use onStart in this case to ensure that the quiz is reconfigured properly if the user made any preference changes.

In both cases, if preferencesChanged is true, onStart calls MainActivityFragment's updateGuessRows (Section 4.7.4) and updateRegions (Section 4.7.5) methods to reconfigure the quiz. To get a reference to the MainActivityFragment so we can call its methods, lines 68–70 use inherited AppCompatActivity method getSupportFragmentManager to get the FragmentManager, then call its findFragmentById method. Next, lines 71–74 call MainActivityFragment's updateGuessRows and updateRegions methods, passing the app's SharedPreferences object as an argument so those methods can load the current preferences. Line 75 resets the quiz and line 76 sets preferencesChanged back to false.

```
60    // called after onCreate completes execution
61    @Override
62    protected void onStart() {
63        super.onStart();
64
65        if (preferencesChanged) {
66            // now that the default preferences have been set,
67            // initialize MainActivityFragment and start the quiz
68            MainActivityFragment quizFragment = (MainActivityFragment)
69                getSupportFragmentManager().findFragmentById(
70                    R.id.quizFragment);
```

Fig. 4.27 | MainActivity overridden Activity method onStart. (Part 1 of 2.)

```
71              quizFragment.updateGuessRows(
72                  PreferenceManager.getDefaultSharedPreferences(this));
73              quizFragment.updateRegions(
74                  PreferenceManager.getDefaultSharedPreferences(this));
75              quizFragment.resetQuiz();
76              preferencesChanged = false;
77          }
78      }
79
```

Fig. 4.27 | MainActivity overridden Activity method onStart. (Part 2 of 2.)

4.6.5 Overridden `Activity` Method `onCreateOptionsMenu`

Overridden `Activity` method `onCreateOptionsMenu` (Fig. 4.28) initializes the Activity's options menu—this method and method `onOptionsItemSelected` (Section 4.6.6) were autogenerated by Android Studio's **Blank Activity** template. The system passes in the `Menu` object where the options will appear. In this app, we want to show the menu only when the app is running in portrait orientation, so we modified this method to check the device's orientation. Line 84 uses the `Activity`'s `Resources` object (returned by inherited method `getResources`) to obtain a `Configuration` object (returned by method `getConfiguration`) that represents the device's current configuration. This object's `public` instance variable `orientation` contains either `Configuration.ORIENTATION_PORTRAIT` or `Configuration.ORIENTATION_LANDSCAPE`. If the device is in portrait orientation (line 87), line 89 creates the menu from `menu_main.xml`—the default menu resource that the IDE defined when you created the project. Inherited `Activity` method `getMenuInflater` returns a `MenuInflater` on which we call `inflate` with two arguments—the resource ID of the menu resource that populates the menu and the `Menu` object in which the menu items will be placed. Returning `true` from `onCreateOptionsMenu` indicates that the menu should be displayed.

```
80      // show menu if app is running on a phone or a portrait-oriented tablet
81      @Override
82      public boolean onCreateOptionsMenu(Menu menu) {
83          // get the device's current orientation
84          int orientation = getResources().getConfiguration().orientation;
85
86          // display the app's menu only in portrait orientation
87          if (orientation == Configuration.ORIENTATION_PORTRAIT) {
88              // inflate the menu
89              getMenuInflater().inflate(R.menu.menu_main, menu);
90              return true;
91          }
92          else
93              return false;
94      }
95
```

Fig. 4.28 | MainActivity overridden Activity method onCreateOptionsMenu.

4.6.6 Overridden Activity Method onOptionsItemSelected

Method onOptionsItemSelected (Fig. 4.29) is called when a menu item is selected. In this app, the default menu provided by the IDE when you created the project contains only the **Settings** menu item, so if this method is called, the user selected **Settings**. Line 99 creates an explicit Intent for launching the SettingsActivity. The Intent constructor used here receives the Context from which the Activity will be launched and the class representing the Activity to launch (SettingsActivity.class). We then pass this Intent to the inherited Activity method startActivity to launch the Activity (line 100).

```
96    // displays the SettingsActivity when running on a phone
97    @Override
98    public boolean onOptionsItemSelected(MenuItem item) {
99        Intent preferencesIntent = new Intent(this, SettingsActivity.class);
100       startActivity(preferencesIntent);
101       return super.onOptionsItemSelected(item);
102   }
103
```

Fig. 4.29 | MainActivity overridden Activity method onOptionsItemSelected.

4.6.7 Anonymous Inner Class That Implements OnSharedPreferenceChangeListener

The preferencesChangeListener objec (Fig. 4.30) is an anonymous-inner-class object that implements the OnSharedPreferenceChangeListener interface. This object was registered in method onCreate to listen for changes to the app's SharedPreferences. When a change occurs, method onSharedPreferenceChanged sets preferencesChanged to true (line 111), then gets a reference to the MainActivityFragment (lines 113–115) so that the quiz can be reset with the new preferences. If the CHOICES preference changed, lines 118–119 call the MainActivityFragment's updateGuessRows and resetQuiz methods.

```
104   // listener for changes to the app's SharedPreferences
105   private OnSharedPreferenceChangeListener preferencesChangeListener =
106       new OnSharedPreferenceChangeListener() {
107           // called when the user changes the app's preferences
108           @Override
109           public void onSharedPreferenceChanged(
110               SharedPreferences sharedPreferences, String key) {
111               preferencesChanged = true; // user changed app settings
112
113               MainActivityFragment quizFragment = (MainActivityFragment)
114                   getSupportFragmentManager().findFragmentById(
115                   R.id.quizFragment);
116
117               if (key.equals(CHOICES)) { // # of choices to display changed
118                   quizFragment.updateGuessRows(sharedPreferences);
```

Fig. 4.30 | Anonymous Inner class that implements OnSharedPreferenceChangeListener. (Part 1 of 2.)

```
119                      quizFragment.resetQuiz();
120               }
121               else if (key.equals(REGIONS)) { // regions to include changed
122                  Set<String> regions =
123                     sharedPreferences.getStringSet(REGIONS, null);
124
125                  if (regions != null && regions.size() > 0) {
126                     quizFragment.updateRegions(sharedPreferences);
127                     quizFragment.resetQuiz();
128                  }
129                  else {
130                     // must select one region--set North America as default
131                     SharedPreferences.Editor editor =
132                        sharedPreferences.edit();
133                     regions.add(getString(R.string.default_region));
134                     editor.putStringSet(REGIONS, regions);
135                     editor.apply();
136
137                     Toast.makeText(MainActivity.this,
138                        R.string.default_region_message,
139                        Toast.LENGTH_SHORT).show();
140                  }
141               }
142
143               Toast.makeText(MainActivity.this,
144                  R.string.restarting_quiz,
145                  Toast.LENGTH_SHORT).show();
146            }
147      };
148 }
```

Fig. 4.30 | Anonymous Inner class that implements `OnSharedPreferenceChangeListener`. (Part 2 of 2.)

If the `REGIONS` preference changed, lines 122–123 get the `Set<String>` containing the enabled regions. `SharedPreferences` method **getStringSet** returns a `Set<String>` for the specified key. The quiz must have at least one region enabled, so if the `Set<String>` is not empty, lines 126–127 call the `MainActivityFragment`'s `updateRegions` and `resetQuiz` methods.

If the `Set<String>` is empty, lines 131–135 update the `REGIONS` preference with North America set as the default region. To obtain the default region's name, line 133 calls `Activity`'s inherited method **getString**, which returns the `String` resource for the specified resource ID (`R.string.default_region`).

To change a `SharedPreferences` object's contents, first call its **edit** method to obtain a `SharedPreferences.Editor` object (lines 131–132), which can add key–value pairs to, remove key–value pairs from, and modify the value associated with a particular key in a `SharedPreferences` file. Line 134 calls `SharedPreferences.Editor` method **putStringSet** to store the contents of regions (the `Set<String>`). Line 135 *commits* (saves) the changes by calling `SharedPreferences.Editor` method **apply**, which immediately makes the changes to the in-memory representation of the `SharedPreferences`, and asynchronously writes the changes to the file in the background. There is also a `commit` method that writes the writes the changes to the file synchronously (immediately).

Lines 137–139 use a `Toast` to indicate that the default region was set. `Toast` method `makeText` receives as arguments the `Context` on which the `Toast` is displayed, the message to display and the duration for which the `Toast` will be displayed. `Toast` method `show` displays the `Toast`. Regardless of which preference changed, lines 143–145 display a `Toast` indicating that the quiz will be reset with the new preferences. Figure 4.31 shows the `Toast` that appears after the user changes the app's preferences.

> Quiz will restart with your new settings

Fig. 4.31 | `Toast` displayed after a preference is changed.

4.7 MainActivityFragment Class

Class `MainActivityFragment` (Figs. 4.32–4.42)—a subclass of the Android Support Library's `Fragment` class (package `android.support.v4.app`)—builds the **Flag Quiz**'s GUI and implements the quiz's logic.

4.7.1 package and import Statements

Figure 4.32 shows the `MainActivityFragment` package statement and `import` statements. Lines 5–36 import the various Java and Android classes and interfaces that the app uses. We've highlighted the key `import` statements, and we discuss the corresponding classes and interfaces in Section 4.3 and as they're encountered in Sections 4.7.2—4.7.11.

```
 1   // MainActivityFragment.java
 2   // Contains the Flag Quiz logic
 3   package com.deitel.flagquiz;
 4
 5   import java.io.IOException;
 6   import java.io.InputStream;
 7   import java.security.SecureRandom;
 8   import java.util.ArrayList;
 9   import java.util.Collections;
10   import java.util.List;
11   import java.util.Set;
12
13   import android.animation.Animator;
14   import android.animation.AnimatorListenerAdapter;
15   import android.app.AlertDialog;
16   import android.app.Dialog;
17   import android.content.DialogInterface;
18   import android.content.SharedPreferences;
19   import android.content.res.AssetManager;
20   import android.graphics.drawable.Drawable;
```

Fig. 4.32 | `MainActivityFragment` package statement, `import` statements. (Part 1 of 2.)

```
21   import android.os.Bundle;
22   import android.support.v4.app.DialogFragment;
23   import android.support.v4.app.Fragment;
24   import android.os.Handler;
25   import android.util.Log;
26   import android.view.LayoutInflater;
27   import android.view.View;
28   import android.view.View.OnClickListener;
29   import android.view.ViewAnimationUtils;
30   import android.view.ViewGroup;
31   import android.view.animation.Animation;
32   import android.view.animation.AnimationUtils;
33   import android.widget.Button;
34   import android.widget.ImageView;
35   import android.widget.LinearLayout;
36   import android.widget.TextView;
37
```

Fig. 4.32 | MainActivityFragment package statement, import statements. (Part 2 of 2.)

4.7.2 Fields

Figure 4.33 lists class MainActivityFragment's static and instance variables. The constant TAG (line 40) is used when we log error messages using class Log (Fig. 4.38) to distinguish this Activity's error messages from others that are being written to the device's log. The constant FLAGS_IN_QUIZ (line 42) represents the number of flags in the quiz.

```
38   public class MainActivityFragment extends Fragment {
39       // String used when logging error messages
40       private static final String TAG = "FlagQuiz Activity";
41
42       private static final int FLAGS_IN_QUIZ = 10;
43
44       private List<String> fileNameList; // flag file names
45       private List<String> quizCountriesList; // countries in current quiz
46       private Set<String> regionsSet; // world regions in current quiz
47       private String correctAnswer; // correct country for the current flag
48       private int totalGuesses; // number of guesses made
49       private int correctAnswers; // number of correct guesses
50       private int guessRows; // number of rows displaying guess Buttons
51       private SecureRandom random; // used to randomize the quiz
52       private Handler handler; // used to delay loading next flag
53       private Animation shakeAnimation; // animation for incorrect guess
54
55       private LinearLayout quizLinearLayout; // layout that contains the quiz
56       private TextView questionNumberTextView; // shows current question #
57       private ImageView flagImageView; // displays a flag
58       private LinearLayout[] guessLinearLayouts; // rows of answer Buttons
59       private TextView answerTextView; // displays correct answer
60
```

Fig. 4.33 | MainActivityFragment fields.

Good Programming Practice 4.1

For readability and modifiability, use String *constants to represent filenames* String *literals (such as those used as the names of files or to log error messages) that do not need to be localized, and thus are not defined in* strings.xml.

Variable fileNameList (line 44) holds the flag-image file names for the currently enabled geographic regions. Variable quizCountriesList (line 45) holds the flag file names for the countries used in the current quiz. Variable regionsSet (line 46) stores the geographic regions that are enabled.

Variable correctAnswer (line 47) holds the flag file name for the current flag's correct answer. Variable totalGuesses (line 48) stores the total number of correct and incorrect guesses the player has made so far. Variable correctAnswers (line 49) is the number of correct guesses so far; this will eventually be equal to FLAGS_IN_QUIZ if the user completes the quiz. Variable guessRows (line 50) is the number of two-Button LinearLayouts displaying the flag answer choices—this is controlled by the app's settings (Section 4.7.4).

Variable random (line 51) is the random-number generator used to randomly pick the flags to include in the quiz and which Button in the two-Button LinearLayouts represents the correct answer. When the user selects a correct answer and the quiz is not over, we use the Handler object handler (line 52) to load the next flag after a short delay.

The Animation shakeAnimation (line 53) holds the dynamically inflated *shake animation* that's applied to the flag image when an incorrect guess is made. Lines 55–59 contain variables that we use to manipulate various GUI components programmatically.

4.7.3 Overridden Fragment Method onCreateView

MainActivityFragment's onCreateView method (Fig. 4.34) inflates the GUI and initializes most of the MainActivityFragment's instance variables—guessRows and regionsSet are initialized when the MainActivity calls MainActivityFragment's updateGuessRows and updateRegions methods. After calling the superclass's onCreateView method (line 65), we inflate the MainActivityFragment's GUI (line 66–67) using the LayoutInflater that method onCreateView receives as an argument. The LayoutInflater's inflate method receives three arguments:

- The layout resource ID indicating the layout to inflate.

- The ViewGroup (layout object) in which the Fragment will be displayed, which is received as onCreateView's second argument.

- A boolean indicating whether or not the inflated GUI needs to be attached to the ViewGroup in the second argument. In a fragment's onCreateView method, this should always be false—the system automatically attaches a fragment to the appropriate host Activity's ViewGroup. Passing true here would cause an exception, because the fragment's GUI is already attached.

Method inflate returns a reference to a View that contains the inflated GUI. We store that in local variable view so that it can be returned by onCreateView after the MainActivityFragment's other instance variables are initialized. [*Note:* We removed the autogenerated, empty, no-argument constructor from this class (which appeared before method onCreateView in the class definition created by the IDE), as the compiler provides a default constructor for any class without constructors.]

```
61    // configures the MainActivityFragment when its View is created
62    @Override
63    public View onCreateView(LayoutInflater inflater, ViewGroup container,
64        Bundle savedInstanceState) {
65      super.onCreateView(inflater, container, savedInstanceState);
66      View view =
67         inflater.inflate(R.layout.fragment_main, container, false);
68
69      fileNameList = new ArrayList<>();        // diamond operator
70      quizCountriesList = new ArrayList<>();
71      random = new SecureRandom();
72      handler = new Handler();
73
74      // load the shake animation that's used for incorrect answers
75      shakeAnimation = AnimationUtils.loadAnimation(getActivity(),
76         R.anim.incorrect_shake);
77      shakeAnimation.setRepeatCount(3); // animation repeats 3 times
78
79      // get references to GUI components
80      quizLinearLayout =
81         (LinearLayout) view.findViewById(R.id.quizLinearLayout);
82      questionNumberTextView =
83         (TextView) view.findViewById(R.id.questionNumberTextView);
84      flagImageView = (ImageView) view.findViewById(R.id.flagImageView);
85      guessLinearLayouts = new LinearLayout[4];
86      guessLinearLayouts[0] =
87         (LinearLayout) view.findViewById(R.id.row1LinearLayout);
88      guessLinearLayouts[1] =
89         (LinearLayout) view.findViewById(R.id.row2LinearLayout);
90      guessLinearLayouts[2] =
91         (LinearLayout) view.findViewById(R.id.row3LinearLayout);
92      guessLinearLayouts[3] =
93         (LinearLayout) view.findViewById(R.id.row4LinearLayout);
94      answerTextView = (TextView) view.findViewById(R.id.answerTextView);
95
96      // configure listeners for the guess Buttons
97      for (LinearLayout row : guessLinearLayouts) {
98         for (int column = 0; column < row.getChildCount(); column++) {
99            Button button = (Button) row.getChildAt(column);
100           button.setOnClickListener(guessButtonListener);
101        }
102     }
103
104     // set questionNumberTextView's text
105     questionNumberTextView.setText(
106        getString(R.string.question, 1, FLAGS_IN_QUIZ));
107     return view; // return the fragment's view for display
108  }
109
```

Fig. 4.34 | MainActivityFragment overridden Fragment method onCreateView.

Lines 69–70 create ArrayList<String> objects that will store the flag-image file names for the currently enabled geographical regions and the names of the countries in the current quiz, respectively. Line 71 creates the SecureRandom object for randomizing the quiz's flags and guess Buttons. Line 72 creates the Handler object handler, which we'll use to delay by two seconds the appearance of the next flag after the user correctly guesses the current flag.

Lines 75–76 dynamically load the *shake animation* that will be applied to the flag when an incorrect guess is made. AnimationUtils static method loadAnimation loads the animation from the XML file represented by the constant R.anim.incorrect_shake. The first argument indicates the Context containing the resources that will be animated—inherited Fragment method getActivity returns the Activity that hosts this Fragment. Activity is an indirect subclass of Context. Line 77 specifies the number of times the animation should repeat with Animation method setRepeatCount.

Lines 80–94 get references to various GUI components that we'll programmatically manipulate. Lines 97–102 get each guess Button from the four guessLinearLayouts and register guessButtonListener (Section 4.7.10) as the OnClickListener—we implement this interface to handle the event raised when the user touches any of the guess Buttons.

Lines 105–106 set the text in questionNumberTextView to the String returned by calling an overloaded version of Fragment's inherited method getString. The first argument to format is the String resource R.string.question, which represents the format String

```
Question %1$d of %2$d
```

This String contains placeholders for two integer values (as described in Section 4.4.5). The remaining arguments are the values to insert in the format String. Line 107 returns the MainActivityFragment's GUI.

4.7.4 Method updateGuessRows

Method updateGuessRows (Fig. 4.35) is called from the app's MainActivity when the app is launched and each time the user changes the number of guess Buttons to display with each flag. Lines 113–114 use the method's SharedPreferences argument to get the String for the key MainActivity.CHOICES—a constant containing the name of the preference in which the SettingsActivityFragment stores the number of guess Buttons to display. Line 115 converts the preference's value to an int and divides it by 2 to determine the value for guessRows, which indicates how many of the guessLinearLayouts should be displayed—each with two guess Buttons. Next, lines 118–119 hide all of the guessLinearLayouts, so that lines 122–123 can show the appropriate guessLinearLayouts based on the value of guessRows. The constant View.GONE (line 119) indicates that Android should not consider the sizes of the specified components when laying out the rest of the components in the layout. There is also the constant View.INVISIBLE, which simply hides the component, and any space allocated to the component remains empty on the screen.

```
110    // update guessRows based on value in SharedPreferences
111    public void updateGuessRows(SharedPreferences sharedPreferences) {
112       // get the number of guess buttons that should be displayed
113       String choices =
114          sharedPreferences.getString(MainActivity.CHOICES, null);
```

Fig. 4.35 | MainActivityFragment method updateGuessRows. (Part 1 of 2.)

```
115          guessRows = Integer.parseInt(choices) / 2;
116
117          // hide all guess button LinearLayouts
118          for (LinearLayout layout : guessLinearLayouts)
119             layout.setVisibility(View.GONE);
120
121          // display appropriate guess button LinearLayouts
122          for (int row = 0; row < guessRows; row++)
123             guessLinearLayouts[row].setVisibility(View.VISIBLE);
124       }
125
```

Fig. 4.35 | MainActivityFragment method updateGuessRows. (Part 2 of 2.)

4.7.5 Method updateRegions

Method updateRegions (Fig. 4.36) is called from the app's MainActivity when the app is launched and each time the user changes the world regions that should be included in the quiz. Lines 128–129 use the method's SharedPreferences argument to get the names of all of the enabled regions as a Set<String>. MainActivity.REGIONS is a constant containing the name of the preference in which the SettingsActivityFragment stores the enabled world regions.

```
126       // update world regions for quiz based on values in SharedPreferences
127       public void updateRegions(SharedPreferences sharedPreferences) {
128          regionsSet =
129             sharedPreferences.getStringSet(MainActivity.REGIONS, null);
130       }
131
```

Fig. 4.36 | MainActivityFragment method updateRegions.

4.7.6 Method resetQuiz

Method resetQuiz (Fig. 4.37) sets up and starts a quiz. Recall that the images for the game are stored in the app's assets folder. To access this folder's contents, the method gets the app's AssetManager (line 135) by calling the parent Activity's **getAssets** method. Next, line 136 clears the fileNameList to prepare to load image file names for only the enabled geographical regions. Lines 140–146 iterate through all the enabled world regions. For each, we use the AssetManager's list method (line 142) to get an array of the flag-image file names, which we store in the String array paths. Lines 144–145 remove the .png extension from each file name and place the names in the fileNameList. AssetManager's list method throws IOExceptions, which are *checked* exceptions (so you must catch or declare the exception). If an exception occurs because the app is unable to access the assets folder, lines 148–150 catch the exception and *log* it for debugging purposes with Android's built-in logging mechanism. Log static method e is used to log error messages. You can see the complete list of Log methods at

http://developer.android.com/reference/android/util/Log.html

```
132    // set up and start the next quiz
133    public void resetQuiz() {
134       // use AssetManager to get image file names for enabled regions
135       AssetManager assets = getActivity().getAssets();
136       fileNameList.clear(); // empty list of image file names
137
138       try {
139          // loop through each region
140          for (String region : regionsSet) {
141             // get a list of all flag image files in this region
142             String[] paths = assets.list(region);
143
144             for (String path : paths)
145                fileNameList.add(path.replace(".png", ""));
146          }
147       }
148       catch (IOException exception) {
149          Log.e(TAG, "Error loading image file names", exception);
150       }
151
152       correctAnswers = 0; // reset the number of correct answers made
153       totalGuesses = 0; // reset the total number of guesses the user made
154       quizCountriesList.clear(); // clear prior list of quiz countries
155
156       int flagCounter = 1;
157       int numberOfFlags = fileNameList.size();
158
159       // add FLAGS_IN_QUIZ random file names to the quizCountriesList
160       while (flagCounter <= FLAGS_IN_QUIZ) {
161          int randomIndex = random.nextInt(numberOfFlags);
162
163          // get the random file name
164          String filename = fileNameList.get(randomIndex);
165
166          // if the region is enabled and it hasn't already been chosen
167          if (!quizCountriesList.contains(filename)) {
168             quizCountriesList.add(filename); // add the file to the list
169             ++flagCounter;
170          }
171       }
172
173       loadNextFlag(); // start the quiz by loading the first flag
174    }
175
```

Fig. 4.37 | MainActivityFragment method resetQuiz.

Next, lines 152–154 reset the counters for the number of correct guesses the user has made (correctAnswers) and the total number of guesses the user has made (total-Guesses) to 0 and clear the quizCountriesList.

Lines 160–171 add 10 (FLAGS_IN_QUIZ) randomly selected file names to the quiz-CountriesList. We get the total number of flags, then randomly generate the index in the range 0 to one less than the number of flags. We use this index to select one image file name from fileNameList. If the quizCountriesList does not already contain that file name, we add it to quizCountriesList and increment the flagCounter. We repeat this process until 10 (FLAGS_IN_QUIZ) unique file names have been selected. Then line 173 calls loadNextFlag (Fig. 4.38) to load the quiz's first flag.

4.7.7 Method loadNextFlag

Method loadNextFlag (Fig. 4.38) loads and displays the next flag and the corresponding set of answer Buttons. The image file names in quizCountriesList have the format

regionName-countryName

without the .png extension. If a *regionName* or *countryName* contains multiple words, they're separated by underscores (_).

```
176    // after the user guesses a correct flag, load the next flag
177    private void loadNextFlag() {
178       // get file name of the next flag and remove it from the list
179       String nextImage = quizCountriesList.remove(0);
180       correctAnswer = nextImage; // update the correct answer
181       answerTextView.setText(""); // clear answerTextView
182
183       // display current question number
184       questionNumberTextView.setText(getString(
185          R.string.question, (correctAnswers + 1), FLAGS_IN_QUIZ));
186
187       // extract the region from the next image's name
188       String region = nextImage.substring(0, nextImage.indexOf('-'));
189
190       // use AssetManager to load next image from assets folder
191       AssetManager assets = getActivity().getAssets();
192
193       // get an InputStream to the asset representing the next flag
194       // and try to use the InputStream
195       try (InputStream stream =
196          assets.open(region + "/" + nextImage + ".png")) {
197          // load the asset as a Drawable and display on the flagImageView
198          Drawable flag = Drawable.createFromStream(stream, nextImage);
199          flagImageView.setImageDrawable(flag);
200
201          animate(false); // animate the flag onto the screen
202       }
203       catch (IOException exception) {
204          Log.e(TAG, "Error loading " + nextImage, exception);
205       }
206
207       Collections.shuffle(fileNameList); // shuffle file names
208
209       // put the correct answer at the end of fileNameList
210       int correct = fileNameList.indexOf(correctAnswer);
211       fileNameList.add(fileNameList.remove(correct));
212
```

Fig. 4.38 | MainActivityFragment method loadNextFlag. (Part 1 of 2.)

```
213        // add 2, 4, 6 or 8 guess Buttons based on the value of guessRows
214        for (int row = 0; row < guessRows; row++) {
215           // place Buttons in currentTableRow
216           for (int column = 0;
217              column < guessLinearLayouts[row].getChildCount();
218              column++) {
219              // get reference to Button to configure
220              Button newGuessButton =
221                 (Button) guessLinearLayouts[row].getChildAt(column);
222              newGuessButton.setEnabled(true);
223
224              // get country name and set it as newGuessButton's text
225              String filename = fileNameList.get((row * 2) + column);
226              newGuessButton.setText(getCountryName(filename));
227           }
228        }
229
230        // randomly replace one Button with the correct answer
231        int row = random.nextInt(guessRows); // pick random row
232        int column = random.nextInt(2); // pick random column
233        LinearLayout randomRow = guessLinearLayouts[row]; // get the row
234        String countryName = getCountryName(correctAnswer);
235        ((Button) randomRow.getChildAt(column)).setText(countryName);
236     }
237
```

Fig. 4.38 | MainActivityFragment method loadNextFlag. (Part 2 of 2.)

Line 179 removes the first name from quizCountriesList and stores it in nextImage. We also save this in correctAnswer so it can be used later to determine whether the user made a correct guess. Next, we clear the answerTextView and display the current question number in the questionNumberTextView (lines 184–185) using the formatted String resource R.string.question.

Line 188 extracts from nextImage the region to be used as the assets subfolder name from which we'll load the image. Next we get the AssetManager, then use it in the try-*with-resources* statement to open an InputStream (package java.io) to read bytes from the flag image's file. We use that stream as an argument to class **Drawable**'s static method **createFromStream**, which creates a Drawable object (package android.graphics.drawable). The Drawable is set as flagImageView's item to display by calling its **setImageDrawable** method. If an exception occurs, we log it for debugging purposes (line 204). Next, we call the animate method with false to animate the next flag and answer Buttons onto the screen (line 201).

Next, line 207 shuffles the fileNameList, and lines 210–211 locate the correctAnswer and move it to the end of the fileNameList—later we'll insert this answer randomly into the one of the guess Buttons.

Lines 214–228 iterate through the Buttons in the guessLinearLayouts for the current number of guessRows. For each Button:

- lines 220–221 get a reference to the next Button

- line 222 enables the Button

- line 225 gets the flag file name from the `fileNameList`
- line 226 sets `Button`'s text with the country name that method `getCountryName` (Section 4.7.8) returns.

Lines 231–235 pick a random row (based on the current number of `guessRows`) and column, then set the text of the corresponding `Button`.

4.7.8 Method `getCountryName`

Method `getCountryName` (Fig. 4.39) parses the country name from the image file name. First, we get a substring starting from the dash (-) that separates the region from the country name. Then we call `String` method `replace` to replace the underscores (_) with spaces.

```
238    // parses the country flag file name and returns the country name
239    private String getCountryName(String name) {
240       return name.substring(name.indexOf('-') + 1).replace('_', ' ');
241    }
242
```

Fig. 4.39 | `MainActivityFragment` method `getCountryName`.

4.7.9 Method `animate`

Method `animate` (Fig. 4.40) executes the *circular reveal* animation on the entire layout (`quizLinearLayout`) of the quiz to transition between questions. Lines 246–247 return immediately for the first question to allow the first question to just appear rather than animate onto the screen. Lines 250–253 calculate the screen coordinates of the center of the quiz UI. Line 256–257 calculate the maximum radius of the circle in the animation (the minimum radius is always 0). The `animate` method accepts one parameter, `animateOut`, and can be used in two ways. Line 262 uses `animateOut` to determine whether the animation will show or hide the quiz.

```
243    // animates the entire quizLinearLayout on or off screen
244    private void animate(boolean animateOut) {
245       // prevent animation into the the UI for the first flag
246       if (correctAnswers == 0)
247          return;
248
249       // calculate center x and center y
250       int centerX = (quizLinearLayout.getLeft() +
251          quizLinearLayout.getRight()) / 2;
252       int centerY = (quizLinearLayout.getTop() +
253          quizLinearLayout.getBottom()) / 2;
254
255       // calculate animation radius
256       int radius = Math.max(quizLinearLayout.getWidth(),
257          quizLinearLayout.getHeight());
258
```

Fig. 4.40 | `MainActivityFragment` method `animate`. (Part 1 of 2.)

```
259        Animator animator;
260
261        // if the quizLinearLayout should animate out rather than in
262        if (animateOut) {
263           // create circular reveal animation
264           animator = ViewAnimationUtils.createCircularReveal(
265              quizLinearLayout, centerX, centerY, radius, 0);
266           animator.addListener(
267              new AnimatorListenerAdapter() {
268                 // called when the animation finishes
269                 @Override
270                 public void onAnimationEnd(Animator animation) {
271                    loadNextFlag();
272                 }
273              }
274           );
275        }
276        else { // if the quizLinearLayout should animate in
277           animator = ViewAnimationUtils.createCircularReveal(
278              quizLinearLayout, centerX, centerY, 0, radius);
279        }
280
281        animator.setDuration(500); // set animation duration to 500 ms
282        animator.start(); // start the animation
283     }
284
```

Fig. 4.40 | MainActivityFragment method animate. (Part 2 of 2.)

If animate is called with the value true, the method will animate the quizLinear-Layout off the screen (lines 264–274). Lines 264–265 create a circular-reveal Animator object by calling ViewAnimationUtils method createCircularReveal. This method takes five parameters:

- The first specifies the View on which to apply the animation (quizLinearLayout).

- The second and third provide the *x*- and *y*-coordinates of the animation circle's center.

- The last two determine the starting and ending radius of the animation's circle.

Because this animates the quizLinearLayout off screen, its starting radius is the calculated radius and its ending radius is 0. Lines 266–274 create and associate an AnimatorListenerAdapter with the Animator. The AnimatorListenerAdapter's onAnimationEnd (lines 269–272) method is called when the animation finishes and loads the next flag (line 271).

If animate is called with the value false, the method will animate the quizLinear-Layout onto the screen at the start of the next question. Lines 277–278 create the Animator by calling the createCircularReveal method, but this time, we specify 0 for the starting radius and the calculated radius for the ending radius. This causes the quizLinearLayout to animate onto the screen rather than off the screen.

Line 281 calls Animator's setDuration method to specify a duration of 500 milliseconds for the animation. Finally, line 282 starts the animation.

4.7.10 Anonymous Inner Class That Implements `OnClickListener`

In Fig. 4.34, lines 97–102 registered guessButtonListener (Fig. 4.41) as the event-handling object for each guess Button. Instance variable guessButtonListener refers to an anonymous-inner-class object that implements interface OnClickListener to respond to Button events. The method receives the clicked Button as parameter v. We get the Button's text (line 290) and the parsed country name (line 291), then increment total-Guesses. If the guess is correct (line 294), we increment correctAnswers. Next, we set the answerTextView's text to the country name and change its color to the color represented by the constant R.color.correct_answer (green), and we call our utility method disableButtons (Section 4.7.11) to disable all the answer Buttons.

```
285    // called when a guess Button is touched
286    private OnClickListener guessButtonListener = new OnClickListener() {
287       @Override
288       public void onClick(View v) {
289          Button guessButton = ((Button) v);
290          String guess = guessButton.getText().toString();
291          String answer = getCountryName(correctAnswer);
292          ++totalGuesses; // increment number of guesses the user has made
293
294          if (guess.equals(answer)) { // if the guess is correct
295             ++correctAnswers; // increment the number of correct answers
296
297             // display correct answer in green text
298             answerTextView.setText(answer + "!");
299             answerTextView.setTextColor(
300                getResources().getColor(R.color.correct_answer,
301                   getContext().getTheme()));
302
303             disableButtons(); // disable all guess Buttons
304
305             // if the user has correctly identified FLAGS_IN_QUIZ flags
306             if (correctAnswers == FLAGS_IN_QUIZ) {
307                // DialogFragment to display quiz stats and start new quiz
308                DialogFragment quizResults =
309                   new DialogFragment() {
310                      // create an AlertDialog and return it
311                      @Override
312                      public Dialog onCreateDialog(Bundle bundle) {
313                         AlertDialog.Builder builder =
314                            new AlertDialog.Builder(getActivity());
315                         builder.setMessage(
316                            getString(R.string.results,
317                               totalGuesses,
318                               (1000 / (double) totalGuesses)));
319
320                         // "Reset Quiz" Button
321                         builder.setPositiveButton(R.string.reset_quiz,
322                            new DialogInterface.OnClickListener() {
```

Fig. 4.41 | Anonymous inner class that implements `OnClickListener`. (Part 1 of 2.)

```
323                              public void onClick(DialogInterface dialog,
324                                  int id) {
325                                  resetQuiz();
326                              }
327                          }
328                      );
329
330                      return builder.create(); // return the AlertDialog
331                  }
332              };
333
334          // use FragmentManager to display the DialogFragment
335          quizResults.setCancelable(false);
336          quizResults.show(getFragmentManager(), "quiz results");
337          }
338          else { // answer is correct but quiz is not over
339              // load the next flag after a 2-second delay
340              handler.postDelayed(
341                  new Runnable() {
342                      @Override
343                      public void run() {
344                          animate(true); // animate the flag off the screen
345                      }
346                  }, 2000); // 2000 milliseconds for 2-second delay
347          }
348      }
349      else { // answer was incorrect
350          flagImageView.startAnimation(shakeAnimation); // play shake
351
352          // display "Incorrect!" in red
353          answerTextView.setText(R.string.incorrect_answer);
354          answerTextView.setTextColor(getResources().getColor(
355              R.color.incorrect_answer, getContext().getTheme()));
356          guessButton.setEnabled(false); // disable incorrect answer
357      }
358      }
359  };
360
```

Fig. 4.41 | Anonymous inner class that implements OnClickListener. (Part 2 of 2.)

If correctAnswers is FLAGS_IN_QUIZ (line 306), the quiz is over. Lines 308–332 create a new anonymous inner class that extends DialogFragment (package android.support.v4.app) and will be used to display the quiz results. The DialogFragment's **onCreateDialog** method uses an AlertDialog.Builder (discussed momentarily) to configure and create an AlertDialog for showing the quiz results, then returns it. When the user touches this dialog's **Reset Quiz** Button, method resetQuiz is called to start a new game (line 325). Line 335 indicates that the dialog is not cancelable—the user must interact with the dialog, because touching outside the dialog or touching the back button will not return the user to the quiz. To display the DialogFragment, line 336 calls its **show** method, passing as arguments the FragmentManager returned by getFragmentManager and a String. The second argument can be used with FragmentManager method **getFragment-**

ByTag to get a reference to the DialogFragment at a later time—we don't use this capability in this app.

If correctAnswers is less than FLAGS_IN_QUIZ, then lines 340–346 call the postDelayed method of Handler object handler. The first argument defines an anonymous inner class that implements the Runnable interface—this represents the task to perform, animate(true), which animates the flags and answer Buttons off the screen and starts the transition to the next question, some number of milliseconds into the future. The second argument is the delay in milliseconds (2000). If the guess is incorrect, line 350 invokes flagImageView's startAnimation method to play the shakeAnimation that was loaded in method onCreateView. We also set the text on answerTextView to display "Incorrect!" in red (lines 353–355), then disable the guessButton that corresponds to the incorrect answer.

Look-and-Feel Observation 4.4
You can set an AlertDialog's title (which appears above the dialog's message) with AlertDialog.Builder method setTitle. According to the Android design guidelines for dialogs (http://developer.android.com/design/building-blocks/dialogs.html), most dialogs do not need titles. A dialog should display a title for "a high-risk operation involving potential loss of data, connectivity, extra charges, and so on." Also, dialogs that display lists of options use the title to specify the dialog's purpose.

Creating and Configuring the AlertDialog
Lines 313–329 use an AlertDialog.Builder to create and configure an AlertDialog. Lines 313–314 create the AlertDialog.Builder, passing the fragment's Activity as the Context argument—the dialog will be displayed in the context of the Activity that hosts the MainActivityFragment. Next, lines 315–318 set the dialog's message to a formatted String showing the quiz results—the resource R.string.results contains placeholders for the total number of guesses and the percentage of the total guesses that were correct.

In this AlertDialog, we need only one button that allows the user to acknowledge the message and reset the quiz. We specify this as the dialog's *positive* Button (lines 321–328)—touching this Button indicates that the user acknowledges the message displayed in the dialog and dismisses the dialog. Method setPositiveButton receives the Button's label (specified with the String resource R.string.reset_quiz) and a reference to the Button's event handler. If the app does not need to respond to the event, you can specify null for the event handler. In this case, we provide an object of an anonymous inner class that implements interface DialogInterface.OnClickListener. You override this interface's onClick method to respond to the event when the user touches the corresponding Button in the dialog.

4.7.11 Method disableButtons
Method disableButtons (Fig. 4.42) iterates through the guess Buttons and disables them. This method is called when the user makes a correct guess.

```
361    // utility method that disables all answer Buttons
362    private void disableButtons() {
363        for (int row = 0; row < guessRows; row++) {
```

Fig. 4.42 | MainActivityFragment method disableButtons. (Part 1 of 2.)

```
364              LinearLayout guessRow = guessLinearLayouts[row];
365              for (int i = 0; i < guessRow.getChildCount(); i++)
366                 guessRow.getChildAt(i).setEnabled(false);
367           }
368        }
369     }
```

Fig. 4.42 | MainActivityFragment method disableButtons. (Part 2 of 2.)

4.8 SettingsActivity Class

Class SettingsActivity (Fig. 4.43) hosts the SettingsActivityFragment when the app is running in portrait orientation. Overridden method onCreate (lines 11–18) calls method setContentView to inflate the GUI defined by activity_settings.xml (represented by the resource R.layout.activity_settings), then displays the Toolbar defined in SettingsActivity's layout. Line 17 displays on the app bar an *up button* that the user can touch to return to the parent MainActivity. The IDE added this line when you added the SettingsActivity to the project and specified its hierarchical parent (Section 4.4.12). We removed from the class the remaining autogenerated code that's not used in this app. You can also remove the unused menu resource menu_settings.xml.

```
 1   // SettingsActivity.java
 2   // Activity to display SettingsActivityFragment on a phone
 3   package com.deitel.flagquiz;
 4
 5   import android.os.Bundle;
 6   import android.support.v7.app.AppCompatActivity;
 7   import android.support.v7.widget.Toolbar;
 8
 9   public class SettingsActivity extends AppCompatActivity {
10      // inflates the GUI, displays Toolbar and adds "up" button
11      @Override
12      protected void onCreate(Bundle savedInstanceState) {
13         super.onCreate(savedInstanceState);
14         setContentView(R.layout.activity_settings);
15         Toolbar toolbar = (Toolbar) findViewById(R.id.toolbar);
16         setSupportActionBar(toolbar);
17         getSupportActionBar().setDisplayHomeAsUpEnabled(true);
18      }
19   }
```

Fig. 4.43 | SettingsActivity displays the SettingsActivityFragment on a phone device and on a tablet device in portrait orientation.

4.9 SettingsActivityFragment Class

Class SettingsActivityFragment (Fig. 4.44) inherits from PreferenceFragment (package android.preference). When the SettingsActivityFragment is created, method onCreate (lines 10–14) builds the preferences GUI by calling inherited PreferenceFragment method **addPreferencesFromResource** to build the preferences GUI from the preferences.xml (Section 4.4.11). As the user interacts with the preferences GUI, the preferences are automatically stored into a `SharedPreferences` file on the device. If the file does not exist, it will be created; otherwise, it will be updated. We removed the other unused autogenerated code from this class.

```
1   // SettingsActivityFragment.java
2   // Subclass of PreferenceFragment for managing app settings
3   package com.deitel.flagquiz;
4
5   import android.os.Bundle;
6   import android.preference.PreferenceFragment;
7
8   public class SettingsActivityFragment extends PreferenceFragment {
9      // creates preferences GUI from preferences.xml file in res/xml
10     @Override
11     public void onCreate(Bundle bundle) {
12        super.onCreate(bundle);
13        addPreferencesFromResource(R.xml.preferences); // load from XML
14     }
15  }
```

Fig. 4.44 | `SettingsActivityFragment` subclass of `PreferenceFragment` displays the app's preferences.

4.10 AndroidManifest.xml

Figure 4.45 shows the **Flag Quiz** app's autogenerated manifest. Each `Activity` in an app must be declared in `AndroidManifest.xml`; otherwise, Android will not know that the `Activity` exists and will not be able to launch it. When you created the app, the IDE declared `MainActivity` in `AndroidManifest.xml` (lines 11–21). The notation

```
.MainActivity
```

in line 12 indicates that the class is in the package specified in line 2 and is shorthand for

```
com.deitel.flagquiz.MainActivity
```

We added line 14, which we'll discuss momentarily.

```
1   <?xml version="1.0" encoding="utf-8"?>
2   <manifest package="com.deitel.flagquiz"
3      xmlns:android="http://schemas.android.com/apk/res/android">
4
5      <application
6         android:allowBackup="true"
7         android:icon="@mipmap/ic_launcher"
8         android:label="@string/app_name"
9         android:supportsRtl="true"
10        android:theme="@style/AppTheme">
11        <activity
12           android:name=".MainActivity"
13           android:label="@string/app_name"
```

Fig. 4.45 | AndroidManifest.xml with SettingsActivity declared. (Part 1 of 2.)

```
14                  android:launchMode="singleTop"
15                  android:theme="@style/AppTheme.NoActionBar">
16                  <intent-filter>
17                      <action android:name="android.intent.action.MAIN"/>
18
19                      <category android:name="android.intent.category.LAUNCHER"/>
20                  </intent-filter>
21              </activity>
22              <activity
23                  android:name=".SettingsActivity"
24                  android:label="@string/title_activity_settings"
25                  android:parentActivityName=".MainActivity"
26                  android:theme="@style/AppTheme.NoActionBar">
27                  <meta-data
28                      android:name="android.support.PARENT_ACTIVITY"
29                      android:value="com.deitel.flagquiz.MainActivity">
30              </activity>
31          </application>
32
33      </manifest>
```

Fig. 4.45 | AndroidManifest.xml with SettingsActivity declared. (Part 2 of 2.)

When you added the SettingsActivity to the project (Section 4.4.1), the IDE added SettingsActivity to the manifest file automatically (lines 22–30). If you were to create a new Activity without using the IDE's tools, you'd have to declare the new Activity by inserting an <activity> element like the one in lines 22–30. For complete manifest file details, visit

> http://developer.android.com/guide/topics/manifest/manifest-
>   intro.html

Launch Mode

Line 14 specifies MainActivity's launchMode. By default each Activity you create uses the "standard" launch mode. In this mode, when Android receives an Intent to launch the Activity, Android creates a new instance of that Activity.

Recall from Section 4.4.12 that you specified SettingsActivity's hierarchical parent. Again, this enables Android to define on the app bar an *up button* that a user can touch to navigate back to the specified parent Activity. When the user touches this button and the parent Activity uses "standard" launch mode, Android uses an Intent to launch the parent Activity. This results in a new instance of MainActivity. This also causes the **Flag Quiz** app to crash in MainActivity's OnSharedPreferenceChangeListener (Section 4.6.7) when it tries to update a quizFragment that no longer exists—it was defined in a different MainActivity instance.

Line 14 fixes this problem by changing MainActivity's launchMode to "singleTop". With this launch mode, when the user touches the *up button*, Android brings the *existing* MainActivity to the foreground, rather than creating a new MainActivity object. For more information on the <activity> element's lauchMode values, visit

> https://developer.android.com/guide/topics/manifest/activity-
>   element.html#lmode

4.11 Wrap-Up

In this chapter, you built a **Flag Quiz** app that tests a user's ability to correctly identify country flags. A key feature of this chapter was using Fragments to create portions of an Activity's GUI. You used two activities to display the MainActivityFragment and the SettingsActivityFragment when the app was running in portrait orientation. You used one Activity to display both Fragments when the app was running on a tablet in landscape orientation—thus, making better use of the available screen real estate. You used a subclass of PreferenceFragment to automatically maintain and persist the app's settings and a subclass of DialogFragment to display an AlertDialog to the user. We discussed portions of a Fragment's lifecycle and showed how to use the FragmentManager to obtain a reference to a Fragment so that you could interact with it programmatically.

In portrait orientation, you provided an icon for the MainActivity's **Settings** menu item. This appeared on the app bar, so the user could touch it to display the SettingsActivity containing the SettingsActivityFragment. To launch the SettingsActivity, you used an explicit Intent. You saw how to obtain preferences from the app's Shared-Preferences file and how to edit that file using a SharedPreferences.Editor.

We showed how to use a Configuration object to determine whether the app was running on a tablet in landscape orientation. We demonstrated how to manage a large number of image resources using subfolders in the app's assets folder and how to access those resources via an AssetManager. You created a Drawable from an image's bytes by reading them from an InputStream, then displayed the Drawable in an ImageView.

You learned about additional subfolders of the app's res folder—menu for storing menu resource files, anim for storing animation resource files and xml for storing XML data files. We discussed how to use qualifiers to create a folder for storing a layout that should be used only on large devices in landscape orientation. We also demonstrated how to use a color state list resource to ensure that the text in the Buttons is readable for both the *enabled* and *disabled* states.

You used Toasts to display minor error messages or informational messages that appear on the screen briefly. To display the next flag in the quiz after a short delay, you used a Handler, which executes a Runnable after a specified number of milliseconds. You learned that a Handler's Runnable executes in the thread that created the Handler (the GUI thread in this app).

We defined an Animation in XML and applied it to the app's ImageView when the user guessed incorrectly to provide visual feedback to the user. We also used ViewAnimationUtils to create a circular reveal Animator for transitioning between questions. You learned how to log exceptions for debugging purposes with Android's built-in logging mechanism and class Log. You also used various classes and interfaces from the java.util package, including List, ArrayList, Collections and Set.

Finally, we presented the app's AndroidManifest.xml file. We discussed the autogenerated <activity> elements. We also changed the MainActivity's launchMode to "singleTop" so that the app used one instance of MainActivity, rather than creating a new one each time the user touches the *up button* on the app bar.

In Chapter 5, we present the **Doodlz** app, which uses Android's graphics capabilities to turn a device's screen into a *virtual canvas*. You'll also learn about Android's immersive mode and printing capabilities.

5

Doodlz App

2D Graphics, Canvas, Bitmap, Accelerometer, SensorManager, Multitouch Events, MediaStore, Printing, Android 6.0 Permissions, Gradle

Objectives

In this chapter you'll:

- Detect when the user touches the screen, moves a finger across the screen and removes a finger from the screen.
- Process multiple touches so the user can draw with multiple fingers at once.
- Use a SensorManager and the accelerometer to detect motion events.
- Use a Paint object to specify the color and width of a line.
- Use Path objects to store each line's data and use a Canvas to draw each line into a Bitmap.
- Create a menu and display menu items on the app bar.
- Use the printing framework and the Android Support Library's PrintHelper class to enable the user to print a drawing.
- Use Android 6.0's new permissions model to request permission for saving an image to external storage.
- Add libraries to an app with the Gradle build system.

5.1 Introduction

The **Doodlz** app enables you to paint by dragging one or more fingers across the screen (Fig. 5.1). The app provides options for setting the drawing color and line width. Additional options allow you to

- clear the screen
- save the current drawing on your device, and
- print the current drawing.

Depending on your device's screen size, some or all of the app's options are displayed as icons directly on the app bar—any that do not fit are displayed as text in the overflow options menu (⋮) that appears on the app bar.

Fig. 5.1 | **Doodlz** app with a finished drawing.

This app introduces Android 6.0's new permissions mechanism. For example, Android requires the user's permission to allow an app to save files (like this app's drawings) on a device. In Android 6.0, rather than prompting the user at installation time with a complete list of permissions the app requires, the app requests each permission individually, only when the permission is required to perform a given task for the first time. In this app, Android prompts for permission the first time the user attempts to save a drawing.

First, you'll test-drive the app. Then we'll overview the technologies used to build it. Next, you'll design the app's GUI. Finally, we'll walk through the app's complete source code, emphasizing the app's new features.

5.2 Test-Driving the Doodlz App in an Android Virtual Device (AVD)

Opening and Running the App
Open Android Studio and open the **Doodlz** app from the Doodlz folder in the book's examples folder, then execute the app in the AVD or on a device. This builds the project and runs the app.

Understanding the App's Options
Figure 5.2(a) and (b) show the app bar and overflow options menu on the Nexus 6 AVD, and Fig. 5.2(c) shows the app bar on the Nexus 9 AVD.

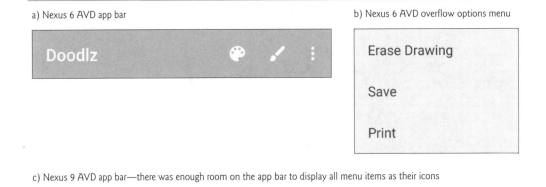

a) Nexus 6 AVD app bar

b) Nexus 6 AVD overflow options menu

c) Nexus 9 AVD app bar—there was enough room on the app bar to display all menu items as their icons

Fig. 5.2 | Doodlz app bar and overflow menu.

This app has the following menu items:

- **Color** ()—Displays a dialog for changing the line color.
- **Line Width** ()—Displays a dialog for changing the thickness of the line that will be drawn as you drag your finger(s) on the screen.
- **Erase Image** ()—First confirms whether you wish to erase the entire image, then clears the drawing area if you do not cancel the action.
- **Save** ()—Saves the image on the device. You can view the image via the Google **Photos** app by opening that app's menu and touching **Device Folders** to see thumbnails of your stored images.[1]

---

1. On some devices you might need to take a picture with the device's camera app before you'll be able to save properly from the **Doodlz** app.

- **Print** (🖨)—Displays a GUI for selecting an available printer so you can print your image or save it as a PDF document (the default).

You'll explore each of these options momentarily.

> **Look-and-Feel Observation 5.1**
>
> *When a menu item is displayed on the app bar, if the menu item has an icon, that icon is displayed; otherwise, the menu item's text is displayed in small capital letters. Any menu items in this app that cannot fit on the app bar are accessible in the drop-down options menu (⋮), which displays the menu items using their text labels.*

Changing the Brush Color to Red

To change the brush color, touch 🎨 on the app bar—or select **Color** from the options menu if the icon is not displayed on the app bar. This displays the **Choose Color** dialog (Fig. 5.3).

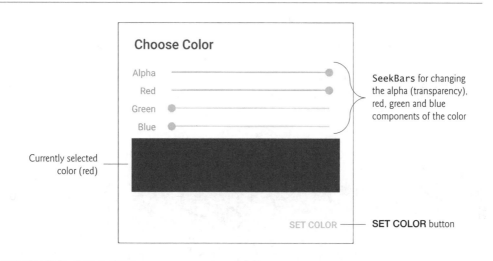

Fig. 5.3 | Changing the drawing color to red.

Colors are defined using the *ARGB color scheme* in which the *alpha* (i.e., *transparency*), red, green and blue components, respectively, are specified by integers in the range 0–255. For alpha, 0 means *completely transparent* and 255 means *completely opaque*. For red, green and blue, 0 means *none* of that color and 255 means the *maximum amount* of that color. The GUI consists of **Alpha**, **Red**, **Green** and **Blue** SeekBars that allow you to select the amount of alpha, red, green and blue, respectively, in the drawing color. You drag the SeekBars to change the color. As you do, the app displays the new color below the Seek-Bars. Select a red color now by dragging the **Red** SeekBar to the right as in Fig. 5.3. Touch the **SET COLOR** button to set this color as the drawing color and dismiss the dialog. If you do not wish to change the color, you can simply touch outside the dialog to dismiss it. You can erase by changing the drawing color to white (i.e., moving all four SeekBars' thumbs to the far right).

Changing the Line Width

To change the line width, touch ✒ on the app bar—or select **Line Width** from the options menu if the icon is not displayed on the app bar. This displays the **Choose Line Width** dialog. Drag the SeekBar for the line width to the right to thicken the line (Fig. 5.4). Touch the **SET LINE WIDTH** button to return to the drawing area.

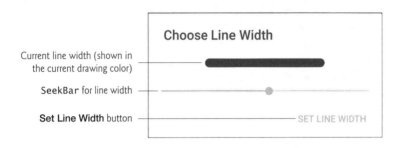

Fig. 5.4 | Changing the line width.

Drawing the Flower Petals

Drag your "finger"—the mouse when using the emulator—on the drawing area to draw flower petals (Fig. 5.5).

Fig. 5.5 | Drawing the flower petals.

Changing the Brush Color to Dark Green

Touch 🎨 or select the **Color** menu item to display the **Choose Color** dialog. Select a dark green color by dragging the **Green** SeekBar to the right and ensuring that the **Red** and **Blue** SeekBars are at the far left (Fig. 5.6(a)).

Changing the Line Width and Drawing the Stem and Leaves

Touch ✒ or select the **Line Width** menu item to display the **Choose Line Width** dialog. Drag the SeekBar for the line width to the right to thicken the line (Fig. 5.6(b)). Draw the flower stem and leaves. Repeat *Steps 9* and *10* for a lighter green color and thinner line, then draw the grass (Fig. 5.7).

a) Selecting dark green as the drawing color

b) Selecting a thicker line

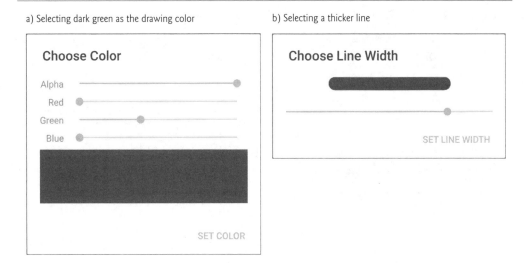

Fig. 5.6 | Changing the color to dark green and making the line thicker.

Fig. 5.7 | Drawing the stem and grass.

Finishing the Drawing
Next, change the drawing color to a semitransparent blue (Fig. 5.8(a)) and select a narrow-er line (Fig. 5.8(b)). Then draw the raindrops (Fig. 5.9).

a) Selecting blue as the drawing color

b) Selecting a thinner line

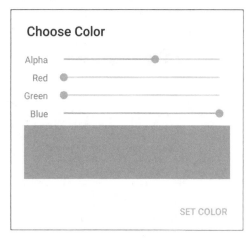

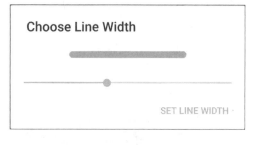

Fig. 5.8 | Changing the line color to blue and narrowing the line.

Fig. 5.9 | Drawing the rain in the new line color and line width.

Saving the Image

You can save your image to the device and view it using the **Photos** app. To do so, touch
🖫 on the app bar—or select **Save** from the options menu if the icon is not displayed on

the app bar. You can then view this image and others stored on the device by opening the **Photos** app.

Printing the Image
To print the image, touch 🖶 on the app bar—or select **Print** from the options menu if the icon is not displayed on the app bar. This displays a dialog of printing options. By default, you can save the image as a PDF document. To choose a printer, tap **Save as PDF** and select from the list of available printers. If no printers appear in the list, you need to configure Google Cloud Print for your printer. For information on this, visit

```
http://www.google.com/cloudprint/learn/
```

5.3 Technologies Overview
This section presents the new technologies that we use in the **Doodlz** app.

5.3.1 Activity and Fragment Lifecycle Methods
A `Fragment`'s lifecycle is tied to that of its parent `Activity`. There are six `Activity` lifecycle methods that have corresponding `Fragment` lifecycle methods—`onCreate`, `onStart`, `onResume`, `onPause`, `onStop` and `onDestroy`. When the system calls these methods on an `Activity`, it will also call the corresponding methods (and potentially other `Fragment` lifecycle methods) on all of the `Activity`'s attached `Fragment`s.

This app uses `Fragment` lifecycle methods `onResume` and `onPause`. An `Activity`'s `onResume` method is called when a `Fragment` is on the screen and ready for the user to interact with it. When an `Activity` hosts `Fragment`s and the `Activity` is resumed, all of its `Fragment`s' `onResume` methods are called. In this app, `MainActivityFragment` overrides `onResume` to enable listening for the accelerometer events so the user can shake the device to erase a drawing (Section 5.7.3).

An `Activity`'s `onPause` method is called when *another* `Activity` receives the focus, which pauses the one that loses the focus and sends it to the background. When an `Activity` hosts `Fragment`s and the `Activity` is paused, all of its `Fragment`s' `onPause` methods are called. In this app, `MainActivityFragment` overrides `onPause` to suspend listening for the shake-to-erase accelerometer events (Section 5.7.4).

Performance Tip 5.1
When an app is paused, it should remove listeners for sensor events so these events are not delivered to the app when it's not on the screen. This saves battery.

We discuss other `Activity` and `Fragment` lifecycle methods as we need them. For more information on the complete `Activity` lifecycle, visit

```
http://developer.android.com/reference/android/app/Activity.html
    #ActivityLifecycle
```

and for more information on the complete `Fragment` lifecycle, visit

```
http://developer.android.com/guide/components/fragments.html
    #Lifecycle
```

5.3.2 Custom `Views`

You can create a *custom view* by extending class `View` or one of its subclasses, as we do with class `DoodleView` (Section 5.8), which extends `View`. To add a custom component to a layout's XML file, you must provide its *fully qualified name* (i.e., its package and class name), so the custom `View`'s class must exist before you add it to the layout. We demonstrate how to create the `DoodleView` class and add it to a layout in Section 5.5.2.

5.3.3 Using `SensorManager` to Listen for Accelerometer Events

In this app, you can shake the device to erase a drawing. Most devices have an accelerometer for detecting device movement. Other currently supported sensors include gravity, gyroscope, light, linear acceleration, magnetic field, orientation, pressure, proximity, rotation vector and temperature. You'll use class `Sensor`'s sensor-type constants to specify the sensors for which your app should receive data. The list of `Sensor` constants can be found at

```
http://developer.android.com/reference/android/hardware/Sensor.html
```

We'll discuss the accelerometer and sensor event handling in Section 5.7. For a complete discussion of Android's other sensors, see the *Sensors Overview* at

```
http://developer.android.com/guide/topics/sensors/
    sensors_overview.html
```

5.3.4 Custom `DialogFragments`

Several previous apps have used `AlertDialogs` in `DialogFragments` to display information to the user or to ask questions and receive responses from the user in the form of `Button` clicks. The `AlertDialogs` you've used so far were created using anonymous inner classes that extended `DialogFragment` and displayed only text and buttons. `AlertDialogs` may also contain custom `Views`. In this app, you'll define three subclasses of `DialogFragment`:

- `ColorDialogFragment` (Section 5.9) displays an `AlertDialog` with a custom `View` containing GUI components for previewing and selecting a new ARGB drawing color.

- `LineWidthDialogFragment` (Section 5.10) displays an `AlertDialog` with a custom `View` containing a GUI for previewing and selecting the line thickness.

- `EraseImageDialogFragment` (Section 5.11) displays a standard `AlertDialog` asking the user to confirm whether the entire image should be erased.

For the `ColorDialogFragment` and `EraseImageDialogFragment`, you'll inflate the custom `View` from a layout resource file. In each of the three `DialogFragment` subclasses, you'll also override the following `Fragment` lifecycle methods:

- `onAttach`—The *first* `Fragment` lifecycle method called when a `Fragment` is attached to a parent `Activity`.

- `onDetach`—The *last* `Fragment` lifecycle method called when a `Fragment` is about to be detached from a parent `Activity`.

Preventing Multiple Dialogs from Appearing at the Same Time
It's possible that the event handler for the shake event could try to display the confirmation dialog for erasing an image when another dialog is already on the screen. To prevent this,

you'll use `onAttach` and `onDetach` to set the value of a `boolean` that indicates whether a dialog is on the screen. When this `boolean`'s value is `true`, we will not allow the event handler for the shake event to display a dialog.

5.3.5 Drawing with Canvas, `Paint` and `Bitmap`

You can use methods of class `Canvas` to draw text, lines and circles. Canvas methods draw on a `View`'s `Bitmap` (both from package `android.graphics`). You can associate a `Canvas` with a `Bitmap`, then use the `Canvas` to draw on the `Bitmap`, which can then be displayed on the screen (Section 5.8). A `Bitmap` also can be saved into a file—we'll use this capability to store drawings in the device's gallery when you touch the **Save** option. Each drawing method in class `Canvas` uses an object of class `Paint` (package `android.graphics`) to specify drawing characteristics, including color, line thickness, font size and more. These capabilities are presented with the `onDraw` method in the `DoodleView` class (Section 5.8.6). For more details on the drawing characteristics you can specify with a `Paint` object, visit

```
http://developer.android.com/reference/android/graphics/Paint.html
```

5.3.6 Processing Multiple Touch Events and Storing Lines in Paths

You can drag one or more fingers across the screen to draw. The app stores the information for each *individual* finger as a `Path` object (package `android.graphics`) that represents line segments and curves. You process *touch events* by overriding the `View` method `onTouchEvent` (Section 5.8.7). This method receives a `MotionEvent` (package `android.view`) that contains the type of touch event that occurred and the ID of the finger (known as a *pointer*) that generated the event. We use the IDs to distinguish the different fingers and add information to the corresponding `Path` objects. We use the type of the touch event to determine whether the user has *touched* the screen, *dragged* across the screen or *lifted a finger* from the screen.

In addition to standard touch-event handling, Android 6.0 provides enhanced support for using a Bluetooth stylus with apps, including access to pressure data and which stylus button the user presses. In this app, for example, you could use a stylus button to specify an erase mode, or you could use the stylus' pressure data to change the stroke thickness dynamically as the user draws. For more information, visit

```
https://developer.android.com/about/versions/marshmallow/android-
    6.0.html#bluetooth-stylus
```

5.3.7 Saving to the Device

The app's **Save** option allows you to save a drawing to the device. You can view the image in the **Photos** app by selecting **Device Folders** from the app's menu to see thumbnails of the stored images—touch a thumbnail to view the full-size image. A `ContentResolver` (package `android.content`) enables the app to read data from and store data on a device. You'll use a `ContentResolver` (Section 5.8.11) and the method `insertImage` of class `MediaStore.Images.Media` to save an image into the device's **Photos** app. The `MediaStore` manages media files (images, audio and video) stored on a device.

5.3.8 Printing and the Android Support Library's `PrintHelper` Class

In this app, we use class `PrintHelper` (Section 5.8.12) from Android's printing framework to print the current drawing. Class `PrintHelper` provides a user interface for selecting a printer, has a method for determining whether a given device supports printing and provides a method for printing a `Bitmap`. `PrintHelper` is part of the *Android Support Library*, which provides new Android features for use in current and older Android versions. The support library also includes additional convenience features, like class `PrintHelper`, that support specific Android versions.

5.3.9 New Android 6.0 (Marshmallow) Permissions Model

Android requires the permission `android.permission.WRITE_EXTERNAL_PERMISSION` before an app can write to external storage. For **Doodlz**, we need this permission to save the image that the user draws.

Android 6.0 (Marshmallow) has a new permissions model that's designed for a better user experience. Before Android 6.0, a user was required *at installation time* to grant in advance all permissions that an app would ever need—this caused many people not to install certain apps. With the new model, the app is installed without asking for *any* permissions. Instead, the user is asked to grant a permission only the first time the corresponding feature is used.

Once the user grants a permission, the app has that permission until:

• the app is reinstalled or

• the user changes the app's permissions via the Android **Settings** app.

You'll learn how to implement the new permissions model in Sections 5.7.8—5.7.9.

5.3.10 Adding Dependencies Using the Gradle Build System

Android Studio uses the Gradle build system to compile your code into an APK file—the installable app. Gradle also handles project dependencies, such as including in the build process any libraries used by the app. For **Doodlz**, you'll add a support library dependency to your project so you can use the `PrintHelper` class for printing an image (Section 5.4.2).

5.4 Creating the Project and Resources

In this section, you'll create the project, import material design icons for the app's menu items and edit the various resources used by the GUI and the app's Java code.

5.4.1 Creating the Project

Create a new **Blank Activity** project. Specify the following values in the **Create New Project** dialog's **New Project** step:

• **Application name:** `Doodlz`

• **Company Domain:** `deitel.com` (or specify your own domain name)

For the remaining steps in the **Create New Project** dialog, use the same settings as in Section 4.4.1. This creates a `MainActivity` that hosts a `Fragment`. The `Fragment` will define the app's drawing area and respond to the user's touches. Follow the steps in Section 2.5.2 to add an app icon to your project.

Once the project is open in Android Studio, in the layout editor, select **Nexus 6** from the virtual-device drop-down list (Fig. 2.11). Also, delete the **Hello world!** TextView in fragment_main.xml and the FloatingActionButton in activity_main.xml.

Use the **Theme Editor** (Section 3.5.2) to specify **Material Blue 500** as the app's primary color, **Material Blue 700** as the dark primary color and **Light blue accent 400** as the accent color. Also, follow the steps in Section 4.4.3 to configure the project for Java SE 7 support.

5.4.2 Gradle: Adding a Support Library to the Project

This app requires the Android Support Library to use the PrintHelper class. To add the support library as a project dependency, follow these steps:

1. Right click the app folder, then select **Open Module Settings**.

2. In the **Project Structure** window that appears, open the **Dependencies** tab.

3. Click the **Add** button (+), then select **Library dependency** to open the **Choose Library Dependency** dialog.

4. Select **support-v4 (com.android.support:support-v4:23.1.0)** from the list, then click **OK**. The dependency will appear in the list in the **Dependencies** tab.

5. Click **OK**. The IDE will display **Gradle project sync in progress...** while the project is being configured to use the Android Support Library.

For more on when to use and how to set up the Android Support Library, visit

```
http://developer.android.com/tools/support-library
http://developer.android.com/tools/support-library/setup.html
```

5.4.3 strings.xml

You created String resources in earlier chapters, so we show only a table of the String resource names and corresponding values here (Fig. 5.10). Double click strings.xml in the res/values folder, then click the **Open editor** link to display the **Translations Editor** for creating these String resources.

Look-and-Feel Observation 5.2
For languages that support uppercase letters, Google's material design specification indicates that a Button's text should use all capital letters (e.g., CANCEL or SET COLOR).

Key	Default Value
button_erase	Erase Image
button_set_color	Set Color
button_set_line_width	Set Line Width
line_imageview_description	This displays the line thickness

Fig. 5.10 | String resources used in the **Doodlz** app. (Part 1 of 2.)

Key	Default Value
`label_alpha`	Alpha
`label_red`	Red
`label_green`	Green
`label_blue`	Blue
`menuitem_color`	Color
`menuitem_delete`	Erase Drawing
`menuitem_line_width`	Line Width
`menuitem_save`	Save
`menuitem_print`	Print
`message_erase`	Erase the drawing?
`message_error_saving`	There was an error saving the image
`message_saved`	Your saved painting can be viewed in the Photos app by selecting Device Folders from that app\'s menu [*Note:* \' is the single-quote (') escape sequence—without the \, the IDE issues the warning "Apostrophe not preceded by \".]
`message_error_printing`	Your device does not support printing
`permission_explanation`	To save an image, the app requires permission to write to external storage
`title_color_dialog`	Choose Color
`title_line_width_dialog`	Choose Line Width

Fig. 5.10 | `String` resources used in the **Doodlz** app. (Part 2 of 2.)

5.4.4 Importing the Material Design Icons for the App's Menu Items

This app's menu specifies icons for each menu item. Menus items that fit on the app bar (which depends on the device) display the corresponding icon. Use the techniques you learned in Section 4.4.9 to import the following material design vector icons:

- 🎨 (`ic_palette_24dp`)
- 🖌 (`ic_brush_24dp`)
- 🗑 (`ic_delete_24dp`)
- 💾 (`ic_save_24dp`)
- 🖨 (`ic_print_24dp`)

The names in parentheses are the names that are displayed as tooltips in the **Vector Asset Studio** dialog when you hover over an image. For each image, open its XML file and change the `fillColor` to

  `@android:color/white`

so that the icons are displayed in white against the app's blue app bar.

5.4.5 `MainActivityFragment` Menu

In Chapter 4, you edited the default menu provided by the IDE to display the **Flag Quiz** app's **Settings** menu item. In this app, you'll define your own menu for the `MainActivityFragment`. You will not use `MainActivity`'s default menu in this app, so you can delete the `menu_main.xml` file in your project's `res/menu` folder. You should also remove the methods `onCreateOptionsMenu` and `onOptionsItemSelected` from class `MainActivity`, as these will not be used.

Menus for Different Android Versions

Keep in mind that the printing capability is not available in versions prior to Android 4.4. If you are developing an app with menus for multiple versions of Android, you may want to create multiple menu resources by using the resource qualifiers discussed in earlier apps. For example, you could create a menu resource for Android versions prior to 4.4 and a separate one for Android versions 4.4 and higher. In the menu resource for pre-Android-4.4, you can omit menu options that are unavailable in earlier Android versions. For more information on creating menu resources, visit

```
http://developer.android.com/guide/topics/ui/menus.html
```

Creating the Menu

To create the menu resource, follow these steps:

1. Right click the `res/menu` folder and select **New > Menu resource file** to open the **New Resource File** dialog.

2. Enter `doodle_fragment_menu.xml` in the **File name** field, and click **OK**. The IDE opens the file in the editor where it displays the file's XML. You must edit the XML directly to add menu items to the menu resource.

3. In this menu, we'll use each menu item's `showAsAction` property to specify that the menu item should be displayed on the app bar if there is room. When working with the Android Support Libraries to provide a backward-compatible app bar, you must use the `showAsAction` attribute from the XML namespace app, rather than the XML namespace android. Edit the `<menu>` element's opening tag to include the **app** XML namespace

```
xmlns:app="http://schemas.android.com/apk/res-auto"
```

4. Add the code for the first menu item in Fig. 5.11 to the XML file. The id of the menu item is `@+id/color`, its `title` property is `@string/menuitem_color`, its `icon` property is `@drawable/ic_palette_24dp` and its `showAsAction` property is `ifRoom`. The value `ifRoom` indicates that Android should display the menu item on the app bar if there's room available; otherwise, the menu item will appear as a text menu item in the overflow options menu at the right side of the app bar. Other `showAsAction` values can be found at

```
http://developer.android.com/guide/topics/resources/menu-
resource.html
```

```
 1  <item
 2      android:id="@+id/color"
 3      android:title="@string/menuitem_color"
 4      android:icon="@drawable/ic_palette_24dp"
 5      app:showAsAction="ifRoom">
 6  </item>
```

Fig. 5.11 | An `<item>` element representing a menu item.

5. Repeat *Step 3* for each of the IDs and titles in Fig. 5.12 to create the menu items for **Line Width**, **Delete**, **Save** and **Print**, then save and close the menu's file. The completed XML for the menu is shown in Fig. 5.13.

Id	Title
@+id/line_width	@string/menuitem_line_width
@+id/delete_drawing	@string/menuitem_delete
@+id/save	@string/menuitem_save
@+id/print	@string/menuitem_print

Fig. 5.12 | Additional menu items for the `MainActivityFragment`.

```
 1  <?xml version="1.0" encoding="utf-8"?>
 2  <menu xmlns:android="http://schemas.android.com/apk/res/android"
 3        xmlns:app="http://schemas.android.com/apk/res-auto">
 4      <item
 5          android:id="@+id/color"
 6          android:title="@string/menuitem_color"
 7          android:icon="@drawable/ic_palette_24dp"
 8          app:showAsAction="ifRoom">
 9      </item>
10
11      <item
12          android:id="@+id/line_width"
13          android:title="@string/menuitem_line_width"
14          android:icon="@drawable/ic_brush_24dp"
15          app:showAsAction="ifRoom">
16      </item>
17
18      <item
19          android:id="@+id/delete_drawing"
20          android:title="@string/menuitem_delete"
21          android:icon="@drawable/ic_delete_24dp"
22          app:showAsAction="ifRoom">
23      </item>
24
```

Fig. 5.13 | `doodle_fragment_menu.xml`. (Part 1 of 2.)

```
25        <item
26           android:id="@+id/save"
27           android:title="@string/menuitem_save"
28           android:icon="@drawable/ic_save_24dp"
29           app:showAsAction="ifRoom">
30        </item>
31
32        <item
33           android:id="@+id/print"
34           android:title="@string/menuitem_print"
35           android:icon="@drawable/ic_print_24dp"
36           app:showAsAction="ifRoom">
37        </item>
38     </menu>
```

Fig. 5.13 | doodle_fragment_menu.xml. (Part 2 of 2.)

5.4.6 Adding a Permission to AndroidManifest.xml

In addition to using Android 6.0's new permissions model in which the app asks the user to grant permissions dynamically, each app also must specify any permissions it uses in the AndroidManifest.xml file. To do so:

1. Expand the project's manifests folder and open AndroidManifest.xml.

2. Inside the <manifest> element and before the <application> element, add

```
<uses-permission
   android:name="android.permission.WRITE_EXTERNAL_STORAGE" />
```

5.5 Building the App's GUI

In this section, you'll create the app's GUI and create the classes for the app's dialogs.

5.5.1 content_main.xml Layout for MainActivity

The content_main.xml layout for this app's MainActivity contains only the MainActivityFragment, which was created automatically when you created the project. For more readable code, we changed the fragment's **id** property:

1. Open content_main.xml in the layout editor's **Design** view.

2. Select the fragment in the **Component Tree**, then change the Fragment's **id** to doodleFragment in the **Properties** window and save the layout.

5.5.2 fragment_main.xml Layout for MainActivityFragment

The fragment_main.xml layout for the MainActivityFragment needs to display only a DoodleView. The layout file was created with a RelativeLayout automatically when you created the project. To change the root element of the layout from a RelativeLayout to a DoodleView, you must first create class DoodleView (a subclass of View), so you can select it when placing the custom view in the layout:

1. Expand the java folder in the **Project** window.

2. Right click the `com.deitel.doodlz` node, then select **New > Java Class**.

3. In the **Create New Class** dialog that appears, enter `DoodleView` in the **Name** field, then click **OK**. The file will open in the editor automatically.

4. In `DoodleView.java`, indicate that class `DoodleView` is a subclass of `View` by adding `extends View` to the class's definition. If the IDE does not add an `import` for `android.view.View`, place the cursor immediately following `extends View`. Next, click the red bulb (💡) that appears above the beginning of class `Doodle-View`'s definition and select **Import Class**.

5. The IDE will display an error indicating that you have not defined a constructor for the new class. To fix this, place the cursor immediately following `extends View`. Click the red bulb (💡) that appears above the beginning of class `Doodle-View`'s definition and select **Create constructor matching super**. In the **Choose Super Class Constructors** dialog, choose the two-argument constructor, then click **OK**. The IDE will add the constructor to the class. You'll add code to this constructor in Section 5.8.3. The two-argument constructor is called by Android when inflating the `DoodleView` from a layout—the second argument specifies the `View` properties set in the layout XML file. You can learn more about class `View`'s constructors at

> `http://developer.android.com/reference/android/view/`
> `View.html#View(android.content.Context)`

6. Switch back to `fragment_main.xml` in the layout editor and click the **Text** tab.

7. Change `RelativeLayout` to `com.deitel.doodlz.DoodleView`.

8. Remove the properties for top, right, bottom and left `padding`—the `DoodleView` should occupy the entire screen.

9. In **Design** view, select **CustomView - com.deitel.doodlz.DoodleView** in the **Component Tree** window, then set the **id** to `doodleView`.

10. Save and close `fragment_main.xml`.

5.5.3 `fragment_color.xml` Layout for `ColorDialogFragment`

The `fragment_color.xml` layout for the `ColorDialogFragment` contains a two-column `GridLayout` that displays a GUI for selecting and previewing a new drawing color. In this section, you'll create `ColorDialogFragment`'s layout and the `ColorDialogFragment` class. To add the `fragment_color.xml` layout:

1. Expand the project's res/layout node in the **Project** window.

2. Right click the `layout` folder and select **New > Layout resource file** to display the **New Resource File** dialog.

3. In the dialog's **File name** field, enter `fragment_color.xml`

4. In the **Root element** field, enter `GridLayout`, then click **OK**.

5. In the **Component Tree** window, select the **GridLayout**.

6. In the **Properties** window, change the **id** value to `colorDialogGridLayout` and the **columnCount** to 2.

7. Using the layout editor's **Palette**, drag **Plain TextViews** and **SeekBars** onto the colorDialogGridLayout node in the **Component Tree** window. Drag the items in the order they're listed in Fig. 5.14 and set each item's **id** as shown in the figure. We'll show you how to add the colorView next.

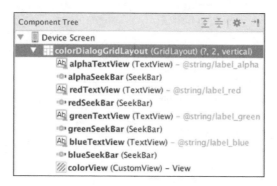

Fig. 5.14 | Component Tree view for fragment_color.xml.

Adding the colorView to the Layout

The colorView does not need its own class—we'll programmatically use methods of class View to change the color displayed in colorView. Android Studio does not provide a drag-and-drop way to add an object of class View to a layout, so you'll need to edit the layout's XML directly to add the colorView. To do so:

1. Click the **Text** tab at the bottom of the layout editor to switch from the **Design** view to the layout's XML text.

2. Add the code in Fig. 5.15 immediately before closing </GridLayout> tag.

```
1    <View
2        android:layout_width="wrap_content"
3        android:layout_height="@dimen/color_view_height"
4        android:id="@+id/colorView"
5        android:layout_column="0"
6        android:layout_columnSpan="2"
7        android:layout_gravity="fill_horizontal"/>
```

Fig. 5.15 | fragment_color.xml.

3. Switch back to the layout editor's **Design** tab.

4. Configure the GUI component properties with the values shown in Fig. 5.16. For the dimension value color_view_height, recall that in the **Resources** dialog, you can click **New Resource** and select **New Dimension Value...** to open the **New Dimension Value Resource** dialog. Specify 80dp for the color_view_height.

5. Save and close fragment_color.xml.

GUI component	Property	Value
colorDialogGridLayout	columnCount	2
	orientation	vertical
	useDefaultMargins	true
	padding top	@dimen/activity_vertical_margin
	padding bottom	@dimen/activity_vertical_margin
	padding left	@dimen/activity_horizontal_margin
	padding right	@dimen/activity_horizontal_margin
alphaTextView	*Layout Parameters*	
	layout:column	0
	layout:gravity	right, center_vertical
	layout:row	0
	Other Properties	
	text	@string/label_alpha
alphaSeekBar	*Layout Parameters*	
	layout:column	1
	layout:gravity	fill_horizontal
	layout:row	0
	Other Properties	
	max	255
redTextView	*Layout Parameters*	
	layout:column	0
	layout:gravity	right, center_vertical
	layout:row	1
	Other Properties	
	text	@string/label_red
redSeekBar	*Layout Parameters*	
	layout:column	1
	layout:gravity	fill_horizontal
	layout:row	1
	Other Properties	
	max	255
greenTextView	*Layout Parameters*	
	layout:column	0
	layout:gravity	right, center_vertical
	layout:row	2
	Other Properties	
	text	@string/label_green
greenSeekBar	*Layout Parameters*	
	layout:column	1
	layout:gravity	fill_horizontal
	layout:row	2
	Other Properties	
	max	255

Fig. 5.16 | Property values for the GUI components in fragment_color.xml. (Part 1 of 2.)

GUI component	Property	Value
blueTextView	*Layout Parameters*	
	layout:column	0
	layout:gravity	right, center_vertical
	layout:row	3
	Other Properties	
	text	@string/label_blue
blueSeekBar	*Layout Parameters*	
	layout:column	1
	layout:gravity	fill_horizontal
	layout:row	3
	Other Properties	
	max	255
colorView	*Layout Parameters*	
	layout:height	@dimen/color_view_height
	layout:column	0
	layout:columnSpan	2
	layout:gravity	fill_horizontal

Fig. 5.16 | Property values for the GUI components in `fragment_color.xml`. (Part 2 of 2.)

Adding Class *ColorDialogFragment* to the Project

To add class `ColorDialogFragment` to the project:

1. In the project's java folder, right click the upper package com.deitel.doodlz and select **New > Java Class** to display the **Create New Class** dialog.

2. In the **Name** field, enter `ColorDialogFragment`.

3. Click **OK** to create the class. You'll create the code for this class in Section 5.9.

5.5.4 fragment_line_width.xml Layout for LineWidthDialogFragment

The `fragment_line_width.xml` layout for the `LineWidthDialogFragment` contains a GridLayout that displays a GUI for selecting and previewing a new line thickness. In this section, you'll create `LineWidthDialogFragment`'s layout and the `LineWidthDialogFragment` class. To add the `fragment_line_width.xml` layout:

1. Expand the project's res/layout node in the **Project** window.

2. Right click the layout folder and select **New > Layout resource file** to display the **New Resource File** dialog.

3. In the dialog's **File name** field, enter `fragment_line_width.xml`

4. In the **Root element** field, enter `GridLayout`, then click **OK**.

5. In the **Component Tree** window, select the **GridLayout**, and change its **id** value to `lineWidthDialogGridLayout`.

6. Using the layout editor's **Palette**, drag an **ImageView** and a **SeekBar** onto the `lineWidthDialogGridLayout` node in the **Component Tree** window so that the window appears as shown in Fig. 5.17. Set each item's **id** as shown in the figure.

Fig. 5.17 | Component Tree view for `fragment_line_width.xml`.

7. Configure the GUI component properties with the values shown in Fig. 5.18. Give the dimension value `line_imageview_height` a value of 50dp.

8. Save and close `fragment_line_width.xml`.

GUI component	Property	Value
lineWidthDialog-GridLayout	column Count	1
	orientation	vertical
	useDefaultMargins	true
	padding top	@dimen/activity_vertical_margin
	padding bottom	@dimen/activity_vertical_margin
	padding left	@dimen/activity_horizontal_margin
	padding right	@dimen/activity_horizontal_margin
widthImageView	*Layout Parameters*	
	layout:height	@dimen/line_imageview_height
	layout:gravity	fill_horizontal
	Other Properties	
	contentDescription	@string/line_imageview_description
widthSeekBar	*Layout Parameters*	
	layout:gravity	fill_horizontal
	Other Properties	
	max	50

Fig. 5.18 | Property values for the GUI components in `fragment_line_width.xml`.

Adding Class LineWidthDialogFragment to the Project
To add class `LineWidthDialogFragment` to the project:

1. In the project's java folder, right click the upper package `com.deitel.doodlz` and select **New > Java Class** to display the **Create New Class** dialog.

2. In the **Name** field, enter `LineWidthDialogFragment`.

3. Click **OK** to create the class.

5.5.5 Adding Class EraseImageDialogFragment

The EraseImageDialogFragment does not require a layout resource, as it will display a simple AlertDialog containing text. To add class EraseImageDialogFragment to the project:

1. In the project's java folder, right click the upper package com.deitel.doodlz and select **New > Java Class** to display the **Create New Class** dialog.

2. In the **Name** field, enter EraseImageDialogFragment.

3. Click **OK** to create the class.

5.6 MainActivity Class

This app consists of six classes:

- MainActivity (discussed below)—This is the parent Activity for the app's Fragments.

- MainActivityFragment (Section 5.7)—Manages the DoodleView and accelerometer event handling.

- DoodleView (Section 5.8)—Provides the drawing, saving and printing capabilities.

- ColorDialogFragment (Section 5.9)—A DialogFragment that's displayed when the user chooses the option to set the drawing color.

- LineWidthDialogFragment (Section 5.10)—A DialogFragment that's displayed when the user chooses the option to set the line width.

- EraseImageDialogFragment (Section 5.11)—A DialogFragment that's displayed when the user chooses the option to erase, or shakes the device to erase, the current drawing.

Class MainActivity's onCreate method (Fig. 5.19) inflates the GUI (line 16) and configures its app bar (lines 17–18), then uses the techniques you learned in Section 4.6.3 to determine the device's size and set MainActivity's orientation. If this app is running on an extra-large device (line 26), we set the orientation to landscape (lines 27–28); otherwise, we set it to portrait (lines 30–31). We removed the other autogenerated methods in class MainActivity, as they're not used in this app.

```
1   // MainActivity.java
2   // Sets MainActivity's layout
3   package com.deitel.doodlz;
4
5   import android.content.pm.ActivityInfo;
6   import android.content.res.Configuration;
7   import android.os.Bundle;
8   import android.support.v7.app.AppCompatActivity;
9   import android.support.v7.widget.Toolbar;
```

Fig. 5.19 | MainActivity class. (Part 1 of 2.)

```
10
11    public class MainActivity extends AppCompatActivity {
12        // configures the screen orientation for this app
13        @Override
14        protected void onCreate(Bundle savedInstanceState) {
15            super.onCreate(savedInstanceState);
16            setContentView(R.layout.activity_main);
17            Toolbar toolbar = (Toolbar) findViewById(R.id.toolbar);
18            setSupportActionBar(toolbar);
19
20            // determine screen size
21            int screenSize =
22                getResources().getConfiguration().screenLayout &
23                Configuration.SCREENLAYOUT_SIZE_MASK;
24
25            // use landscape for extra large tablets; otherwise, use portrait
26            if (screenSize == Configuration.SCREENLAYOUT_SIZE_XLARGE)
27                setRequestedOrientation(
28                    ActivityInfo.SCREEN_ORIENTATION_LANDSCAPE);
29            else
30                setRequestedOrientation(
31                    ActivityInfo.SCREEN_ORIENTATION_PORTRAIT);
32        }
33    }
```

Fig. 5.19 | MainActivity class. (Part 2 of 2.)

5.7 MainActivityFragment Class

The MainActivityFragment (Sections 5.7.1—5.7.10) displays the DoodleView (Section 5.8), manages the menu options displayed on the app bar and in the options menu, and manages the sensor event handling for the app's *shake-to-erase* feature.

5.7.1 package Statement, import Statements and Fields

Section 5.3 discussed the key new classes and interfaces used by MainActivityFragment. We've highlighted these classes and interfaces in Fig. 5.20. DoodleView variable doodle-View (line 24) represents the drawing area. Accelerometer information is delivered to the app as float values. The float variables in lines 25–27 are used to calculate changes in the device's acceleration to determine when a *shake event* occurs (so we can ask whether the user would like to erase the drawing). Line 28 defines a boolean variable with the default value false that will be used throughout this class to specify when there's a dialog displayed on the screen. We use this to prevent multiple dialogs from being displayed simultaneously—for example, if the **Choose Color** dialog is displayed and the user accidentally shakes the device, the dialog for erasing the image should *not* be displayed. The constant in line 31 is used to ensure that small device movements (which happen frequently) are *not* interpreted as shakes—we picked this constant via trial and error by shaking the app on several different types of devices. The constant in line 35 is used to identify the request for the permission needed to save the user's drawing.

```
1   // MainActivityFragment.java
2   // Fragment in which the DoodleView is displayed
3   package com.deitel.doodlz;
4
5   import android.Manifest;
6   import android.app.AlertDialog;
7   import android.content.Context;
8   import android.content.DialogInterface;
9   import android.content.pm.PackageManager;
10  import android.hardware.Sensor;
11  import android.hardware.SensorEvent;
12  import android.hardware.SensorEventListener;
13  import android.hardware.SensorManager;
14  import android.os.Bundle;
15  import android.support.v4.app.Fragment;
16  import android.view.LayoutInflater;
17  import android.view.Menu;
18  import android.view.MenuInflater;
19  import android.view.MenuItem;
20  import android.view.View;
21  import android.view.ViewGroup;
22
23  public class MainActivityFragment extends Fragment {
24     private DoodleView doodleView; // handles touch events and draws
25     private float acceleration;
26     private float currentAcceleration;
27     private float lastAcceleration;
28     private boolean dialogOnScreen = false;
29
30     // value used to determine whether user shook the device to erase
31     private static final int ACCELERATION_THRESHOLD = 100000;
32
33     // used to identify the request for using external storage, which
34     // the save image feature needs
35     private static final int SAVE_IMAGE_PERMISSION_REQUEST_CODE = 1;
36
```

Fig. 5.20 | MainActivityFragment class package statement, import statements and fields.

5.7.2 Overridden Fragment Method onCreateView

Method onCreateView (Fig. 5.21) inflates MainActivityFragment's GUI and initializes the instance variables. A Fragment can place items in the app's app bar and options menu. To do so, the Fragment must call its setHasOptionsMenu method with the argument true. If the parent Activity also has options menu items, then the Activity's and the Fragment's items will be placed on the app bar or in the options menu (based on their settings).

```
37     // called when Fragment's view needs to be created
38     @Override
39     public View onCreateView(LayoutInflater inflater, ViewGroup container,
40        Bundle savedInstanceState) {
```

Fig. 5.21 | Overriding Fragment method onCreateView. (Part 1 of 2.)

```
41        super.onCreateView(inflater, container, savedInstanceState);
42        View view =
43           inflater.inflate(R.layout.fragment_main, container, false);
44
45        setHasOptionsMenu(true); // this fragment has menu items to display
46
47        // get reference to the DoodleView
48        doodleView = (DoodleView) view.findViewById(R.id.doodleView);
49
50        // initialize acceleration values
51        acceleration = 0.00f;
52        currentAcceleration = SensorManager.GRAVITY_EARTH;
53        lastAcceleration = SensorManager.GRAVITY_EARTH;
54        return view;
55     }
56
```

Fig. 5.21 | Overriding Fragment method onCreateView. (Part 2 of 2.)

Line 48 gets a reference to the DoodleView, then lines 51–53 initialize the instance variables that help calculate acceleration changes to determine whether the user shook the device. We initially set variables currentAcceleration and lastAcceleration to SensorManager's GRAVITY_EARTH constant, which represents the acceleration due to Earth's gravity. SensorManager also provides constants for other planets in the solar system, for the moon and for other entertaining values, which you can see at

```
http://developer.android.com/reference/android/hardware/
   SensorManager.html
```

5.7.3 Methods onResume and enableAccelerometerListening

Accelerometer listening should be enabled only when the MainActivityFragment is visible. For this reason, we override Fragment lifecycle method onResume (Fig. 5.22, lines 58–62), which is called when the Fragment is on the screen and ready for the user to interact with it. Method onResume calls method enableAccelerometerListening (lines 65–75) to begin listening for accelerometer events. A SensorManager is used to register listeners for accelerometer events.

Method enableAccelerometerListening first uses Activity's getSystemService method to retrieve the system's SensorManager service, which enables the app to interact with the device's sensors. Lines 72–74 then register to receive accelerometer events using SensorManager's registerListener method, which receives three arguments:

- The SensorEventListener that responds to the events (defined in Section 5.7.5).

- A Sensor object representing the type of sensor data the app wishes to receive— this is retrieved by calling SensorManager's **getDefaultSensor** method and passing a Sensor-type constant (Sensor.TYPE_ACCELEROMETER in this app).

- The rate at which Android delivers sensor events— SENSOR_DELAY_NORMAL indicates the default rate. A faster rate can be used to get more accurate data, but this is also more CPU and battery intensive.

```
57    // start listening for sensor events
58    @Override
59    public void onResume() {
60       super.onResume();
61       enableAccelerometerListening(); // listen for shake event
62    }
63
64    // enable listening for accelerometer events
65    private void enableAccelerometerListening() {
66       // get the SensorManager
67       SensorManager sensorManager =
68          (SensorManager) getActivity().getSystemService(
69             Context.SENSOR_SERVICE);
70
71       // register to listen for accelerometer events
72       sensorManager.registerListener(sensorEventListener,
73          sensorManager.getDefaultSensor(Sensor.TYPE_ACCELEROMETER),
74          SensorManager.SENSOR_DELAY_NORMAL);
75    }
76
```

Fig. 5.22 | Methods onResume and enableAccelerometerListening.

5.7.4 Methods onPause and disableAccelerometerListening

To ensure that accelerometer listening is disabled when the MainActivityFragment is not on the screen, we override Fragment lifecycle method onPause (Fig. 5.23, lines 78–82), which calls method disableAccelerometerListening (lines 85–94). Method disable-AccelerometerListening uses class SensorManager's unregisterListener method to stop listening for accelerometer events.

```
77    // stop listening for accelerometer events
78    @Override
79    public void onPause() {
80       super.onPause();
81       disableAccelerometerListening(); // stop listening for shake
82    }
83
84    // disable listening for accelerometer events
85    private void disableAccelerometerListening() {
86       // get the SensorManager
87       SensorManager sensorManager =
88          (SensorManager) getActivity().getSystemService(
89             Context.SENSOR_SERVICE);
90
91       // stop listening for accelerometer events
92       sensorManager.unregisterListener(sensorEventListener,
93          sensorManager.getDefaultSensor(Sensor.TYPE_ACCELEROMETER));
94    }
95
```

Fig. 5.23 | Methods onPause and disableAccelerometerListening.

5.7.5 Anonymous Inner Class for Processing Accelerometer Events

Figure 5.24 overrides SensorEventListener method onSensorChanged (lines 100–123) to process accelerometer events. If the user moves the device, this method determines whether the movement was enough to be considered a shake. If so, line 121 calls method confirmErase (Section 5.7.6) to display an EraseImageDialogFragment (Section 5.11) and confirm whether the user really wants to erase the image. Interface SensorEventListener also contains method onAccuracyChanged (line 127)—we don't use this method in this app, so we provide an empty body because the method is required by the interface.

```
96      // event handler for accelerometer events
97      private final SensorEventListener sensorEventListener =
98         new SensorEventListener() {
99            // use accelerometer to determine whether user shook device
100           @Override
101           public void onSensorChanged(SensorEvent event) {
102              // ensure that other dialogs are not displayed
103              if (!dialogOnScreen) {
104                 // get x, y, and z values for the SensorEvent
105                 float x = event.values[0];
106                 float y = event.values[1];
107                 float z = event.values[2];
108
109                 // save previous acceleration value
110                 lastAcceleration = currentAcceleration;
111
112                 // calculate the current acceleration
113                 currentAcceleration = x * x + y * y + z * z;
114
115                 // calculate the change in acceleration
116                 acceleration = currentAcceleration *
117                    (currentAcceleration - lastAcceleration);
118
119                 // if the acceleration is above a certain threshold
120                 if (acceleration > ACCELERATION_THRESHOLD)
121                    confirmErase();
122              }
123           }
124
125           // required method of interface SensorEventListener
126           @Override
127           public void onAccuracyChanged(Sensor sensor, int accuracy) {}
128        };
129
```

Fig. 5.24 | Anonymous inner class that implements interface SensorEventListener to process accelerometer events.

The user can shake the device even when dialogs are already displayed on the screen. For this reason, onSensorChanged first checks whether a dialog is displayed (line 103). This test ensures that no other dialogs are displayed; otherwise, onSensorChanged simply returns. This is important because the sensor events occur in a different thread of execution. Without this test, we'd be able to display the confirmation dialog for erasing the image when another dialog is on the screen.

The `SensorEvent` parameter contains information about the sensor change that occurred. For accelerometer events, this parameter's `values` array contains three elements representing the acceleration (in *meters/second²*) in the *x* (left/right), *y* (up/down) and *z* (forward/backward) directions. A description and diagram of the coordinate system used by the `SensorEvent` API is available at

```
http://developer.android.com/reference/android/hardware/
SensorEvent.html
```

This link also describes the real-world meanings for a `SensorEvent`'s *x*, *y* and *z* values for each different `Sensor`.

Lines 105–107 store the acceleration values. It's important to handle sensor events quickly or to copy the event data (as we did here) because the array of sensor values is *reused* for each sensor event. Line 110 stores the last value of `currentAcceleration`. Line 113 sums the squares of the x, y and z acceleration values and stores them in `currentAcceleration`. Then, using the `currentAcceleration` and `lastAcceleration` values, we calculate a value (`acceleration`) that can be compared to our `ACCELERATION_THRESHOLD` constant. If the value is greater than the constant, the user moved the device enough for this app to consider the movement a shake. In this case, we call method `confirmErase`.

5.7.6 Method `confirmErase`

Method `confirmErase` (Fig. 5.25) simply creates an `EraseImageDialogFragment` (Section 5.11) and uses the `DialogFragment` method `show` to display it.

```
130     // confirm whether image should be erased
131     private void confirmErase() {
132         EraseImageDialogFragment fragment = new EraseImageDialogFragment();
133         fragment.show(getFragmentManager(), "erase dialog");
134     }
135
```

Fig. 5.25 | Method `confirmErase` displays an `EraseImageDialogFragment`.

5.7.7 Overridden Fragment Methods `onCreateOptionsMenu` and `onOptionsItemSelected`

Figure 5.26 overrides `Fragment`'s `onCreateOptionsMenu` method (lines 137–141) to add the options to the method's `Menu` argument using the method's `MenuInflater` argument. When the user selects a menu item, `Fragment` method `onOptionsItemSelected` (lines 144–169) responds to the selection.

We use the `MenuItem` argument's `getItemID` method (line 147) to get the resource ID of the selected menu item, then take different actions based on the selection. The actions are as follows:

- For `R.id.color`, lines 149–150 create and show a `ColorDialogFragment` (Section 5.9) to allow the user to select a new drawing color.

- For R.id.line_width, lines 153–155 create and show a LineWidthDialogFragment (Section 5.10) to allow the user to select a new line width.

- For R.id.delete_drawing, line 158 calls method confirmErase (Section 5.7.6) to display an EraseImageDialogFragment (Section 5.11) and confirm whether the user really wants to erase the image.

- For R.id.save, line 161 calls the saveImage method to save the painting as an image stored in the device's **Photos** after checking for and, if necessary, requesting permission to write to external storage.

- For R.id.print, line 164 calls doodleView's printImage method to allow the user to save the image as a PDF or to print the image.

```
136    // displays the fragment's menu items
137    @Override
138    public void onCreateOptionsMenu(Menu menu, MenuInflater inflater) {
139       super.onCreateOptionsMenu(menu, inflater);
140       inflater.inflate(R.menu.doodle_fragment_menu, menu);
141    }
142
143    // handle choice from options menu
144    @Override
145    public boolean onOptionsItemSelected(MenuItem item) {
146       // switch based on the MenuItem id
147       switch (item.getItemId()) {
148          case R.id.color:
149             ColorDialogFragment colorDialog = new ColorDialogFragment();
150             colorDialog.show(getFragmentManager(), "color dialog");
151             return true; // consume the menu event
152          case R.id.line_width:
153             LineWidthDialogFragment widthDialog =
154                new LineWidthDialogFragment();
155             widthDialog.show(getFragmentManager(), "line width dialog");
156             return true; // consume the menu event
157          case R.id.delete_drawing:
158             confirmErase(); // confirm before erasing image
159             return true; // consume the menu event
160          case R.id.save:
161             saveImage(); // check permission and save current image
162             return true; // consume the menu event
163          case R.id.print:
164             doodleView.printImage(); // print the current images
165             return true; // consume the menu event
166       }
167
168       return super.onOptionsItemSelected(item);
169    }
170
```

Fig. 5.26 | Overridden Fragment methods onCreateOptionsMenu and onOptionsItemSelected.

5.7.8 Method saveImage

Method saveImage (Fig. 5.27) is called by the onOptionsItemSelected method when the user selects the **Save** option in the options menu. The saveImage method implements part of the new Android 6.0 permissions model that first checks whether the app has the required permission before performing a task. If not, the app requests permission from the user before attempting to perform the task.

Lines 176–178 check whether the app does not yet have permission to write to external storage so that it can save the image. If the app does not have the permission android.permission.WRITE_EXTERNAL_STORAGE, lines 181–182 use the built-in shouldShowRequestPermissionRationale method to determine whether an explanation of why the app needs this permission should be displayed. The method returns true when it would be helpful to explain to the user why the app requires permission—for example, if the user denied the permission previously. If so, lines 183–203 create and display a dialog with the explanation. When the user clicks the dialog's **OK** button, lines 195–197 request the android.permission.WRITE_EXTERNAL_STORAGE permission using the inherited Fragment method requestPermissions. If an explanation is not necessary—for example, if this is the first time the app needs the permission—lines 207–209 immediately request the permission.

```
171    // requests the permission needed for saving the image if
172    // necessary or saves the image if the app already has permission
173    private void saveImage() {
174       // checks if the app does not have permission needed
175       // to save the image
176       if (getContext().checkSelfPermission(
177          Manifest.permission.WRITE_EXTERNAL_STORAGE) !=
178          PackageManager.PERMISSION_GRANTED) {
179
180          // shows an explanation of why permission is needed
181          if (shouldShowRequestPermissionRationale(
182             Manifest.permission.WRITE_EXTERNAL_STORAGE)) {
183             AlertDialog.Builder builder =
184                new AlertDialog.Builder(getActivity());
185
186             // set Alert Dialog's message
187             builder.setMessage(R.string.permission_explanation);
188
189             // add an OK button to the dialog
190             builder.setPositiveButton(android.R.string.ok,
191                new DialogInterface.OnClickListener() {
192                   @Override
193                   public void onClick(DialogInterface dialog, int which) {
194                      // request permission
195                      requestPermissions(new String[]{
196                         Manifest.permission.WRITE_EXTERNAL_STORAGE},
197                         SAVE_IMAGE_PERMISSION_REQUEST_CODE);
198                   }
199                }
200             );
201
```

Fig. 5.27 | Method saveImage. (Part 1 of 2.)

```
202                // display the dialog
203                builder.create().show();
204            }
205            else {
206                // request permission
207                requestPermissions(
208                    new String[]{Manifest.permission.WRITE_EXTERNAL_STORAGE},
209                    SAVE_IMAGE_PERMISSION_REQUEST_CODE);
210            }
211        }
212        else { // if app already has permission to write to external storage
213            doodleView.saveImage(); // save the image
214        }
215    }
216
```

Fig. 5.27 | Method saveImage. (Part 2 of 2.)

The requestPermissions method receives a String array of permissions the app is requesting and an integer (SAVE_IMAGE_PERMISSION_REQUEST_CODE) that's used to identify this request for permission. When requestPermissions is called, Android displays a dialog (Fig. 5.28) that allows the user to **DENY** or **ALLOW** the requested permissions. The system invokes the callback method onRequestPermissionsResult (Section 5.7.9) to process the user's response. If the app already has the requested permission, line 213 calls the DoodleView's saveImage method to save the image.

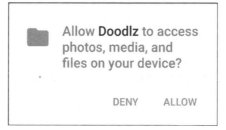

Fig. 5.28 | Dialog enabling the user to deny or allow writing to external storage.

5.7.9 Overridden Method onRequestPermissionsResult

Method onRequestPermissionsResult (Fig. 5.29) receives a permission requestCode for the request that was made and passes it to the switch in lines 224–229, which executes appropriate code for the request. This app has only one permission request, so the switch statement has only one case identified by the SAVE_IMAGE_PERMISSION_REQUEST_CODE constant. For apps that require multiple permissions you should specify unique values for each permission when you call method requestPermissions. Line 226 checks whether the user granted the app permission to write to external storage. If so, line 227 calls the DoodleView's saveImage method to save the image.

Software Engineering Observation 5.1

*If the user attempts to save the image and denies permission, the next time the user attempts to save, the permission dialog will contain a **Never ask again** checkbox. If the user checks this and denies permission, then attempts to save in the future, method onRequestPermissionResult will be called with PackageManager.PERMISSION_DENIED as an argument. A production app should handle this case and tell the user how to change the app's permissions via the **Settings** app.*

```
217    // called by the system when the user either grants or denies the
218    // permission for saving an image
219    @Override
220    public void onRequestPermissionsResult(int requestCode,
221        String[] permissions, int[] grantResults) {
222        // switch chooses appropriate action based on which feature
223        // requested permission
224        switch (requestCode) {
225            case SAVE_IMAGE_PERMISSION_REQUEST_CODE:
226                if (grantResults[0] == PackageManager.PERMISSION_GRANTED)
227                    doodleView.saveImage(); // save the image
228                return;
229        }
230    }
231
```

Fig. 5.29 | Overridden Fragment method onRequestPermissionsResult.

5.7.10 Methods getDoodleView and setDialogOnScreen

Methods getDoodleView and setDialogOnScreen (Fig. 5.30) are called by methods of the app's DialogFragment subclasses. Method getDoodleView returns a reference to this Fragment's DoodleView so that a DialogFragment can set the drawing color, set the line width or clear the image. Method setDialogOnScreen is called by Fragment lifecycle methods of the app's DialogFragment subclasses to indicate when a dialog is on the screen.

Software Engineering Observation 5.2

*This app's Fragments interact with one another directly. We chose this tightly coupled approach for simplicity in this app. Generally, a parent Activity manages an app's Fragment interactions. To pass data to a Fragment, the Activity provides a Bundle of arguments. Each Fragment class typically provides an interface of callback methods that the Activity implements. When the Fragment needs to notify its parent Activity of a state change, the Fragment calls the appropriate callback method. These techniques make Fragments more reusable across activities. We'll demonstrate these techniques in Chapter 9's **Address Book** app.*

```
232    // returns the DoodleView
233    public DoodleView getDoodleView() {
234        return doodleView;
235    }
```

Fig. 5.30 | Methods getDoodleView and setDialogOnScreen. (Part 1 of 2.)

```
236
237     // indicates whether a dialog is displayed
238     public void setDialogOnScreen(boolean visible) {
239        dialogOnScreen = visible;
240     }
241  }
```

Fig. 5.30 | Methods getDoodleView and setDialogOnScreen. (Part 2 of 2.)

5.8 DoodleView Class

The DoodleView class (Sections 5.8.1—5.8.12) processes the user's touches and draws the corresponding lines.

5.8.1 package Statement and import Statements

Figure 5.31 lists class DoodleView's package statement and import statements. The new classes and interfaces are highlighted here. Many of these were discussed in Section 5.3, and the rest are discussed as we use them throughout class DoodleView.

```
1    // DoodleView.java
2    // Main View for the Doodlz app.
3    package com.deitel.doodlz;
4
5    import android.content.Context;
6    import android.graphics.Bitmap;
7    import android.graphics.Canvas;
8    import android.graphics.Color;
9    import android.graphics.Paint;
10   import android.graphics.Path;
11   import android.graphics.Point;
12   import android.provider.MediaStore;
13   import android.support.v4.print.PrintHelper;
14   import android.util.AttributeSet;
15   import android.view.Gravity;
16   import android.view.MotionEvent;
17   import android.view.View;
18   import android.widget.Toast;
19
20   import java.util.HashMap;
21   import java.util.Map;
22
```

Fig. 5.31 | DoodleView package statement and import statements.

5.8.2 static and Instance Variables

Class DoodleView's static and instance variables (Fig. 5.32) are used to manage the data for the set of lines that the user is currently drawing and to draw those lines. Line 34 creates the pathMap, which maps each finger ID (known as a pointer) to a corresponding Path object for the lines currently being drawn. Line 35 creates the previousPointMap, which maintains the last point for each finger—as each finger moves, we draw a line from its cur-

rent point to its previous point. We discuss the other fields as we use them in class DoodleView.

```
23   // custom View for drawing
24   public class DoodleView extends View {
25       // used to determine whether user moved a finger enough to draw again
26       private static final float TOUCH_TOLERANCE = 10;
27
28       private Bitmap bitmap; // drawing area for displaying or saving
29       private Canvas bitmapCanvas; // used to to draw on the bitmap
30       private final Paint paintScreen; // used to draw bitmap onto screen
31       private final Paint paintLine; // used to draw lines onto bitmap
32
33       // Maps of current Paths being drawn and Points in those Paths
34       private final Map<Integer, Path> pathMap = new HashMap<>();
35       private final Map<Integer, Point> previousPointMap = new HashMap<>();
36
```

Fig. 5.32 | DoodleView static and instance variables.

5.8.3 Constructor

The constructor (Fig. 5.33) initializes several of the class's instance variables—the two
Maps are initialized in their declarations in Fig. 5.32. Line 40 of Fig. 5.33 creates the Paint
object paintScreen that will be used to display the user's drawing on the screen, and line
43 creates the Paint object paintLine that specifies the settings for the line(s) the user is
currently drawing. Lines 44–48 specify the settings for the paintLine object. We pass
true to Paint's setAntiAlias method to enable *anti-aliasing* which smooths the edges of
the lines. Next, we set the Paint's style to Paint.Style.STROKE with Paint's setStyle
method. The style can be STROKE, FILL or FILL_AND_STROKE for a line, a filled shape without a border and a filled shape with a border, respectively. The default option is
Paint.Style.FILL. We set the line's width using Paint's setStrokeWidth method. This
sets the app's *default line width* to five pixels. We also use Paint's setStrokeCap method
to round the ends of the lines with Paint.Cap.ROUND.

```
37       // DoodleView constructor initializes the DoodleView
38       public DoodleView(Context context, AttributeSet attrs) {
39           super(context, attrs); // pass context to View's constructor
40           paintScreen = new Paint(); // used to display bitmap onto screen
41
42           // set the initial display settings for the painted line
43           paintLine = new Paint();
44           paintLine.setAntiAlias(true); // smooth edges of drawn line
45           paintLine.setColor(Color.BLACK); // default color is black
46           paintLine.setStyle(Paint.Style.STROKE); // solid line
47           paintLine.setStrokeWidth(5); // set the default line width
48           paintLine.setStrokeCap(Paint.Cap.ROUND); // rounded line ends
49       }
50
```

Fig. 5.33 | DoodleView constructor.

5.8.4 Overridden `View` Method `onSizeChanged`

The `DoodleView`'s size is not determined until it's inflated and added to the `MainActivi-ty`'s `View` hierarchy; therefore, we can't determine the size of the drawing `Bitmap` in on-Create. So, we override `View` method `onSizeChanged` (Fig. 5.34), which is called when the `DoodleView`'s size changes—e.g., when it's added to an `Activity`'s `View` hierarchy or when the user rotates the device. In this app, `onSizeChanged` is called only when the `DoodleView` is added to the `Doodlz` `Activity`'s `View` hierarchy, because the app always dis-plays in portrait on phones and small tablets, and in landscape on large tablets.

Software Engineering Observation 5.3

In apps that support both portrait and landscape orientations, `onSizeChanged` is called each time the user rotates the device. In this app, that would result in a new `Bitmap` each tim the method is called. When replacing a `Bitmap`, you should call the prior `Bitmap`'s `recycle` method to release its resources.

```
51      // creates Bitmap and Canvas based on View's size
52      @Override
53      public void onSizeChanged(int w, int h, int oldW, int oldH) {
54          bitmap = Bitmap.createBitmap(getWidth(), getHeight(),
55              Bitmap.Config.ARGB_8888);
56          bitmapCanvas = new Canvas(bitmap);
57          bitmap.eraseColor(Color.WHITE); // erase the Bitmap with white
58      }
59
```

Fig. 5.34 | Overridden `View` method `onSizeChanged`.

Bitmap's `static` `createBitmap` method creates a `Bitmap` of the specified width and height—here we use the `DoodleView`'s width and height as the `Bitmap`'s dimensions. The last argument to `createBitmap` is the `Bitmap`'s encoding, which specifies how each pixel in the `Bitmap` is stored. The constant `Bitmap.Config.ARGB_8888` indicates that each pixel's color is stored in four bytes (one byte each for the alpha, red, green and blue values) of the pixel's color. Next, we create a new `Canvas` that's used to draw shapes directly to the `Bitmap`. Finally, we use `Bitmap`'s `eraseColor` method to fill the `Bitmap` with white pixels—the default `Bitmap` background is black.

5.8.5 Methods `clear`, `setDrawingColor`, `getDrawingColor`, `setLineWidth` and `getLineWidth`

Figure 5.35 defines methods `clear` (lines 61–66), `setDrawingColor` (lines 69–71), `get-DrawingColor` (lines 74–76), `setLineWidth` (lines 79–81) and `getLineWidth` (lines 84–86), which are called from the `MainActivityFragment`. Method `clear`, which we use in the `EraseImageDialogFragment`, empties the `pathMap` and `previousPointMap`, erases the `Bitmap` by setting all of its pixels to white, then calls the inherited `View` method `invali-date` to indicate that the `View` needs to be redrawn. Then, the system automatically deter-mines when the `View`'s `onDraw` method should be called. Method `setDrawingColor` changes the current drawing color by setting the color of the `Paint` object `paintLine`.

Paint's `setColor` method receives an `int` that represents the new color in ARGB format. Method `getDrawingColor` returns the current color, which we use in the `ColorDialog-Fragment`. Method `setLineWidth` sets `paintLine`'s stroke width to the specified number of pixels. Method `getLineWidth` returns the current stroke width, which we use in the `LineWidthDialogFragment`.

```
60     // clear the painting
61     public void clear() {
62        pathMap.clear(); // remove all paths
63        previousPointMap.clear(); // remove all previous points
64        bitmap.eraseColor(Color.WHITE); // clear the bitmap
65        invalidate(); // refresh the screen
66     }
67
68     // set the painted line's color
69     public void setDrawingColor(int color) {
70        paintLine.setColor(color);
71     }
72
73     // return the painted line's color
74     public int getDrawingColor() {
75        return paintLine.getColor();
76     }
77
78     // set the painted line's width
79     public void setLineWidth(int width) {
80        paintLine.setStrokeWidth(width);
81     }
82
83     // return the painted line's width
84     public int getLineWidth() {
85        return (int) paintLine.getStrokeWidth();
86     }
87
```

Fig. 5.35 | DoodleView methods `clear`, `setDrawingColor`, `getDrawingColor`, `setLineWidth` and `getLineWidth`.

5.8.6 Overridden View Method onDraw

When a `View` needs to be *redrawn*, its `onDraw` method is called. Figure 5.36 overrides `onDraw` to display `bitmap` (the `Bitmap` that contains the drawing) on the `DoodleView` by calling the `Canvas` argument's **`drawBitmap`** method. The first argument is the `Bitmap` to draw, the next two arguments are the *x-y* coordinates where the upper-left corner of the `Bitmap` should be placed on the `View` and the last argument is the `Paint` object that specifies the drawing characteristics. Lines 95–96 then loop through and display the `Paths` that are currently being drawn. For each `Integer` key in the `pathMap`, we pass the corresponding `Path` to `Canvas`'s **`drawPath`** method to draw the `Path` using the `paintLine` object, which defines the line *width* and *color*.

```
88      // perform custom drawing when the DoodleView is refreshed on screen
89      @Override
90      protected void onDraw(Canvas canvas) {
91          // draw the background screen
92          canvas.drawBitmap(bitmap, 0, 0, paintScreen);
93
94          // for each path currently being drawn
95          for (Integer key : pathMap.keySet())
96              canvas.drawPath(pathMap.get(key), paintLine); // draw line
97      }
98
```

Fig. 5.36 | Overridden View method onDraw.

5.8.7 Overridden View Method onTouchEvent

Method onTouchEvent (Fig. 5.37) is called when the View receives a touch event. Android supports *multitouch*—that is, having multiple fingers touching the screen. At any time, the user can touch the screen with more fingers or remove fingers from the screen. For this reason, each finger—known as a *pointer*—has a unique ID that identifies it across touch events. We'll use that ID to locate the corresponding Path objects that represent each line currently being drawn. These Paths are stored in pathMap.

```
99      // handle touch event
100     @Override
101     public boolean onTouchEvent(MotionEvent event) {
102         int action = event.getActionMasked(); // event type
103         int actionIndex = event.getActionIndex(); // pointer (i.e., finger)
104
105         // determine whether touch started, ended or is moving
106         if (action == MotionEvent.ACTION_DOWN ||
107             action == MotionEvent.ACTION_POINTER_DOWN) {
108             touchStarted(event.getX(actionIndex), event.getY(actionIndex),
109                 event.getPointerId(actionIndex));
110         }
111         else if (action == MotionEvent.ACTION_UP ||
112             action == MotionEvent.ACTION_POINTER_UP) {
113             touchEnded(event.getPointerId(actionIndex));
114         }
115         else {
116             touchMoved(event);
117         }
118
119         invalidate(); // redraw
120         return true;
121     }
122
```

Fig. 5.37 | Overridden View method onTouchEvent.

MotionEvent's **getActionMasked** method (line 102) returns an int representing the MotionEvent type, which you can use with constants from class MotionEvent to determine how to handle each event. MotionEvent's **getActionIndex** method (line 103) returns an integer index representing which finger caused the event. This index is *not* the finger's unique ID—it's simply the index at which that finger's information is located in this MotionEvent object. To get the finger's unique ID that persists across MotionEvents until the user removes that finger from the screen, we'll use MotionEvent's **getPointerID** method (lines 109 and 113), passing the finger index as an argument.

If the action is MotionEvent.ACTION_DOWN or MotionEvent.ACTION_POINTER_DOWN (lines 106–107), the user *touched the screen with a new finger*. The first finger to touch the screen generates a MotionEvent.ACTION_DOWN event, and all other fingers generate MotionEvent.ACTION_POINTER_DOWN events. For these cases, we call the touchStarted method (Fig. 5.38) to store the initial coordinates of the touch. If the action is Motion-Event.ACTION_UP or MotionEvent.ACTION_POINTER_UP, the user *removed a finger from the screen*, so we call method touchEnded (Fig. 5.40) to draw the completed Path to the bitmap so that we have a permanent record of that Path. For all other touch events, we call method touchMoved (Fig. 5.39) to draw the lines. After the event is processed, line 119 (of Fig. 5.37) calls the inherited View method invalidate to redraw the screen, and line 120 returns true to indicate that the event has been processed.

5.8.8 touchStarted Method

The touchStarted method (Fig. 5.38) is called when a finger first *touches* the screen. The coordinates of the touch and its ID are supplied as arguments. If a Path already exists for the given ID (line 129), we call Path's **reset** method to *clear* any existing points so we can *reuse* the Path for a new stroke. Otherwise, we create a new Path, add it to pathMap, then add a new Point to the previousPointMap. Lines 142–144 call Path's **moveTo** method to set the Path's starting coordinates and specify the new Point's x and y values.

```
123    // called when the user touches the screen
124    private void touchStarted(float x, float y, int lineID) {
125        Path path; // used to store the path for the given touch id
126        Point point; // used to store the last point in path
127
128        // if there is already a path for lineID
129        if (pathMap.containsKey(lineID)) {
130            path = pathMap.get(lineID); // get the Path
131            path.reset(); // resets the Path because a new touch has started
132            point = previousPointMap.get(lineID); // get Path's last point
133        }
134        else {
135            path = new Path();
136            pathMap.put(lineID, path); // add the Path to Map
137            point = new Point(); // create a new Point
138            previousPointMap.put(lineID, point); // add the Point to the Map
139        }
140
141        // move to the coordinates of the touch
142        path.moveTo(x, y);
```

Fig. 5.38 | touchStarted method of class DoodleView. (Part 1 of 2.)

```
143        point.x = (int) x;
144        point.y = (int) y;
145    }
146
```

Fig. 5.38 | touchStarted method of class DoodleView. (Part 2 of 2.)

5.8.9 touchMoved Method

The touchMoved method (Fig. 5.39) is called when the user moves one or more fingers across the screen. The system MotionEvent passed from onTouchEvent contains touch information for multiple moves on the screen if they occur at the same time. MotionEvent method **getPointerCount** (line 150) returns the number of touches this MotionEvent describes. For each, we store the finger's ID (line 152) in pointerID, and store the finger's corresponding index in this MotionEvent (line 153) in pointerIndex. Then we check whether there's a corresponding Path in pathMap (line 156). If so, we use MotionEvent's getX and getY methods to get the last coordinates for this *drag* event for the specified pointerIndex. We get the corresponding Path and last Point for the pointerID from each respective HashMap, then calculate the difference between the last point and the current point—we want to update the Path *only* if the user has moved a distance that's greater than our TOUCH_TOLERANCE constant. We do this because many devices are sensitive enough to generate MotionEvents indicating small movements when the user is attempting to hold a finger motionless on the screen. If the user moved a finger further than the TOUCH_TOLERANCE, we use Path's **quadTo** method (lines 173–174) to add a geometric curve (specifically a *quadratic Bezier curve*) from the previous Point to the new Point. We then update the most recent Point for that finger.

```
147        // called when the user drags along the screen
148        private void touchMoved(MotionEvent event) {
149            // for each of the pointers in the given MotionEvent
150            for (int i = 0; i < event.getPointerCount(); i++) {
151                // get the pointer ID and pointer index
152                int pointerID = event.getPointerId(i);
153                int pointerIndex = event.findPointerIndex(pointerID);
154
155                // if there is a path associated with the pointer
156                if (pathMap.containsKey(pointerID)) {
157                    // get the new coordinates for the pointer
158                    float newX = event.getX(pointerIndex);
159                    float newY = event.getY(pointerIndex);
160
161                    // get the path and previous point associated with
162                    // this pointer
163                    Path path = pathMap.get(pointerID);
164                    Point point = previousPointMap.get(pointerID);
165
```

Fig. 5.39 | touchMoved method of class DoodleView. (Part 1 of 2.)

```
166                    // calculate how far the user moved from the last update
167                    float deltaX = Math.abs(newX - point.x);
168                    float deltaY = Math.abs(newY - point.y);
169
170                    // if the distance is significant enough to matter
171                    if (deltaX >= TOUCH_TOLERANCE || deltaY >= TOUCH_TOLERANCE) {
172                       // move the path to the new location
173                       path.quadTo(point.x, point.y, (newX + point.x) / 2,
174                          (newY + point.y) / 2);
175
176                       // store the new coordinates
177                       point.x = (int) newX;
178                       point.y = (int) newY;
179                    }
180                 }
181              }
182           }
183
```

Fig. 5.39 | touchMoved method of class DoodleView. (Part 2 of 2.)

5.8.10 touchEnded Method

The touchEnded method (Fig. 5.40) is called when the user lifts a finger from the screen. The method receives the ID of the finger (lineID) for which the touch just ended as an argument. Line 186 gets the corresponding Path. Line 187 calls the bitmapCanvas's draw-Path method to draw the Path on the Bitmap object named bitmap before we call Path's reset method to clear the Path. Resetting the Path does not erase its corresponding painted line from the screen, because those lines have already been drawn to the bitmap that's displayed to the screen. The lines that are currently being drawn by the user are displayed on top of that bitmap.

```
184    // called when the user finishes a touch
185    private void touchEnded(int lineID) {
186       Path path = pathMap.get(lineID); // get the corresponding Path
187       bitmapCanvas.drawPath(path, paintLine); // draw to bitmapCanvas
188       path.reset(); // reset the Path
189    }
190
```

Fig. 5.40 | touchEnded method of class DoodleView.

5.8.11 Method saveImage

Method saveImage (Fig. 5.41) saves the current drawing. Line 194 creates a filename for the image, then lines 197–199 store the image in the device's **Photos** app by calling class MediaStore.Images.Media's insertImage method. The method receives four arguments:

- a ContentResolver that the method uses to locate where the image should be stored on the device
- the Bitmap to store

- the name of the image

- a description of the image

Method `insertImage` returns a `String` representing the image's location on the device, or null if the image could not be saved. Lines 201–217 check whether the image was saved and display an appropriate `Toast`.

```
191    // save the current image to the Gallery
192    public void saveImage() {
193        // use "Doodlz" followed by current time as the image name
194        final String name = "Doodlz" + System.currentTimeMillis() + ".jpg";
195
196        // insert the image on the device
197        String location = MediaStore.Images.Media.insertImage(
198            getContext().getContentResolver(), bitmap, name,
199            "Doodlz Drawing");
200
201        if (location != null) {
202            // display a message indicating that the image was saved
203            Toast message = Toast.makeText(getContext(),
204                R.string.message_saved,
205                Toast.LENGTH_SHORT);
206            message.setGravity(Gravity.CENTER, message.getXOffset() / 2,
207                message.getYOffset() / 2);
208            message.show();
209        }
210        else {
211            // display a message indicating that there was an error saving
212            Toast message = Toast.makeText(getContext(),
213                R.string.message_error_saving, Toast.LENGTH_SHORT);
214            message.setGravity(Gravity.CENTER, message.getXOffset() / 2,
215                message.getYOffset() / 2);
216            message.show();
217        }
218    }
219
```

Fig. 5.41 | `DoodleView` method `saveImage`.

5.8.12 Method `printImage`

Method `printImage` (Fig. 5.42) uses the Android Support Library's `PrintHelper` class to print the current drawing—this is available only on devices running Android 4.4 or higher. Line 222 first confirms that printing support is available on the device. If so, line 224 creates a `PrintHelper` object. Next, line 227 specifies the image's *scale mode*—`PrintHelper.SCALE_MODE_FIT` indicates that the image should fit within the printable area of the paper. There's also the scale mode `PrintHelper.SCALE_MODE_FILL`, which causes the image to fill the paper, possibly cutting off a portion of the image. Finally, line 228 calls `PrintHelper` method **printBitmap**, passing as arguments the print job name (used by the printer to identify the print) and the `Bitmap` containing the image to print. This displays Android's print dialog, which allows the user to choose whether to save the image as a PDF document on the device or to print it to an available printer.

```
220      // print the current image
221      public void printImage() {
222         if (PrintHelper.systemSupportsPrint()) {
223            // use Android Support Library's PrintHelper to print image
224            PrintHelper printHelper = new PrintHelper(getContext());
225
226            // fit image in page bounds and print the image
227            printHelper.setScaleMode(PrintHelper.SCALE_MODE_FIT);
228            printHelper.printBitmap("Doodlz Image", bitmap);
229         }
230         else {
231            // display message indicating that system does not allow printing
232            Toast message = Toast.makeText(getContext(),
233               R.string.message_error_printing, Toast.LENGTH_SHORT);
234            message.setGravity(Gravity.CENTER, message.getXOffset() / 2,
235               message.getYOffset() / 2);
236            message.show();
237         }
238      }
239   }
```

Fig. 5.42 | DoodleView method printImage.

5.9 ColorDialogFragment Class

Class ColorDialogFragment (Figs. 5.43–5.47) extends DialogFragment to create an AlertDialog for setting the drawing color. The class's instance variables (lines 18–23) are used to reference the GUI controls for selecting the new color, displaying a preview of it and storing the color as a 32-bit int value that represents the color's ARGB values.

```
1   // ColorDialogFragment.java
2   // Allows user to set the drawing color on the DoodleView
3   package com.deitel.doodlz;
4
5   import android.app.Activity;
6   import android.app.AlertDialog;
7   import android.app.Dialog;
8   import android.content.DialogInterface;
9   import android.graphics.Color;
10  import android.os.Bundle;
11  import android.support.v4.app.DialogFragment;
12  import android.view.View;
13  import android.widget.SeekBar;
14  import android.widget.SeekBar.OnSeekBarChangeListener;
15
16  // class for the Select Color dialog
17  public class ColorDialogFragment extends DialogFragment {
18     private SeekBar alphaSeekBar;
19     private SeekBar redSeekBar;
```

Fig. 5.43 | ColorDialogFragment's package statement, import statements and instance variables. (Part 1 of 2.)

```
20       private SeekBar greenSeekBar;
21       private SeekBar blueSeekBar;
22       private View colorView;
23       private int color;
24
```

Fig. 5.43 | ColorDialogFragment's package statement, import statements and instance variables. (Part 2 of 2.)

5.9.1 Overridden DialogFragment Method onCreateDialog

Method onCreateDialog (Fig. 5.44) inflates the custom View (lines 31–32) defined by fragment_color.xml containing the GUI for selecting a color, then attaches that View to the AlertDialog by calling AlertDialog.Builder's setView method (line 33). Lines 39–47 get references to the dialog's SeekBars and colorView. Next, lines 50–53 register colorChangedListener (Fig. 5.47) as the listener for the SeekBars' events.

```
25       // create an AlertDialog and return it
26       @Override
27       public Dialog onCreateDialog(Bundle bundle) {
28          // create dialog
29          AlertDialog.Builder builder =
30             new AlertDialog.Builder(getActivity());
31          View colorDialogView = getActivity().getLayoutInflater().inflate(
32             R.layout.fragment_color, null);
33          builder.setView(colorDialogView); // add GUI to dialog
34
35          // set the AlertDialog's message
36          builder.setTitle(R.string.title_color_dialog);
37
38          // get the color SeekBars and set their onChange listeners
39          alphaSeekBar = (SeekBar) colorDialogView.findViewById(
40             R.id.alphaSeekBar);
41          redSeekBar = (SeekBar) colorDialogView.findViewById(
42             R.id.redSeekBar);
43          greenSeekBar = (SeekBar) colorDialogView.findViewById(
44             R.id.greenSeekBar);
45          blueSeekBar = (SeekBar) colorDialogView.findViewById(
46             R.id.blueSeekBar);
47          colorView = colorDialogView.findViewById(R.id.colorView);
48
49          // register SeekBar event listeners
50          alphaSeekBar.setOnSeekBarChangeListener(colorChangedListener);
51          redSeekBar.setOnSeekBarChangeListener(colorChangedListener);
52          greenSeekBar.setOnSeekBarChangeListener(colorChangedListener);
53          blueSeekBar.setOnSeekBarChangeListener(colorChangedListener);
54
55          // use current drawing color to set SeekBar values
56          final DoodleView doodleView = getDoodleFragment().getDoodleView();
57          color = doodleView.getDrawingColor();
```

Fig. 5.44 | Overridden DialogFragment method onCreateDialog. (Part 1 of 2.)

```
58        alphaSeekBar.setProgress(Color.alpha(color));
59        redSeekBar.setProgress(Color.red(color));
60        greenSeekBar.setProgress(Color.green(color));
61        blueSeekBar.setProgress(Color.blue(color));
62
63        // add Set Color Button
64        builder.setPositiveButton(R.string.button_set_color,
65           new DialogInterface.OnClickListener() {
66              public void onClick(DialogInterface dialog, int id) {
67                 doodleView.setDrawingColor(color);
68              }
69           }
70        );
71
72        return builder.create(); // return dialog
73     }
74
```

Fig. 5.44 | Overridden DialogFragment method onCreateDialog. (Part 2 of 2.)

Line 56 (Fig. 5.44) calls method getDoodleFragment (Fig. 5.45) to get a reference to the DoodleFragment, then calls the MainActivityFragment's getDoodleView method to get the DoodleView. Lines 57–61 get the DoodleView's current drawing color, then use it to set each SeekBar's value. Color's static methods **alpha**, **red**, **green** and **blue** extract the ARGB values from the color, and SeekBar's setProgress method positions the thumbs. Lines 64–70 configure the AlertDialog's positive button to set the DoodleView's new drawing color. Line 72 returns the AlertDialog.

5.9.2 Method getDoodleFragment

Method getDoodleFragment (Fig. 5.45) simply uses the FragmentManager to get a reference to the DoodleFragment.

```
75     // gets a reference to the MainActivityFragment
76     private MainActivityFragment getDoodleFragment() {
77        return (MainActivityFragment) getFragmentManager().findFragmentById(
78           R.id.doodleFragment);
79     }
80
```

Fig. 5.45 | Method getDoodleFragment.

5.9.3 Overridden Fragment Lifecycle Methods onAttach and onDetach

When the ColorDialogFragment is added to a parent Activity, method onAttach (Fig. 5.46, lines 82–89) is called. Line 85 gets a reference to the MainActivityFragment. If that reference is not null, line 88 calls MainActivityFragment's setDialogOnScreen method to indicate that the **Choose Color** dialog is now displayed. When the ColorDialogFragment is removed from a parent Activity, method onDetach (lines 92–99) is called. Line 98 calls MainActivityFragment's setDialogOnScreen method to indicate that the **Choose Color** dialog is no longer on the screen.

```
81      // tell MainActivityFragment that dialog is now displayed
82      @Override
83      public void onAttach(Activity activity) {
84          super.onAttach(activity);
85          MainActivityFragment fragment = getDoodleFragment();
86
87          if (fragment != null)
88              fragment.setDialogOnScreen(true);
89      }
90
91      // tell MainActivityFragment that dialog is no longer displayed
92      @Override
93      public void onDetach() {
94          super.onDetach();
95          MainActivityFragment fragment = getDoodleFragment();
96
97          if (fragment != null)
98              fragment.setDialogOnScreen(false);
99      }
100
```

Fig. 5.46 | Overridden Fragment lifecycle methods onAttach and onDetach.

5.9.4 Anonymous Inner Class That Responds to the Events of the Alpha, Red, Green and Blue SeekBars

Figure 5.47 defines an anonymous inner class that implements interface OnSeekBar-ChangeListener to respond to events when the user adjusts the SeekBars in the **Choose Color** Dialog. This was registered as the SeekBars' event handler in Fig. 5.44 (lines 50–53). Method onProgressChanged (Fig. 5.47, lines 105–114) is called when the position of a SeekBar's thumb changes. If the user moved a SeekBar's thumb (line 109), lines 110–112 store the new color. Class Color's static method **argb** combines the SeekBars' values into a Color and returns the appropriate color as an int. We then use class View's **set-BackgroundColor** method to update the colorView with a color that matches the current state of the SeekBars.

```
101     // OnSeekBarChangeListener for the SeekBars in the color dialog
102     private final OnSeekBarChangeListener colorChangedListener =
103         new OnSeekBarChangeListener() {
104             // display the updated color
105             @Override
106             public void onProgressChanged(SeekBar seekBar, int progress,
107                 boolean fromUser) {
108
```

Fig. 5.47 | Anonymous inner class that implements interface OnSeekBarChangeListener to respond to the events of the alpha, red, green and blue SeekBars. (Part 1 of 2.)

```
109                  if (fromUser) // user, not program, changed SeekBar progress
110                     color = Color.argb(alphaSeekBar.getProgress(),
111                        redSeekBar.getProgress(), greenSeekBar.getProgress(),
112                        blueSeekBar.getProgress());
113                  colorView.setBackgroundColor(color);
114               }
115
116               @Override
117               public void onStartTrackingTouch(SeekBar seekBar) {} // required
118
119               @Override
120               public void onStopTrackingTouch(SeekBar seekBar) {} // required
121            };
122      }
```

Fig. 5.47 | Anonymous inner class that implements interface OnSeekBarChangeListener to respond to the events of the alpha, red, green and blue SeekBars. (Part 2 of 2.)

5.10 LineWidthDialogFragment Class

Class LineWidthDialogFragment (Fig. 5.48) extends DialogFragment to create an Alert-Dialog for setting the line width. The class is similar to class ColorDialogFragment, so we discuss only the key differences here. The class's only instance variable is an ImageView (line 21) in which we draw a line showing the current line-width setting.

```
1    // LineWidthDialogFragment.java
2    // Allows user to set the drawing color on the DoodleView
3    package com.deitel.doodlz;
4
5    import android.app.Activity;
6    import android.app.AlertDialog;
7    import android.app.Dialog;
8    import android.content.DialogInterface;
9    import android.graphics.Bitmap;
10   import android.graphics.Canvas;
11   import android.graphics.Paint;
12   import android.os.Bundle;
13   import android.support.v4.app.DialogFragment;
14   import android.view.View;
15   import android.widget.ImageView;
16   import android.widget.SeekBar;
17   import android.widget.SeekBar.OnSeekBarChangeListener;
18
19   // class for the Select Line Width dialog
20   public class LineWidthDialogFragment extends DialogFragment {
21      private ImageView widthImageView;
22
```

Fig. 5.48 | Class LineWidthDialogFragment. (Part 1 of 3.)

```
23      // create an AlertDialog and return it
24      @Override
25      public Dialog onCreateDialog(Bundle bundle) {
26         // create the dialog
27         AlertDialog.Builder builder =
28            new AlertDialog.Builder(getActivity());
29         View lineWidthDialogView =
30            getActivity().getLayoutInflater().inflate(
31               R.layout.fragment_line_width, null);
32         builder.setView(lineWidthDialogView); // add GUI to dialog
33
34         // set the AlertDialog's message
35         builder.setTitle(R.string.title_line_width_dialog);
36
37         // get the ImageView
38         widthImageView = (ImageView) lineWidthDialogView.findViewById(
39            R.id.widthImageView);
40
41         // configure widthSeekBar
42         final DoodleView doodleView = getDoodleFragment().getDoodleView();
43         final SeekBar widthSeekBar = (SeekBar)
44            lineWidthDialogView.findViewById(R.id.widthSeekBar);
45         widthSeekBar.setOnSeekBarChangeListener(lineWidthChanged);
46         widthSeekBar.setProgress(doodleView.getLineWidth());
47
48         // add Set Line Width Button
49         builder.setPositiveButton(R.string.button_set_line_width,
50            new DialogInterface.OnClickListener() {
51               public void onClick(DialogInterface dialog, int id) {
52                  doodleView.setLineWidth(widthSeekBar.getProgress());
53               }
54            }
55         );
56
57         return builder.create(); // return dialog
58      }
59
60      // return a reference to the MainActivityFragment
61      private MainActivityFragment getDoodleFragment() {
62         return (MainActivityFragment) getFragmentManager().findFragmentById(
63            R.id.doodleFragment);
64      }
65
66      // tell MainActivityFragment that dialog is now displayed
67      @Override
68      public void onAttach(Activity activity) {
69         super.onAttach(activity);
70         MainActivityFragment fragment = getDoodleFragment();
71
72         if (fragment != null)
73            fragment.setDialogOnScreen(true);
74      }
```

Fig. 5.48 | Class LineWidthDialogFragment. (Part 2 of 3.)

```
75
76      // tell MainActivityFragment that dialog is no longer displayed
77      @Override
78      public void onDetach() {
79         super.onDetach();
80         MainActivityFragment fragment = getDoodleFragment();
81
82         if (fragment != null)
83            fragment.setDialogOnScreen(false);
84      }
85
86      // OnSeekBarChangeListener for the SeekBar in the width dialog
87      private final OnSeekBarChangeListener lineWidthChanged =
88         new OnSeekBarChangeListener() {
89            final Bitmap bitmap = Bitmap.createBitmap(
90               400, 100, Bitmap.Config.ARGB_8888);
91            final Canvas canvas = new Canvas(bitmap); // draws into bitmap
92
93            @Override
94            public void onProgressChanged(SeekBar seekBar, int progress,
95               boolean fromUser) {
96               // configure a Paint object for the current SeekBar value
97               Paint p = new Paint();
98               p.setColor(
99                  getDoodleFragment().getDoodleView().getDrawingColor());
100              p.setStrokeCap(Paint.Cap.ROUND);
101              p.setStrokeWidth(progress);
102
103              // erase the bitmap and redraw the line
104              bitmap.eraseColor(
105                 getResources().getColor(android.R.color.transparent,
106                    getContext().getTheme()));
107              canvas.drawLine(30, 50, 370, 50, p);
108              widthImageView.setImageBitmap(bitmap);
109           }
110
111           @Override
112           public void onStartTrackingTouch(SeekBar seekBar) {} // required
113
114           @Override
115           public void onStopTrackingTouch(SeekBar seekBar) {} // required
116        };
117 }
```

Fig. 5.48 | Class LineWidthDialogFragment. (Part 3 of 3.)

5.10.1 Method onCreateDialog

Method onCreateDialog (lines 24–58) inflates the custom View (lines 29–31) defined by fragment_line_width.xml that displays the GUI for selecting the line width, then attaches that View to the AlertDialog by calling AlertDialog.Builder's setView method (line 32). Lines 38–39 get a reference to the ImageView in which the sample line will be drawn. Next, lines 42–46 get a reference to the widthSeekBar, register lineWidthChanged (lines 87–116) as the SeekBar's listener and set the SeekBar's current value to the current line width. Lines 49–55 define the dialog's positive button to call the DoodleView's setLine-Width method when the user touches the **Set Line Width** button. Line 57 returns the AlertDialog for display.

5.10.2 Anonymous Inner Class That Responds to the Events of the widthSeekBar

Lines 87–116 define the lineWidthChanged OnSeekBarChangeListener that responds to events when the user adjusts the SeekBar in the **Choose Line Width** dialog. Lines 89–90 create a Bitmap on which to display a sample line representing the selected line thickness. Line 91 creates a Canvas for drawing on the Bitmap. Method onProgressChanged (lines 93–109) draws the sample line based on the current drawing color and the SeekBar's value. First, lines 97–101 configure a Paint object for drawing the sample line. Class Paint's setStrokeCap method (line 100) specifies the appearance of the line ends—in this case, they're rounded (Paint.Cap.ROUND). Lines 104–106 clear bitmap's background to the predefined Android color android.R.color.transparent with Bitmap method eraseColor. We use canvas to draw the sample line. Finally, line 108 displays bitmap in the widthImageView by passing it to ImageView's setImageBitmap method.

5.11 EraseImageDialogFragment Class

Class EraseImageDialogFragment (Fig. 5.49) extends DialogFragment to create an AlertDialog that confirms whether the user really wants to erase the entire image. The class is similar to class ColorDialogFragment and LineWidthDialogFragment, so we discuss only method onCreateDialog (lines 15–35) here. The method creates an AlertDialog with **Erase Image** and **Cancel** button. Lines 24–30 configure the **Erase Image** button as the positive button—when the user touches this, line 27 in the button's listener calls the DoodleView's clear method to erase the image. Line 33 configures **Cancel** as the negative button—when the user touches this, the dialog is dismissed. In this case, we use the predefined Android String resource android.R.string.cancel. For other predefined String resources, visit

http://developer.android.com/reference/android/R.string.html

Line 34 returns the AlertDialog.

```
 1   // EraseImageDialogFragment.java
 2   // Allows user to erase image
 3   package com.deitel.doodlz;
 4
 5   import android.app.Activity;
 6   import android.app.AlertDialog;
 7   import android.app.Dialog;
 8   import android.support.v4.app.DialogFragment;
 9   import android.content.DialogInterface;
10   import android.os.Bundle;
11
```

Fig. 5.49 | Class EraseImageDialogFragment. (Part 1 of 2.)

```
12  // class for the Erase Image dialog
13  public class EraseImageDialogFragment extends DialogFragment {
14     // create an AlertDialog and return it
15     @Override
16     public Dialog onCreateDialog(Bundle bundle) {
17        AlertDialog.Builder builder =
18           new AlertDialog.Builder(getActivity());
19
20        // set the AlertDialog's message
21        builder.setMessage(R.string.message_erase);
22
23        // add Erase Button
24        builder.setPositiveButton(R.string.button_erase,
25           new DialogInterface.OnClickListener() {
26              public void onClick(DialogInterface dialog, int id) {
27                 getDoodleFragment().getDoodleView().clear(); // clear image
28              }
29           }
30        );
31
32        // add cancel Button
33        builder.setNegativeButton(android.R.string.cancel, null);
34        return builder.create(); // return dialog
35     }
36
37     // gets a reference to the MainActivityFragment
38     private MainActivityFragment getDoodleFragment() {
39        return (MainActivityFragment) getFragmentManager().findFragmentById(
40           R.id.doodleFragment);
41     }
42
43     // tell MainActivityFragment that dialog is now displayed
44     @Override
45     public void onAttach(Activity activity) {
46        super.onAttach(activity);
47        MainActivityFragment fragment = getDoodleFragment();
48
49        if (fragment != null)
50           fragment.setDialogOnScreen(true);
51     }
52
53     // tell MainActivityFragment that dialog is no longer displayed
54     @Override
55     public void onDetach() {
56        super.onDetach();
57        MainActivityFragment fragment = getDoodleFragment();
58
59        if (fragment != null)
60           fragment.setDialogOnScreen(false);
61     }
62  }
```

Fig. 5.49 | Class EraseImageDialogFragment. (Part 2 of 2.)

5.12 Wrap-Up

In this chapter, you built the **Doodlz** app, which enables users to paint by dragging one or more fingers across the screen. You implemented a shake-to-erase feature by using Android's SensorManager to register a SensorEventListener that responds to accelerometer events, and you learned that Android supports many other sensors.

You created subclasses of DialogFragment for displaying custom Views in AlertDialogs. You also overrode the Fragment lifecycle methods onAttach and onDetach, which are called when a Fragment is attached to or detached from a parent Activity, respectively.

We showed how to associate a Canvas with a Bitmap, then use the Canvas to draw into the Bitmap. We demonstrated how to handle multitouch events, so the app could respond to multiple fingers being dragged across the screen at the same time. You stored the information for each individual finger as a Path. You processed the touch events by overriding the View method onTouchEvent, which receives a MotionEvent containing the event type and the ID of the pointer (finger) that generated the event. We used the IDs to distinguish among the fingers and add information to the corresponding Path objects.

You used a ContentResolver and the MediaStore.Images.Media.insertImage method to save an image onto the device. To enable this feature, you used Android 6.0's new permissions model to request permission from the user to save to external storage.

We showed how to use the printing framework to allow users to print their drawings. You used the Android Support Library's PrintHelper class to print a Bitmap. The PrintHelper displayed a user interface for selecting a printer or saving the image into a PDF document. To incorporate Android Support Library features into the app, you used Gradle to specify the app's dependency on features from that library.

In Chapter 6, you'll create a **Cannon Game** using multithreading and frame-by-frame animation. You'll handle touch gestures to fire a cannon. You'll also learn how to create a game loop that updates the display as fast as possible to create smooth animations and to make the game feel like it executes at the same speed regardless of a given device's processor speed.

Cannon Game App

Manual Frame-By-Frame Animation, Graphics, Sound, Threading, SurfaceView and SurfaceHolder, Immersive Mode and Full-Screen

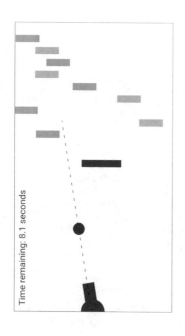

Time remaining: 8.1 seconds

Objectives

In this chapter you'll:

- Create a simple game app that's easy to code and fun to play.

- Create a custom SurfaceView subclass for displaying the game's graphics from a separate thread of execution.

- Draw graphics using Paints and a Canvas.

- Override View's onTouchEvent method to fire a cannonball when the user touches the screen.

- Perform simple collision detection.

- Add sound to your app using a SoundPool and the AudioManager.

- Override Fragment lifecycle method onDestroy.

- Use immersive mode to enable the game to occupy the entire screen, but still allow the user to access the system bars.

6.1 Introduction

The **Cannon Game**[1] app challenges you to destroy nine targets before a ten-second time limit expires (Fig. 6.1). The game consists of four types of visual components—a *cannon* that you control, a *cannonball*, nine *targets* and a *blocker* that defends the targets. You aim

---

1. We'd like to thank Prof. Hugues Bersini—author of a French-language object-oriented programming book for Éditions Eyrolles, Secteur Informatique—for sharing with us his suggested refactoring of our original **Cannon Game** app. We used this as inspiration for our own refactoring in the latest versions of this app in this book and *iOS® 8 for Programmers: An App-Driven Approach*.

and fire the cannon by *touching* the screen—the cannon then aims at the touched point and fires the cannonball in a straight line in that direction.

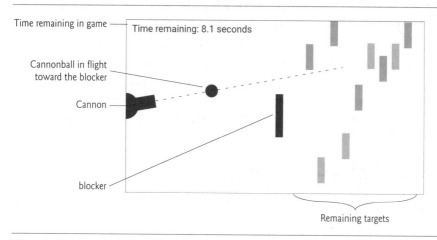

Fig. 6.1 | Completed **Cannon Game** app.

Each time you destroy a target, a three-second time bonus is *added* to your remaining time, and each time you hit the blocker, a two-second time penalty is *subtracted* from your remaining time. You win by destroying all nine target sections before you run out of time—if the timer reaches zero, you lose. At the end of the game, the app displays an AlertDialog indicating whether you won or lost, and shows the number of shots fired and the elapsed time (Fig. 6.2).

Fig. 6.2 | **Cannon Game** app AlertDialogs showing a win and a loss.

When you fire the cannon, the game plays a *firing sound*. When a cannonball hits a target, a *glass-breaking sound* plays and that target disappears. When the cannonball hits the blocker, a *hit sound* plays and the cannonball bounces back. The blocker cannot be destroyed. Each of the targets and the blocker move *vertically* at different speeds, changing direction when they hit the top or bottom of the screen.

[*Note:* The Android Emulator performs slowly on some computers. For the best experience, you should test this app on an Android device. On a slow emulator, the cannonball will sometimes appear to pass through the blocker or targets.]

6.2 Test-Driving the Cannon Game App

Opening and Running the App

Open Android Studio and open the **Cannon Game** app from the CannonGame folder in the book's examples folder, then execute the app in the AVD or on a device. This builds the project and runs the app.

Playing the Game

Tap the screen to aim and fire the cannon. You can fire a cannonball only if there is not another cannonball on the screen. If you're running on an AVD, the mouse is your "finger." Destroy all of the targets as fast as you can—the game ends if the timer runs out or you destroy all nine targets.

6.3 Technologies Overview

This section presents the new technologies that we use in the **Cannon Game** app in the order they're encountered in the chapter.

6.3.1 Using the Resource Folder res/raw

Media files, such as the sounds used in the **Cannon Game** app, are placed in the app's resource folder **res/raw**. Section 6.4.5 discusses how to create this folder. You'll copy the app's sound files into it.

6.3.2 Activity and Fragment Lifecycle Methods

We introduced Activity and Fragment lifecycle methods in Section 5.3.1. This app uses Fragment lifecycle method onDestroy. When an Activity is shut down, its **onDestroy** method is called, which in turn calls the **onDestroy** methods of all the Fragments hosted by the Activity. We use this method in the MainActivityFragment to release the CannonView's sound resources.

Error-Prevention Tip 6.1

Method onDestroy is not guaranteed to be called, so it should be used only to release resources, not to save data. The Android documentation recommends that you save data in methods onPause or onSaveInstanceState.

6.3.3 Overriding View Method onTouchEvent

Users interact with this app by touching the device's screen. A touch aligns the cannon to face the touch point on the screen, then fires the cannon. To process simple touch events for the CannonView, you'll override View method **onTouchEvent** (Section 6.13.14), then use constants from class MotionEvent (package android.view) to test which type of event occurred and process it accordingly.

6.3.4 Adding Sound with SoundPool and AudioManager

An app's sound effects are managed with a SoundPool (package android.media), which can be used to *load*, *play* and *unload* sounds. Sounds are played using one of Android's audio streams for *alarms*, *music*, *notifications*, *phone rings*, *system sounds*, *phone calls* and more. You'll configure and create a `SoundPool` object using a `SoundPool.Builder` object. You'll also use an `AudioAttributes.Builder` object to create an `AudioAttributes` object that will be associated with the `SoundPool`. We call the `AudioAttributes`'s `setUsage` method to designate the audio as game audio. The Android documentation recommends that games use the *music audio stream* to play sounds, because that stream's volume can be controlled via the device's volume buttons. In addition, we use the `Activity`'s `setVolume-ControlStream` method to allow the game's volume to be controlled with the device's volume buttons. The method receives a constant from class `AudioManager` (package `android.media`), which provides access to the device's volume and phone-ringer controls.

6.3.5 Frame-by-Frame Animation with Threads, `SurfaceView` and `SurfaceHolder`

This app *performs its animations manually* by updating the game elements from a separate thread of execution. To do this, we use a subclass of `Thread` with a `run` method that directs our custom `CannonView` to update the positions of the game's elements, then draws them. The `run` method drives the *frame-by-frame animations*—this is known as the game loop.

All updates to an app's user interface must be performed in the GUI thread of execution, because GUI components are not thread safe—updates performed outside the GUI thread can corrupt the GUI. Games, however, often require complex logic that should be performed in separate threads of execution, and those threads often need to draw to the screen. For such cases, Android provides class `SurfaceView`—a subclass of `View` that provides a dedicated drawing area in which other threads can display graphics on the screen in a thread-safe manner.

> **Performance Tip 6.1**
> *It's important to minimize the amount of work you do in the GUI thread to ensure that the GUI remains responsive and does not display ANR (Application Not Responding) dialogs.*

You manipulate a `SurfaceView` via an object of class `SurfaceHolder`, which enables you to obtain a `Canvas` on which you can draw graphics. Class `SurfaceHolder` also provides methods that give a thread *exclusive access* to the `Canvas` for drawing—only one thread at a time can draw to a `SurfaceView`. Each `SurfaceView` subclass should implement the interface `SurfaceHolder.Callback`, which contains methods that are called when the `SurfaceView` is *created*, *changed* (e.g., its size or orientation changes) or *destroyed*.

6.3.6 Simple Collision Detection

The `CannonView` performs simple *collision detection* to determine whether the cannonball has collided with any of the `CannonView`'s edges, with the blocker or with a section of the target. These techniques are presented in Section 6.13.11.

Game-development frameworks typically provide more sophisticated "pixel-perfect" collision-detection capabilities. Many such frameworks are available (free and fee-based) for developing the simplest 2D games to the most complex 3D console-style games (such as games for Sony's PlayStation® and Microsoft's Xbox®). Figure 6.3 lists a few game-development frameworks—there are dozens more. Many support multiple platforms, including Android and iOS. Some require C++ or other programming languages.

Game-development frameworks

AndEngine—http://www.andengine.org
Cocos2D—http://code.google.com/p/cocos2d-android
GameMaker—http://www.yoyogames.com/studio
libgdx—https://libgdx.badlogicgames.com
Unity—http://www.unity3d.com
Unreal Engine—http://www.unrealengine.com

Fig. 6.3 | Game-development frameworks.

6.3.7 Immersive Mode

To immerse users in games, game developers often use full-screen themes, such as

```
Theme.Material.Light.NoActionBar.Fullscreen
```

that display only the bottom system bar. In landscape orientation on phones, that system bar appears at the screen's right edge.

In Android 4.4 (KitKat), Google added support for full-screen *immersive mode* (Section 6.13.16), which enables an app to take advantage of the entire screen. When an app is in immersive mode, the user can swipe down from the top of the screen to display the system bars temporarily. If the user does not interact with the system bars, they disappear after a few seconds.

6.4 Building the GUI and Resource Files

In this section, you'll create the app's resource files, GUI layout files and classes.

6.4.1 Creating the Project

For this app, you'll add a Fragment and its layout manually—much of the autogenerated code in the **Blank Activity** template with a Fragment is not needed in the **Cannon Game**. Create a new project using the **Empty Activity** template. In the **Create New Project** dialog's **New Project** step, specify

- **Application name:** Cannon Game
- **Company Domain:** deitel.com (or specify your own domain name)

In the layout editor, select **Nexus 6** from the virtual-device drop-down list (Fig. 2.11). Once again, we'll use this device as the basis for our design. Also, delete the **Hello world!** TextView from activity_main.xml. As you've done previously, add an app icon to your project.

Configure the App for Landscape Orientation
The **Cannon** game is designed for only landscape orientation. Follow the steps you performed in Section 3.7 to set the screen orientation, but this time set android:screenOrientation to landscape rather than portrait.

6.4.2 Adjusting the Theme to Remove the App Title and App Bar

As we noted in Section 6.3.7, game developers often use full-screen themes, such as

```
Theme.Material.Light.NoActionBar.Fullscreen
```

that display only the bottom system bar, which in landscape orientation appears at the screen's right edge. The AppCompat themes do not include a full-screen theme by default, but you can modify the app's theme to achieve this. To do so:

1. Open styles.xml.

2. Add the following lines to the <style> element:

```
<item name="windowNoTitle">true</item>
<item name="windowActionBar">false</item>
<item name="android:windowFullscreen">true</item>
```

The first line indicates that the title (usually the app's name) should not be displayed. The second indicates that the app bar should not be displayed. The last line indicates that the app should use the full screen.

6.4.3 strings.xml

You created String resources in earlier chapters, so we show here only a table of the String resource names and corresponding values (Fig. 6.4). Double click strings.xml in the res/values folder, then click the **Open editor** link to display the **Translations Editor** for creating these String resources.

Key	Value
results_format	Shots fired: %1$d\nTotal time: %2$.1f
reset_game	Reset Game
win	You win!
lose	You lose!
time_remaining_format	Time remaining: %.1f seconds

Fig. 6.4 | String resources used in the **Cannon Game** app.

6.4.4 Colors

This app draws targets of alternating colors on the Canvas. For this app, we added the following dark blue and yellow color resources to colors.xml:

```
<color name="dark">#1976D2</color>
<color name="light">#FFE100</color>
```

6.4.5 Adding the Sounds to the App

As we mentioned previously, sound files are stored in the app's res/raw folder. This app uses three sound files—blocker_hit.wav, target_hit.wav and cannon_fire.wav—which are located with the book's examples in the sounds folder. To add these files to your project:

1. Right click the app's res folder, then select **New > Android resource directory**, to open the **New Resource Directory** dialog

2. In the **Resource type** drop-down, select raw. The **Directory name** will automatically change to raw.

3. Click **OK** to create the folder.

4. Copy and paste the sound files into the res/raw folder. In the **Copy** dialog that appears, click **OK**.

6.4.6 Adding Class `MainActivityFragment`

Next, you'll add class `MainActivityFragment` to the project:

1. In the **Project** window, right click the **com.deitel.cannongame** node and select **New > Fragment > Fragment (Blank)**.

2. For **Fragment Name** specify `MainActivityFragment` and for **Fragment Layout Name** specify `fragment_main`.

3. Uncheck the checkboxes for **Include fragment factory methods?** and **Include interface callbacks?**

By default, `fragment_main.xml` contains a `FrameLayout` that displays a `TextView`. A `FrameLayout` is designed to display one `View`, but can also be used to layer views. Remove the `TextView`—in this app, the `FrameLayout` will display the `CannonView`.

6.4.7 Editing `activity_main.xml`

In this app, `MainActivity`'s layout displays only `MainActivityFragment`. Edit the layout as follows:

1. Open `activity_main.xml` in the layout editor and switch to the **Text** tab.

2. Change `RelativeLayout` to `fragment` and remove the padding properties so that the `fragment` element will fill the entire screen.

3. Switch to **Design** view, select **fragment** in the **Component Tree**, then set the **id** to `fragment`.

4. Set the **name** to `com.deitel.cannongame.MainActivityFragment`—rather than typing this, you can click the ellipsis button to the right of the **name** property's value field, then select the class from the **Fragments** dialog that appears.

Recall that the layout editor's **Design** view can show a preview of a fragment displayed in a particular layout. If you do not specify which fragment to preview in `MainActivity`'s layout, the layout editor displays a **"Rendering Problems"** message. To specify the fragment to preview, right click the fragment—either in **Design** view or in the **Component Tree** and click **Choose Preview Layout....** Then, in the **Resources** dialog, select the name of the fragment layout.

6.4.8 Adding the `CannonView` to `fragment_main.xml`

You'll now add the `CannonView` to `fragment_main.xml`. You first must create `CannonView.java`, so that you can select class `CannonView` when placing a **CustomView** in the layout. Follow these steps to create `CannonView.java` and add the `CannonView` to the layout:

1. Expand the java folder in the Project window.

2. Right click package com.deitel.cannongame's folder, then select **New > Java Class**.

3. In the **Create New Class** dialog that appears, enter CannonView in the **Name** field, then click **OK**. The file will open in the editor automatically.

4. In CannonView.java, indicate that CannonView extends SurfaceView. If the import statement for the android.view.SurfaceView class does not appear, place the cursor at the end of the class name SurfaceView. Click the red bulb menu (💡) that appears above the beginning of the line and select **Import Class**.

5. Place the cursor at the end of SurfaceView if you have not already done so. Click the red bulb menu that appears and select **Create constructor matching super**. Choose the two-argument constructor in the list in the **Choose Super Class Constructors** dialog that appears, then click **OK**. The IDE will add the constructor to the file automatically.

6. Switch back to fragment_main.xml's **Design** view in the layout editor.

7. Click **CustomView** in the **Custom** section of the **Palette**.

8. In the **Views** dialog that appears, select CannonView (com.deitel.cannongame), then click **OK**.

9. Hover over and click the FrameLayout in the **Component Tree**. The **view (Custom-View)**—which is a CannonView—should appear in the **Component Tree** within the FrameLayout.

10. Ensure that **view (CustomView)** is selected in the **Component Tree** window. In the **Properties** window, set **layout:width** and **layout:height** to match_parent.

11. In the **Properties** window, change the **id** from view to cannonView.

12. Save and close fragment_main.xml.

6.5 Overview of This App's Classes

This app consists of eight classes:

- MainActivity (the Activity subclass; Section 6.6)—Hosts the MainActivityFragment.

- MainActivityFragment (Section 6.7)—Displays the CannonView.

- GameElement (Section 6.8)—The superclass for items that move up and down (Blocker and Target) or across (Cannonball) the screen.

- Blocker (Section 6.9)—Represents a blocker, which makes destroying targets more challenging.

- Target (Section 6.10)—Represents a target that can be destroyed by a cannonball.

- Cannon (Section 6.11)—Represents the cannon, which fires a cannonball each time the user touches the screen.

- Cannonball (Section 6.12)—Represents a cannonball that the cannon fires when the user touches the screen.

- CannonView (Section 6.13)—Contains the game's logic and coordinates the behaviors of the Blocker, Targets, Cannonball and Cannon.

You must create the classes GameElement, Blocker, Target, Cannonball and Cannon. For each class, right click the package folder com.deitel.cannongame in the project's app/java folder and select **New > Java Class**. In the **Create New Class** dialog, enter the name of the class in the **Name** field and click **OK**.

6.6 MainActivity Subclass of Activity

Class MainActivity (Fig. 6.5) is the host for the **Cannon Game** app's MainActivityFragment. In this app, we override only the Activity method onCreate, which inflates the GUI. We deleted the autogenerated MainActivity methods that managed its menu, because the menu is not used in this app.

```
1   // MainActivity.java
2   // MainActivity displays the MainActivityFragment
3   package com.deitel.cannongame;
4
5   import android.support.v7.app.AppCompatActivity;
6   import android.os.Bundle;
7
8   public class MainActivity extends AppCompatActivity {
9      // called when the app first launches
10     @Override
11     protected void onCreate(Bundle savedInstanceState) {
12        super.onCreate(savedInstanceState);
13        setContentView(R.layout.activity_main);
14     }
15  }
```

Fig. 6.5 | MainActivity class displays the MainActivityFragment.

6.7 MainActivityFragment Subclass of Fragment

Class MainActivityFragment (Fig. 6.6) overrides four Fragment methods:

- onCreateView (lines 17–28)—As you learned in Section 4.3.3, this method is called after a Fragment's onCreate method to build and return a View containing the Fragment's GUI. Lines 22–23 inflate the GUI. Line 26 gets a reference to the MainActivityFragment's CannonView so that we can call its methods.

- onActivityCreated (lines 31–37)—This method is called after the Fragment's host Activity is created. Line 36 calls the Activity's setVolumeControlStream method to allow the game's volume to be controlled by the device's volume buttons. There are seven sound streams identified by AudioManager constants, but the music stream (AudioManager.STREAM_MUSIC) is recommended for sound in games, because this stream's volume can be controlled via the device's buttons.

- onPause (lines 40–44)—When the MainActivity is sent to the *background* (and thus, paused), MainActivityFragment's onPause method executes. Line 43 calls the CannonView's stopGame method (Section 6.13.12) to stop the game loop.

- onDestroy (lines 47–51)—When the MainActivity is destroyed, its onDestroy method calls MainActivityFragment's onDestroy. Line 50 calls the CannonView's releaseResources method to release the sound resources (Section 6.13.12).

```java
1  // MainActivityFragment.java
2  // MainActivityFragment creates and manages a CannonView
3  package com.deitel.cannongame;
4
5  import android.media.AudioManager;
6  import android.os.Bundle;
7  import android.support.v4.app.Fragment;
8  import android.view.LayoutInflater;
9  import android.view.View;
10 import android.view.ViewGroup;
11
12 public class MainActivityFragment extends Fragment {
13    private CannonView cannonView; // custom view to display the game
14
15    // called when Fragment's view needs to be created
16    @Override
17    public View onCreateView(LayoutInflater inflater, ViewGroup container,
18       Bundle savedInstanceState) {
19       super.onCreateView(inflater, container, savedInstanceState);
20
21       // inflate the fragment_main.xml layout
22       View view =
23          inflater.inflate(R.layout.fragment_main, container, false);
24
25       // get a reference to the CannonView
26       cannonView = (CannonView) view.findViewById(R.id.cannonView);
27       return view;
28    }
29
30    // set up volume control once Activity is created
31    @Override
32    public void onActivityCreated(Bundle savedInstanceState) {
33       super.onActivityCreated(savedInstanceState);
34
35       // allow volume buttons to set game volume
36       getActivity().setVolumeControlStream(AudioManager.STREAM_MUSIC);
37    }
38
39    // when MainActivity is paused, terminate the game
40    @Override
41    public void onPause() {
42       super.onPause();
43       cannonView.stopGame(); // terminates the game
44    }
45
46    // when MainActivity is paused, MainActivityFragment releases resources
47    @Override
48    public void onDestroy() {
```

Fig. 6.6 | MainActivityFragment creates and manages the CannonView. (Part 1 of 2.)

```
49          super.onDestroy();
50          cannonView.releaseResources();
51      }
52  }
```

Fig. 6.6 | MainActivityFragment creates and manages the CannonView. (Part 2 of 2.)

6.8 Class GameElement

Class GameElement (Fig. 6.7)—the superclass of the Blocker, Target and Cannonball—contains the common data and functionality of an object that moves in the **Cannon Game** app.

```
1   // GameElement.java
2   // Represents a rectangle-bounded game element
3   package com.deitel.cannongame;
4
5   import android.graphics.Canvas;
6   import android.graphics.Paint;
7   import android.graphics.Rect;
8
9   public class GameElement {
10      protected CannonView view; // the view that contains this GameElement
11      protected Paint paint = new Paint(); // Paint to draw this GameElement
12      protected Rect shape; // the GameElement's rectangular bounds
13      private float velocityY; // the vertical velocity of this GameElement
14      private int soundId; // the sound associated with this GameElement
15
16      // public constructor
17      public GameElement(CannonView view, int color, int soundId, int x,
18          int y, int width, int length, float velocityY) {
19          this.view = view;
20          paint.setColor(color);
21          shape = new Rect(x, y, x + width, y + length); // set bounds
22          this.soundId = soundId;
23          this.velocityY = velocityY;
24      }
25
26      // update GameElement position and check for wall collisions
27      public void update(double interval) {
28          // update vertical position
29          shape.offset(0, (int) (velocityY * interval));
30
31          // if this GameElement collides with the wall, reverse direction
32          if (shape.top < 0 && velocityY < 0 ||
33              shape.bottom > view.getScreenHeight() && velocityY > 0)
34              velocityY *= -1; // reverse this GameElement's velocity
35      }
36
```

Fig. 6.7 | GameElement class represents a rectangle-bounded game element. (Part 1 of 2.)

```
37       // draws this GameElement on the given Canvas
38       public void draw(Canvas canvas) {
39          canvas.drawRect(shape, paint);
40       }
41
42       // plays the sound that corresponds to this type of GameElement
43       public void playSound() {
44          view.playSound(soundId);
45       }
46    }
```

Fig. 6.7 | GameElement class represents a rectangle-bounded game element. (Part 2 of 2.)

6.8.1 Instance Variables and Constructor

The GameElement constructor receives a reference to the CannonView (Section 6.13), which implements the game's logic and draws the game elements. The constructor receives an int representing the GameElement's 32-bit color, and an int representing the ID of a sound that's associated with this GameElement. The CannonView stores all of the sounds in the game and provides an ID for each. The constructor also receives

- ints for the x and y position of the GameElement's upper-left corner

- ints for its width and height, and

- an initial vertical velocity, velocityY, of this GameElement.

Line 20 sets the paint object's color, using the int representation of the color passed to the constructor. Line 21 calculates the GameElement's bounds and stores them in a Rect object that represents a rectangle.

6.8.2 Methods update, draw, and playSound

A GameElement has the following methods:

- update (lines 27–35)—In each iteration of the game loop, this method is called to update the GameElement's position. Line 29 updates the vertical position of shape, based on the vertical velocity (velocityY) and the elapsed time between calls to update, which the method receives as the parameter interval. Lines 32–34 check whether this GameElement is colliding with the top or bottom edge of the screen and, if so, reverse its vertical velocity.

- draw (lines 38–40)—This method is called when a GameElement needs to be re-drawn on the screen. The method receives a Canvas and draws this GameElement as a rectangle on the screen—we'll override this method in class Cannonball to draw a circle instead. The GameElement's paint instance variable specifies the rectangle's color, and the GameElement's shape specifies the rectangle's bounds on the screen.

- playSound (lines 43–45)—Every game element has an associated sound that can be played by calling method playSound. This method passes the value of the soundId instance variable to the CannonView's playSound method. Class Cannon-View loads and maintains references to the game's sounds.

6.9 Blocker Subclass of GameElement

Class Blocker (Fig. 6.8)—a subclass of GameElement—represents the blocker, which makes it more difficult for the player to destroy targets. Class Blocker's missPenalty is subtracted from the remaining game time if the Cannonball collides with the Blocker. The getMissPenalty method (lines 17–19) returns the missPenalty—this method is called from CannonView's testForCollisions method when subtracting the missPenalty from the remaining time (Section 6.13.11). The Blocker constructor (lines 9–14) passes its arguments and the ID for the blocker-hit sound (CannonView.BLOCKER_SOUND_ID) to the superclass constructor (line 11), then initializes missPenalty.

```
1   // Blocker.java
2   // Subclass of GameElement customized for the Blocker
3   package com.deitel.cannongame;
4
5   public class Blocker extends GameElement {
6       private int missPenalty; // the miss penalty for this Blocker
7
8       // constructor
9       public Blocker(CannonView view, int color, int missPenalty, int x,
10          int y, int width, int length, float velocityY) {
11          super(view, color, CannonView.BLOCKER_SOUND_ID, x, y, width, length,
12              velocityY);
13          this.missPenalty = missPenalty;
14      }
15
16      // returns the miss penalty for this Blocker
17      public int getMissPenalty() {
18          return missPenalty;
19      }
20  }
```

Fig. 6.8 | Blocker subclass of GameElement.

6.10 Target Subclass of GameElement

Class Target (Fig. 6.9)—a subclass of GameElement—represents a target that the player can destroy. Class Target's hitPenalty is added to the remaining game time if the Cannonball collides with a Target. The getHitReward method (lines 17–19) returns the hitReward—this method is called from CannonView's testForCollisions method when adding the hitReward to the remaining time (Section 6.13.11). The Target constructor (lines 9–14) passes its arguments and the ID for the target-hit sound (Cannon-View.TARGET_SOUND_ID) to the super constructor (line 11), then initializes hitReward.

```
1   // Target.java
2   // Subclass of GameElement customized for the Target
3   package com.deitel.cannongame;
4
```

Fig. 6.9 | Target subclass of GameElement. (Part 1 of 2.)

```
5   public class Target extends GameElement {
6      private int hitReward; // the hit reward for this target
7
8      // constructor
9      public Target(CannonView view, int color, int hitReward, int x, int y,
10        int width, int length, float velocityY) {
11        super(view, color, CannonView.TARGET_SOUND_ID, x, y, width, length,
12           velocityY);
13        this.hitReward = hitReward;
14     }
15
16     // returns the hit reward for this Target
17     public int getHitReward() {
18        return hitReward;
19     }
20  }
```

Fig. 6.9 | Target subclass of GameElement. (Part 2 of 2.)

6.11 Cannon Class

The Cannon class (Figs. 6.10–6.14) represents the cannon in the **Cannon Game** app. The cannon has a base and a barrel, and it can fire a cannonball.

6.11.1 Instance Variables and Constructor

The Cannon constructor (Fig. 6.10) has four parameters. It receives

- the CannonView that this Cannon is in (view),
- the radius of the Cannon's base (baseRadius),
- the length of the Cannon's barrel (barrelLength) and
- the width of the Cannon's barrel (barrelWidth).

Line 25 sets the width of the Paint object's stroke so that the barrel will be drawn with the given barrelWidth. Line 27 aligns the Cannon's barrel to be initially parallel with the top and bottom edges of the screen. The Cannon class has a Point barrelEnd that's used to draw the barrel, barrelAngle to store the current angle of the barrel, and cannonball to store the Cannonball that was most recently fired if it's still on the screen.

```
1   // Cannon.java
2   // Represents Cannon and fires the Cannonball
3   package com.deitel.cannongame;
4
5   import android.graphics.Canvas;
6   import android.graphics.Color;
7   import android.graphics.Paint;
8   import android.graphics.Point;
9
```

Fig. 6.10 | Cannon instance variables and constructor. (Part I of 2.)

```
10   public class Cannon {
11      private int baseRadius; // Cannon base's radius
12      private int barrelLength; // Cannon barrel's length
13      private Point barrelEnd = new Point(); // endpoint of Cannon's barrel
14      private double barrelAngle; // angle of the Cannon's barrel
15      private Cannonball cannonball; // the Cannon's Cannonball
16      private Paint paint = new Paint(); // Paint used to draw the cannon
17      private CannonView view; // view containing the Cannon
18
19      // constructor
20      public Cannon(CannonView view, int baseRadius, int barrelLength,
21         int barrelWidth) {
22         this.view = view;
23         this.baseRadius = baseRadius;
24         this.barrelLength = barrelLength;
25         paint.setStrokeWidth(barrelWidth); // set width of barrel
26         paint.setColor(Color.BLACK); // Cannon's color is Black
27         align(Math.PI / 2); // Cannon barrel facing straight right
28      }
29
```

Fig. 6.10 | Cannon instance variables and constructor. (Part 2 of 2.)

6.11.2 Method align

Method align (Fig. 6.11) aims the cannon. The method receives as an argument the barrel angle in radians. We use the cannonLength and the barrelAngle to determine the *x*- and *y*-coordinate values for the endpoint of the cannon's barrel, barrelEnd—this is used to draw a line from the cannon base's center at the left edge of the screen to the cannon's barrel endpoint. Line 32 stores the barrelAngle so that the ball can be fired at angle later.

```
30      // aligns the Cannon's barrel to the given angle
31      public void align(double barrelAngle) {
32         this.barrelAngle = barrelAngle;
33         barrelEnd.x = (int) (barrelLength * Math.sin(barrelAngle));
34         barrelEnd.y = (int) (-barrelLength * Math.cos(barrelAngle)) +
35            view.getScreenHeight() / 2;
36      }
37
```

Fig. 6.11 | Cannon method align.

6.11.3 Method fireCannonball

The fireCannonball method (Fig. 6.12) fires a Cannonball across the screen at the Cannon's current trajectory (barrelAngle). Lines 41–46 calculate the horizontal and vertical components of the Cannonball's velocity. Lines 49–50 calculate the radius of the Cannonball, which is CannonView.CANNONBALL_RADIUS_PERCENT of the screen height. Lines 53–56 "load the cannon" (that is, construct a new Cannonball and position it inside the Cannon). Finally, we play the Cannonball's firing sound (line 58).

```
38       // creates and fires Cannonball in the direction Cannon points
39       public void fireCannonball() {
40          // calculate the Cannonball velocity's x component
41          int velocityX = (int) (CannonView.CANNONBALL_SPEED_PERCENT *
42             view.getScreenWidth() * Math.sin(barrelAngle));
43
44          // calculate the Cannonball velocity's y component
45          int velocityY = (int) (CannonView.CANNONBALL_SPEED_PERCENT *
46             view.getScreenWidth() * -Math.cos(barrelAngle));
47
48          // calculate the Cannonball's radius
49          int radius = (int) (view.getScreenHeight() *
50             CannonView.CANNONBALL_RADIUS_PERCENT);
51
52          // construct Cannonball and position it in the Cannon
53          cannonball = new Cannonball(view, Color.BLACK,
54             CannonView.CANNON_SOUND_ID, -radius,
55             view.getScreenHeight() / 2 - radius, radius, velocityX,
56             velocityY);
57
58          cannonball.playSound(); // play fire Cannonball sound
59       }
60
```

Fig. 6.12 | Cannon method fireCannonball.

6.11.4 Method draw

The draw method (Fig. 6.13) draws the Cannon on the screen. We draw the Cannon in two parts. First we draw the Cannon's barrel, then the Cannon's base.

```
61       // draws the Cannon on the Canvas
62       public void draw(Canvas canvas) {
63          // draw cannon barrel
64          canvas.drawLine(0, view.getScreenHeight() / 2, barrelEnd.x,
65             barrelEnd.y, paint);
66
67          // draw cannon base
68          canvas.drawCircle(0, (int) view.getScreenHeight() / 2,
69             (int) baseRadius, paint);
70       }
71
```

Fig. 6.13 | Cannon method draw.

Drawing the Cannon Barrel with **Canvas** *Method* **drawLine**

We use Canvas's **drawLine** method to display the Cannon barrel (lines 64–65). This method receives five parameters—the first four represent the *x-y* coordinates of the line's start and end, and the last is the Paint object specifying the line's characteristics, such as its thickness. Recall that paint was configured to draw the barrel with the thickness given in the constructor (Fig. 6.10, line 25).

*Drawing the Cannon Base with **Canvas** Method **drawCircle***

Lines 68–69 use Canvas's drawCircle method to draw the Cannon's half-circle base by drawing a circle that's centered at the left edge of the screen. Because a circle is displayed based on its center point, half of this circle is drawn off the left side of the SurfaceView.

6.11.5 Methods getCannonball and removeCannonball

Figure 6.14 shows the getCannonball and removeCannonball methods. The getCannonball method (lines 73–75) returns the current Cannonball instance, which Cannon stores. A cannonball value of null means that currently no Cannonball exists in the game. The CannonView uses this method to avoid firing a Cannonball if another Cannonball is already on the screen (Section 6.13.8, Fig. 6.26). The removeCannonball method (lines 78–80 of Fig. 6.14) removes the CannnonBall from the game by setting cannonball to null. The CannonView uses this method to remove the Cannonball from the game when it destroys a Target or after it leaves the screen (Section 6.13.11, Fig. 6.29).

```
72      // returns the Cannonball that this Cannon fired
73      public Cannonball getCannonball() {
74         return cannonball;
75      }
76
77      // removes the Cannonball from the game
78      public void removeCannonball() {
79         cannonball = null;
80      }
81   }
```

Fig. 6.14 | CannonView methods getCannonball and removeCannonball.

6.12 Cannonball Subclass of GameElement

The Cannonball subclass of GameElement (Sections 6.12.1—6.12.4) represents a cannonball fired from the cannon.

6.12.1 Instance Variables and Constructor

The Cannonball constructor (Fig. 6.15) receives the cannonball's radius rather than width and height in the GameElement constructor. Lines 15–16 call super with width and height values calculated from the radius. The constructor also receives the horizontal velocity of the Cannonball, velocityX, in addition to its vertical velocity, velocityY. Line 18 initializes onScreen to true because the Cannonball is initially on the screen.

```
1    // Cannonball.java
2    // Represents the Cannonball that the Cannon fires
3    package com.deitel.cannongame;
4
5    import android.graphics.Canvas;
6    import android.graphics.Rect;
```

Fig. 6.15 | Cannonball instance variables and constructor. (Part 1 of 2.)

```
7
8   public class Cannonball extends GameElement {
9      private float velocityX;
10     private boolean onScreen;
11
12     // constructor
13     public Cannonball(CannonView view, int color, int soundId, int x,
14        int y, int radius, float velocityX, float velocityY) {
15        super(view, color, soundId, x, y,
16           2 * radius, 2 * radius, velocityY);
17        this.velocityX = velocityX;
18        onScreen = true;
19     }
20
```

Fig. 6.15 | Cannonball instance variables and constructor. (Part 2 of 2.)

6.12.2 Methods getRadius, collidesWith, isOnScreen, and reverseVelocityX

Method getRadius (Fig. 6.16, lines 22–24) returns the Cannonball's radius by finding half the distance between the shape.right and shape.left bounds of the Cannonball's shape. Method isOnScreen (lines 32–34) returns true if the Cannonball is on the screen.

```
21     // get Cannonball's radius
22     private int getRadius() {
23        return (shape.right - shape.left) / 2;
24     }
25
26     // test whether Cannonball collides with the given GameElement
27     public boolean collidesWith(GameElement element) {
28        return (Rect.intersects(shape, element.shape) && velocityX > 0);
29     }
30
31     // returns true if this Cannonball is on the screen
32     public boolean isOnScreen() {
33        return onScreen;
34     }
35
36     // reverses the Cannonball's horizontal velocity
37     public void reverseVelocityX() {
38        velocityX *= -1;
39     }
40
```

Fig. 6.16 | Cannonball methods getRadius, collidesWith, isOnScreen and reverseVelocityX.

Checking for Collisions with Another GameElement with the collidesWith Method
The collidesWith method (line 27–29) checks whether the cannonball has *collided* with the given GameElement. We perform simple *collision detection*, based on the rectangular

boundary of the Cannonball. Two conditions must be met if the Cannonball is colliding with the GameElement:

- The Cannonball's bounds, which are stored in the shape Rect, must intersect the bounds of the given GameElement's shape. Rect's intersects method is used to check if the bounds of the Cannonball and the given GameElement intersect.

- The Cannonball must be moving horizontally towards the given GameElement. The Cannonball travels from left to right (unless it hits the blocker). If velocityX (the horizontal velocity) is positive, the Cannonball is moving left-to-right toward the given GameElement.

Reversing the *Cannonball's* Horizontal Velocity with *reverseVelocityX*

The reverseVelocityX method reverses the horizontal velocity of the Cannonball by multiplying velocityX by -1. If the collidesWith method returns true, CannonView method testForCollisions calls reverseVelocityX to reverse the ball's horizontal velocity, so the cannonball bounces back toward the cannon (Section 6.13.11).

6.12.3 Method update

The update method (Fig. 6.17) first calls the superclass's update method (line 44) to update the Cannonball's vertical velocity and to check for vertical collisions. Line 47 uses Rect's **offset** method to horizontally translate the bounds of this Cannonball. We multiply its horizontal velocity (velocityX) by the amount of time that passed (interval) to determine the translation amount. Lines 50–53 set onScreen to false if the Cannonball hits one of the screen's edges.

```
41    // updates the Cannonball's position
42    @Override
43    public void update(double interval) {
44        super.update(interval); // updates Cannonball's vertical position
45
46        // update horizontal position
47        shape.offset((int) (velocityX * interval), 0);
48
49        // if Cannonball goes off the screen
50        if (shape.top < 0 || shape.left < 0 ||
51            shape.bottom > view.getScreenHeight() ||
52            shape.right > view.getScreenWidth())
53            onScreen = false; // set it to be removed
54    }
55
```

Fig. 6.17 | Overridden GameElement method update.

6.12.4 Method draw

The draw method (Fig. 6.18) overrides GameElement's draw method and uses Canvas's drawCircle method to draw the Cannonball in its current position. The first two arguments represent the coordinates of the circle's *center*. The third argument is the circle's *radius*. The last argument is the Paint object specifying the circle's drawing characteristics.

```
56      // draws the Cannonball on the given canvas
57      @Override
58      public void draw(Canvas canvas) {
59         canvas.drawCircle(shape.left + getRadius(),
60            shape.top + getRadius(), getRadius(), paint);
61      }
62   }
```

Fig. 6.18 | Overridden GameElement method draw.

6.13 CannonView Subclass of SurfaceView

Class CannonView (Figs. 6.19–6.33) is a custom subclass of View that implements the **Cannon Game**'s logic and draws game objects on the screen.

6.13.1 package and import Statements

Figure 6.19 lists the package statement and the import statements for class CannonView. Section 6.3 discussed the key new classes and interfaces that class CannonView uses. We've highlighted them in Fig. 6.19.

```
1    // CannonView.java
2    // Displays and controls the Cannon Game
3    package com.deitel.cannongame;
4
5    import android.app.Activity;
6    import android.app.AlertDialog;
7    import android.app.Dialog;
8    import android.app.DialogFragment;
9    import android.content.Context;
10   import android.content.DialogInterface;
11   import android.graphics.Canvas;
12   import android.graphics.Color;
13   import android.graphics.Paint;
14   import android.graphics.Point;
15   import android.media.AudioAttributes;
16   import android.media.SoundPool;
17   import android.os.Build;
18   import android.os.Bundle;
19   import android.util.AttributeSet;
20   import android.util.Log;
21   import android.util.SparseIntArray;
22   import android.view.MotionEvent;
23   import android.view.SurfaceHolder;
24   import android.view.SurfaceView;
25   import android.view.View;
26
27   import java.util.ArrayList;
28   import java.util.Random;
29
```

Fig. 6.19 | CannonView class's package and import statements. (Part 1 of 2.)

```
30   public class CannonView extends SurfaceView
31      implements SurfaceHolder.Callback {
32
```

Fig. 6.19 | CannonView class's package and import statements. (Part 2 of 2.)

6.13.2 Instance Variables and Constants

Figure 6.20 lists the large number of class CannonView's constants and instance variables. We'll explain each as we encounter it in the discussion. Many of the constants are used in calculations that scale the game elements' sizes based on the screen's dimensions.

```
33      private static final String TAG = "CannonView"; // for logging errors
34
35      // constants for game play
36      public static final int MISS_PENALTY = 2; // seconds deducted on a miss
37      public static final int HIT_REWARD = 3; // seconds added on a hit
38
39      // constants for the Cannon
40      public static final double CANNON_BASE_RADIUS_PERCENT = 3.0 / 40;
41      public static final double CANNON_BARREL_WIDTH_PERCENT = 3.0 / 40;
42      public static final double CANNON_BARREL_LENGTH_PERCENT = 1.0 / 10;
43
44      // constants for the Cannonball
45      public static final double CANNONBALL_RADIUS_PERCENT = 3.0 / 80;
46      public static final double CANNONBALL_SPEED_PERCENT = 3.0 / 2;
47
48      // constants for the Targets
49      public static final double TARGET_WIDTH_PERCENT = 1.0 / 40;
50      public static final double TARGET_LENGTH_PERCENT = 3.0 / 20;
51      public static final double TARGET_FIRST_X_PERCENT = 3.0 / 5;
52      public static final double TARGET_SPACING_PERCENT = 1.0 / 60;
53      public static final double TARGET_PIECES = 9;
54      public static final double TARGET_MIN_SPEED_PERCENT = 3.0 / 4;
55      public static final double TARGET_MAX_SPEED_PERCENT = 6.0 / 4;
56
57      // constants for the Blocker
58      public static final double BLOCKER_WIDTH_PERCENT = 1.0 / 40;
59      public static final double BLOCKER_LENGTH_PERCENT = 1.0 / 4;
60      public static final double BLOCKER_X_PERCENT = 1.0 / 2;
61      public static final double BLOCKER_SPEED_PERCENT = 1.0;
62
63      // text size 1/18 of screen width
64      public static final double TEXT_SIZE_PERCENT = 1.0 / 18;
65
66      private CannonThread cannonThread; // controls the game loop
67      private Activity activity; // to display Game Over dialog in GUI thread
68      private boolean dialogIsDisplayed = false;
69
70      // game objects
71      private Cannon cannon;
```

Fig. 6.20 | CannonView class's static and instance variables. (Part 1 of 2.)

```
72      private Blocker blocker;
73      private ArrayList<Target> targets;
74
75      // dimension variables
76      private int screenWidth;
77      private int screenHeight;
78
79      // variables for the game loop and tracking statistics
80      private boolean gameOver; // is the game over?
81      private double timeLeft; // time remaining in seconds
82      private int shotsFired; // shots the user has fired
83      private double totalElapsedTime; // elapsed seconds
84
85      // constants and variables for managing sounds
86      public static final int TARGET_SOUND_ID = 0;
87      public static final int CANNON_SOUND_ID = 1;
88      public static final int BLOCKER_SOUND_ID = 2;
89      private SoundPool soundPool; // plays sound effects
90      private SparseIntArray soundMap; // maps IDs to SoundPool
91
92      // Paint variables used when drawing each item on the screen
93      private Paint textPaint; // Paint used to draw text
94      private Paint backgroundPaint; // Paint used to clear the drawing area
95
```

Fig. 6.20 | CannonView class's static and instance variables. (Part 2 of 2.)

6.13.3 Constructor

Figure 6.21 shows class CannonView's constructor. When a View is inflated, its constructor is called with a Context and an AttributeSet as arguments. The Context is the Activity that displays the MainActivityFragment containing the CannonView, and the Attribute-Set (package android.util) contains the CannonView attribute values that are set in the layout's XML document. These arguments are passed to the superclass constructor (line 96) to ensure that the custom View is properly configured with the values of any standard View attributes specified in the XML. Line 99 stores a reference to the MainActivity so we can use it at the end of a game to display an AlertDialog from the GUI thread. Though we chose to store the Activity reference, we can access this at any time by calling the inherited View method getContext.

```
96      // constructor
97      public CannonView(Context context, AttributeSet attrs) {
98          super(context, attrs); // call superclass constructor
99          activity = (Activity) context; // store reference to MainActivity
100
101         // register SurfaceHolder.Callback listener
102         getHolder().addCallback(this);
103
```

Fig. 6.21 | CannonView constructor. (Part 1 of 2.)

```
104        // configure audio attributes for game audio
105        AudioAttributes.Builder attrBuilder = new AudioAttributes.Builder();
106        attrBuilder.setUsage(AudioAttributes.USAGE_GAME);
107
108        // initialize SoundPool to play the app's three sound effects
109        SoundPool.Builder builder = new SoundPool.Builder();
110        builder.setMaxStreams(1);
111        builder.setAudioAttributes(attrBuilder.build());
112        soundPool = builder.build();
113
114        // create Map of sounds and pre-load sounds
115        soundMap = new SparseIntArray(3); // create new SparseIntArray
116        soundMap.put(TARGET_SOUND_ID,
117           soundPool.load(context, R.raw.target_hit, 1));
118        soundMap.put(CANNON_SOUND_ID,
119           soundPool.load(context, R.raw.cannon_fire, 1));
120        soundMap.put(BLOCKER_SOUND_ID,
121           soundPool.load(context, R.raw.blocker_hit, 1));
122
123        textPaint = new Paint();
124        backgroundPaint = new Paint();
125        backgroundPaint.setColor(Color.WHITE);
126     }
127
```

Fig. 6.21 | CannonView constructor. (Part 2 of 2.)

Registering the *SurfaceHolder.Callback Listener*

Line 102 registers this (i.e., the CannonView) as the SurfaceHolder.Callback that receives method calls when the SurfaceView is *created*, *updated* and *destroyed*. Inherited
SurfaceView method **getHolder** returns the SurfaceHolder object for managing the SurfaceView, and SurfaceHolder method **addCallback** stores the object that implements interface SurfaceHolder.Callback.

Configuring the *SoundPool* and Loading the Sounds

Lines 105–121 configure the sounds that we use in the app. First we create an AudioAt-
tributes.Builder object (line 105) and call the setUsage method (line 106), which receives a constant that represents what the audio will be used for. For this app, we use the
AudioAttribute.USAGE_GAME constant, which indicates that the audio is being used as
game audio. Next, we create a SoundPool.Builder object (line 109), which will enable us
to create the SoundPool that's used to load and play the app's sound effects. Next, we call
SoundPool.Builder's setMaxStreams method (line 110), which takes an argument that
represents the maximum number of simultaneous sound streams that can play at once. We
play only one sound at a time, so we pass 1. Some more complex games might play many
sounds at the same time. We then call AudioAttributes.Builder's setAudioAttributes
method (line 111) to use the audio attributes with the SoundPool object after creating it.

Line 115 creates a SparseIntArray (soundMap), which maps integer keys to integer
values. SparseIntArray is similar to—but more efficient than—a HashMap<Integer,
Integer> for small numbers of key–value pairs. In this case, we map the sound keys
(defined in Fig. 6.20, lines 86–88) to the loaded sounds' IDs, which are represented by the

return values of the SoundPool's load method (called in Fig. 6.21, lines 117, 119 and 121). Each sound ID can be used to *play* a sound (and later to return its resources to the system). SoundPool method load receives three arguments—the application's Context, a resource ID representing the sound file to load and the sound's priority. According to the documentation for this method, the last argument is not currently used and should be specified as 1.

Creating the **Paint** Objects Used to Draw the Background and Timer Text
Lines 123–124 create the Paint objects that are used when drawing the game's background and **Time remaining** text. The text color defaults to black and line 125 sets the background color to white.

6.13.4 Overriding View Method onSizeChanged

Figure 6.22 overrides class View's onSizeChanged method, which is called whenever the View's size changes, including when the View is first added to the View hierarchy as the layout is inflated. This app always displays in landscape mode, so onSizeChanged is called only once when the activity's onCreate method inflates the GUI. The method receives the View's new width and height and its old width and height. The first time this method is called, the old width and height are 0. Lines 138–139 configure the textPaint object, which is used to draw the **Time remaining** text. Line 138 sets the size of the text to be TEXT_SIZE_PERCENT of the height of the screen (screenHeight). We arrived at the value for TEXT_SIZE_PERCENT and the other scaling factors in Fig. 6.20 via trial and error, choosing values that made the game elements look nice on the screen.

```
128     // called when the size of the SurfaceView changes,
129     // such as when it's first added to the View hierarchy
130     @Override
131     protected void onSizeChanged(int w, int h, int oldw, int oldh) {
132         super.onSizeChanged(w, h, oldw, oldh);
133
134         screenWidth = w; // store CannonView's width
135         screenHeight = h; // store CannonView's height
136
137         // configure text properties
138         textPaint.setTextSize((int) (TEXT_SIZE_PERCENT * screenHeight));
139         textPaint.setAntiAlias(true); // smoothes the text
140     }
141
```

Fig. 6.22 | Overriding View method onSizeChanged.

6.13.5 Methods getScreenWidth, getScreenHeight, and playSound

In Fig. 6.23, the methods getScreenWidth and getScreenHeight return the width and height of the screen, which are updated in the onSizeChanged method (Fig. 6.22). Using soundPool's play method, the playSound method (lines 153–155) plays the sound in soundMap with the given soundId, which was associated with the sound when soundMap was constructed (Fig. 6.21, lines 113–119). The soundId is used as the soundMap key to locate the sound's ID in the SoundPool. An object of class GameElement can call the play-Sound method to play its sound.

```
142     // get width of the game screen
143     public int getScreenWidth() {
144         return screenWidth;
145     }
146
147     // get height of the game screen
148     public int getScreenHeight() {
149         return screenHeight;
150     }
151
152     // plays a sound with the given soundId in soundMap
153     public void playSound(int soundId) {
154         soundPool.play(soundMap.get(soundId), 1, 1, 1, 0, 1f);
155     }
156
```

Fig. 6.23 | CannonView methods getScreenWidth, getScreenHeight and playSound.

6.13.6 Method newGame

Method newGame (Fig. 6.24) resets the instance variables that are used to control the game. Lines 160–163 create a new Cannon object with

- a base radius of CANNON_BASE_RADIUS_PERCENT of the screen height,

- a barrel length of CANNON_BARREL_LENGTH_PERCENT of the screen width and

- a barrel width of CANNON_BARREL_WIDTH_PERCENT of the screen height.

```
157     // reset all the screen elements and start a new game
158     public void newGame() {
159         // construct a new Cannon
160         cannon = new Cannon(this,
161             (int) (CANNON_BASE_RADIUS_PERCENT * screenHeight),
162             (int) (CANNON_BARREL_LENGTH_PERCENT * screenWidth),
163             (int) (CANNON_BARREL_WIDTH_PERCENT * screenHeight));
164
165         Random random = new Random(); // for determining random velocities
166         targets = new ArrayList<>(); // construct a new Target list
167
168         // initialize targetX for the first Target from the left
169         int targetX = (int) (TARGET_FIRST_X_PERCENT * screenWidth);
170
171         // calculate Y coordinate of Targets
172         int targetY = (int) ((0.5 - TARGET_LENGTH_PERCENT / 2) *
173             screenHeight);
174
```

Fig. 6.24 | CannonView method newGame. (Part 1 of 2.)

```
175         // add TARGET_PIECES Targets to the Target list
176         for (int n = 0; n < TARGET_PIECES; n++) {
177
178            // determine a random velocity between min and max values
179            // for Target n
180            double velocity = screenHeight * (random.nextDouble() *
181               (TARGET_MAX_SPEED_PERCENT - TARGET_MIN_SPEED_PERCENT) +
182               TARGET_MIN_SPEED_PERCENT);
183
184            // alternate Target colors between dark and light
185            int color = (n % 2 == 0) ?
186               getResources().getColor(R.color.dark,
187                  getContext().getTheme()) :
188               getResources().getColor(R.color.light,
189                  getContext().getTheme());
190
191            velocity *= -1; // reverse the initial velocity for next Target
192
193            // create and add a new Target to the Target list
194            targets.add(new Target(this, color, HIT_REWARD, targetX, targetY,
195               (int) (TARGET_WIDTH_PERCENT * screenWidth),
196               (int) (TARGET_LENGTH_PERCENT * screenHeight),
197               (int) velocity));
198
199            // increase the x coordinate to position the next Target more
200            // to the right
201            targetX += (TARGET_WIDTH_PERCENT + TARGET_SPACING_PERCENT) *
202               screenWidth;
203         }
204
205         // create a new Blocker
206         blocker = new Blocker(this, Color.BLACK, MISS_PENALTY,
207            (int) (BLOCKER_X_PERCENT * screenWidth),
208            (int) ((0.5 - BLOCKER_LENGTH_PERCENT / 2) * screenHeight),
209            (int) (BLOCKER_WIDTH_PERCENT * screenWidth),
210            (int) (BLOCKER_LENGTH_PERCENT * screenHeight),
211            (float) (BLOCKER_SPEED_PERCENT * screenHeight));
212
213         timeLeft = 10; // start the countdown at 10 seconds
214
215         shotsFired = 0; // set the initial number of shots fired
216         totalElapsedTime = 0.0; // set the time elapsed to zero
217
218         if (gameOver) {// start a new game after the last game ended
219            gameOver = false; // the game is not over
220            cannonThread = new CannonThread(getHolder()); // create thread
221            cannonThread.start(); // start the game loop thread
222         }
223
224         hideSystemBars();
225      }
226
```

Fig. 6.24 | CannonView method newGame. (Part 2 of 2.)

Line 165 creates a new Random object that's used to randomize the Target velocities. Line 166 creates a new ArrayList of Targets. Line 169 initializes targetX to the number of pixels from the left that the first Target will be positioned on the screen. The first Target is positioned TARGET_FIRST_X_PERCENT of the way across the screen. Lines 172–173 initialize targetY with a value to vertically center all Targets on the screen. Lines 176–203 construct TARGET_PIECES (9) new Targets and add them to targets. Lines 180–182 set the velocity of the new Target to a random value between the screen height percentages TARGET_MIN_SPEED_PERCENT and TARGET_MAX_SPEED_PERCENT. Lines 185–189 set the color of the new Target to alternate between the R.color.dark and R.color.light colors and alternate between positive and negative vertical velocities. Line 191 reverses the target velocity for each new target so that some targets move up to start and some move down. The new Target is constructed and added to targets (lines 194–197). The Target is given a width of TARGET_WIDTH_PERCENT of the screen width and a height of TARGET_HEIGHT_PERCENT of the screen height. Finally, targetX is incremented to position the next Target.

A new Blocker is constructed and stored in blocker in lines 206–211. The Blocker is positioned BLOCKER_X_PERCENT of the screen width from the left and is vertically centered on the screen to start the game. The Blocker's width is BLOCKER_WIDTH_PERCENT of the screen width and the Blocker's height is BLOCKER_HEIGHT_PERCENT of the screen height. The Blocker's speed is BLOCKER_SPEED_PERCENT of the screen height.

If variable gameOver is true, which occurs only *after* the first game completes, line 219 resets gameOver and lines 220–221 create a new CannonThread and call its start method to begin the *game loop* that controls the game. Line 224 calls method hideSystemBars (Section 6.13.16) to put the app in immersive mode—this hides the system bars and enables the user to display them at any time by swiping down from the top of the screen.

6.13.7 Method updatePositions

Method updatePositions (Fig. 6.25) is called by the CannonThread's run method (Section 6.13.15) to update the on-screen elements' positions and to perform simple *collision detection*. The new locations of the game elements are calculated based on the elapsed time in milliseconds between the previous and current animation frames. This enables the game to update the amount by which each game element moves, based on the device's *refresh rate*. We discuss this in more detail when we cover game loops in Section 6.13.15.

```
227    // called repeatedly by the CannonThread to update game elements
228    private void updatePositions(double elapsedTimeMS) {
229       double interval = elapsedTimeMS / 1000.0; // convert to seconds
230
231       // update cannonball's position if it is on the screen
232       if (cannon.getCannonball() != null)
233          cannon.getCannonball().update(interval);
234
235       blocker.update(interval); // update the blocker's position
236
237       for (GameElement target : targets)
238          target.update(interval); // update the target's position
```

Fig. 6.25 | CannonView method updatePositions. (Part 1 of 2.)

```
239
240        timeLeft -= interval; // subtract from time left
241
242        // if the timer reached zero
243        if (timeLeft <= 0) {
244           timeLeft = 0.0;
245           gameOver = true; // the game is over
246           cannonThread.setRunning(false); // terminate thread
247           showGameOverDialog(R.string.lose); // show the losing dialog
248        }
249
250        // if all pieces have been hit
251        if (targets.isEmpty()) {
252           cannonThread.setRunning(false); // terminate thread
253           showGameOverDialog(R.string.win); // show winning dialog
254           gameOver = true;
255        }
256     }
257
```

Fig. 6.25 | CannonView method updatePositions. (Part 2 of 2.)

Elapsed Time Since the Last Animation Frame

Line 229 converts the elapsed time since the last animation frame from milliseconds to seconds. This value is used to modify the positions of various game elements.

Updating the Cannonball, Blocker and Target Positions

To update the positions of the GameElements, lines 232–238 call the update methods of the Cannonball (if there is one on the screen), the Blocker and all of the remaining Targets. The update method receives the time elapsed since the previous frame so that the positions can be updated by the correct amount for the interval.

Updating the Time Left and Determining Whether Time Ran Out

We decrease timeLeft by the time that has passed since the prior animation frame (line 240). If timeLeft has reached zero, the game is over, so we set timeLeft to 0.0 just in case it was negative; otherwise, sometimes a negative final time would display on the screen. Then we set gameOver to true, terminate the CannonThread by calling its setRunning method with the argument false and call method showGameOverDialog with the String resource ID representing the losing message.

6.13.8 Method alignAndFireCannonball

When the user touches the screen, method onTouchEvent (Section 6.13.14) calls align-AndFireCannonball (Fig. 6.26). Lines 267–272 calculate the angle necessary to aim the cannon at the touch point. Line 275 calls Cannon's align method to aim the cannon with trajectory angle. Finally, if the Cannonball exists and is on the screen, lines 280–281 fire the Cannonball and increment shotsFired.

```
258     // aligns the barrel and fires a Cannonball if a Cannonball is not
259     // already on the screen
260     public void alignAndFireCannonball(MotionEvent event) {
261         // get the location of the touch in this view
262         Point touchPoint = new Point((int) event.getX(),
263             (int) event.getY());
264
265         // compute the touch's distance from center of the screen
266         // on the y-axis
267         double centerMinusY = (screenHeight / 2 - touchPoint.y);
268
269         double angle = 0; // initialize angle to 0
270
271         // calculate the angle the barrel makes with the horizontal
272         angle = Math.atan2(touchPoint.x, centerMinusY);
273
274         // point the barrel at the point where the screen was touched
275         cannon.align(angle);
276
277         // fire Cannonball if there is not already a Cannonball on screen
278         if (cannon.getCannonball() == null ||
279             !cannon.getCannonball().isOnScreen()) {
280             cannon.fireCannonball();
281             ++shotsFired;
282         }
283     }
284
```

Fig. 6.26 | CannonView method alignAndFireCannonball.

6.13.9 Method showGameOverDialog

When the game ends, the showGameOverDialog method (Fig. 6.27) displays a Dialog-Fragment (using the techniques you learned in Section 4.7.10) containing an Alert-Dialog that indicates whether the player won or lost, the number of shots fired and the total time elapsed. The call to method setPositiveButton (lines 301–311) creates a reset button for starting a new game.

```
285     // display an AlertDialog when the game ends
286     private void showGameOverDialog(final int messageId) {
287         // DialogFragment to display game stats and start new game
288         final DialogFragment gameResult =
289             new DialogFragment() {
290                 // create an AlertDialog and return it
291                 @Override
292                 public Dialog onCreateDialog(Bundle bundle) {
293                     // create dialog displaying String resource for messageId
294                     AlertDialog.Builder builder =
295                         new AlertDialog.Builder(getActivity());
296                     builder.setTitle(getResources().getString(messageId));
297
```

Fig. 6.27 | CannonView method showGameOverDialog. (Part 1 of 2.)

```
298              // display number of shots fired and total time elapsed
299              builder.setMessage(getResources().getString(
300                 R.string.results_format, shotsFired, totalElapsedTime));
301              builder.setPositiveButton(R.string.reset_game,
302                 new DialogInterface.OnClickListener() {
303                    // called when "Reset Game" Button is pressed
304                    @Override
305                    public void onClick(DialogInterface dialog,
306                       int which) {
307                       dialogIsDisplayed = false;
308                       newGame(); // set up and start a new game
309                    }
310                 }
311              );

313              return builder.create(); // return the AlertDialog
314           }
315        };

317        // in GUI thread, use FragmentManager to display the DialogFragment
318        activity.runOnUiThread(
319           new Runnable() {
320              public void run() {
321                 showSystemBars(); // exit immersive mode
322                 dialogIsDisplayed = true;
323                 gameResult.setCancelable(false); // modal dialog
324                 gameResult.show(activity.getFragmentManager(), "results");
325              }
326           }
327        );
328     }
329
```

Fig. 6.27 | CannonView method showGameOverDialog. (Part 2 of 2.)

The onClick method of the Button's listener indicates that the dialog is no longer displayed and calls newGame to set up and start a new game. A dialog must be displayed from the GUI thread, so lines 318–327 call Activity method **runOnUiThread** to specify a Runnable that should execute in the GUI thread as soon as possible. The argument is an object of an anonymous inner class that implements Runnable. The Runnable's run method calls method showSystemBars (Section 6.13.16) to remove the app from immersive mode, then indicates that the dialog is displayed and displays it.

6.13.10 Method drawGameElements

The method drawGameElements (Fig. 6.28) draws the Cannon, Cannonball, Blocker and Targets on the SurfaceView using the Canvas that the CannonThread (Section 6.13.15) obtains from the SurfaceView's SurfaceHolder.

Clearing the Canvas with Method drawRect

First, we call Canvas's **drawRect** method (lines 333–334) to clear the Canvas so that the game elements can be displayed in their new positions. The method receives the rectangle's

```
330    // draws the game to the given Canvas
331    public void drawGameElements(Canvas canvas) {
332       // clear the background
333       canvas.drawRect(0, 0, canvas.getWidth(), canvas.getHeight(),
334          backgroundPaint);
335
336       // display time remaining
337       canvas.drawText(getResources().getString(
338          R.string.time_remaining_format, timeLeft), 50, 100, textPaint);
339
340       cannon.draw(canvas); // draw the cannon
341
342       // draw the GameElements
343       if (cannon.getCannonball() != null &&
344          cannon.getCannonball().isOnScreen())
345          cannon.getCannonball().draw(canvas);
346
347       blocker.draw(canvas); // draw the blocker
348
349       // draw all of the Targets
350       for (GameElement target : targets)
351          target.draw(canvas);
352    }
353
```

Fig. 6.28 | CannonView method drawGameElements.

upper-left *x-y* coordinates, width and height, and the Paint object that specifies the drawing characteristics—recall that backgroundPaint sets the drawing color to white.

Displaying the Time Remaining with **Canvas** *Method* **drawText**
Next, we call Canvas's **drawText** method (lines 337–338) to display the time remaining in the game. We pass as arguments the String to be displayed, the *x*- and *y*-coordinates at which to display it and the textPaint (configured in Fig. 6.22, lines 138–139) to describe how the text should be rendered (that is, the text's font size, color and other attributes).

Drawing the **Cannon,** **Cannonball,** **Blocker** *and* **Target**s *with the* **draw** *Method*
Lines 339–350 draw the Cannon, the Cannonball (if it is on the screen), the Blocker, and each of the Targets. Each of these elements is drawn by calling its draw method and passing in canvas.

6.13.11 Method testForCollisions
The testForCollisions method (Fig. 6.29) checks whether the Cannonball is colliding with any of the Targets or with the Blocker, and applies certain effects in the game if a collision occurs. Lines 359–360 check whether a Cannonball is on the screen. If so, line 362 calls the Cannonball's collidesWith method to determine whether the Cannonball is colliding with a Target. If ther is a collision, line 363 calls the Target's playSound method to play the target-hit sound, line 366 increments timeLeft by the hit reward associated with the Target, and lines 368–369 remove the Cannonball and Target from the screen. Line 370 decrements n to ensure the target that's now in position n gets tested for a colli-

sion. Line 376 destroys the Cannonball associated with Cannon if it's not on the screen. If the Cannonball is still on the screen, lines 380–381 call collidesWith again to determine whether the Cannonball is colliding with the Blocker. If so, line 382 calls the Blocker's playSound method to play the blocker-hit sound, line 385 reverses the cannonball's horizontal velocity by calling class Cannonball's reverseVelocityX method, and line 388 decrements timeLeft by the miss penalty associated with the Blocker.

```
354    // checks if the ball collides with the Blocker or any of the Targets
355    // and handles the collisions
356    public void testForCollisions() {
357       // remove any of the targets that the Cannonball
358       // collides with
359       if (cannon.getCannonball() != null &&
360          cannon.getCannonball().isOnScreen()) {
361          for (int n = 0; n < targets.size(); n++) {
362             if (cannon.getCannonball().collidesWith(targets.get(n))) {
363                targets.get(n).playSound(); // play Target hit sound
364
365                // add hit rewards time to remaining time
366                timeLeft += targets.get(n).getHitReward();
367
368                cannon.removeCannonball(); // remove Cannonball from game
369                targets.remove(n); // remove the Target that was hit
370                --n; // ensures that we don't skip testing new target n
371                break;
372             }
373          }
374       }
375       else { // remove the Cannonball if it should not be on the screen
376          cannon.removeCannonball();
377       }
378
379       // check if ball collides with blocker
380       if (cannon.getCannonball() != null &&
381          cannon.getCannonball().collidesWith(blocker)) {
382          blocker.playSound(); // play Blocker hit sound
383
384          // reverse ball direction
385          cannon.getCannonball().reverseVelocityX();
386
387          // deduct blocker's miss penalty from remaining time
388          timeLeft -= blocker.getMissPenalty();
389       }
390    }
391
```

Fig. 6.29 | CannonView method testForCollisions.

6.13.12 Methods stopGame and releaseResources

Class MainActivityFragment's onPause and onDestroy methods (Section 6.13) call class CannonView's stopGame and releaseResources methods (Fig. 6.30), respectively. Method stopGame (lines 393–396) is called from the main Activity to stop the game when the

Activity's onPause method is called—for simplicity, we don't store the game's state in this example. Method releaseResources (lines 399–402) calls the SoundPool's release method to release the resources associated with the SoundPool.

```
392    // stops the game: called by CannonGameFragment's onPause method
393    public void stopGame() {
394       if (cannonThread != null)
395          cannonThread.setRunning(false); // tell thread to terminate
396    }
397
398    // release resources: called by CannonGame's onDestroy method
399    public void releaseResources() {
400       soundPool.release(); // release all resources used by the SoundPool
401       soundPool = null;
402    }
403
```

Fig. 6.30 | CannonView methods stopGame and releaseResources.

6.13.13 Implementing the SurfaceHolder.Callback Methods

Figure 6.31 implements the surfaceChanged, surfaceCreated and surfaceDestroyed methods of interface SurfaceHolder.Callback. Method surfaceChanged has an empty body in this app because the app is *always* displayed in landscape orientation. This method is called when the SurfaceView's size or orientation changes, and would typically be used to redisplay graphics based on those changes.

```
404    // called when surface changes size
405    @Override
406    public void surfaceChanged(SurfaceHolder holder, int format,
407       int width, int height) { }
408
409    // called when surface is first created
410    @Override
411    public void surfaceCreated(SurfaceHolder holder) {
412       if (!dialogIsDisplayed) {
413          newGame(); // set up and start a new game
414          cannonThread = new CannonThread(holder); // create thread
415          cannonThread.setRunning(true); // start game running
416          cannonThread.start(); // start the game loop thread
417       }
418    }
419
420    // called when the surface is destroyed
421    @Override
422    public void surfaceDestroyed(SurfaceHolder holder) {
423       // ensure that thread terminates properly
424       boolean retry = true;
425       cannonThread.setRunning(false); // terminate cannonThread
426
```

Fig. 6.31 | Implementing the SurfaceHolder.Callback methods. (Part 1 of 2.)

```
427         while (retry) {
428             try {
429                 cannonThread.join(); // wait for cannonThread to finish
430                 retry = false;
431             }
432             catch (InterruptedException e) {
433                 Log.e(TAG, "Thread interrupted", e);
434             }
435         }
436     }
437
```

Fig. 6.31 | Implementing the SurfaceHolder.Callback methods. (Part 2 of 2.)

Method surfaceCreated (lines 410–418) is called when the SurfaceView is created—e.g., when the app first loads or when it resumes from the background. We use surfaceCreated to create and start the CannonThread to begin the game loop. Method surfaceDestroyed (lines 421–436) is called when the SurfaceView is destroyed—e.g., when the app terminates. We use surfaceDestroyed to ensure that the CannonThread terminates properly. First, line 425 calls CannonThread's setRunning method with false as an argument to indicate that the thread should *stop*, then lines 427–435 wait for the thread to *terminate*. This ensures that no attempt is made to draw to the SurfaceView once surfaceDestroyed completes execution.

6.13.14 Overriding View Method onTouchEvent

In this example, we override View method onTouchEvent (Fig. 6.32) to determine when the user touches the screen. The MotionEvent parameter contains information about the event that occurred. Line 442 uses the MotionEvent's getAction method to determine which type of touch event occurred. Then, lines 445–446 determine whether the user touched the screen (MotionEvent.ACTION_DOWN) or dragged a finger across the screen (MotionEvent.ACTION_MOVE). In either case, line 448 calls the cannonView's alignAnd-FireCannonball method to aim and fire the cannon toward that touch point. Line 451 then returns true to indicate that the touch event was handled.

```
438     // called when the user touches the screen in this activity
439     @Override
440     public boolean onTouchEvent(MotionEvent e) {
441         // get int representing the type of action which caused this event
442         int action = e.getAction();
443
444         // the user touched the screen or dragged along the screen
445         if (action == MotionEvent.ACTION_DOWN ||
446             action == MotionEvent.ACTION_MOVE) {
447             // fire the cannonball toward the touch point
448             alignAndFireCannonball(e);
449         }
450
```

Fig. 6.32 | Overriding View method onTouchEvent. (Part 1 of 2.).

```
451        return true;
452    }
453
```

Fig. 6.32 | Overriding View method onTouchEvent. (Part 2 of 2.).

6.13.15 CannonThread: Using a Thread to Create a Game Loop

Figure 6.33 defines a subclass of Thread which updates the game. The thread maintains a reference to the SurfaceView's SurfaceHolder (line 456) and a boolean indicating whether the thread is *running*.

```
454    // Thread subclass to control the game loop
455    private class CannonThread extends Thread {
456        private SurfaceHolder surfaceHolder; // for manipulating canvas
457        private boolean threadIsRunning = true; // running by default
458
459        // initializes the surface holder
460        public CannonThread(SurfaceHolder holder) {
461            surfaceHolder = holder;
462            setName("CannonThread");
463        }
464
465        // changes running state
466        public void setRunning(boolean running) {
467            threadIsRunning = running;
468        }
469
470        // controls the game loop
471        @Override
472        public void run() {
473            Canvas canvas = null; // used for drawing
474            long previousFrameTime = System.currentTimeMillis();
475
476            while (threadIsRunning) {
477                try {
478                    // get Canvas for exclusive drawing from this thread
479                    canvas = surfaceHolder.lockCanvas(null);
480
481                    // lock the surfaceHolder for drawing
482                    synchronized(surfaceHolder) {
483                        long currentTime = System.currentTimeMillis();
484                        double elapsedTimeMS = currentTime - previousFrameTime;
485                        totalElapsedTime += elapsedTimeMS / 1000.0;
486                        updatePositions(elapsedTimeMS); // update game state
487                        testForCollisions(); // test for GameElement collisions
488                        drawGameElements(canvas); // draw using the canvas
489                        previousFrameTime = currentTime; // update previous time
490                    }
491                }
```

Fig. 6.33 | Nested class CannonThread manages the game loop, updating the game elements every TIME_INTERVAL milliseconds. (Part 1 of 2.)

```
492                 finally {
493                     // display canvas's contents on the CannonView
494                     // and enable other threads to use the Canvas
495                     if (canvas != null)
496                         surfaceHolder.unlockCanvasAndPost(canvas);
497                 }
498             }
499         }
500     }
```

Fig. 6.33 | Nested class CannonThread manages the game loop, updating the game elements every TIME_INTERVAL milliseconds. (Part 2 of 2.)

The class's run method (lines 471–499) drives the *frame-by-frame animations*—this is known as the *game loop*. Each update of the game elements on the screen is performed, based on the number of milliseconds that have passed since the last update. Line 474 gets the system's current time in milliseconds when the thread begins running. Lines 476–498 loop until threadIsRunning is false.

First we obtain the Canvas for drawing on the SurfaceView by calling SurfaceHolder method lockCanvas (line 479). Only one thread at a time can draw to a SurfaceView. To ensure this, you must first *lock* the SurfaceHolder by specifying it as the expression in the parentheses of a synchronized block (line 482). Next, we get the current time in milliseconds, then calculate the elapsed time and add that to the total time so far—this will be used to help display the amount of time left in the game. Line 486 calls method update-Positions to move all the game elements, passing the elapsed time in milliseconds as an argument. This ensures that the game operates at the same speed *regardless of how fast the device is*. If the time between frames is larger (i.e, the device is slower), the game elements will move further when each frame of the animation is displayed. If the time between frames is smaller (i.e, the device is faster), the game elements will move less when each frame of the animation is displayed. Line 487 calls testForCollisions to determine whether the Cannonball collided with the Blocker or a Target:

- If a collision occurs with the Blocker, testForCollisions reverses the Cannonball's velocity.

- If a collision occurs with a Target, testForCollisions removes the Cannonball.

Finally, line 488 calls the drawGameElements method to draw the game elements using the SurfaceView's Canvas, and line 489 stores the currentTime as the previousFrameTime to prepare to calculate the elapsed time between this animation frame and the *next*.

6.13.16 Methods hideSystemBars and showSystemBars

This app uses *immersive mode*—at any time during game play, the user can view the system bars by swiping down from the top of the screen. Immersive mode is available only on devices running Android 4.4 or higher. So, methods hideSystemBars and showSystemBars (Fig. 6.34) first check whether the device's Android version—Build.VERSION_SDK_INT—is greater than or equal to Build.VERSION_CODES_KITKAT—the constant for Android 4.4 (API level 19). If so, both methods use View method setSystemUiVisibility to configure the system bars and app bar (though we already hid the app bar by modifying this app's theme). To hide the system bars and app bar and place the UI into immersive mode, you pass to `setSystemUiVisibility` the constants that are combined via the bitwise OR (|) operator in lines 505–510. To show the system bars and app bar, you pass to `setSystem-UiVisibility` the constants that are combined in lines 517–519. These combinations of `View` constants ensure that the `CannonView` is *not* resized each time the system bars and app bar are hidden and redisplayed. Instead, the system bars and app bar *overlay* the `Cannon-View`—that is, part of the `CannonView` is temporarily hidden when the system bars are on the screen. For more information on immersive mode, visit

```
http://developer.android.com/training/system-ui/immersive.html
```

```
501   // hide system bars and app bar
502   private void hideSystemBars() {
503      if (Build.VERSION.SDK_INT >= Build.VERSION_CODES.KITKAT)
504         setSystemUiVisibility(
505            View.SYSTEM_UI_FLAG_LAYOUT_STABLE |
506            View.SYSTEM_UI_FLAG_LAYOUT_HIDE_NAVIGATION |
507            View.SYSTEM_UI_FLAG_LAYOUT_FULLSCREEN |
508            View.SYSTEM_UI_FLAG_HIDE_NAVIGATION |
509            View.SYSTEM_UI_FLAG_FULLSCREEN |
510            View.SYSTEM_UI_FLAG_IMMERSIVE);
511   }
512
513   // show system bars and app bar
514   private void showSystemBars() {
515      if (Build.VERSION.SDK_INT >= Build.VERSION_CODES.KITKAT)
516         setSystemUiVisibility(
517            View.SYSTEM_UI_FLAG_LAYOUT_STABLE |
518            View.SYSTEM_UI_FLAG_LAYOUT_HIDE_NAVIGATION |
519            View.SYSTEM_UI_FLAG_LAYOUT_FULLSCREEN);
520   }
521 }
```

Fig. 6.34 | DoodleView methods hideSystemBars and showSystemBars.

6.14 Wrap-Up

In this chapter, you created the **Cannon Game** app, which challenges the player to destroy nine targets before a 10-second time limit expires. The user aims and fires the cannon by touching the screen. To draw on the screen from a separate thread, you created a custom view by extending class `SurfaceView`. You learned that custom component class names must be fully qualified in the XML layout element that represents the component. We presented additional `Fragment` lifecycle methods. You learned that method `onPause` is called when a `Fragment` is paused and method `onDestroy` is called when the `Fragment` is destroyed. You handled touches by overriding `View`'s `onTouchEvent` method. You added sound effects to the app's `res/raw` folder and managed them with a `SoundPool`. You also used the system's `AudioManager` service to obtain the device's current music volume and use it as the playback volume.

This app manually performs its animations by updating the game elements on a `Sur-faceView` from a separate thread of execution. To do this, you extended class `Thread` and created a `run` method that displays graphics by calling methods of class `Canvas`. You used the `SurfaceView`'s `SurfaceHolder` to obtain the appropriate `Canvas`. You also learned how to build a game loop that controls a game, based on the amount of time that has elapsed between animation frames, so that the game will operate at the same overall speed on all devices, regardless of their processor speeds. Finally, you used immersive mode to enable the app to use the entire screen.

In Chapter 7, you'll build the **WeatherViewer** app. You'll use web services to interact with the 16-day weather forecast web service from `OpenWeatherMap.org`. Like many of today's web services, the `OpenWeatherMap.org` web service will return the forecast data in JavaScript Object Notation (JSON) format. You'll process the response using the `JSONObject` and `JSONArray` classes from the `org.json` package. You'll then display the daily forecast in a `ListView`.

7

WeatherViewer App

REST Web Services, AsyncTask, HttpUrlConnection, Processing JSON Responses, JSONObject, JSONArray, ListView, ArrayAdapter, ViewHolder Pattern, TextInputLayout, FloatingActionButton

Objectives

In this chapter you'll:

- Use the free OpenWeatherMap.org REST web services to get a 16-day weather forecast for a city specified by the user.

- Use an AsyncTask and an HttpUrlConnection to invoke a REST web service or to download an image in a separate thread and deliver results to the GUI thread.

- Process a JSON response using package org.json classes JSONObjects and JSONArrays.

- Define an ArrayAdapter that specifies the data to display in a ListView.

- Use the ViewHolder pattern to reuse views that scroll off the screen in a ListView, rather than creating new views.

- Use the material design components TextInputLayout, Snackbar and FloatingActionButton from the Android Design Support Library.

7.1 Introduction

The **WeatherViewer** app (Fig. 7.1) uses the free `OpenWeatherMap.org` REST web services to obtain a specified city's 16-day weather forecast. The app receives the weather data in *JSON (JavaScript Object Notation)* data format. The list of weather data is displayed in a `ListView`—a view that displays a scrollable list of items. In this app, you'll use a custom list-item format to display:

- a weather-condition icon
- the day of the week with a text description of that day's weather
- the day's low and high temperatures (in °F), and
- the humidity percentage.

The preceding items represent a subset of the returned forecast data. For details of the data returned by the 16-day weather forecast API, visit:

```
http://openweathermap.org/forecast16
```

For a list of all weather data APIs provided by `OpenWeatherMap.org`, visit:

```
http://openweathermap.org/api
```

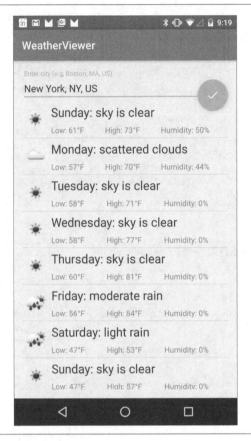

Fig. 7.1 | Weather Viewer app displaying the New York, NY, US weather forecast.

7.2 Test-Driving the WeatherViewer App

Opening and Running the App

Open Android Studio and open the **WeatherViewer** app from the WeatherViewer folder in the book's examples folder. Before running this app, you must add your own OpenWeatherMap.org API key. See Section 7.3.1 for information on how to obtain your key and where you should place it in the project. *This is required before you can run the app.* After adding your API key to the project, execute the app in the AVD or on a device.

Viewing a City's 16-Day Weather Forecast

When the app first executes, the EditText at the top of the user interface receives the focus and the virtual keyboard displays so you can enter a city name (Fig. 7.2). You should consider following the city with a comma and the country code. In this case, we entered New York, NY, US to locate the weather for New York, NY in the United States. Once you've entered the city, touch the circular FloatingActionButton containing the done icon (✓) to submit the city to the app, which then requests that city's 16-day weather forecast (shown in Fig. 7.1).

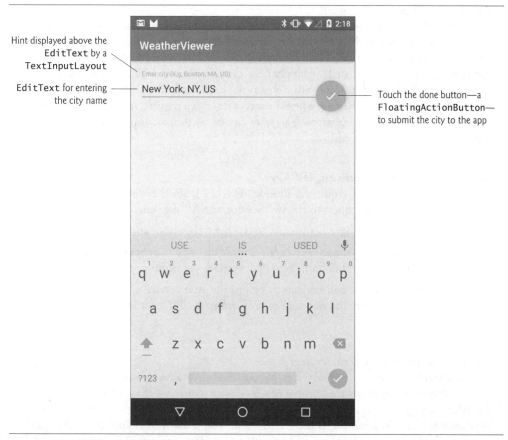

Hint displayed above the
EditText by a
TextInputLayout

EditText for entering
the city name

Touch the done button—a
FloatingActionButton—
to submit the city to the app

Fig. 7.2 | Entering a city.

7.3 Technologies Overview

This section introduces the features you'll use to build the **WeatherViewer** app.

7.3.1 Web Services

This chapter introduces web services, which promote software portability and reusability in applications that operate over the Internet. A web service is a software component that can be accessed over a network.

The machine on which a web service resides is the web service host. The client—in this case the **WeatherViewer** app—sends a request over a network to the web service host, which processes the request and returns a response over the network to the client. This distributed computing benefits systems in various ways. For example, an app can access data on demand via a web service, rather than storing the data directly on the device. Similarly, an app lacking the processing power to perform specific computations could use a web service to take advantage of another system's superior resources.

REST Web Services

Representational State Transfer (REST) refers to an architectural style for implementing web services—often called RESTful web services. Many of today's most popular free and fee-based web services are RESTful. Though REST itself is not a standard, RESTful web services use web standards, such as HyperText Transfer Protocol (HTTP), which is used by web browsers to communicate with web servers. Each method in a RESTful web service is identified by a unique URL. So, when the server receives a request, it immediately knows what operation to perform. Such web services can be used in an app or even entered directly into a web browser's address bar.

Web Services Often Require an API Key

Using a web service often requires a unique API key from the web service's provider. When your app makes a request to the web service, the API key enables the provider to:

- confirm that you have permission to use the web service and
- track your usage—many web services limit the total number of requests you can make in a specific timeframe (e.g., per second, per minute, per hour, etc.).

Some web services require authentication before the web service gives the app an API key—in effect, you log into the web service programmatically, before being allowed to use the web service.

OpenWeatherMap.org Web Services

The OpenWeatherMap.org web services we use in the **WeatherViewer** app are free, but OpenWeatherMap.org limits the number of web service requests—these limits are currently 1200 requests-per-minute and 1.7 million requests-per-day. OpenWeatherMap.org is a *freemium* service—in addition to the free tier that you'll use in this app, they offer paid tiers with higher request limits, more frequent data updates and other features. For additional information about the OpenWeatherMap.org web services, visit:

```
http://openweathermap.org/api
```

OpenWeatherMap.org Web Service License

OpenWeatherMap.org uses a creative commons public license for its web services. For the license terms, visit:

```
http://creativecommons.org/licenses/by-sa/2.0/
```

For more information about the license terms, see the Licenses section at

```
http://openweathermap.org/terms
```

Obtaining an OpenWeatherMap.org API Key

Before running this app, you must obtain your own OpenWeatherMap.org API key from

```
http://openweathermap.org/register
```

After registering, copy the hexadecimal API key from the confirmation web page, then replace YOUR_API_KEY in strings.xml with the key.

7.3.2 JavaScript Object Notation (JSON) and the org.json Package

JavaScript Object Notation (JSON) is an alternative to XML for representing data. JSON is a text-based data-interchange format used to represent objects in JavaScript as collections of name/value pairs represented as Strings. JSON is a simple format that makes objects easy to create, read and parse and, because it's much less verbose than XML, allows programs to transmit data efficiently across the Internet. Each JSON object is represented as a list of property names and values contained in curly braces, in the following format:

> *{propertyName1: value1, propertyName2: value2}*

Each property name is a String. Arrays are represented in JSON with square brackets in the following format:

> *[value1, value2, value3]*

Each array element can be a String, number, JSON object, true, false or null. Figure 7.3 sample JSON returned by OpenWeatherMap.org's daily forecast web service used in this app—this particular sample contains two days of weather data (lines 15–57).

```
 1   {
 2      "city": {
 3         "id": 5128581,
 4         "name": "New York",
 5         "coord": {
 6            "lon": -74.005966,
 7            "lat": 40.714272
 8         },
 9         "country": "US",
10         "population": 0
11      },
12      "cod": "200",
13      "message": 0.0102,
14      "cnt": 2,
15      "list": [{ // you'll use this array of objects to get the daily weather
16         "dt": 1442419200,
17         "temp": {
18            "day": 79.9,
19            "min": 71.74,
20            "max": 82.53,
21            "night": 71.85,
22            "eve": 82.53,
23            "morn": 71.74
24         },
25         "pressure": 1037.39,
26         "humidity": 64,
27         "weather": [{
28            "id": 800,
29            "main": "Clear",
30            "description": "sky is clear",
31            "icon": "01d"
32         }],
```

Fig. 7.3 | Sample JSON from the OpenWeatherMap.org daily forecast web service. (Part 1 of 2.)

```
33          "speed": 0.92,
34          "deg": 250,
35          "clouds": 0
36      }, { // end of first array element and beginning of second one
37          "dt": 1442505600,
38          "temp": {
39             "day": 79.92,
40             "min": 66.72,
41             "max": 83.1,
42             "night": 70.79,
43             "eve": 81.99,
44             "morn": 66.72
45          },
46          "pressure": 1032.46,
47          "humidity": 62,
48          "weather": [{
49             "id": 800,
50             "main": "Clear",
51             "description": "sky is clear",
52             "icon": "01d"
53          }],
54          "speed": 1.99,
55          "deg": 224,
56          "clouds": 0
57      }] // end of second array element and end of array
58  }
```

Fig. 7.3 | Sample JSON from the `OpenWeatherMap.org` daily forecast web service. (Part 2 of 2.)

There are many properties in the JSON object returned by the daily forecast. We use only the `"list"` property—an array of JSON objects representing the forecasts for up to 16 days (7 by default, unless you specify otherwise). Each `"list"` array element contains many properties of which we use:

- `"dt"`—a `long` integer containing the date/time stamp represented as the number of seconds since January 1, 1970 GMT. We convert this into a day name.

- `"temp"`—a JSON object containing `double` properties representing the day's temperatures. We use only the minimum (`"min"`) and maximum (`"max"`) temperatures, but the web service also returns the average daytime (`"day"`), nighttime (`"night"`), evening (`"eve"`) and morning (`"morn"`) temperatures.

- `"humidity"`—an `int` representing the humidity percentage.

- `"weather"`—a JSON object containing several properties, including a description of the conditions (`"description"`) and the name of an icon that represents the conditions (`"icon"`).

org.json *Package*

You'll use the following classes from the `org.json` package to process the JSON data that the app receives (Section 7.7.6):

- `JSONObject`—One of this class's constructors converts a `String` of JSON data into a `JSONObject` containing a `Map<String, Object>` that maps the JSON keys to their corresponding values. You access the JSON properties in your code via JSONObject's *get* methods, which enable you to obtain a JSON key's value as one of the types JSONObject, JSONArray, Object, boolean, double, int, long or String.

- JSONArray—This class represents a JSON array and provides methods for accessing its elements. The "list" property in the OpenWeatherMap.org response will be manipulated as a JSONArray.

7.3.3 HttpUrlConnection Invoking a REST Web Service

To invoke the OpenWeatherMap.org daily forecast web service, you'll convert the web service's URL String into a URL object, then use the URL to open an HttpUrlConnection (Section 7.7.5). This will make the HTTP request to the web service. To receive the JSON response, you'll read all the data from the HttpUrlConnection's InputStream and place it in a String. We'll show you how to convert that to a JSONObject for processing.

7.3.4 Using AsyncTask to Perform Network Requests Outside the GUI Thread

You should perform *long-running operations* or operations that *block* execution until they complete (e.g., network, file and database access) *outside* the GUI thread. This helps maintain application responsiveness and avoid *Activity Not Responding (ANR) dialogs* that appear when Android thinks the GUI is not responsive. Recall from Chapter 6, however, that updates to an app's user interface must be performed in the GUI thread, because GUI components are not thread safe.

To perform long-running tasks that result in updates to the GUI, Android provides class **AsyncTask** (package android.os), which performs the long-running operation in one thread and delivers the results to the GUI thread. The details of creating and manipulating threads are handled for you by class AsyncTask, as are communicating the results from the AsyncTask to the GUI thread. We'll use two AsyncTask subclasses in this app—one will invoke the OpenWeatherMap.org web service (Section 7.7.5) and the other will download a weather-condition image (Section 7.6.5).

7.3.5 ListView, ArrayAdapter and the View-Holder Pattern

This app displays the weather data in a ListView (package android.widget)—a scrollable list of items. ListView is a subclass of **AdapterView** (package android.widget), which represents a view that get's its data from a data source via an **Adapter** object (package android.widget). In this app, we use a subclass of **ArrayAdapter** (package android.widget) to create an object that populates the ListView using data from an ArrayList collection object (Section 7.6). When the app updates the ArrayList with weather data, we'll call the ArrayAdapter's **notifyDataSetChanged** method to indicate that the underlying data in the ArrayList has changed. The adapter then notifies the ListView to update its list of displayed items. This is known as data binding. Several types of AdapterViews can be bound to data using an Adapter. In Chapter 9, you'll learn how to bind database data to a ListView. For more details on data binding in Android and several tutorials, visit

http://developer.android.com/guide/topics/ui/binding.html

View-Holder Pattern

By default, a ListView can display one or two TextViews. In this app, you'll customize the ListView items to display an ImageView and several TextViews in a custom layout. Creating custom ListView items involves the expensive runtime overhead of creating new objects dynamically. For large lists with complex list-item layouts and for which the user is scrolling rapidly, this overhead can prevent smooth scrolling. To reduce this overhead, as ListView items scroll off the screen, Android reuses those list items for the new ones that are scrolling onto the screen. For complex item layouts, you can take advantage of the existing GUI components in the reused list items to increase a ListView's performance.

To do this, we introduce the view-holder pattern in which you create a class (typically named ViewHolder) containing instance variables for the views that display a ListView item's data. When a ListView item is created, you also create a ViewHolder object and initialize its instance variables with references to the item's nested views. You then store that ViewHolder object with the ListView item, which is a View. Class View's **setTag** method allows you to add any Object to a View. This Object is then available to you via the View's **getTag** method. We'll specify as the tag the ViewHolder object that contains references to the ListView item's nested views.

As a new item is about to scroll onto the screen, the ListView checks whether a reusable view is available. If not, we inflate the new item's view from a layout XML file, then store references to the GUI components in a ViewHolder object. Then we'll use setTag to set that ViewHolder object as the tag for the ListView item. If there is a reusable item available, we'll get that item's tag with getTag, which will return the existing ViewHolder object that was created previously for that ListView item. Regardless of how we obtain the ViewHolder object, we'll then display data in the ViewHolder's referenced views.

7.3.6 FloatingActionButton

Users touch buttons to initiate actions. With material design in Android 5.0, Google introduced the floating action button (Google refers to this as the "FAB") as a button that floats over the app's user interface—that is, it has a higher material-design elevation than the rest of the user interface—and that specifies an important action. For example, a contacts app might use a floating action button containing a + icon to promote the action for adding a new contact. In this app, we use a floating action button containing a done icon (✓) to enable the user to submit a city to the app and obtain that city's forecast. With Android 6.0 and the new Android Design Support Library, Google formalized the floating action button as class FloatingActionButton (package android.support.design.widget). In Android Studio 1.4, Google reimplemented the app templates to use material design, and most new template include a FloatingActionButton by default.

FloatingActionButton is a subclass of ImageView, which enables a FloatingActionButton to display an image. The material design guidelines suggest that you position a FloatingActionButton at least 16dp from the edges of a phone device and at least 24dp from the edges of a tablet device—the default app templates configure this for you. For more details about how and when you should use a FloatingActionButton, visit:

```
https://www.google.com/design/spec/components/buttons-floating-
   action-button.html
```

7.3.7 `TextInputLayout`

In this app, you'll use an `EditText` to enable the user to enter the city for which you'd like to obtain a weather forecast. To help the user understand an `EditText`'s purpose, you can provide hint text that's displayed when the `EditText` is empty. Once the user starts entering text, the hint disappears—possibly causing the user to forget the `EditText`'s purpose.

The Android Design Support Library's `TextInputLayout` (package `android.support.design.widget`) solves this problem. In a `TextInputLayout`, when the `EditText` receives the focus, the `TextInputLayout` animates the hint text from it's original size to a smaller size that's displayed above the `EditText` so that the user can enter data and see the hint (Fig. 7.2). In this app, the `EditText` receives the focus as the app begins executing, so the `TextInputLayout` immediately moves the hint above the `EditText`.

7.3.8 Snackbar

A `Snackbar` (package `android.support.design.widget`) is a material design component similar in concept to a `Toast`. In addition to appearing on the screen for a specified time limit, `Snackbar`s are also interactive. Users can swipe them away to dismiss them. A `Snackbar` also can have an associated action to perform when the user touches the `Snackbar`. In this app, we'll use a `Snackbar` to display informational messages.

7.4 Building the App's GUI and Resource Files

In this section, we review the new features in the GUI and resource files for the **Weather Viewer** app.

7.4.1 Creating the Project

Create a new project using the template **Blank Activity**. In the **Create New Project** dialog's **New Project** step, specify:

- **Application name:** `WeatherViewer`
- **Company Domain:** `deitel.com` (or specify your own domain name)

For the remaining steps in the **Create New Project** dialog, use the same settings as in Section 2.3. Follow the steps in Section 2.5.2 to add an app icon to your project. Also, follow the steps in Section 4.4.3 to configure Java SE 7 support for the project.

7.4.2 `AndroidManifest.xml`

The **WeatherViewer** is designed for only portrait orientation. Follow the steps you performed in Section 3.7 to set the `android:screenOrientation` property to `portrait`. In addition, add the following Internet-access permission to the `<manifest>` element before its nested `<application>` element:

```
<uses-permission android:name="android.permission.INTERNET" />
```

This allows the app to access the Internet, which is required to invoke a web service.

Permissions That Are Automatically Granted in Android 6.0
The new Android 6.0 permissions model (introduced in Chapter 5) automatically grants the Internet permission at installation time, because Internet access is considered a funda-

mental capability in today's apps. In Android 6.0, the Internet permission and many others that, according to Google, are not "great risk to the user's privacy or security" are granted automatically at installation time—these permissions are grouped into the category PROTECTION_NORMAL. For a complete list of such permissions, visit:

```
https://developer.android.com/preview/features/runtime-
    permissions.html#best-practices
```

Android does not ask users to grant such permissions, nor can users revoke such permissions from the app. For this reason, your code does not need to check whether the app has a given PROTECTION_NORMAL permission. You must still request these permissions in AndroidManifest.xml, however, for backward compatibility with earlier Android versions.

7.4.3 strings.xml

Double click strings.xml in the res/values folder, then click the **Open editor** link to display the **Translations Editor** and create the String resources in Fig. 7.4.

Key	Value
api_key	*Use your own OpenWeatherMap.org API key for this resource's value.*
web_service_url	http://api.openweathermap.org/data/2.5/forecast/daily?q=
invalid_url	Invalid URL
weather_condition_image	A graphical representation of the weather conditions
high_temp	High: %s
low_temp	Low: %s
day_description	%1$s: %2$s
humidity	Humidity: %s
hint_text	Enter city (e.g, Boston, MA, US)
read_error	Unable to read weather data
connect_error	Unable to connect to OpenWeatherMap.org

Fig. 7.4 | String resources used in the **WeatherViewer** app.

7.4.4 colors.xml

The Android Studio **Blank Activity** template customizes the app's primary, dark primary and accent colors. In this app, we changed the template's accent color (colorAccent) to a blue shade (hexadecimal value #448AFF) in colors.xml.

7.4.5 activity_main.xml

The Android Studio **Blank Activity** template breaks MainActivity's GUI into two files:

- activity_main.xml defines the activity's Toolbar (the app bar replacement in an AppCompatActivity) and a FloatingActionButton, which is positioned in the bottom-right corner by default.

- content_main.xml defines the rest of MainActivity's GUI and is included in the activity_main.xml file via an <include> element.

Make the following changes to `activity_main.xml` for this app:

1. Add the **id** `coordinatorLayout` to the `CoordinatorLayout`—you'll use this to specify the layout in which a `Snackbar` will be displayed.

2. Add the material design done (✓) button to the project via the **Vector Asset Studio** (as you did in Section 4.4.9), then specify this new icon for the predefined `FloatingActionButton`'s **src** property.

3. Edit the layout's XML to configure several `FloatingActionButton` properties that are not available via the **Properties** window. Change the `layout_gravity` from `bottom|end` to `top|end` so that the `FloatingActionButton` appears at the top right of the user interface.

4. To move the button to overlap the `EditText`'s right edge, define a new dimension resource named `fab_margin_top` with the value 90dp. Using this dimension resource and the `fab_margin` dimension resource defined by the **Blank Activity** template to define the following `FloatingActionButton` margins:

```
android:layout_marginTop="@dimen/fab_margin_top"
android:layout_marginEnd="@dimen/fab_margin"
android:layout_marginBottom="@dimen/fab_margin"
android:layout_marginStart="@dimen/fab_margin"
```

5. Finally, remove the `FloatingActionButton`'s `layout_margin` that was predefined by the **Blank Activity** template.

7.4.6 content_main.xml

This layout is included into `activity_main.xml` and defines `MainActivity`'s primary GUI. Perform the following steps:

1. Remove the default `TextView` defined by the **Blank Activity** template and change the `RelativeLayout` to a vertical `LinearLayout`.

2. Next, insert a `TextInputLayout`. In the layout editor's **Design** view, click **CustomView** in the **Custom** section. In the dialog that appears, begin typing `TextInputLayout` to search the list of custom GUI components. Once the IDE highlights `TextInputLayout`, click **OK**, then in the **Component Tree**, click the `LinearLayout` to insert the `TextInputLayout` as a nested layout.

3. To add an `EditText` to the `TextInputLayout`, switch to the layout editor's **Text** view, then change the `TextInputLayout` element's closing `/>` to `>`, position the cursor to the right of the `>`, press *Enter* and type `</`. The IDE will auto-complete the closing tag. Between the `TextInputLayout`'s starting and ending tags, type `<EditText`. The IDE will show an auto-complete window with `EditText` selected. Press *Enter* to insert an `EditText`, then set its `layout_width` to `match_parent` and `layout_height` to `wrap_content`. In **Design** view, set the `EditText`'s **id** to `locationEditText`, check its **singleLine** property's checkbox and set its **hint** property to the `String` resource `hint_text`.

4. To complete the layout, drag a `ListView` onto the `LinearLayout` in the **Component Tree**. Set its **layout:width** to `match_parent`, its **layout:height** to `0dp`, its **layout:weight** to 1 and its **id** to `weatherListView`. Recall that the **layout:height** value

0dp is recommended by the IDE for more efficient rendering when using the **layout:weight** to determine a View's height.

7.4.7 list_item.xml

You'll now add the list_item.xml layout to the project and define the custom layout for displaying weather data in a ListView item (Fig. 7.5). This layout will be inflated by the WeatherArrayAdapter to create the user interface for new ListView items (Section 7.6.4).

Horizontal LinearLayout containing an ImageView and GridLayout

Two row and three column GridLayout containing four TextViews

Fig. 7.5 | Layout for one day's weather displayed in a ListView item.

*Step 1: Creating the Layout File and Customizing the **LinearLayout**'s Orientation*
Create the list_item.xml layout file by performing the following steps:

1. Right click the project's layout folder, and select **New > Layout resource file**.

2. Enter list_item.xml in the **File name** field of the **New Resource File** dialog.

3. Ensure that LinearLayout is specified in the **Root element** field, then click **OK**. The list_item.xml file will appear in the layout directory in the **Project** window and will open in the layout editor.

4. Select the LinearLayout and change its orientation to horizontal—this layout will consist of an ImageView and a GridLayout containing the other views.

*Step 2: Adding the **ImageView** for Displaying a Weather-Condition Icon*
Perform the following steps to add and configure the ImageView:

1. Drag an ImageView from the **Palette** onto the LinearLayout in the **Component Tree**.

2. Set the **id** to conditionImageView.

3. Set the **layout:width** to 50dp—define the dimension resource image_side_length for this value.

4. Set the **layout:height** to match_parent—the ImageView's height will match the ListView item's height.

5. Set the **contentDescription** to the String resource weather_condition_image that you created in Section 7.4.3.

6. Set the **scaleType** to fitCenter—the icon will fit within the ImageView's bounds and be centered horizontally and vertically.

Step 3: Adding the GridLayout for Displaying the TextViews
Perform the following steps to add and configure the GridLayout:

1. Drag a GridLayout from the **Palette** onto the LinearLayout in the **Component Tree**.

2. Set the **columnCount** to 3 and the **rowCount** to 2.

3. Set the **layout:width** to 0dp—this GridLayout's width will be determined by the **layout:weight**.

4. Set the **layout:height** to match_parent—the GridLayout's height will match the ListView item's height.

5. Set the **layout:weight** to 1—the GridLayout's width will occupy all remaining horizontal space in its parent LinearLayout.

6. Check the **useDefaultMargins** property to add the default spacing between the GridLayout's cells.

Step 4: Adding the TextViews
Perform the following steps to add and configure the four TextViews:

1. Drag a **Large Text** onto the GridLayout in the **Component Tree** and set its **id** to dayTextView, its **layout:column** to 0 and its **layout:columnSpan** to 3.

2. Drag three **Plain TextViews** onto the GridLayout in the **Component Tree** and set their **ids** to lowTextView, hiTextView and humidityTextView, respectively. Set each of these TextViews' **layout:row** to 1 and **layout:columnWeight** to 1. These TextViews will all appear in the GridLayout's second row and, because they all have the same **layout:columnWeight**, the columns will be sized equally.

3. Set lowTextView's **layout:column** to 0, hiTextView's **layout:column** to 1 and humidityTextView's **layout:column** to 2.

This completes the list_item.xml layout. You do not need to change the **text** property of any of the TextViews—their text will be set programmatically.

7.5 Class Weather

This app consists of three classes that are discussed in Sections 7.5—7.7:

- Class Weather (this section) represents one day's weather data. Class MainActivity will convert the JSON weather data into an ArrayList<Weather>.

- Class WeatherArrayAdapter (Section 7.6) defines a custom ArrayAdapter subclass for binding the ArrayList<Weather> to the MainActivity's ListView. ListView items are indexed from 0 and each ListView item's nested views are populated with data from the Weather object at the same index in the ArrayList<Weather>.

- Class MainActivity (Section 7.7) defines the app's user interface and the logic for interacting with the OpenWeatherMap.org daily forecast web service and processing the JSON response.

In this section, we focus on class Weather.

7.5.1 package Statement, import Statements and Instance Variables

Figure 7.6 contains the package statement, import statements and class Weather's instance variables. You'll use classes from the java.text and java.util packages (lines 5–8) to convert the timestamp for each day's weather into that day's name (Monday, Tuesday, etc.). The instance variables are declared final, because they do not need to be modified after they're initialized. We also made them public—recall that Java Strings are immutable, so even though the instance variables are public, their values cannot change.

```
 1    // Weather.java
 2    // Maintains one day's weather information
 3    package com.deitel.weatherviewer;
 4
 5    import java.text.NumberFormat;
 6    import java.text.SimpleDateFormat;
 7    import java.util.Calendar;
 8    import java.util.TimeZone;
 9
10    class Weather {
11       public final String dayOfWeek;
12       public final String minTemp;
13       public final String maxTemp;
14       public final String humidity;
15       public final String description;
16       public final String iconURL;
17
```

Fig. 7.6 | Weather class package statement, import statements and instance variables.

7.5.2 Constructor

The Weather constructor (Fig. 7.7) initializes the class's instance variables:

- The NumberFormat object creates Strings from numeric values. Lines 22–23 configure the object to round floating-point values to whole numbers.

- Line 25 calls our utility method convertTimeStampToDay (Section 7.5.3) to get the String day name and initialize dayOfWeek.

- Lines 26–27 format the day's minimum and maximum temperature values as whole numbers using the numberFormat object. We append °F to the end of each formatted String, as we'll request Fahrenheit temperatures—the Unicode escape sequence \u00B0 represents the degree symbol (°). The OpenWeatherMap.org APIs also support Kelvin (the default) and Celsius temperature formats.

- Lines 28–29 get a NumberFormat for locale-specific percentage formatting, then use it to format the humidity percentage. The web service returns this percentage as a whole number, so we divide that by 100.0 for formatting—in the U.S. locale, 1.00 is formatted as 100%, 0.5 is formatted as 50%, etc.

- Line 30 initializes the weather condition description.

- Lines 31–32 create a URL String representing the weather condition image for the day's weather—this will be used to download the image.

```
18       // constructor
19       public Weather(long timeStamp, double minTemp, double maxTemp,
20          double humidity, String description, String iconName) {
21          // NumberFormat to format double temperatures rounded to integers
22          NumberFormat numberFormat = NumberFormat.getInstance();
23          numberFormat.setMaximumFractionDigits(0);
24
25          this.dayOfWeek = convertTimeStampToDay(timeStamp);
26          this.minTemp = numberFormat.format(minTemp) + "\u00B0F";
27          this.maxTemp = numberFormat.format(maxTemp) + "\u00B0F";
28          this.humidity =
29             NumberFormat.getPercentInstance().format(humidity / 100.0);
30          this.description = description;
31          this.iconURL =
32             "http://openweathermap.org/img/w/" + iconName + ".png";
33       }
34
```

Fig. 7.7 | Weather class constructor.

7.5.3 Method convertTimeStampToDay

Utility method convertTimeStampToDay (Fig. 7.8) receives as its argument a long value representing the number of seconds since January 1, 1970 GMT—the standard way time is represented on Linux systems (Android is based on Linux). To perform the conversion:

- Line 37 gets a Calendar object for manipulating dates and times, then line 38 calls method setTimeInMillis to set the time using the timestamp argument. The timestamp is in seconds so we multiply by 1000 to convert it to milliseconds.

- Line 39 gets the default TimeZone object, which we use to adjust the time, based on the device's time zone (lines 42–43).

- Line 46 creates a SimpleDateFormat that formats a Date object. The constructor argument "EEEE" formats the Date as just the day name (Monday, Tuesday, etc.). For a complete list of formats, visit:

      http://developer.android.com/reference/java/text/
         SimpleDateFormat.html

- Line 47 formats and returns the day name. Calendar's getTime method returns a Date object containing the time. This Date is passed to the SimpleDateFormat's format method to get the day name.

```
35       // convert timestamp to a day's name (e.g., Monday, Tuesday, ...)
36       private static String convertTimeStampToDay(long timeStamp) {
37          Calendar calendar = Calendar.getInstance(); // create Calendar
38          calendar.setTimeInMillis(timeStamp * 1000); // set time
39          TimeZone tz = TimeZone.getDefault(); // get device's time zone
40
```

Fig. 7.8 | Weather method convertTimeStampToDay. (Part 1 of 2.)

```
41          // adjust time for device's time zone
42          calendar.add(Calendar.MILLISECOND,
43             tz.getOffset(calendar.getTimeInMillis()));
44
45          // SimpleDateFormat that returns the day's name
46          SimpleDateFormat dateFormatter = new SimpleDateFormat("EEEE");
47          return dateFormatter.format(calendar.getTime());
48       }
49    }
```

Fig. 7.8 | Weather method convertTimeStampToDay. (Part 2 of 2.)

7.6 Class WeatherArrayAdapter

Class WeatherArrayAdapter defines a subclass of ArrayAdapter for binding an Array-
List<Weather> to the MainActivity's ListView.

7.6.1 package Statement and import Statements

Figure 7.9 contains WeatherArrayAdapter's package statement and import statements.
We'll discuss the imported types as we encounter them.

　　This app's ListView items require a custom layout. Each item contains an image (the
weather-condition icon) and text representing the day, weather description, low temperature, high temperature and humidity. To map weather data to ListView items, we extend
class ArrayAdapter (line 23) so that we can override ArrayAdapter method getView to
configure a custom layout for each ListView item.

```
1    // WeatherArrayAdapter.java
2    // An ArrayAdapter for displaying a List<Weather>'s elements in a ListView
3    package com.deitel.weatherviewer;
4
5    import android.content.Context;
6    import android.graphics.Bitmap;
7    import android.graphics.BitmapFactory;
8    import android.os.AsyncTask;
9    import android.view.LayoutInflater;
10   import android.view.View;
11   import android.view.ViewGroup;
12   import android.widget.ArrayAdapter;
13   import android.widget.ImageView;
14   import android.widget.TextView;
15
16   import java.io.InputStream;
17   import java.net.HttpURLConnection;
18   import java.net.URL;
19   import java.util.HashMap;
20   import java.util.List;
21   import java.util.Map;
22
23   class WeatherArrayAdapter extends ArrayAdapter<Weather> {
```

Fig. 7.9 | WeatherArrayAdapter class package statement and import statements.

7.6.2 Nested Class ViewHolder

Nested class ViewHolder (Fig. 7.10) defines instance variables that class WeatherArray-Adapter accesses directly when manipulating ViewHolder objects. When a ListView item is created, we'll associate a new ViewHolder object with that item. If there's an existing ListView item that's being reused, we'll simply obtain that item's ViewHolder object.

```
24      // class for reusing views as list items scroll off and onto the screen
25      private static class ViewHolder {
26          ImageView conditionImageView;
27          TextView dayTextView;
28          TextView lowTextView;
29          TextView hiTextView;
30          TextView humidityTextView;
31      }
32
```

Fig. 7.10 | Nested class ViewHolder.

7.6.3 Instance Variable and Constructor

Figure 7.11 defines class WeatherArrayAdapter's instance variable and constructor. We use the instance variable bitmaps (line 34)—a Map<String, Bitmap>—to cache previously loaded weather-condition images, so they do not need to be re-downloaded as the user scrolls through the weather forecast. The cached images will remain in memory until Android terminates the app. The constructor (lines 37–39) simply calls the superclass's three-argument constructor, passing the Context (i.e., the activity in which the ListView is displayed) and the List<Weather> (the List of data to display) as the first and third arguments. The second superclass constructor argument represents a layout resource ID for a layout that contains a TextView in which a ListView item's data is displayed. The argument -1 indicates that we use a custom layout in this app, so we can display more than just one TextView.

```
33      // stores already downloaded Bitmaps for reuse
34      private Map<String, Bitmap> bitmaps = new HashMap<>();
35
36      // constructor to initialize superclass inherited members
37      public WeatherArrayAdapter(Context context, List<Weather> forecast) {
38          super(context, -1, forecast);
39      }
40
```

Fig. 7.11 | WeatherArrayAdapter class instance variable and constructor.

7.6.4 Overridden ArrayAdapter Method getView

Method getView (Fig. 7.12) is called to get the View that displays a ListView item's data. Overriding this method enables you to map data to a custom ListView item. The method receives the ListView item's position, the View (convertView) representing that List-View item and that ListView item's parent as arguments. By manipulating convertView, you can customize the ListView item's contents. Line 45 calls the inherited ArrayAdapter method getItem to get from the List<Weather> the Weather object that will be displayed.

Line 47 defines the `ViewHolder` variable that will be set to a new `ViewHolder` object or an existing one, depending on whether method `getView`'s `convertView` argument is `null`.

```
41   // creates the custom views for the ListView's items
42   @Override
43   public View getView(int position, View convertView, ViewGroup parent) {
44       // get Weather object for this specified ListView position
45       Weather day = getItem(position);
46
47       ViewHolder viewHolder; // object that reference's list item's views
48
49       // check for reusable ViewHolder from a ListView item that scrolled
50       // offscreen; otherwise, create a new ViewHolder
51       if (convertView == null) { // no reusable ViewHolder, so create one
52           viewHolder = new ViewHolder();
53           LayoutInflater inflater = LayoutInflater.from(getContext());
54           convertView =
55               inflater.inflate(R.layout.list_item, parent, false);
56           viewHolder.conditionImageView =
57               (ImageView) convertView.findViewById(R.id.conditionImageView);
58           viewHolder.dayTextView =
59               (TextView) convertView.findViewById(R.id.dayTextView);
60           viewHolder.lowTextView =
61               (TextView) convertView.findViewById(R.id.lowTextView);
62           viewHolder.hiTextView =
63               (TextView) convertView.findViewById(R.id.hiTextView);
64           viewHolder.humidityTextView =
65               (TextView) convertView.findViewById(R.id.humidityTextView);
66           convertView.setTag(viewHolder);
67       }
68       else { // reuse existing ViewHolder stored as the list item's tag
69           viewHolder = (ViewHolder) convertView.getTag();
70       }
71
72       // if weather condition icon already downloaded, use it;
73       // otherwise, download icon in a separate thread
74       if (bitmaps.containsKey(day.iconURL)) {
75           viewHolder.conditionImageView.setImageBitmap(
76               bitmaps.get(day.iconURL));
77       }
78       else {
79           // download and display weather condition image
80           new LoadImageTask(viewHolder.conditionImageView).execute(
81               day.iconURL);
82       }
83
84       // get other data from Weather object and place into views
85       Context context = getContext(); // for loading String resources
86       viewHolder.dayTextView.setText(context.getString(
87           R.string.day_description, day.dayOfWeek, day.description));
88       viewHolder.lowTextView.setText(
89           context.getString(R.string.low_temp, day.minTemp));
```

Fig. 7.12 | Overridden `ArrayAdapter` method `getView`. (Part 1 of 2.)

```
90          viewHolder.hiTextView.setText(
91              context.getString(R.string.high_temp, day.maxTemp));
92          viewHolder.humidityTextView.setText(
93              context.getString(R.string.humidity, day.humidity));
94
95          return convertView; // return completed list item to display
96       }
97
```

Fig. 7.12 | Overridden ArrayAdapter method getView. (Part 2 of 2.)

If convertView is null, line 52 creates a new ViewHolder object to store references to a new ListView item's views. Next, line 53 gets the Context's LayoutInflator, which we use in lines 54–55 to inflate the ListView item's layout. The first argument is the layout to inflate (R.layout.list_item), the second is the layout's parent ViewGroup to which the layout's views will be attached and the last argument is a boolean indicating whether the views should be attached automatically. In this case, the third argument is false, because the ListView calls method getView to obtain the item's View, then attaches it to the ListView. Lines 56–65 get references to the views in the newly inflated layout and set the ViewHolder's instance variables. Line 66 sets the new ViewHolder object as the List-View item's tag to store the ViewHolder with the ListView item for future use.

If convertView is not null, the ListView is reusing a ListView item that scrolled off the screen. In this case, line 69 gets the current ListView item's tag, which is the View-Holder that was previously attached to that ListView item.

After creating or getting the ViewHolder, lines 74–93 set the data for the ListItem's views. Lines 74–82 determine if the weather-condition image was previously downloaded, in which case the bitmaps object will contain a key for the Weather object's iconURL. If so, lines 75–76 get the existing Bitmap from bitmaps and set the conditionImageView's image. Otherwise, lines 80–81 create a new LoadImageTask (Section 7.6.5) to download the image in a separate thread. The task's **execute** method receives the iconURL and initiates the task. Lines 86–93 set the Strings for the ListView item's TextViews. Finally, line 95 returns the ListView item's configured View.

Software Engineering Observation 7.1

Every time an AsyncTask is required, you must create a new object of your AsyncTask type—each AsyncTask can be executed only once.

7.6.5 AsyncTask Subclass for Downloading Images in a Separate Thread

Nested class LoadImageTask (Fig. 7.13) extends class AsyncTask and defines how to download a weather-condition image in a separate thread, then return the image to the GUI thread for display in the ListView item's ImageView.

```
98       // AsyncTask to load weather condition icons in a separate thread
99       private class LoadImageTask extends AsyncTask<String, Void, Bitmap> {
100         private ImageView imageView; // displays the thumbnail
```

Fig. 7.13 | AsyncTask subclass for downloading images in a separate thread. (Part 1 of 2.)

```
101
102      // store ImageView on which to set the downloaded Bitmap
103      public LoadImageTask(ImageView imageView) {
104         this.imageView = imageView;
105      }
106
107      // load image; params[0] is the String URL representing the image
108      @Override
109      protected Bitmap doInBackground(String... params) {
110         Bitmap bitmap = null;
111         HttpURLConnection connection = null;
112
113         try {
114            URL url = new URL(params[0]); // create URL for image
115
116            // open an HttpURLConnection, get its InputStream
117            // and download the image
118            connection = (HttpURLConnection) url.openConnection();
119
120            try (InputStream inputStream = connection.getInputStream()) {
121               bitmap = BitmapFactory.decodeStream(inputStream);
122               bitmaps.put(params[0], bitmap); // cache for later use
123            }
124            catch (Exception e) {
125               e.printStackTrace();
126            }
127         }
128         catch (Exception e) {
129            e.printStackTrace();
130         }
131         finally {
132            connection.disconnect(); // close the HttpURLConnection
133         }
134
135         return bitmap;
136      }
137
138      // set weather condition image in list item
139      @Override
140      protected void onPostExecute(Bitmap bitmap) {
141         imageView.setImageBitmap(bitmap);
142      }
143   }
144 }
```

Fig. 7.13 | AsyncTask subclass for downloading images in a separate thread. (Part 2 of 2.)

AsyncTask is a generic type that requires three type parameters:

- The first is the variable-length parameter-list type (String) for AsyncTask's doInBackground method, which you *must* overload (lines 108–136). When you call the task's execute method, it creates a thread in which doInBackground performs the task. This app passes the weather-condition icon's URL String as the argument to the AsyncTask's execute method (Fig. 7.12, lines 80–81).

- The second is the variable-length parameter-list type for the AsyncTask's onProgressUpdate method. This method executes in the GUI thread and is used to receive *intermediate updates* of the specified type from a long-running task. Overriding this method is optional. We don't use it in this example, so we specify type Void here and ignore this type parameter.

- The third is the type of the task's result (Bitmap), which is passed to AsyncTask's onPostExecute method (139–143). This method executes in the GUI thread and enables the ListView item's ImageView to display the AsyncTask's results. The ImageView to update is specified as an argument to class LoadImageTask's constructor (lines 103–105) and stored in the instance variable at line 100.

A key benefit of using an AsyncTask is that it handles the details of creating threads and executing its methods on the appropriate threads for you, so that you do not have to interact with the threading mechanism directly.

Downloading the Weather-Condition Image
Method doInBackground uses an HttpURLConnection to download the weather-condition image. Line 114 converts the URL String that was passed to the AsyncTask's execute method (params[0]) into a URL object. Next, line 118 calls class URL's method openConnection to get an HttpURLConnection—the cast is required, because the method returns a URLConnection. Method openConnection requests the content specified by URL. Line 120 gets the HttpURLConnection's InputStream, which we pass to BitmapFactory method decodeStream to read the image's bytes and return a Bitmap object containing the image (line 121). Line 122 caches the downloaded image in the bitmaps Map for potential reuse and line 132 calls HttpURLConnection's inherited method disconnect to close the connection and release its resources. Line 135 returns the downloaded Bitmap, which is then passed to onPostExecute—in the GUI thread—to display the image.

7.7 Class MainActivity

Class MainActivity defines the app's user interface, the logic for interacting with the OpenWeatherMap.org daily forecast web service and the logic for processing the JSON response from the web service. The nested AsyncTask subclass GetWeatherTask performs the web service request in a separate thread (Section 7.7.5). MainActivity does not require a menu in this app, so we removed the methods onCreateOptionsMenu and onOptionsItemSelected from the autogenerated code.

7.7.1 package Statement and import Statements

Figure 7.14 contains MainActivity's package statement and import statements. We'll discuss the imported types as we encounter them.

```
1   // MainActivity.java
2   // Displays a 16-dayOfWeek weather forecast for the specified city
3   package com.deitel.weatherviewer;
```

Fig. 7.14 | Class MainActivity's package statement and import statements. (Part I of 2.)

```
4
5    import android.content.Context;
6    import android.os.AsyncTask;
7    import android.os.Bundle;
8    import android.support.design.widget.FloatingActionButton;
9    import android.support.design.widget.Snackbar;
10   import android.support.v7.app.AppCompatActivity;
11   import android.support.v7.widget.Toolbar;
12   import android.view.View;
13   import android.view.inputmethod.InputMethodManager;
14   import android.widget.EditText;
15   import android.widget.ListView;
16
17   import org.json.JSONArray;
18   import org.json.JSONException;
19   import org.json.JSONObject;
20
21   import java.io.BufferedReader;
22   import java.io.IOException;
23   import java.io.InputStreamReader;
24   import java.net.HttpURLConnection;
25   import java.net.URL;
26   import java.net.URLEncoder;
27   import java.util.ArrayList;
28   import java.util.List;
29
```

Fig. 7.14 | Class MainActivity's package statement and import statements. (Part 2 of 2.)

7.7.2 Instance Variables

Class MainActivity (Fig. 7.15) extends class AppCompatActivity and defines three instance variables:

- weatherList (line 32) is an ArrayList<Weather> that stores the Weather objects—each represents one day in the daily forecast.

- weatherArrayAdapter will refer to a WeatherArrayAdapter object (Section 7.6) that binds the weatherList to the ListView's items.

- weatherListView will refer to MainActivity's ListView.

```
30   public class MainActivity extends AppCompatActivity {
31       // List of Weather objects representing the forecast
32       private List<Weather> weatherList = new ArrayList<>();
33
34       // ArrayAdapter for binding Weather objects to a ListView
35       private WeatherArrayAdapter weatherArrayAdapter;
36       private ListView weatherListView; // displays weather info
37
```

Fig. 7.15 | Class MainActivity's instance variables.

7.7.3 Overridden Activity Method onCreate

Overridden method onCreate (Fig. 7.15) configures MainActivity's GUI. Lines 41–45 were generated by Android Studio when you chose the **Blank Activity** template while creating this project. These lines inflate the GUI, create the app's Toolbar and attach the Toolbar to the activity. Recall that an AppCompatActivity must provide its own Toolbar, because app bars (formerly called action bars) are not supported in early versions of Android.

Lines 48–50 configure the weatherListView's ListAdapter—in this case, an object of the WeatherArrayAdapter subclass of ArrayAdapter. ListView method **setAdapter** connects the WeatherArrayAdapter to the ListView for populating the ListView's items.

```
38    // configure Toolbar, ListView and FAB
39    @Override
40    protected void onCreate(Bundle savedInstanceState) {
41       super.onCreate(savedInstanceState);
42       // autogenerated code to inflate layout and configure Toolbar
43       setContentView(R.layout.activity_main);
44       Toolbar toolbar = (Toolbar) findViewById(R.id.toolbar);
45       setSupportActionBar(toolbar);
46
47       // create ArrayAdapter to bind weatherList to the weatherListView
48       weatherListView = (ListView) findViewById(R.id.weatherListView);
49       weatherArrayAdapter = new WeatherArrayAdapter(this, weatherList);
50       weatherListView.setAdapter(weatherArrayAdapter);
51
52       // configure FAB to hide keyboard and initiate web service request
53       FloatingActionButton fab =
54          (FloatingActionButton) findViewById(R.id.fab);
55       fab.setOnClickListener(new View.OnClickListener() {
56          @Override
57          public void onClick(View view) {
58             // get text from locationEditText and create web service URL
59             EditText locationEditText =
60                (EditText) findViewById(R.id.locationEditText);
61             URL url = createURL(locationEditText.getText().toString());
62
63             // hide keyboard and initiate a GetWeatherTask to download
64             // weather data from OpenWeatherMap.org in a separate thread
65             if (url != null) {
66                dismissKeyboard(locationEditText);
67                GetWeatherTask getLocalWeatherTask = new GetWeatherTask();
68                getLocalWeatherTask.execute(url);
69             }
70             else {
71                Snackbar.make(findViewById(R.id.coordinatorLayout),
72                   R.string.invalid_url, Snackbar.LENGTH_LONG).show();
73             }
74          }
75       });
76    }
77
```

Fig. 7.16 | Overridden Activity method onCreate.

Lines 53–75 configure the FloatingActionButton from the **Blank Activity** template. The onClick listener method was autogenerated by Android Studio, but we reimplemented its body for this app. We get a reference to the app's EditText then use it in line 61 to get the user's input. We pass that to method createURL (Section 7.7.4) to create the URL representing the web service request that will return the city's weather forecast.

If the URL is created successfully, line 66 programmatically hides the keyboard by calling method dismissKeyboard (Section 7.7.4). Line 67 then creates a new GetWeatherTask to obtain the weather forecast in a separate thread and line 68 executes the task, passing the URL of the web service request as an argument to AsyncTask method execute. If the URL is not created successfully, lines 71–72 create a Snackbar indicating that the URL was invalid.

7.7.4 Methods dismissKeyboard and createURL

Figure 7.17 contains MainActivity methods dismissKeyboard and createURL. Method dismissKeyboard (lines 79–83) is called to hide the soft keyboard when the user touches the FloatingActionButton to submit a city to the app. Android provides a service for managing the keyboard programmatically. You can obtain a reference to this service (and many other Android services) by calling the inherited Context method getSystemService with the appropriate constant—Context.INPUT_METHOD_SERVICE in this case. This method can return objects of many different types, so you must cast its return value to the appropriate type—InputMethodManager (package android.view.inputmethod). To dismiss the keyboard, call InputMethodManager method hideSoftInputFromWindow (line 82).

```
78    // programmatically dismiss keyboard when user touches FAB
79    private void dismissKeyboard(View view) {
80       InputMethodManager imm = (InputMethodManager) getSystemService(
81          Context.INPUT_METHOD_SERVICE);
82       imm.hideSoftInputFromWindow(view.getWindowToken(), 0);
83    }
84
85    // create openweathermap.org web service URL using city
86    private URL createURL(String city) {
87       String apiKey = getString(R.string.api_key);
88       String baseUrl = getString(R.string.web_service_url);
89
90       try {
91          // create URL for specified city and imperial units (Fahrenheit)
92          String urlString = baseUrl + URLEncoder.encode(city, "UTF-8") +
93             "&units=imperial&cnt=16&APPID=" + apiKey;
94          return new URL(urlString);
95       }
96       catch (Exception e) {
97          e.printStackTrace();
98       }
99
100      return null; // URL was malformed
101   }
102
```

Fig. 7.17 | MainActivity methods dismissKeyboard and createURL.

Method createURL (lines 86–101) assembles the String representation of the URL for the web service request (lines 92–93). Then line 94 attempts to create and return a URL object initialized with the URL String. In line 93, we add parameters to the web service query

```
&units=imperial&cnt=16&APPID=
```

The units parameter can be imperial (for Fahrenheit temperatures), metric (for Celsius) or standard (for Kelvin)—standard is the default if you do not include the units parameter. The cnt parameter specifies how many days should be included in the forecast. The maximum is 16 and the default is 7—providing an invalid number of days results in a seven-day forecast. Finally the APPID parameter is for your OpenWeatherMap.org API key, which we load into the app from the String resource api_key. By default, the forecast is returned in JSON format, but you can add the mode parameter with the value XML or HTML, to receive XML formatted data or a web page, respectively.

7.7.5 AsyncTask Subclass for Invoking a Web Service

Nested AsyncTask subclass GetWeatherTask (Fig. 7.18) performs the web service request and processes the response in a separate thread, then passes the forecast information as a JSONObject to the GUI thread for display.

```
103    // makes the REST web service call to get weather data and
104    // saves the data to a local HTML file
105    private class GetWeatherTask
106       extends AsyncTask<URL, Void, JSONObject> {
107
108       @Override
109       protected JSONObject doInBackground(URL... params) {
110          HttpURLConnection connection = null;
111
112          try {
113             connection = (HttpURLConnection) params[0].openConnection();
114             int response = connection.getResponseCode();
115
116             if (response == HttpURLConnection.HTTP_OK) {
117                StringBuilder builder = new StringBuilder();
118
119                try (BufferedReader reader = new BufferedReader(
120                   new InputStreamReader(connection.getInputStream()))) {
121
122                   String line;
123
124                   while ((line = reader.readLine()) != null) {
125                      builder.append(line);
126                   }
127                }
128                catch (IOException e) {
129                   Snackbar.make(findViewById(R.id.coordinatorLayout),
130                      R.string.read_error, Snackbar.LENGTH_LONG).show();
131                   e.printStackTrace();
132                }
```

Fig. 7.18 | AsyncTask subclass for invoking a web service. (Part 1 of 2.)

```
133
134                return new JSONObject(builder.toString());
135            }
136            else {
137                Snackbar.make(findViewById(R.id.coordinatorLayout),
138                    R.string.connect_error, Snackbar.LENGTH_LONG).show();
139            }
140        }
141        catch (Exception e) {
142            Snackbar.make(findViewById(R.id.coordinatorLayout),
143                R.string.connect_error, Snackbar.LENGTH_LONG).show();
144            e.printStackTrace();
145        }
146        finally {
147            connection.disconnect(); // close the HttpURLConnection
148        }
149
150        return null;
151    }
152
153    // process JSON response and update ListView
154    @Override
155    protected void onPostExecute(JSONObject weather) {
156        convertJSONtoArrayList(weather); // repopulate weatherList
157        weatherArrayAdapter.notifyDataSetChanged(); // rebind to ListView
158        weatherListView.smoothScrollToPosition(0); // scroll to top
159    }
160 }
161
```

Fig. 7.18 | AsyncTask subclass for invoking a web service. (Part 2 of 2.)

For class GetWeatherTask the three generic type parameters are:

- URL for the variable-length parameter-list type of AsyncTask's doInBackground method (lines 108–51)—the URL of the web service request is passed as the only argument to the GetWeatherTask's execute method.

- Void for the variable-length parameter-list type for the onProgressUpdate method—once again, we do not use this method.

- JSONObject for the type of the task's result, which is passed to onPostExecute (154–159) in the GUI thread to display the results.

Line 113 in doInBackground creates the HttpURLConnection that's used to invoke the REST web service. As in Section 7.6.5, simply opening the connection makes the request. Line 114 gets the response code from the web server. If the response code is HttpURLConnection.HTTP_OK, the REST web service was invoked properly and there is a response to process. In this case, lines 119–126 get the HttpURLConnection's InputStream, wrap it in a BufferedReader, read each line of text from the response and append it to a StringBuilder. Then, line 134 converts the JSON String in the StringBuilder to a JSONObject and return it to the GUI thread. Line 147 disconnects the HttpURLConnection.

If there's an error reading the weather data or connecting to the web service, lines 129–130, 137–138 or 142–143 display a Snackbar indicating the problem that occurred.

These problems might occur if the device loses its network access in the middle of a request or if the device does not have network access in the first place—for example, if the device is in airplane mode.

When `onPostExecute` is called in the GUI thread, line 156 calls method `convertJSONtoArrayList` (Section 7.7.6) to extract the weather data from the `JSONObject` and place it in the `weatherList`. Then line 157 calls the `ArrayAdapter`'s `notifyDataSetChanged` method, which causes the `weatherListView` to update itself with the new data. Line 158 calls `ListView` method `smoothScrollToPosition` to reposition the `ListView`'s first item to the top of the `ListView`—this ensures that the new weather forecast's first day is shown at the top.

7.7.6 Method `convertJSONtoArrayList`

In Section 7.3.2, we discussed the JSON returned by the `OpenWeatherMap.org` daily weather forecast web service. Method `convertJSONtoArrayList` (Fig. 7.19) extracts this weather data from its `JSONObject` argument. First, line 164 clears the `weatherList` of any existing `Weather` objects. Processing JSON data in a `JSONObject` or `JSONArray` can result in `JSONExceptions`, so lines 168–188 are placed in a `try` block.

```
162    // create Weather objects from JSONObject containing the forecast
163    private void convertJSONtoArrayList(JSONObject forecast) {
164        weatherList.clear(); // clear old weather data
165
166        try {
167            // get forecast's "list" JSONArray
168            JSONArray list = forecast.getJSONArray("list");
169
170            // convert each element of list to a Weather object
171            for (int i = 0; i < list.length(); ++i) {
172                JSONObject day = list.getJSONObject(i); // get one day's data
173
174                // get the day's temperatures ("temp") JSONObject
175                JSONObject temperatures = day.getJSONObject("temp");
176
177                // get day's "weather" JSONObject for the description and icon
178                JSONObject weather =
179                    day.getJSONArray("weather").getJSONObject(0);
180
181                // add new Weather object to weatherList
182                weatherList.add(new Weather(
183                    day.getLong("dt"), // date/time timestamp
184                    temperatures.getDouble("min"), // minimum temperature
185                    temperatures.getDouble("max"), // maximum temperature
186                    day.getDouble("humidity"), // percent humidity
187                    weather.getString("description"), // weather conditions
188                    weather.getString("icon"))); // icon name
189            }
190        }
```

Fig. 7.19 | `MainActivity` method `convertJSONtoArrayList`. (Part 1 of 2.)

```
191          catch (JSONException e) {
192             e.printStackTrace();
193          }
194       }
195   }
```

Fig. 7.19 | `MainActivity` method `convertJSONtoArrayList`. (Part 2 of 2.)

Line 168 obtains the `"list"` `JSONArray` by calling `JSONObject` method `getJSONArray` with the name of the array property as an argument. Next, lines 171–189 create a `Weather` object for every element in the `JSONArray`. `JSONArray` method `length` returns the array's number of elements (line 171).

Next, line 172 gets a `JSONObject` representing one day's forecast from the `JSONArray` by calling method `getJSONObject`, which receives an index as its argument. Line 175 gets the `"temp"` JSON object, which contains the day's temperature data. Lines 178–179 get the `"weather"` JSON array, then get the array's first element which contains the day's weather description and icon.

Lines 182–188 create a `Weather` object and add it to the `weatherList`. Line 183 uses `JSONObject` method `getLong` to get the day's timestamp (`"dt"`), which the Weather constructor converts to the day name. Lines 184–186 call `JSONObject` method `getDouble` to get the minimum (`"min"`) and maximum (`"max"`) temperatures from the `temperatures` object and the `"humidity"` percentage from the day object. Finally, lines 187–188 use `getString` to get the weather description and the weather-condition icon `String`s from the `weather` object.

7.8 Wrap-Up

In this chapter, you built the **WeatherViewer** app. The app obtained a city's 16-day weather forecast from web services provided by `OpenWeatherMap.org` and displayed the forecast in a `ListView`. We discussed the architectural style for implementing web services known as Representational State Transfer (REST). You learned that apps use web standards, such as HyperText Transfer Protocol (HTTP), to invoke RESTful web services and receive their responses.

The `OpenWeatherMap.org` web service used in this app returned the forecast as a `String` in JavaScript Object Notation (JSON) format. You learned that JSON is a text-based format in which objects are represented as collections of name/value pairs. You used the classes `JSONObject` and `JSONArray` from the `org.json` package to process the JSON data.

To invoke the web service, you converted the web service's URL `String` into a `URL` object. You then used the `URL` to open an `HttpUrlConnection` that invoked the web service via an HTTP request. The app read all the data from the `HttpUrlConnection`'s `Input-Stream` and placed it in a `String`, then converted that `String` to a `JSONObject` for processing. We demonstrated how to perform long-running operations outside the GUI thread and receive their results in the GUI thread by using `AsyncTask` objects. This is particularly important for web-service requests, which have indeterminate response times.

You displayed the weather data in a `ListView`, using a subclass of `ArrayAdapter` to supply the data for each `ListView` item. We showed how to improve a `ListView`'s performance via the view-holder pattern by reusing existing ListView items' views as the items scroll off the screen.

Finally, you used several material-design features from the Android Design Support Library's—a TextInputLayout to keep an EditText's hint on the screen even after the user began entering text, a FloatingActionButton to enable the user to submit input and a Snackbar to display an informational message to the user.

In Chapter 8, we build the **Twitter® Searches** app. Many mobile apps display lists of items, just as we did in this app. In Chapter 8, you'll do this by using a RecyclerView that obtains data from an ArrayList<String>. For large data sets, RecyclerView is more efficient than ListView. You'll also store app data as user preferences and learn how to launch the device's web browser to display a web page.

8

Twitter® Searches App

SharedPreferences, SharedPreferences.Editor,
Implicit Intents, Intent Choosers, RecyclerView,
RecyclerView.Adapter, RecyclerView.ViewHolder,
RecyclerView.ItemDecoration

Objectives

In this chapter you'll:

- Use SharedPreferences to store key–value pairs of data associated with an app.

- Use an implicit Intent to open a website in a browser.

- Use an implicit Intent to display an intent chooser containing a list of apps that can share text.

- Display a scrolling list of items in a RecyclerView.

- Use a subclass of RecyclerView.Adapter to specify a RecyclerView's data.

- Use a subclass of RecyclerView.ViewHolder to implement the view-holder pattern for a RecyclerView.

- Use a subclass of RecyclerView.ItemDecoration to display lines between a RecyclerView's items.

- Use an AlertDialog.Builder object to create an AlertDialog that displays a list of options.

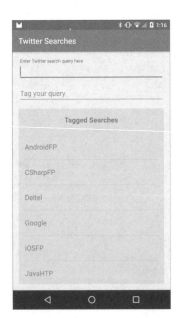

Outline

8.1 Introduction

Twitter's search mechanism makes it easy to follow trending topics being discussed by Twitter's 300+ million active monthly users[1] (there are over one billion total Twitter accounts[2]). Searches can be fine-tuned using Twitter's *search operators* (Section 8.2), often resulting in lengthy search strings that are time consuming and cumbersome to enter on a mobile device. The **Twitter® Searches** app (Fig. 8.1) allows you to save your favorite search queries with easy-to-remember short tag names (Fig. 8.1(a)) that are displayed as a scrollable list. You can then scroll through your saved searches and simply touch a tag name to quickly view tweets on a given topic (Fig. 8.1(b)). As you'll see, the app also allows you to *share, edit* and *delete* saved searches.

---

1. `https://about.twitter.com/company`.

2. `http://www.businessinsider.com/twitter-monthly-active-users-2015-7?r=UK&IR=T`.

a) App with several saved searches   b) App after the user touches "**Deitel**"

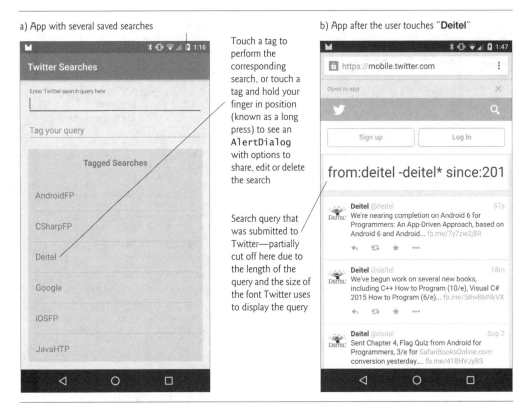

Touch a tag to perform the corresponding search, or touch a tag and hold your finger in position (known as a long press) to see an `AlertDialog` with options to share, edit or delete the search

Search query that was submitted to Twitter—partially cut off here due to the length of the query and the size of the font Twitter uses to display the query

Fig. 8.1 | Twitter Searches app.

The app supports both portrait and landscape orientations. In the **Flag Quiz** app, you did this by providing separate layouts for each orientation. In the **Doodlz** app, you did this by programmatically setting the orientation. In this app, we support both orientations by designing a GUI that *dynamically* adjusts, based on the current orientation.

First, you'll test-drive the app. Then we'll overview the technologies we used to build it. Next, we'll design the app's GUI. Finally, we'll walk through the app's complete source code, discussing the new features in more detail.

8.2 Test-Driving the App

Opening and Running the App
Open Android Studio and open the **Twitter Searches** app from the `TwitterSearches` folder in the book's examples folder, then execute the app in the AVD or on a device. This builds the project and runs the app (Fig. 8.2).

8.2.1 Adding a Favorite Search

Touch the top `EditText`, then enter `from:deitel` as the search query—the `from:` operator locates tweets from a specified Twitter account. Figure 8.3 shows several Twitter search

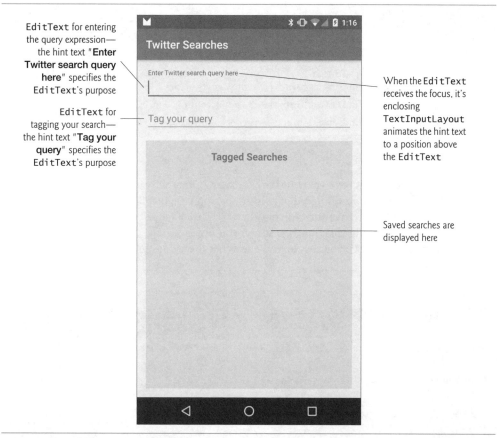

EditText for entering the query expression—the hint text "**Enter Twitter search query here**" specifies the EditText's purpose

EditText for tagging your search—the hint text "**Tag your query**" specifies the EditText's purpose

When the EditText receives the focus, it's enclosing TextInputLayout animates the hint text to a position above the EditText

Saved searches are displayed here

Fig. 8.2 | Twitter Searches app when it first executes.

operators—multiple operators can be used to construct more complex queries. A complete list can be found at

```
http://bit.ly/TwitterSearchOperators
```

Example	Finds tweets containing
google android	Implicit *logical and* operator—Finds tweets containing google *and* android.
google OR android	Logical OR operator—Finds tweets containing google *or* android *or both*.
"how to program"	String in quotes("")—Finds tweets containing "how to program".
android ?	? (question mark)—Finds tweets asking questions about android.
google -android	- (minus sign)—Finds tweets containing google but not android.
android :)	:) (happy face)—Finds *positive attitude* tweets containing android.
android :(	:((sad face)—Finds *negative attitude* tweets containing android.

Fig. 8.3 | Some Twitter search operators. (Part 1 of 2.)

Example	Finds tweets containing
`since:2013-10-01`	Finds tweets that occurred *on or after* the specified date, which must be in the form YYYY-MM-DD.
`near:"New York City"`	Finds tweets that were sent near "New York City".
`from:GoogleCode`	Finds tweets from the Twitter account @GoogleCode.
`to:GoogleCode`	Finds tweets to the Twitter account @GoogleCode.

Fig. 8.3 | Some Twitter search operators. (Part 2 of 2.)

In the bottom `EditText` enter `Deitel` as the tag for the search query (Fig. 8.4(a)). This will be the *short name* displayed in a list in the app's **Tagged Searches** section. Touch the *save* button (🔘) to save the search—the tag "Deitel" appears in the list under the **Tagged Searches** heading (Fig. 8.4(b)). When you save a search, the soft keyboard is dismissed so that you can see your list of saved searches (Section 8.5.5).

a) Entering a Twitter search and search tag   b) App after saving the search and search tag

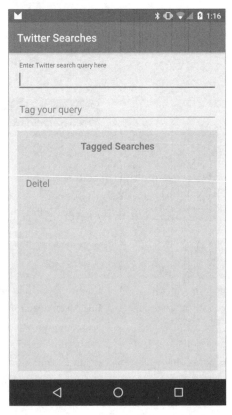

Fig. 8.4 | Entering a Twitter search.

8.2.2 Viewing Twitter Search Results

To view the search results, touch the tag "**Deitel**." This launches the device's web browser and passes a URL that represents the saved search to the Twitter website. Twitter obtains the search query from the URL, then returns the tweets that match the query (if any) as a web page. The web browser then displays the results page (Fig. 8.5). When you're done viewing the results, touch the back button (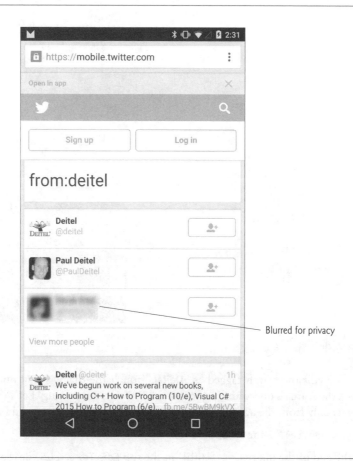) to return to the **Twitter Searches** app where you can save more searches, and edit, delete and share previously saved searches. For the `"from:deitel"` query, Twitter shows relevant user accounts containing `deitel` in the account name and recent tweets from those accounts.

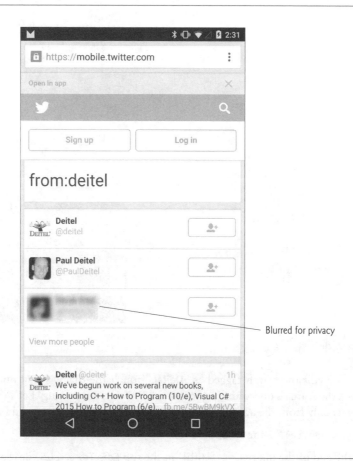

Fig. 8.5 | Viewing search results for `from:deitel`—we blurred one Twitter account for privacy.

8.2.3 Editing a Search

You may also *share*, *edit* or *delete* a search. To see these options, *long press* the search's tag— that is, touch the tag and keep your finger on the screen until the dialog containing **Share**, **Edit** and **Delete** options appears. If you're using an AVD, click and hold the left mouse button on the search tag to perform a long press. When you long press "**Deitel**," the `Alert-`

Dialog in Fig. 8.6(a) displays the **Share**, **Edit** and **Delete** options for the search tagged as "**Deitel**." If you don't wish to perform any of these tasks, touch **CANCEL**.

<table>
<tr>
<td>a) Selecting **Edit** to edit an existing search</td>
<td>b) Editing the "**Deitel**" saved search</td>
</tr>
<tr>
<td></td>
<td></td>
</tr>
</table>

Fig. 8.6 | Editing a saved search.

To edit the search tagged as "**Deitel**," touch the dialog's **Edit** option. The app then loads the search's query and tag into the `EditText`s for editing. Let's restrict our search to tweets only from the account `@deitel` since September 1, 2015. Add a space then

```
-deitel* since:2015-06-01
```

to the end of the query (Fig. 8.6(b)) in the top `EditText`. The `-deitel*` deletes from the results tweets from accounts that begin with `"deitel"` but followed by other characters. The `since:` operator restricts the search results to tweets that occurred *on or after* the specified date (in the form yyyy-mm-dd). Touch the *save* button (🔘) to update the saved search, then view the updated results (Fig. 8.7) by touching **Deitel** in the **Tagged Searches** section of the app. [*Note:* Changing the tag name will create a *new* search, which is useful if you want to create a new query that's based on a previously saved query.]

Fig. 8.7 | Viewing the updated "**Deitel**" search results.

8.2.4 Sharing a Search

Android makes it easy for you to share various types of information from an app via e-mail, instant messaging (SMS), Facebook, Google+, Twitter and more. In this app, you can share a favorite search by *long pressing* the search's tag and selecting **Share** from the Alert-Dialog that appears. This displays a so-called intent chooser (Fig. 8.8(a)), which can vary, based on the type of content you're sharing and the apps that can handle that content. In this app we're sharing text, and the intent chooser on our phone shows many apps capable of handling text. If no apps can handle the content, the intent chooser will display a message saying so. If only one app can handle the content, that app will launch without you having to select which app to use from the intent chooser. For this test-drive, we touched **Gmail**. Figure 8.8(b) shows the **Gmail** app's **Compose** screen with the from address, e-mail subject and body pre-populated. We blurred the **From** email address for privacy in the screen capture.

a) Intent chooser showing share options

b) Gmail app **Compose** screen for an e-mail containing the "**Deitel**" search

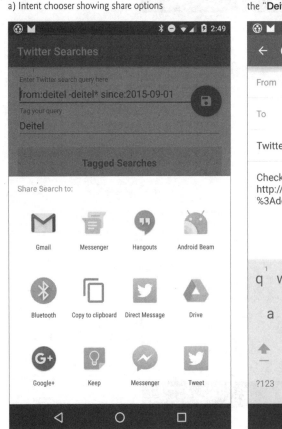

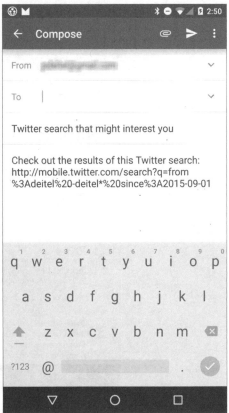

Fig. 8.8 | Sharing a search via e-mail—the Gmail **Compose** window shows your email address by default (blurred for privacy here), positions the cursor in the **To** field so you can enter the recipient's email address and prepopulates the email's subject and content.

8.2.5 Deleting a Search

To delete a search, *long press* the search's tag and select **Delete** from the AlertDialog that appears. The app prompts you to confirm that you'd like to delete the search (Fig. 8.9)—touching **CANCEL** returns you to the main screen *without* deleting the search. Touching **DELETE** deletes the search.

Are you sure you want to delete the search "Deitel"?

CANCEL   DELETE

Fig. 8.9 | AlertDialog confirming a delete.

8.2.6 Scrolling Through Saved Searches

Figure 8.10 shows the app after we've saved several favorite searches—six of which are currently visible. The app allows you to scroll through your favorite searches if there are more than can be displayed on the screen at once. Unlike desktop apps, touch-screen apps do not typically display scrollbars to indicate scrollable areas of the screen. To scroll, simply *drag* or *flick* your finger (or the mouse in an AVD) up or down in the list of **Tagged Searches**. Also, rotate the device to *landscape* orientation to see that the GUI dynamically adjusts.

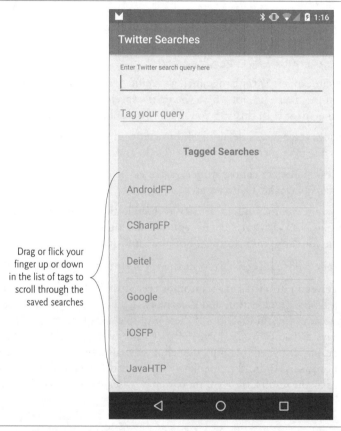

Drag or flick your finger up or down in the list of tags to scroll through the saved searches

Fig. 8.10 | App with more searches than can be displayed on the screen.

8.3 Technologies Overview

This section introduces the features you'll use to build the **Twitter Searches** app.

8.3.1 Storing Key–Value Data in a SharedPreferences File

Each app can have `SharedPreferences` files containing key–value pairs associated with the app—each key enables you to quickly look up a corresponding value. Chapter 4's **Flag Quiz** app stored the app's preferences in a `SharedPreferences` file on the device. That app's `PreferenceFragment` created the `SharedPreferences` file for you. In this app, you'll create and manage a `SharedPreferences` file called `searches` in which you'll store the pairs of tags (the keys) and Twitter search queries (the *values*) that the user creates. Once again, you'll use a `SharedPreferences.Editor` to make changes to the tag–query pairs.

> **Performance Tip 8.1**
> *This app does not store a lot of data, so we read the saved searches from the device in* Main-
> Activity's *onCreate method. Lengthy data access should not be done in the UI thread; otherwise, the app will display an Application Not Responding (ANR) dialog—typically after five seconds of preventing the user from interacting with the app. For information on designing responsive apps, see* `http://developer.android.com/training/articles/perf-anr.html` *and consider using* AsyncTasks *as shown in Chapter 7.*

8.3.2 Implicit Intents and Intent Choosers

In Chapter 4, you used an explicit `Intent` to launch a specific `Activity` in the same app. Android also supports implicit `Intents` for which you do *not* specify explicitly which component should handle the `Intent`. In this app you'll use two implicit `Intents`:

- one that launches the device's default web browser to display Twitter search results, based on a search query embedded in a URL, and

- one that enables the user to choose from a variety of apps that can share text, so the user can share a favorite Twitter search.

In either case, if the system cannot find an activity to handle the action, then method `startActivity` throws an `ActivityNotFoundException`. It's a good practice to handle this exception to prevent your app from crashing. For more information on `Intents`, visit

```
http://developer.android.com/guide/components/intents-filters.html
```

When Android receives an implicit `Intent`, it finds every installed app containing an `Activity` that can handle the given action and data type. If there is only one, Android launches the appropriate `Activity` in that app. If there multiple apps that can handle the `Intent`, Android displays a dialog from which the user can choose which app should handle the `Intent`. For example, when this app's user chooses a saved search and the device contains only one web browser, Android immediately launches that web browser to perform the search and display the results. If two or more web browsers are installed, however, the user must select which browser should perform this task.

8.3.3 RecyclerView

In Chapter 7, you used a `ListView` to display a weather forecast—a limited set of data. Many mobile apps display extensive lists of information. For example, an e-mail app displays a list of e-mails, an address-book app displays a list of contacts, a news app displays a list of headlines, etc. In each case, the user touches an item in the list to see more information—e.g., the content of the selected e-mail, the details of the selected contact or the text of the selected news story.

RecyclerView vs. ListView

In this app, you'll display the scrollable list of tagged searches using a `RecyclerView` (package `android.support.v7.widget`)—a flexible, customizable view that enables you to control how an app displays a scrolling list of data. `RecyclerView` was designed as a better

ListView. It provides better separation of the data's presentation from the RecyclerView's capabilities for reusing views (Section 8.3.4), as well as more flexible customization options (Section 8.3.5) for presenting the RecyclerView's items. For example, a ListView's items are always displayed in a vertical list, whereas a RecyclerView has layout managers that can display the items in a vertical list or in a grid. You can even define your own custom layout manager.

RecyclerView *Layout Managers*

For this app, the RecyclerView will use a LinearLayoutManager—a subclass of RecyclerView.LayoutManager—to specify that the items will appear in a vertical list, and the list items will each display a search's tag as a String in a TextView. You also can design custom layouts for a RecyclerView's items.

8.3.4 RecyclerView.Adapter and RecyclerView.ViewHolder

In Chapter 7, we used a subclass of Adapter to bind data to the ListView. We also introduced the view-holder pattern for reusing views that scroll off-screen. Recall that we created a class called ViewHolder (Section 8.6.2) that maintained references to the views in a ListView item. The Adapter subclass stored a ViewHolder object with each ListView item so that we could reuse the ListView item's views. You're not required to use this pattern, but doing so is recommended to increase the ListView's scrolling performance.

RecyclerView formalizes the view-holder pattern by making it required. You'll create a RecyclerView.Adapter subclass to bind the RecyclerView's list items to data in a List (Section 8.6). Each RecyclerView item has a corresponding object of a subclass of class RecyclerView.ViewHolder (Section 8.6.2) that maintains references to the item's view(s) for reuse. The RecyclerView and its RecyclerView.Adapter work together to recycle the view(s) for items that scroll off the screen.

8.3.5 RecyclerView.ItemDecoration

Class ListView automatically displays a horizontal line between items, but RecyclerView does not provide any default decorations. To display horizontal lines between the items, you'll define a subclass of RecyclerView.ItemDecoration that draws divider lines onto the RecyclerView (Section 8.7).

8.3.6 Displaying a List of Options in an AlertDialog

This app enables the user to long touch a RecyclerView item to display an AlertDialog containing a list of options from which the user can select only one. You'll use an AlertDialog.Builder's setItems method to specify a String array resource containing names of the option to display and to set the event handler that's called when the user touches one of the options.

8.4 Building the App's GUI and Resource Files

In this section, you'll build the **Twitter Searches** app's GUI and resource files. Recall from Section 8.3.3 that RecyclerView does not define how to render its list items. So you'll also create a layout that defines a list item's GUI. The RecyclerView will inflate this layout as necessary when creating list items.

8.4.1 Creating the Project

Create a new project using the **Blank Activity** template. Fragments are not required for this app, so when you configure the **Blank Activity**, do not check the **Use a Fragment** checkbox. Specify the following values in the **Create New Project** dialog's **New Project** step:

- **Application name:** Twitter Searches
- **Company Domain:** deitel.com (or specify your own domain name)

Follow the steps you used in earlier apps to add an app icon to your project. Delete the **Hello world!** TextView from the content_main.xml, as it's not used. Also, follow the steps in Section 4.4.3 to configure Java SE 7 support for the project.

8.4.2 AndroidManifest.xml

Most users will launch this app so that they can perform an existing saved search. When the first focusable GUI component in an activity is an EditText, Android gives that component the focus when the activity is displayed. When an EditText receives the focus, its corresponding virtual keyboard is displayed unless a hardware keyboard is present. In this app, we want to prevent the soft keyboard from being displayed until the user touches one of the app's EditTexts. To do so, follow the steps in Section 3.7 for setting the window-SoftInputMode option, but set its value to stateAlwaysHidden.

8.4.3 Adding the RecyclerView Library

This app uses new material-design user-interface components from the Android Design Support Library, including the TextInputLayout, FloatingActionButton, and the RecyclerView. Android Studio's new app templates are already configured with Android Design Support Library support for TextInputLayout and FloatingActionButton. To use RecyclerView, however, you must update the app's dependencies to include the RecyclerView library:

1. Right click the project's **app** folder and select **Open Module Settings** to open the **Project Structure** window.

2. Open the **Dependencies** tab, then click the add icon (+) and select **Library Dependency** to open the **Choose Library Dependency** dialog.

3. Select the **recyclerview-v7** library in the list, then click **OK**. The library will appear in the **Dependencies** tab's list.

4. In the **Project Structure** window, click **OK**.

The IDE updates the project's build.gradle file—the one that appears in the project's **Gradle Scripts** node as **build.gradle (Module: app)**—to specify the new dependency. The Gradle build tool then makes the libraries available for use in your project.

8.4.4 colors.xml

For this app, we changed the app's default accent color (used for the EditTexts, TextInputLayouts and FloatingActionButton) and added a color resource for the background color in the **Tagged Searches** area of the screen. Open colors.xml and replace the hexadecimal value for the `colorAccent` resource with #FF5722, then add a new color resource named `colorTaggedSearches` with the value #BBDEFB.

8.4.5 `strings.xml`

Add the `String` resources in Fig. 8.11 to `strings.xml`.

Key	Default Value
query_prompt	Enter Twitter search query here
tag_prompt	Tag your query
save_description	Touch this button to save your tagged search
tagged_searches	Tagged Searches
search_URL	http://mobile.twitter.com/search?q=
share_edit_delete_title	Share, Edit or Delete the search tagged as \"%s\"
cancel	Cancel
share_subject	Twitter search that might interest you
share_message	Check out the results of this Twitter search: %s
share_search	Share Search to:
confirm_message	Are you sure you want to delete the search \"%s\"?
delete	Delete

Fig. 8.11 | String resources used in the **Twitter Searches** app.

8.4.6 `arrays.xml`

Recall from Chapter 4 that array resources are normally defined in `arrays.xml`. Follow the steps in Section 4.4.6 to create an `arrays.xml` file, then add the resource in (Fig. 8.12) to the file.

Array resource name	Values
dialog_items	Share, Edit, Delete

Fig. 8.12 | String array resources defined in `arrays.xml`.

8.4.7 `dimens.xml`

Add the dimension resource shown in Fig. 8.13 to the `dimens.xml` file.

Resource name	Value
fab_margin_top	90dp

Fig. 8.13 | Dimension resources in `dimens.xml`.

8.4.8 Adding the Save Button Icon

Use Android Studio's **Vector Asset Studio** (Section 4.4.9) to add the material design save icon (; located in the **Content** group) to the project—this will be used as the `Floating-ActionButton`'s icon. After adding the vector icon, go to the project's `res/drawable` folder, open the icon's XML file and change the `<path>` element's `android:fillColor` value to

```
"@android:color/white"
```

This will make the icon more visible against the app's accent color, which is applied to the `FloatingActionButton` by the app's theme.

8.4.9 `activity_main.xml`

In this section, you'll customize the `FloatingActionButton` that's built into Android Studio's **Blank Activity** app template. By default, the button contains an email icon and is positioned the bottom-right of `MainActivity`'s layout. You'll replace the email icon with the save icon that you added in Section 8.4.8 and reposition the button at the layout's top right. Perform the following steps:

1. Open `activity_main.xml` and, in **Design** view, select the `FloatingActionButton` in the **Component Tree**.

2. Set the **contentDescription** property to the `save_description` String resource and set the **src** property to the `ic_save_24dp` Drawable resource.

At the time of this writing, Android Studio does not display layout properties for components from the Android Design Support Library, so any changes to these properties must be implemented directly in the layout's XML. Switch to **Text** view, then:

3. Change the `layout_gravity` property's value from `"bottom|end"` to `"top|end"` so that the `FloatingActionButton`'s moves to the top of the layout.

4. Change the name of the `layout_margin` property to `layout_marginEnd` so it applies only to the `FloatingActionButton`'s right side (or left side for right-to-left languages).

5. Add the following line to the `FloatingActionButton`'s XML element to specify a new value for its top margin—this moves the button down from the top of the layout over the part of the GUI defined by `content_main.xml`:

```
android:layout_marginTop="@dimen/fab_margin_top"
```

8.4.10 `content_main.xml`

The `RelativeLayout` in this app's `content_main.xml` contains two `TextInputLayouts` and a `LinearLayout` that, in turn, contains a `TextView` and a `RecyclerView`. Use the layout editor and the **Component Tree** window to form the layout structure shown in Fig. 8.14. As you create the GUI components, set their **ids** as specified in the figure. There are several components in this layout that do not require **ids**, as the app's Java code does not reference them directly.

Fig. 8.14 | Twitter Searches GUI's components labeled with their **id** property values.

Step 1: Adding the queryTextInputLayout and Its Nested EditText

Add the queryTextInputLayout and its nested EditText as follows:

1. Insert a TextInputLayout. In the layout editor's **Design** view, click **CustomView** in the **Palette**'s **Custom** section. In the dialog that appears, begin typing TextInputLayout to search the list of custom GUI components. Once the IDE highlights TextInputLayout, click **OK**, then in the **Component Tree**, click the RelativeLayout to insert the TextInputLayout as a nested layout. Select the TextInputLayout and set its **id** to queryTextInputLayout.

2. To add an EditText to the TextInputLayout, switch to the layout editor's **Text** view, then change the TextInputLayout element's closing /> to >, position the cursor to the right of the >, press *Enter* and type </. The IDE will auto-complete the closing tag. Between the TextInputLayout's starting and ending tags, type <EditText. The IDE will show an auto-complete window with EditText selected. Press *Enter* to insert an EditText, then set its layout_width to match_parent and layout_height to wrap_content.

3. Switch back to **Design** view, then in the **Component Tree**, select the EditText and set its **imeOptions** to actionNext (the keyboard displays a ⊙ button to jump to the next EditText), its **hint** to the String resource query_prompt and check its **singleLine** property's checkbox. To view the **imeOptions** property, you must first click the **Show expert properties** button (▼) at the top of the **Properties** window.

Step 2: Adding the `tagTextInputLayout` and Its Nested `EditText`

Using the techniques from the previous step, add the `tagTextInputLayout` and its nested `EditText`, with the following changes:

1. After adding the `TextInputLayout`, set its **id** to `tagTextInputLayout`.

2. In **Text** view, add the following line to the `tagTextInputLayout`'s XML element to indicate that this `TextInputLayout` should appear below the `queryTextInputLayout`:

   ```
   android:layout_below="@id/queryTextInputLayout"
   ```

3. In **Design** view, set the `String` resource `tag_prompt` as the `tagTextInputLayout` `EditText`'s **hint**.

4. Set the `EditText`'s **imeOptions** to `actionDone`—for this option, the keyboard displays a ✓ button to dismiss the keyboard.

Step 3: Adding the `LinearLayout`

Next, add a `LinearLayout` below the `tagTextInputLayout`:

1. In **Design** view, drag a **LinearLayout (vertical)** onto the **RelativeLayout** node in the **Component Tree**.

2. In the **Properties** window, expand the **layout:alignComponent** property's node, then click the value field to the right of **top:bottom** and select `tagTextInputLayout`. This indicates that the top of the `LinearLayout` will be placed below the bottom of the `tagTextInputLayout`.

Step 4: Adding the `LinearLayout`'s Nested `TextView` and `RecyclerView`

Finally, add the `LinearLayout`'s nested `TextView` and `RecyclerView`:

1. Drag a **Medium Text** onto the **LinearLayout (vertical)** node in the **Component Tree**, then set its **layout:width** to `match_parent`, its **text** to the `String` resource named `tagged_searches`, its **gravity** to `center_horizontal` and its **textStyle** to `bold`. Also, expand its **padding** property and set **top** and **bottom** to the dimension resource named `activity_vertical_margin`.

2. Next, you'll insert a `RecyclerView`. In the layout editor's **Design** view, click **CustomView** in the **Palette**'s **Custom** section. In the dialog that appears, begin typing `RecyclerView` to search the list of custom GUI components. Once the IDE highlights `RecyclerView`, click **OK**, then in the **Component Tree**, click the `LinearLayout` to insert the `RecyclerView` as a nested view.

3. Select the `RecyclerView` in the **Component Tree**, then set its **id** to `recyclerView`, its **layout:width** to `match_parent`, its **layout:height** to `0dp` and its **layout:weight** to `1`—the `RecyclerView` will fill all remaining vertical space in the `LinearLayout`. Also, expand the `RecyclerView`'s **padding** property and set **left** and **right** to the dimension resource named `activity_horizontal_margin`.

8.4.11 RecyclerView Item's Layout: `list_item.xml`

When populating a `RecyclerView` with data, you must specify each list item's layout. The list items in this app each display the tag name of one saved search. You'll now create a new layout that contains only a `TextView` with the appropriate formatting. Perform the following steps:

1. In the **Project** window, expand the project's `res` folder, then right click the `layout` folder and select **New > Layout resource file** to display the **New Resource File** dialog.

2. In the **File name** field, specify `list_item.xml`.

3. In the **Root element** field, specify `TextView`.

4. Click **OK**. The new `list_item.xml` file will appear in the `res/layout` folder.

The IDE opens the new layout in the layout editor. Select the `TextView` in the **Component Tree** window, set its **id** to `textView`, then set the following properties:

- **layout:width**—`match_parent`

- **layout:height**—`?android:attr/listPreferredItemHeight`—This value is a predefined Android resource that represents a list item's preferred height for a touchable view.[3]

Look-and-Feel Observation 8.1
The Android design guidelines specify that the minimum recommended size for a touchable item on the screen is 48dp-by-48dp. For more information on GUI sizing and spacing, see `https://www.google.com/design/spec/layout/metrics-keylines.html`*.*

- **gravity**—`center_vertical`

- **textAppearance**—`?android:attr/textAppearanceMedium`—This is the predefined theme resource that specifies the font size for medium-sized text.

Other Predefined Android Resources
There are many predefined Android resources like the ones used to set the **height** and **textAppearance** for a list item. You can view the complete list at:

```
http://developer.android.com/reference/android/R.attr.html
```

To use a value in your layouts, specify it in the format

```
?android:attr/resourceName
```

8.5 MainActivity Class

This app consists of three classes:

- Class `MainActivity`—which we discuss in this section—configures the app's GUI and defines the app's logic.

- Class `SearchesAdapter` (Section 8.6) is a subclass of `RecyclerView.Adapter` that defines how to bind the tag names for the user's searches to the `RecyclerView`'s items. Class `MainActivity`'s `onCreate` method creates an object of class `SearchesAdapter` as the `RecyclerView`'s adapter.

---

3. At the time of this writing, you must set this directly in the XML due to an Android Studio bug that erroneously appends `dp` to the end of this property value when you set it via the **Properties** window.

- Class `ItemDivider` (Section 8.7) is a subclass of `RecyclerView.ItemDecoration` that the `RecyclerView` uses to draw a horizontal line between items.

Sections 8.5.1—8.5.10 discuss class `MainActivity` in detail. This app does not need a menu, so we removed the `MainActivity` methods `onCreateOptionsMenu` and `onOptions-ItemSelected`, and the corresponding menu resource from the project's res/menu folder.

8.5.1 package and import Statements

Figure 8.15 shows `MainActivity`'s package and import statements. We discuss the imported types in Section 8.3 and as we encounter them in class `MainActivity`.

```
 I  // MainActivity.java
 2  // Manages your favorite Twitter searches for easy
 3  // access and display in the device's web browser
 4  package com.deitel.twittersearches;
 5
 6  import android.app.AlertDialog;
 7  import android.content.Context;
 8  import android.content.DialogInterface;
 9  import android.content.Intent;
10  import android.content.SharedPreferences;
11  import android.net.Uri;
12  import android.os.Bundle;
13  import android.support.design.widget.FloatingActionButton;
14  import android.support.design.widget.TextInputLayout;
15  import android.support.v7.app.AppCompatActivity;
16  import android.support.v7.widget.LinearLayoutManager;
17  import android.support.v7.widget.RecyclerView;
18  import android.support.v7.widget.Toolbar;
19  import android.text.Editable;
20  import android.text.TextWatcher;
21  import android.view.View;
22  import android.view.View.OnClickListener;
23  import android.view.View.OnLongClickListener;
24  import android.view.inputmethod.InputMethodManager;
25  import android.widget.EditText;
26  import android.widget.TextView;
27
28  import java.util.ArrayList;
29  import java.util.Collections;
30  import java.util.List;
31
```

Fig. 8.15 | MainActivity's package and import statements.

8.5.2 MainActivity Fields

As in the **WeatherViewer** app, class `MainActivity` (Fig. 8.16) extends `AppCompatActivity` (line 32) so that it can display an app bar and use other `AppCompat` library features on devices running past or current Android versions. The static String constant SEARCHES (line 34) represents the name of a `SharedPreferences` file that will store tag–query pairs on the device.

```
32   public class MainActivity extends AppCompatActivity {
33      // name of SharedPreferences XML file that stores the saved searches
34      private static final String SEARCHES = "searches";
35
36      private EditText queryEditText; // where user enters a query
37      private EditText tagEditText; // where user enters a query's tag
38      private FloatingActionButton saveFloatingActionButton; // save search
39      private SharedPreferences savedSearches; // user's favorite searches
40      private List<String> tags; // list of tags for saved searches
41      private SearchesAdapter adapter; // for binding data to RecyclerView
42
```

Fig. 8.16 | MainActivity fields.

Lines 36–41 define MainActivity's instance variables:

- Lines 36–37 declare EditTexts that we'll use to access the queries and tags that the user enters as input.

- Line 38 declares a FloatingActionButton that the user touches to save a search. In the **Blank Activity** app template, this was declared as a local variable in method onCreate (Section 8.5.3)—we renamed it and made it an instance variable, so we can hide the button when the EditTexts are empty and show it when the Edit-Texts both contain input.

- Line 39 declares the SharedPreferences instance variable savedSearches, which we'll use to manipulate the tag–query pairs representing the user's saved searches.

- Line 40 declares the List<String> tags that will store the sorted tag names for the user's searches.

- Line 41 declares the SearchesAdapter instance variable adapter, which will refer to the RecyclerView.Adapter subclass object that provides data to the RecyclerView.

8.5.3 Overriden Activity Method onCreate

Overridden Activity method onCreate (Fig. 8.17) initializes the Activity's instance variables and configures the GUI components. Lines 52–57 obtain references to the queryEditText and tagEditText and, for each, register a TextWatcher (Section 8.5.4) that's notified when the user enters or removes characters in the EditTexts.

```
43      // configures the GUI and registers event listeners
44      @Override
45      protected void onCreate(Bundle savedInstanceState) {
46         super.onCreate(savedInstanceState);
47         setContentView(R.layout.activity_main);
48         Toolbar toolbar = (Toolbar) findViewById(R.id.toolbar);
49         setSupportActionBar(toolbar);
```

Fig. 8.17 | Overridden Activity method onCreate. (Part 1 of 2.)

```
50
51      // get references to the EditTexts and add TextWatchers to them
52      queryEditText = ((TextInputLayout) findViewById(
53          R.id.queryTextInputLayout)).getEditText();
54      queryEditText.addTextChangedListener(textWatcher);
55      tagEditText = ((TextInputLayout) findViewById(
56          R.id.tagTextInputLayout)).getEditText();
57      tagEditText.addTextChangedListener(textWatcher);
58
59      // get the SharedPreferences containing the user's saved searches
60      savedSearches = getSharedPreferences(SEARCHES, MODE_PRIVATE);
61
62      // store the saved tags in an ArrayList then sort them
63      tags = new ArrayList<>(savedSearches.getAll().keySet());
64      Collections.sort(tags, String.CASE_INSENSITIVE_ORDER);
65
66      // get reference to the RecyclerView to configure it
67      RecyclerView recyclerView =
68          (RecyclerView) findViewById(R.id.recyclerView);
69
70      // use a LinearLayoutManager to display items in a vertical list
71      recyclerView.setLayoutManager(new LinearLayoutManager(this));
72
73      // create RecyclerView.Adapter to bind tags to the RecyclerView
74      adapter = new SearchesAdapter(
75          tags, itemClickListener, itemLongClickListener);
76      recyclerView.setAdapter(adapter);
77
78      // specify a custom ItemDecorator to draw lines between list items
79      recyclerView.addItemDecoration(new ItemDivider(this));
80
81      // register listener to save a new or edited search
82      saveFloatingActionButton =
83          (FloatingActionButton) findViewById(R.id.fab);
84      saveFloatingActionButton.setOnClickListener(saveButtonListener);
85      updateSaveFAB(); // hides button because EditTexts initially empty
86  }
87
```

Fig. 8.17 | Overridden Activity method onCreate. (Part 2 of 2.)

Getting a *SharedPreferences* Object

Line 60 uses the method **getSharedPreferences** (inherited indirectly from class Context) to get a SharedPreferences object that can read existing *tag–query pairs* (if any) from the searches file. The first argument indicates the name of the file that contains the data. The second argument specifies the file's access-level and can be set to:

- MODE_PRIVATE—Accessible *only* to this app. In most cases, you'll use this option.

- MODE_WORLD_READABLE—Any app on the device can *read* the file.

- MODE_WORLD_WRITABLE—Any app on the device can *write* to the file.

These constants can be combined with the bitwise OR operator (|).

*Getting the Keys Stored in the **SharedPreferences** Object*

We'd like to display the search tags alphabetically so the user can easily find a search to perform. First, line 63 gets the Strings representing the keys in the SharedPreferences object and stores them in tags (an ArrayList<String>). SharedPreferences method getAll returns all the saved searches as a Map (package java.util)—a collection of key–value pairs. We then call method keySet on the Map object to get all the keys as a Set<String> (package java.util)—a collection of unique values. The result is used to initialize tags.

*Sorting the **ArrayList** of Tags*

Line 64 uses Collections.sort to sort tags. Since the user could enter tags using mixtures of uppercase and lowercase letters, we perform a *case-insensitive sort* by passing the predefined Comparator<String> object String.CASE_INSENSITIVE_ORDER as the second argument to Collections.sort.

*Configuring the **RecyclerView***

Lines 67–79 configure the RecyclerView:

- Lines 67–68 get a reference to the RecyclerView.

- A RecyclerView can arrange its items for display in difference ways. For this app, we use the LinearLayoutManager to display the items in a vertical list. The LinearLayoutManager's constructor receives a Context object, which is the MainActivity in this case. Line 71 creates a LinearLayoutManager calls RecyclerView method setLayoutManager to set the new object as the RecyclerView's layout manager.

- Lines 74–75 create a SearchesAdapter (Section 8.6)—a subclass of RecyclerView.Adapter—that will supply data for display in the RecyclerView. Line 76 calls RecyclerView method setAdapter to specify that the SearchesAdapter will supply the RecyclerView's data.

- Line 79 creates a subclass of RecyclerView.ItemDecoration named ItemDivider (Section 8.7) and passes the object to RecyclerView method addItemDecoration. This enables the RecyclerView to draw a horizontal line decoration between list items.

*Registering a Listener for the **FloatingActionButton***

Lines 82–85 obtain a reference to the saveFloatingActionButton and register its OnClickListener. Instance variable saveButtonListener refers to an *anonymous-inner-class object* that implements interface View.OnClickListener (Section 8.5.5). Line 85 calls method updateSaveFAB (Section 8.5.4), which initially hides the saveFloatingActionButton, because the EditTexts are empty when onCreate is first called—the button displays only when both EditTexts contain input.

8.5.4 TextWatcher Event Handler and Method updateSaveFAB

Figure 8.18 defines an anonymous inner class that implements interface TextWatcher (lines 89–103). The TextWatcher's onTextChanged method calls updateSaveFAB when the contents change in either of the app's EditTexts. Lines 54 and 57 (Fig. 8.17) register the instance variable textWatcher as the listener for the EditTexts events.

```
88      // hide/show saveFloatingActionButton based on EditTexts' contents
89      private final TextWatcher textWatcher = new TextWatcher() {
90         @Override
91         public void beforeTextChanged(CharSequence s, int start, int count,
92            int after) { }
93
94         // hide/show the saveFloatingActionButton after user changes input
95         @Override
96         public void onTextChanged(CharSequence s, int start, int before,
97            int count) {
98            updateSaveFAB();
99         }
100
101        @Override
102        public void afterTextChanged(Editable s) { }
103     };
104
105     // shows or hides the saveFloatingActionButton
106     private void updateSaveFAB() {
107        // check if there is input in both EditTexts
108        if (queryEditText.getText().toString().isEmpty() ||
109           tagEditText.getText().toString().isEmpty())
110           saveFloatingActionButton.hide();
111        else
112           saveFloatingActionButton.show();
113     }
114
```

Fig. 8.18 | TextWatcher event handler and method updateSaveFAB.

The updatedSaveFAB method (Fig. 8.18, lines 106–113) checks whether there's text in both EditTexts (lines 108–109). If either (or both) of the EditTexts is empty, line 110 calls the FloatingActionButton's hide method to hide the button, because both the query and tag are required before a tag–query pair can be saved. If both contain text, line 112 calls the FloatingActionButton's show method, to display the button so the user can touch it to store a tag–query pair.

8.5.5 saveButton's OnClickListener

Figure 8.19 defines instance variable saveButtonListener, which refers to an anonymous inner class object that implements the interface OnClickListener. Line 84 (Fig. 8.17) registered saveButtonListener as the saveFloatingActionButton's event handler. Lines 119–135 (Fig. 8.19) override interface OnClickListener's onClick method. Lines 121–122 get the Strings from the EditTexts. If the user entered a query and a tag (line 124):

- lines 126–128 hide the soft keyboard

- line 130 calls method addTaggedSearch (Section 8.5.6) to store the tag–query pair

- lines 131–132 clear the two EditTexts, and

- line 133 calls the queryEditText's requestFocus method to position the input cursor in the queryEditText.

```
115    // saveButtonListener save a tag-query pair into SharedPreferences
116    private final OnClickListener saveButtonListener =
117       new OnClickListener() {
118          // add/update search if neither query nor tag is empty
119          @Override
120          public void onClick(View view) {
121             String query = queryEditText.getText().toString();
122             String tag = tagEditText.getText().toString();
123
124             if (!query.isEmpty() && !tag.isEmpty()) {
125                // hide the virtual keyboard
126                ((InputMethodManager) getSystemService(
127                   Context.INPUT_METHOD_SERVICE)).hideSoftInputFromWindow(
128                      view.getWindowToken(), 0);
129
130                addTaggedSearch(tag, query); // add/update the search
131                queryEditText.setText(""); // clear queryEditText
132                tagEditText.setText(""); // clear tagEditText
133                queryEditText.requestFocus(); // queryEditText gets focus
134             }
135          }
136       };
137
```

Fig. 8.19 | Anonymous inner class that implements the saveButton's OnClickListener to save a new or updated search.

8.5.6 addTaggedSearch Method

The event handler in Fig. 8.19 calls method addTaggedSearch (Fig. 8.20) to add a new search to savedSearches or to modify an existing search.

```
138    // add new search to file, then refresh all buttons
139    private void addTaggedSearch(String tag, String query) {
140       // get a SharedPreferences.Editor to store new tag/query pair
141       SharedPreferences.Editor preferencesEditor = savedSearches.edit();
142       preferencesEditor.putString(tag, query); // store current search
143       preferencesEditor.apply(); // store the updated preferences
144
145       // if tag is new, add to and sort tags, then display updated list
146       if (!tags.contains(tag)) {
147          tags.add(tag); // add new tag
148          Collections.sort(tags, String.CASE_INSENSITIVE_ORDER);
149          adapter.notifyDataSetChanged(); // update tags in RecyclerView
150       }
151    }
152
```

Fig. 8.20 | MainActivity's addTaggedSearch method.

*Editing a **SharedPreferences** Object's Contents*

Recall from Section 4.6.7 that to change a SharedPreferences object's contents, you must first call its edit method to obtain a SharedPreferences.Editor object (Fig. 8.20, line 141), which can add key–value pairs to, remove key–value pairs from, and modify the value associated with a particular key in a SharedPreferences file. Line 142 calls Shared-Preferences.Editor method **putString** to save the search's tag (the key) and query (the corresponding value)—if the tag already exists in the SharedPreferences this updates the value. Line 143 commits the changes by calling SharedPreferences.Editor method apply to make the changes to the file.

Notifying the RecyclerView.Adapter That Its Data Has Changed

When the user adds a new search, the RecyclerView should be updated to display it. Line 146 determines whether a new tag was added. If so, lines 147–148 add the new search's tag to tags, then sort tags. Line 149 calls the RecyclerView.Adapter's notifyDataSet-Changed method to indicate that the underlying data in tags has changed. As with a List-View adapter, the RecyclerView.Adapter then notifies the RecyclerView to update its list of displayed items.

8.5.7 Anonymous Inner Class That Implements View.OnClickListener to Display Search Results

Figure 8.21 defines instance variable itemClickListener, which refers to an anonymous inner-class object that implements interface OnClickListener (a nested interface of class View). Lines 156–168 override the interface's onClick method. The method's argument is the View that the user touched—in this case, the TextView that displays a search tag in the RecyclerView.

```
153    // itemClickListener launches web browser to display search results
154    private final OnClickListener itemClickListener =
155       new OnClickListener() {
156          @Override
157          public void onClick(View view) {
158             // get query string and create a URL representing the search
159             String tag = ((TextView) view).getText().toString();
160             String urlString = getString(R.string.search_URL) +
161                Uri.encode(savedSearches.getString(tag, ""), "UTF-8");
162
163             // create an Intent to launch a web browser
164             Intent webIntent = new Intent(Intent.ACTION_VIEW,
165                Uri.parse(urlString));
166
167             startActivity(webIntent); // show results in web browser
168          }
169       };
170
```

Fig. 8.21 | Anonymous inner class that implements View.OnClickListener to display search results.

Getting String Resources

Line 159 gets the text of the View that the user touched in the RecyclerView—this is the tag for a search. Lines 160–161 create a String containing the Twitter search URL and the query to perform. Line 160 calls Activity's inherited method getString with one argument to get the String resource named search_URL, then we append the query String to it.

Getting *Strings from a* **SharedPreferences** *Object*
We append the result of line 161 to the search URL to complete the urlString. Shared-Preferences method getString returns the query associated with the tag. If the tag does not already exist, the second argument ("" in this case) is returned. Line 161 passes the query to Uri method encode, which *escapes* any special URL characters (such as ?, /, :, etc.) and returns a so-called *URL-encoded* String. Class Uri (uniform resource identifier) of package android.net enables us to convert a URL into the format required by an Intent that launches the device's web browser.[4] This is important to ensure that the Twitter web server that receives the request can parse the URL properly to obtain the search query.

Creating an **Intent** to Launch the Device's Web Browser
Lines 164–165 create a new Intent, which we'll use to launch the device's web browser and display the search results. In Chapter 4, you used an explicit Intent to launch another activity in the same app. Here you'll use an implicit Intent to launch another app. The first argument of Intent's constructor is a constant describing the action to perform. Intent.ACTION_VIEW indicates that we'd like to display a representation of the Intent's data. Many constants are defined in the Intent class describing actions such as *searching, choosing, sending* and *playing*:

```
http://developer.android.com/reference/android/content/Intent.html
```

The second argument (line 165) is a Uri representing the *data* for which to perform the action. Class Uri's parse method converts a String representing a URL (uniform resource locator) to a Uri.

Starting an **Activity** for an **Intent**
Line 167 passes the Intent to the inherited Activity method startActivity, which starts an Activity that can perform the specified *action* for the given *data*. In this case, because we've specified to view a URI, the Intent launches the device's web browser to display the corresponding web page. This page shows the results of the supplied Twitter search.

8.5.8 Anonymous Inner Class That Implements View.OnLongClickListener to Share, Edit or Delete a Search
Figure 8.22 defines instance variable itemLongClickListener, which refers to an anonymous inner-class object that implements interface OnLongClickListener. Lines 175–216 override interface OnLongClickListener's onLongClick method.

---

4. A Uniform Resource Identifier (URI) uniquely identifies a resource on a network. One common type of URI is a Uniform Resource Locator (URL) that identifies items on the Web, such as web pages, image files, web service methods and more.

```
171    // itemLongClickListener displays a dialog allowing the user to share
172    // edit or delete a saved search
173    private final OnLongClickListener itemLongClickListener =
174       new OnLongClickListener() {
175          @Override
176          public boolean onLongClick(View view) {
177             // get the tag that the user long touched
178             final String tag = ((TextView) view).getText().toString();
179
180             // create a new AlertDialog
181             AlertDialog.Builder builder =
182                new AlertDialog.Builder(MainActivity.this);
183
184             // set the AlertDialog's title
185             builder.setTitle(
186                getString(R.string.share_edit_delete_title, tag));
187
188             // set list of items to display and create event handler
189             builder.setItems(R.array.dialog_items,
190                new DialogInterface.OnClickListener() {
191                   @Override
192                   public void onClick(DialogInterface dialog, int which) {
193                      switch (which) {
194                         case 0: // share
195                            shareSearch(tag);
196                            break;
197                         case 1: // edit
198                            // set EditTexts to match chosen tag and query
199                            tagEditText.setText(tag);
200                            queryEditText.setText(
201                               savedSearches.getString(tag, ""));
202                            break;
203                         case 2: // delete
204                            deleteSearch(tag);
205                            break;
206                      }
207                   }
208                }
209             );
210
211             // set the AlertDialog's negative Button
212             builder.setNegativeButton(getString(R.string.cancel), null);
213
214             builder.create().show(); // display the AlertDialog
215             return true;
216          }
217       };
218
```

Fig. 8.22 | Anonymous inner class that implements View.OnLongClickListener.

final *Local Variables for Use in Anonymous Inner Classes*

Line 178 assigns to final local variable tag the text of the item the user *long pressed*—final is required for any local variable or method parameter used in an anonymous inner class.

AlertDialog That Displays a List of Items
Lines 181–186 create an AlertDialog.Builder and set the dialog's title to a formatted String (R.string.share_edit_delete_title) in which tag replaces the format specifier. Line 186 calls Activity's inherited method getString that receives multiple arguments— a String resource ID representing a format String and the values that should replace the format specifiers in the format String. In addition to buttons, an AlertDialog can display a list of items. Lines 189–209 use AlertDialog.Builder method setItems to specify that the dialog should display the array of Strings R.array.dialog_items and to define an anonymous inner class object that responds when the user touches any item in the list.

Event Handler for the Dialog's List of Items
The anonymous inner class in lines 190–208 determines which item the user selected in the dialog's list and performs the appropriate action. If the user selects **Share**, shareSearch is called (line 195). If the user selects **Edit**, lines 199–201 display the search's query and tag in the EditTexts. If the user selects **Delete**, deleteSearch is called (line 204).

Configuring the Negative Button and Displaying the Dialog
Line 212 configures the dialog's negative button. When the negative button's event handler is null, touching the negative button simply dismisses the dialog. Line 214 creates and shows the dialog.

8.5.9 shareSearch Method

Method shareSearch (Fig. 8.23) is called when the user selects to share a search (Fig. 8.22). Lines 222–223 create a String representing the search to share. Lines 226–232 create and configure an Intent that allows the user to send the search URL using an Activity that can handle the Intent.ACTION_SEND.

```
219      // allow user to choose an app for sharing URL of a saved search
220      private void shareSearch(String tag) {
221         // create the URL representing the search
222         String urlString = getString(R.string.search_URL) +
223            Uri.encode(savedSearches.getString(tag, ""), "UTF-8");
224
225         // create Intent to share urlString
226         Intent shareIntent = new Intent();
227         shareIntent.setAction(Intent.ACTION_SEND);
228         shareIntent.putExtra(Intent.EXTRA_SUBJECT,
229            getString(R.string.share_subject));
230         shareIntent.putExtra(Intent.EXTRA_TEXT,
231            getString(R.string.share_message, urlString));
232         shareIntent.setType("text/plain");
233
234         // display apps that can share plain text
235         startActivity(Intent.createChooser(shareIntent,
236            getString(R.string.share_search)));
237      }
238
```

Fig. 8.23 | MainActivity's shareSearch method.

Adding Extras to an **Intent**

An Intent includes a Bundle of *extras*—additional information that's passed to the Activity that handles the Intent. For example, an e-mail Activity can receive *extras* representing the e-mail's subject, CC and BCC addresses, and the body text. Lines 228–231 use Intent method **putExtra** to add to the Intent's Bundle key–value pairs representing the extras. The method's first argument is a String key representing the purpose of the extra and the second argument is the corresponding extra data. Extras may be primitive type values, primitive type arrays, entire Bundle objects and more—see class Intent's documentation for a complete list of the putExtra overloads.

The extra at lines 228–229 specifies an e-mail's subject with the String resource R.string.share_subject. For an Activity that does *not* use a subject (such as sharing on a social network), this extra is ignored. The extra at lines 230–231 represents the text to share—a formatted String in which the urlString is substituted into the String resource R.string.share_message. Line 232 sets the Intent's MIME type to text/plain—such data can be handled by any Activity capable of sending plain text messages.

Displaying an Intent Chooser

To display the *intent chooser* shown in Fig. 8.8(a), we pass the Intent and a String title to Intent's static **createChooser** method (lines 235–236). The intent chooser's title is specified by the second argument (R.string.share_search). It's important to set this title to remind the user to select an appropriate Activity. You cannot control the apps installed on a user's phone or the Intent filters that can launch those apps, so it's possible that incompatible activities could appear in the chooser. Method createChooser returns an Intent that we pass to startActivity to display the intent chooser.

8.5.10 deleteSearch Method

The deleteSearch method (Fig. 8.24) is called when the user long presses a search tag and selects **Delete** from the dialog displayed by the code in Fig. 8.22. Before deleting the search, the app displays an AlertDialog to confirm the delete operation. Line 243 (Fig. 8.24) sets the dialog's title to a formatted String in which tag replaces the format specifier in the String resource R.string.confirm_message. Line 246 configures the dialog's negative button to dismiss the dialog. Lines 249–264 configure the dialog's positive button to remove the search. Line 252 removes the tag from the tags collection, and lines 255–258 use a SharedPreferences.Editor to remove the search from the app's SharedPreferences. Line 261 then notifies the RecyclerView.Adapter that the underlying data has changed so that the RecyclerView can update its displayed list of items.

```
239    // deletes a search after the user confirms the delete operation
240    private void deleteSearch(final String tag) {
241       // create a new AlertDialog and set its message
242       AlertDialog.Builder confirmBuilder = new AlertDialog.Builder(this);
243       confirmBuilder.setMessage(getString(R.string.confirm_message, tag));
244
245       // configure the negative (CANCEL) Button
246       confirmBuilder.setNegativeButton(getString(R.string.cancel), null);
```

Fig. 8.24 | MainActivity's deleteSearch method. (Part 1 of 2.)

```
247
248        // configure the positive (DELETE) Button
249        confirmBuilder.setPositiveButton(getString(R.string.delete),
250           new DialogInterface.OnClickListener() {
251              public void onClick(DialogInterface dialog, int id) {
252                 tags.remove(tag); // remove tag from tags
253
254                 // get SharedPreferences.Editor to remove saved search
255                 SharedPreferences.Editor preferencesEditor =
256                    savedSearches.edit();
257                 preferencesEditor.remove(tag); // remove search
258                 preferencesEditor.apply(); // save the changes
259
260                 // rebind tags to RecyclerView to show updated list
261                 adapter.notifyDataSetChanged();
262              }
263           }
264        );
265
266        confirmBuilder.create().show(); // display AlertDialog
267     }
268 }
```

Fig. 8.24 | MainActivity's deleteSearch method. (Part 2 of 2.)

8.6 SearchesAdapter Subclass of RecyclerView.Adapter

This section presents the RecyclerView.Adapter that binds the items in MainActivity's List<String> named tags to the app's RecyclerView.

8.6.1 package Statement, import statements, Instance Variables and Constructor

Figure 8.25 shows the beginning of class SearchesAdapter's definition. The class extends generic class RecyclerView.Adapter, using as its type argument the nested class SearchesAdapter.ViewHolder (defined in Section 8.6.2). The instance variables in lines 17–18 maintain references to the event listeners (defined in class MainActivity) that are registered for each RecyclerView item. The instance variable in line 21 maintains a reference to MainActivity's List<String> that contains the tag names to display.

```
1  // SearchesAdapter.java
2  // Subclass of RecyclerView.Adapter for binding data to RecyclerView items
3  package com.deitel.twittersearches;
4
5  import android.support.v7.widget.RecyclerView;
6  import android.view.LayoutInflater;
7  import android.view.View;
```

Fig. 8.25 | SearchesAdapter package statement, import statements, instance variables and constructor. (Part 1 of 2.)

```
 8   import android.view.ViewGroup;
 9   import android.widget.TextView;
10
11   import java.util.List;
12
13   public class SearchesAdapter
14      extends RecyclerView.Adapter<SearchesAdapter.ViewHolder> {
15
16      // listeners from MainActivity that are registered for each list item
17      private final View.OnClickListener clickListener;
18      private final View.OnLongClickListener longClickListener;
19
20      // List<String> used to obtain RecyclerView items' data
21      private final List<String> tags; // search tags
22
23      // constructor
24      public SearchesAdapter(List<String> tags,
25         View.OnClickListener clickListener,
26         View.OnLongClickListener longClickListener) {
27         this.tags = tags;
28         this.clickListener = clickListener;
29         this.longClickListener = longClickListener;
30      }
31
```

Fig. 8.25 | SearchesAdapter package statement, import statements, instance variables and constructor. (Part 2 of 2.)

8.6.2 Nested ViewHolder Subclass of RecyclerView.ViewHolder

Every item in a RecyclerView must be wrapped in its own RecyclerView.ViewHolder. For this app, we defined a RecyclerView.ViewHolder called ViewHolder (Fig. 8.26). The ViewHolder constructor (line 39–48) receives a View object and listeners for that View's OnClick and OnLongClick events. The View represents an item in the RecyclerView, which is passed to the superclass's constructor (line 42). Line 43 stores a reference to the TextView for the item. Line 46 registers the TextView's OnClickListener, which displays the search results for that TextView's tag. Line 47 registers the TextView's OnLongClick-Listener, which opens the **Share**, **Edit** or **Delete** dialog for that TextView's tag. The constructor is called when the RecyclerView.Adapter creates a new list item method onCreateViewHolder (Section 8.6.3).

```
32      // nested subclass of RecyclerView.ViewHolder used to implement
33      // the view-holder pattern in the context of a RecyclerView--the logic
34      // of recycling views that have scrolled offscreen is handled for you
35      public static class ViewHolder extends RecyclerView.ViewHolder {
36         public final TextView textView;
37
```

Fig. 8.26 | SearchesAdapter nested ViewHolder subclass of RecyclerView.ViewHolder. (Part 1 of 2.)

```
38          // configures a RecyclerView item's ViewHolder
39          public ViewHolder(View itemView,
40             View.OnClickListener clickListener,
41             View.OnLongClickListener longClickListener) {
42             super(itemView);
43             textView = (TextView) itemView.findViewById(R.id.textView);
44
45             // attach listeners to itemView
46             itemView.setOnClickListener(clickListener);
47             itemView.setOnLongClickListener(longClickListener);
48          }
49       }
50
```

Fig. 8.26 | SearchesAdapter nested ViewHolder subclass of RecyclerView.ViewHolder. (Part 2 of 2.)

8.6.3 Overridden RecyclerView.Adapter Methods

Figure 8.27 defines the overridden RecyclerView.Adapter methods onCreateViewHolder (lines 52–61), onBindViewHolder (lines 64–67) and getItemCount (lines 70–73).

```
51       // sets up new list item and its ViewHolder
52       @Override
53       public ViewHolder onCreateViewHolder(ViewGroup parent,
54          int viewType) {
55          // inflate the list_item layout
56          View view = LayoutInflater.from(parent.getContext()).inflate(
57             R.layout.list_item, parent, false);
58
59          // create a ViewHolder for current item
60          return (new ViewHolder(view, clickListener, longClickListener));
61       }
62
63       // sets the text of the list item to display the search tag
64       @Override
65       public void onBindViewHolder(ViewHolder holder, int position) {
66          holder.textView.setText(tags.get(position));
67       }
68
69       // returns the number of items that adapter binds
70       @Override
71       public int getItemCount() {
72          return tags.size();
73       }
74    }
```

Fig. 8.27 | SearchesAdapter overridden RecyclerView.Adapter methods onCreateViewHolder, onBindViewHolder and getItemCount.

*Overriding the **onCreateViewHolder** Method*

The RecyclerView calls its RecyclerView.Adapter's onCreateViewHolder method (lines 52–61) to inflate the layout for each RecyclerView item (lines 56–57) and wrap it in an object of the RecyclerView.ViewHolder subclass named ViewHolder (line 60). This new ViewHolder object is then returned to the RecyclerView for display.

*Overriding the **onBindViewHolder** Method*

The RecyclerView calls its RecyclerView.Adapter's onBindViewHolder method (lines 64–67) to set the data that's displayed for a particular RecyclerView item. The method receives:

- an object of our custom subclass of RecyclerView.ViewHolder containing the Views in which data will be displayed—in this case, one TextView—and

- an int representing the item's position in the RecyclerView.

Line 66 sets the TextView's text to the String in tags at the given position.

*Overriding the **getItemCount** Method*

The RecyclerView calls its RecyclerView.Adapter's getItemCount method (lines 70–73) to obtain the total number of items that that the RecyclerView needs to display—in this case, the number of items in tags (line 72).

8.7 ItemDivider Subclass of RecyclerView.ItemDecoration

A RecyclerView.ItemDecoration object draws *decorations*—such as separators between items—on a RecyclerView. The RecyclerView.ItemDecoration subclass ItemDivider (Fig. 8.28) draws divider lines between list items. Lines 17–18 in the constructor obtain the predefined Android Drawable resource android.R.attr.listDivider, which is the standard Android list-item divider used by default in ListViews.

```
1  // ItemDivider.java
2  // Class that defines dividers displayed between the RecyclerView items;
3  // based on Google's sample implementation at bit.ly/DividerItemDecoration
4  package com.deitel.twittersearches;
5
6  import android.content.Context;
7  import android.graphics.Canvas;
8  import android.graphics.drawable.Drawable;
9  import android.support.v7.widget.RecyclerView;
10 import android.view.View;
11
12 class ItemDivider extends RecyclerView.ItemDecoration {
13     private final Drawable divider;
14
```

Fig. 8.28 | ItemDivider subclass of RecyclerView.ItemDecoration for displaying a horizontal line between items in the RecyclerView. (Part 1 of 2.)

```
15      // constructor loads built-in Android list item divider
16      public ItemDivider(Context context) {
17         int[] attrs = {android.R.attr.listDivider};
18         divider = context.obtainStyledAttributes(attrs).getDrawable(0);
19      }
20
21      // draws the list item dividers onto the RecyclerView
22      @Override
23      public void onDrawOver(Canvas c, RecyclerView parent,
24         RecyclerView.State state) {
25         super.onDrawOver(c, parent, state);
26
27         // calculate left/right x-coordinates for all dividers
28         int left = parent.getPaddingLeft();
29         int right = parent.getWidth() - parent.getPaddingRight();
30
31         // for every item but the last, draw a line below it
32         for (int i = 0; i < parent.getChildCount() - 1; ++i) {
33            View item = parent.getChildAt(i); // get ith list item
34
35            // calculate top/bottom y-coordinates for current divider
36            int top = item.getBottom() + ((RecyclerView.LayoutParams)
37               item.getLayoutParams()).bottomMargin;
38            int bottom = top + divider.getIntrinsicHeight();
39
40            // draw the divider with the calculated bounds
41            divider.setBounds(left, top, right, bottom);
42            divider.draw(c);
43         }
44      }
45   }
```

Fig. 8.28 | `ItemDivider` subclass of `RecyclerView.ItemDecoration` for displaying a horizontal line between items in the `RecyclerView`. (Part 2 of 2.)

Overriding the onDrawOver Method

As the user scrolls through the `RecyclerView`'s items, the `RecyclerView`'s contents are repeatedly redrawn to display the items in their new positions on the screen. As part of this process, the `RecyclerView` calls its `RecyclerView.ItemDecoration`'s onDrawOver method (lines 22–44) to draw the decorations on the `RecyclerView`. The method receives:

- a Canvas for drawing the decorations on the `RecyclerView`.

- the `RecyclerView` object on which the Canvas draws

- the `RecyclerView.State`—an object that stores information passed between various `RecyclerView` components. In this app, we simply pass this value to the superclass's onDrawOver method (line 25).

Lines 28–29 calculate the left and right *x*-coordinates that are used to specify the bound's of the Drawable that will be displayed. The left *x*-coordinate is determined by calling the `RecyclerView`'s getPaddingLeft method, which returns the amount of padding between the `RecyclerView`'s left edge and its content. The right *x*-coordinate is determined by calling the RecyclerView's getWidth method and subtracting the result of calling the RecyclerView's getPaddingRight method, which returns the amount of padding between the RecyclerView's right edge and its content.

Lines 32–43 draw the dividers on the RecyclerView's Canvas by iterating through all but the last item and drawing the dividers below each item. Line 33 gets and stores the current RecyclerView item. Lines 36–37 calculate one divider's top *y*-coordinate, using the item's bottom *y*-coordinate plus the item's margin. Line 38 calculates the divider's bottom *y*-coordinate, using the top *y*-coordinate plus the divider's height—returned by Drawable method getIntrinsicHeight. Line 41 sets the divider's bounds and line 42 draws it to the Canvas.

8.8 A Note on Fabric: Twitter's New Mobile Development Platform

In Chapter 7, you used REST web services to obtain a weather forecast. Twitter provides extensive REST web services that enable you to integrate Twitter functionality into your apps. Using these web services requires a Twitter developer account and special authentication. The focus of this chapter is not on how to use Twitter's web services. For this reason, the app performs searches as if you enter them directly on the Twitter website in the web browser. The Twitter website then returns the results directly to the device's web browser for display.

Working with the Twitter web services directly using Chapter 7's techniques can be challenging. Twitter recognized this and now offers Fabric—a robust mobile development platform for Android and iOS. Fabric encapsulates the Twitter web services's details in libraries that you incorporate into your projects, making it easier for developers to add Twitter capabilities to their apps. In addition, you can add mobile identity management (called Digits; for user sign-in to websites and apps), advertising-based monetization capabilities (called MoPub) and app crash reporting (called Crashlytics).

To use Fabric, sign up at

```
https://get.fabric.io/
```

and install the Android Studio plug-in. Once installed, you simply click the plug-in's icon on the Android Studio toolbar and it walks you through the steps that add the Fabric libraries to your project. The preceding website also provides extensive Fabric documentation and tutorials.

8.9 Wrap-Up

In this chapter, you created the **Twitter Searches** app. You used a SharedPreferences file to store and manipulate key–value pairs representing the user's saved Twitter searches.

We introduced the RecyclerView (from package android.support.v7.widget)—a flexible, customizable view that enables you to control how an app displays a scrolling list of data. You learned that RecyclerViews support different layout managers and arranged this app's RecyclerView items vertically using a LinearLayoutManager—a subclass of RecyclerView.LayoutManager.

We once again used the view-holder pattern for reusing views that scroll off-screen. You learned that RecyclerView formalizes the view–holder pattern, making it required. You created a subclass of RecyclerView.Adapter to bind the RecyclerView's list items to data. You also created a subclass of RecyclerView.ViewHolder to maintains references to each list item's view for reuse. To display decorations between a RecyclerView's items, you defined a subclass of RecyclerView.ItemDecoration to draw divider lines onto the RecyclerView.

You used two implicit Intents for which you did not specify the precise component that should handle each Intent. You used one to launch the device's default web browser to display Twitter search results, based on a search query embedded in a URL, and that displayed an Intent chooser, enabling the user to select from a variety of apps that could share text.

Finally, you displayed an AlertDialog containing a list of options from which the user could select only one. You used an AlertDialog.Builder's setItems method to specify a String array resource containing names of the option to display and to set the event handler that was called when the user touched one of the options.

In Chapter 9, we build the database-driven **Address Book** app, which provides quick and easy access to stored contact information and the ability to add contacts, delete contacts and edit existing contacts. You'll learn how to dynamically swap Fragments in a GUI and provide layouts that optimize screen real estate on phones and tablets.

9

Address Book App

FragmentTransactions and the Fragment Back Stack, SQLite, SQLiteDatabase, SQLiteOpenHelper, ContentProvider, ContentResolver, Loader, LoaderManager, Cursor and GUI Styles

Objectives

In this chapter you'll:

- Use FragmentTransactions and the back stack to dynamically attach Fragments to and detach Fragments from the GUI.

- Use a RecyclerView to display data from a database.

- Create and open databases with SQLiteOpenHelper.

- Use a ContentProvider and a SQLiteDatabase object to interact with data in a SQLite database.

- Use a ContentResolver to invoke methods of a ContentProvider to perform tasks with a database.

- Use a LoaderManager and Loaders to perform database access asynchronously outside the GUI thread.

- Use Cursors to manipulate database query results.

- Define styles containing common GUI attributes and values, then apply them to multiple GUI components.

Outline

9.1 Introduction

The **Address Book** app (Fig. 9.1) provides convenient access to contact information that's stored in a SQLite database on the device. You can:

- scroll through an alphabetical contact list
- view a contact's details by touching a contact's name in the contact list
- add new contacts
- edit or delete existing contacts.

The app provides a separate tablet layout (Fig. 9.2) that always displays the contact list in one third of the screen and uses the screen's remaining two thirds to display either the selected contact's data or the screen for adding and editing a contact.

a) Contact list

b) Details displayed after the user touches **Paul** in the contact list

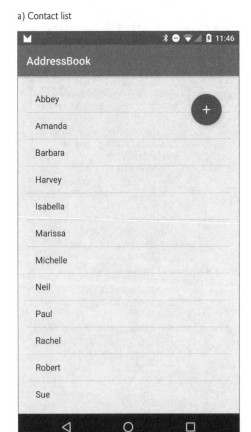

Fig. 9.1 | Contact list and a selected contact's details.

a) In landscape orientation on a phone or tablet, the app bar icons are displayed with their text

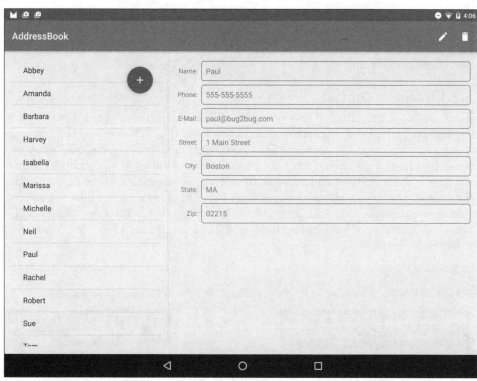

Fig. 9.2 | Address Book running in landscape on a tablet.

This app presents several new technologies:

- You'll dynamically add Fragments to and remove Fragments from an Activity's GUI using FragmentTransactions. You'll also take advantage of the Fragment back stack to enable back-button support, so the user can navigate backward through the Fragments that have been displayed.
- You'll display database data in a RecyclerView.
- You'll create and open a database with a subclass of SQLiteOpenHelper.
- You'll use a ContentProvider, a ContentResolver and a SQLiteDatabase object to perform database insert, update, delete and query operations.
- You'll use a LoaderManager and Loaders to perform database access asynchronously outside the GUI thread and to receive those results in the GUI thread.
- Finally, you'll define styles containing common GUI attributes and values, then apply them to multiple GUI components.

First, you'll test-drive the app. Then we'll overview the technologies we used to build it. Next, you'll create the app's GUI and resource files. Finally, we'll present and walk through the app's complete source code, discussing the app's new features in more detail.

9.2 Test-Driving the Address Book App

Opening and Running the App
Open Android Studio and open the **Address Book** app from the AddressBook folder in the book's examples folder, then execute the app in the AVD or on a device. This builds the project and runs the app.

9.2.1 Adding a Contact

The first time you run the app, the contact list will be empty. Touch the ➕ FloatingAction-tionButton to display the screen for adding a new entry (Fig. 9.3). The app requires each contact to have a name, so the save (▯) FloatingActionButton appears only when the **Name** EditText is not empty. After adding the contact's information, touch ▯ to store the contact in the database and return to the app's main screen. If you choose not to add the contact, you can simply touch the device's back button to return to the main screen. Add more contacts if you wish. On a tablet, after adding a contact, the new contact's details are displayed next to the contact list (Fig. 9.2). Notice that on tablets, the contact list is always displayed.

---

a) Touch the FloatingActionButton to add a new contact

b) Fragment for adding the contact

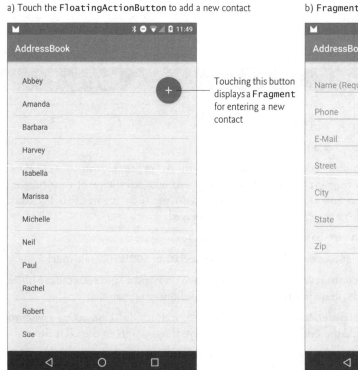

Touching this button displays a **Fragment** for entering a new contact

Fig. 9.3 | Adding a contact to the database.

9.2.2 Viewing a Contact

On a phone or phone AVD, touch the name of the contact you just added to view that contact's details (as you saw in Fig. 9.1). Again, on a tablet, the details are displayed automatically to the right of the contact list (Fig. 9.2).

9.2.3 Editing a Contact

While viewing the contact's details, touch ✏ on the app bar to display a screen of Edit-Texts that are prepopulated with the contact's data (Fig. 9.4). Edit the data as necessary, then touch the FloatingActionButton 🔲 to store the updated contact in the database and return to the app's main screen. If you choose not to edit the contact, you can simply touch the device's back button (◁) to return to the prior screen. On a tablet, after editing a contact, the updated contact details are displayed to the right of the contact list.

a) Details for a contact   b) **Fragment** for editing the contact

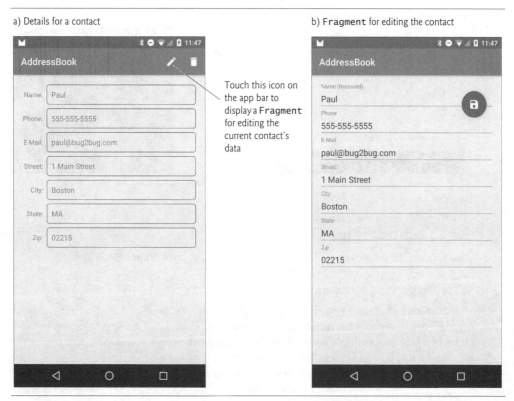

Touch this icon on the app bar to display a **Fragment** for editing the current contact's data

Fig. 9.4 | Editing a contact's data.

9.2.4 Deleting a Contact

While viewing the contact's details, touch 🗑 on the app bar to delete the contact. A dialog will ask you to confirm this action (Fig. 9.5). Touching **DELETE** removes the contact from the database and the app will display the updated contact list. Touching **CANCEL** retains the contact.

a) Details for a contact   b) Deleting the selected contact

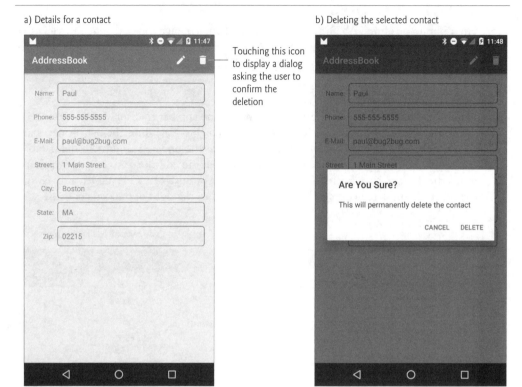

Touching this icon to display a dialog asking the user to confirm the deletion

Fig. 9.5 | Deleting a contact from the database.

9.3 Technologies Overview

This section introduces the features you'll use to build the **Address Book** app.

9.3.1 Displaying Fragments with FragmentTransactions

In earlier apps that used Fragments, you declared each Fragment in an Activity's layout or, for a DialogFragment, called its show method to create it. The **Flag Quiz** app demonstrated how to use multiple activities to host each of the app's Fragments on a phone device, and a single Activity to host multiple Fragments on a tablet device.

In this app, you'll use only one Activity to host all of the app's Fragments. On a phone-sized device, you'll display one Fragment at a time. On a tablet, you'll always display the Fragment containing the contact list and display the Fragments for viewing, adding and editing contacts as they're needed. To do this, you'll use the FragmentManager and FragmentTransactions to dynamically display Fragments. In addition, you'll use Android's Fragment back stack—a data structure that stores Fragments in last-in-first-out (LIFO) order—to provide automatic support for Android's back button (◁). This enables users to go back to prior Fragments via the back button. For more information on Fragments and FragmentTransactions, visit:

```
http://developer.android.com/guide/components/fragments.html
```

9.3.2 Communicating Data Between a Fragment and a Host Activity

To communicate data between Fragments and a host Activity or the Activity's other Fragments, it's considered best practice to do so through the host Activity—this makes the Fragments more reusable, because they do not refer to one another directly. Typically, each Fragment defines an *interface* of *callback methods* that are implemented in the host Activity. We'll use this technique to enable this app's MainActivity to be notified when the user:

- selects a contact to display,
- touches the contact-list Fragment's add (✚) FloatingActionButton,
- touches the contact details Fragment's ✏ or 🗑 actions,
- or touches 💾 to finish editing an existing contact or adding a new one.

9.3.3 Manipulating a SQLite Database

The contact information is stored in a SQLite database. According to www.sqlite.org, SQLite is one of the world's most widely deployed database engines. You'll use a subclass of SQLiteOpenHelper (package android.database.sqlite) to simplify creating the database and to obtain a SQLiteDatabase object (package android.database.sqlite) for manipulating the database's contents. Database queries are performed with Structured Query Language (SQL). Query results are managed via a Cursor (package android.database). For more information on SQLite in Android, visit:

```
http://developer.android.com/guide/topics/data/data-storage.html#db
```

9.3.4 ContentProviders and ContentResolvers

A ContentProvider (package android.provider) exposes an app's data for use in that app or in other apps. Android provides various built-in ContentProviders. For example, your apps can interact with data from the Android **Contacts** and **Calendar** apps. There are also ContentProviders for various telephony features, the media store (e.g., for images/video) and the user dictionary (used with Android's predictive text-input capabilities).

In addition to exposing data to other apps, ContentProviders also enable your app to provide custom search suggestions when a user performs searches on a device and are used to support copy-and-paste operations between apps.

In this app, we use a ContentProvider to help access the database asynchronously outside the GUI thread—this is required when working with Loaders and the LoaderManager (introduced in Section 9.3.5). You'll define a subclass of ContentProvider that specifies how to:

- query the database to locate a specific contact or all the contacts
- insert a new contact into the database
- update an existing contact in the database, and
- delete an existing contact from the database.

The ContentProvider will use a subclass of SQLiteOpenHelper to create the database and to obtain SQLiteDatabase objects to perform the preceding tasks. When changes are made to the database, the ContentProvider will notify listeners of those changes so data can be updated in the GUI.

Uris

The ContentProvider will define Uris that help determine the tasks to perform. For example, in this app the ContentProvider's query method is used for two different queries—one that returns a Cursor for a single contact and one that returns a Cursor for the names of all contacts in the database.

ContentResolver

To invoke the ContentProvider's query, insert, update and delete capabilities, we'll use the corresponding methods of the Activity's built-in ContentResolver (package android.content). The ContentProvider and ContentResolver handle communication for you—including between apps if your ContentProvider exposes its data to other apps. As you'll see, the ContentResolver's methods receive as their first argument a Uri that specifies the ContentProvider to access. Each ContentResolver method invokes the corresponding method of the ContentProvider, which uses the Uri to help determine the task to perform. For more information on ContentProviders and ContentResolvers, see:

```
http://developer.android.com/guide/topics/providers/content-
    providers.html
```

9.3.5 Loader and LoaderManager—Asynchronous Database Access

As we've stated previously, long-running operations or operations that block execution until they complete (e.g., file and database access) should be performed outside the GUI thread. This helps maintain application responsiveness and avoid Activity Not Responding (ANR) dialogs that appear when Android determines that the GUI is not responsive. Loaders and the LoaderManager help you perform asynchronous data access from any Activity or Fragment.

Loaders

A Loader (package android.content) performs asynchronous data access. When interacting with a ContentProvider to load and manipulate data, you'll typically use a CursorLoader—a subclass of AsyncTaskLoader that uses an AsyncTask to perform the data access in a separate thread. Loaders also:

- Watch for changes to the corresponding data source and make the updated data available to the corresponding Activity or Fragment.

- Reconnect to the last Loader's Cursor, rather than perform a new query, when a configuration change occurs.

LoaderManager and LoaderManager.LoaderCallbacks

An Activity's or Fragment's Loaders are created and managed by its LoaderManager (package android.app), which ties each Loader's lifecycle to its Activity's or Fragment's lifecycle. In addition, a LoaderManager invokes methods of the LoaderManager.LoaderCallbacks interface to notify an Activity or Fragment when a Loader

- should be created,

- finishes loading its data, or

- is reset and the data is no longer available.

You'll use Loaders and LoaderManagers in several of this app's Fragment subclasses. For more information about Loaders and LoaderManagers, see:

```
http://developer.android.com/guide/components/loaders.html
```

9.3.6 Defining Styles and Applying Them to GUI Components

You can define common GUI component attribute–value pairs as style resources (Section 9.4.5). You can then apply the styles to all components that share those values (Section 9.4.9) by using the style attribute. Any subsequent changes you make to a style are automatically applied to all GUI components that use it. We use this to style the TextViews that display a contact's information. For more information on styles, visit:

```
http://developer.android.com/guide/topics/ui/themes.html
```

9.3.7 Specifying a TextView Background

By default TextViews do not have a border. To define one, you can specify a Drawable as the value for the TextView's android:background attribute. The Drawable could be an image, but in this app you'll define a Drawable as a shape in a resource file (Section 9.4.6). Like an image, the resource file for such a Drawable is defined in one (or more) of the app's drawable folders. For more information on drawable resources, visit:

```
http://developer.android.com/guide/topics/resources/drawable-
   resource.html
```

9.4 Building the GUI and Resource Files

In this section, you'll create the **Address Book** app's additional Java source-code files, resource files and GUI layout files.

9.4.1 Creating the Project

Create a new project using the **Blank Activity** template. When configuring the project, check the **Use a Fragment** checkbox. Specify the following values in the **Create New Project** dialog's **New Project** step:

- **Application name:** Address Book
- **Company Domain:** deitel.com (or specify your own domain name)

Follow the steps you used in earlier apps to add an app icon to your project. Follow the steps in Section 4.4.3 to configure Java SE 7 support for the project. Follow the steps in Section 8.4.3 to add the RecyclerView library to this project. In colors.xml, change the colorAccent color's value to #FF4081.

9.4.2 Creating the App's Classes

When you create this project, Android Studio defines the classes MainActivity and MainActivityFragment for you. In this app, we renamed MainActivityFragment as ContactsFragment. To do so:

1. Open class MainActivityFragment in the editor.

2. Right click the class name and select **Refactor > Rename....** The IDE highlights the class name for editing.

3. Type ContactsFragment and press *Enter*. The IDE renames the class and its constructor, and changes class's file name.

Package com.deitel.addressbook

This app consists of seven additional classes that you must add to the project (**File > New > Java Class**). The additional classes in package com.deitel.addressbook are:

- Class ContactsAdapter is a subclass of RecyclerView.Adapter that supplies data to the ContactsFragment's RecyclerView.

- Class AddEditFragment is a subclass of Fragment that provides a GUI for adding a new contact or editing an existing one.

- Class DetailFragment is a subclass of Fragment that displays one contact's data and provides menu items for editing and deleting that contact.

- Class ItemDivider is a subclass of RecyclerView.ItemDecoration that the ContactsFragment's RecyclerView uses to draw a horizontal line between items. This class is identical to the one in Section 8.7, so you can simply copy this class from the **Twitter Searches** app's project and paste it into the **app > java > com.deitel.addressbook** node in the **Project** window.

Package com.deitel.addressbook.data

This class also defines a nested package named com.deitel.addressbook.data that contains the classes used to manipulate this app's database. To create the package:

1. In the **Project** window, right click the package com.deitel.addressbook and select **New > Package**.

2. Type data as the new package name to create the com.deitel.addressbook.data package.

Next add the following classes to the com.deitel.addressbook.data package:

- Class DatabaseDescription describes the database's contacts table.

- Class AddressBookDatabaseHelper is a subclass of SQLiteOpenHelper that creates the database and is used to access the database.

- Class AddressBookContentProvider is a subclass of ContentProvider that defines how to manipulate the database. To create this class, use **New > Other > Content Provider**. For **URI authorities** specify com.deitel.addressbook.data and uncheck the **Exported** checkbox, then click **Finish**. Unchecking **Exported** indicates that this ContentProvider is for use only in this app. The IDE defines a subclass of ContentProvider and overrides its required methods. In addition, the IDE declares the ContentProvider AndroidManifest.xml as a <provider> element nested in the <application> element. This is *required* to register the ContentProvider with the Android operating system—not only for use in this app, but for use in other apps (when the ContentProvider is exported).

We overview all of the classes in Section 9.5 and discuss their details in Sections 9.6—9.13.

9.4.3 Add the App's Icons

Use Android Studio's **Vector Asset Studio** (Section 4.4.9) to add the material design save (█), add (➕), edit (✏) and delete (🗑) icons to the project—this will be used as the FloatingActionButton's icon. After adding the vector icons, go to the project's res/ drawable folder, open each icon's XML file and change the `<path>` element's android:fillColor to

```
    "@android:color/white"
```

9.4.4 strings.xml

Figure 9.6 shows this app's String resource names and corresponding values. Double click strings.xml in the res/values folder to display the resource editor for creating these String resources.

Resource name	Value
menuitem_edit	Edit
menuitem_delete	Delete
hint_name_required	Name (Required)
hint_email	E-Mail
hint_phone	Phone
hint_street	Street
hint_city	City
hint_state	State
hint_zip	Zip
label_name	Name:
label_email	E-Mail:
label_phone	Phone:
label_street	Street:
label_city	City:
label_state	State:
label_zip	Zip:
confirm_title	Are You Sure?
confirm_message	This will permanently delete the contact
button_cancel	Cancel
button_delete	Delete
contact_added	Contact added successfully
contact_not_added	Contact was not added due to an error
contact_updated	Contact updated
contact_not_updated	Contact was not updated due to an error

Fig. 9.6 | String resources used in the **Address Book** app. (Part 1 of 2.)

Resource name	Value
invalid_query_uri	Invalid query Uri:
invalid_insert_uri	Invalid insert Uri:
invalid_update_uri	Invalid update Uri:
invalid_delete_uri	Invalid delete Uri:
insert_failed	Insert failed: s

Fig. 9.6 | String resources used in the **Address Book** app. (Part 2 of 2.)

9.4.5 styles.xml

In this section, you'll define the styles for the DetailFragment's TextViews that display a contact's information (Section 9.4.9). Like other resources, style resources are placed in the app's res/values folder. When you create a project, the IDE creates a styles.xml file containing predefined styles. Each new style you create specifies a name that's used to apply that style to GUI components and one or more items specifying property values to apply. To create the new styles, in the app's res/values folder, open the styles.xml file then add the code in Fig. 9.7 before the file's closing </resources> tag. When you're done, save and close styles.xml.

```
 1    <style name="ContactLabelTextView">
 2        <item name="android:layout_width">wrap_content</item>
 3        <item name="android:layout_height">wrap_content</item>
 4        <item name="android:layout_gravity">right|center_vertical</item>
 5    </style>
 6
 7    <style name="ContactTextView">
 8        <item name="android:layout_width">wrap_content</item>
 9        <item name="android:layout_height">wrap_content</item>
10        <item name="android:layout_gravity">fill_horizontal</item>
11        <item name="android:textSize">16sp</item>
12        <item name="android:background">@drawable/textview_border</item>
13    </style>
```

Fig. 9.7 | New styles for formatting the DetailFragment's TextViews.

Lines 1–5 define a new style named ContactLabelTextView that defines values for the layout properties layout_width, layout_height and layout_gravity. You'll apply this style to the DetailFragment's TextViews displayed to the left of each piece of a contact's information. Each new style consists of a style element containing item elements. The style's name is used to apply it. An item element's name specifies the property to set and its value is assigned to that property when the style is applied to a view. Lines 7–13 define another new style named ContactTextView that will be applied to the Detail-Fragment's TextViews that display the contact's information. Line 12 sets the property android:background to the drawable resource defined in Section 9.4.6.

9.4.6 `textview_border.xml`

The `style` `ContactTextView` that you created in the preceding section defines the appearance of the `TextViews` that are used to display a contact's details. You specified a `Drawable` (i.e., an image or graphic) named `@drawable/textview_border` as the value for the `TextView`'s `android:background` attribute. In this section, you'll define that `Drawable` in the app's `res/drawable` folder. To define the `Drawable`:

1. Right click the `res/drawable` folder and select **New > Drawable resource file**.

2. Specify `textview_border.xml` as the **File name** and click **OK**.

3. Replace the file's contents with the XML code in Fig. 9.8.

```
 1   <?xml version="1.0" encoding="utf-8"?>
 2   <shape xmlns:android="http://schemas.android.com/apk/res/android"
 3      android:shape="rectangle">
 4      <corners android:radius="5dp"/>
 5      <stroke android:width="1dp" android:color="#555"/>
 6      <padding android:top="10dp" android:left="10dp" android:bottom="10dp"
 7         android:right="10dp"/>
 8   </shape>
```

Fig. 9.8 | XML representation of a `Drawable` that's used to place a border on a `TextView`.

The **shape** element's `android:shape` attribute (line 3) can have the value `"rectangle"` (used in this example), `"oval"`, `"line"` or `"ring"`. The **corners** element (line 4) specifies the rectangle's corner radius, which rounds the corners. The **stroke** element (line 5) defines the rectangle's line width and line color. The **padding** element (lines 6–7) specifies the spacing around the content in the element to which this `Drawable` is applied. You must specify the top, left, bottom and right padding amounts separately. The complete details of defining shapes can be viewed at:

> http://developer.android.com/guide/topics/resources/drawable-
> resource.html#Shape

9.4.7 `MainActivity`'s Layout

By default, `MainActivity`'s layout contains a `FloatingActionButton` and includes the layout file `content_main.xml`. In this app, we provide `FloatingActionButtons` as needed in the app's `Fragments`. For this reason, open `activity_main.xml` in the `res/layout` folder and remove the predefined `FloatingActionButton`. Also, set the `CoordinatorLayout`'s id to `coordinatorLayout`—we use this when displaying `SnackBars`. Remove the code that configures the `FloatingActionButton` from `MainActivity`'s `onCreate` method.

Phone Layout: content_main.xml
In this app, you'll provide two `content_main.xml` layouts to be included into `MainActivity`—one for phone-sized devices and one for tablet-sized devices. For the phone layout, open `content_main.xml` in the `res/layout` folder and replace its contents with the XML in Fig. 9.9. `MainActivity` dynamically displays the app's `Fragments` in the `FrameLayout` named `fragmentContainer`. This layout fills the available space in `MainActivity`'s layout with 16dp padding on all sides. The `app:layout_behavior` property (line 20) is used by

activity_main.xml's CoordinatorLayout to manage interactions between its views. Setting this property ensures that the contents of the FrameLayout scroll below the Toolbar defined in activity_main.xml.

```
9    <FrameLayout
10       android:id="@+id/fragmentContainer"
11       xmlns:android="http://schemas.android.com/apk/res/android"
12       xmlns:app="http://schemas.android.com/apk/res-auto"
13       xmlns:tools="http://schemas.android.com/tools"
14       android:layout_width="match_parent"
15       android:layout_height="match_parent"
16       android:paddingBottom="@dimen/activity_vertical_margin"
17       android:paddingLeft="@dimen/activity_horizontal_margin"
18       android:paddingRight="@dimen/activity_horizontal_margin"
19       android:paddingTop="@dimen/activity_vertical_margin"
20       app:layout_behavior="@string/appbar_scrolling_view_behavior"
21       tools:context=".MainActivity"/>
```

Fig. 9.9 | content_main.xml used on a phone device.

Tablet Layout: content_main.xml for Large Devices

Create the new tablet layout content_main.xml (as in Section 4.5.4). This layout should use a horizontal LinearLayout containing a ContactsFragment and an empty FrameLayout as shown in Fig. 9.10. Create the divider_margin resource (16dp) used in lines 24 and 32. This LinearLayout uses several properties that we have not discussed previously:

- divider (line 9)—This property specifies a drawable resource that's used to separate items in the LinearLayout. In this case, we use the predefined Android drawable theme resource ?android:listDivider. The ?android: indicates that the LinearLayout should use the list divider defined in the current theme.

- showDividers (line 15)—This property is used with the divider property to specify where the dividers appear—in this case, middle indicates that the dividers should appear only between the LinearLayout's elements. You can also display a divider before the first item in the layout (beginning) and after the last item (end), and you can combine these values using |.

- weightSum (line 16)—This helps allocate the horizontal space between the ContactsFragment and FrameLayout. Setting weightSum to 3, then setting the ContactsFragment's and FrameLayout's layout_weights to 1 and 2, respectively, indicates that the ContactsFragment should occupy one-third of the LinearLayout's width and the FrameLayout should occupy the remaining two-thirds.

```
1    <?xml version="1.0" encoding="utf-8"?>
2    <LinearLayout
3       xmlns:android="http://schemas.android.com/apk/res/android"
4       xmlns:app="http://schemas.android.com/apk/res-auto"
5       xmlns:tools="http://schemas.android.com/tools"
6       android:layout_width="match_parent"
```

Fig. 9.10 | content_main.xml used on a tablet device. (Part I of 2.)

```
 7          android:layout_height="match_parent"
 8          android:baselineAligned="false"
 9          android:divider="?android:listDivider"
10          android:orientation="horizontal"
11          android:paddingBottom="@dimen/activity_vertical_margin"
12          android:paddingLeft="@dimen/activity_horizontal_margin"
13          android:paddingRight="@dimen/activity_horizontal_margin"
14          android:paddingTop="@dimen/activity_vertical_margin"
15          android:showDividers="middle"
16          android:weightSum="3"
17          app:layout_behavior="@string/appbar_scrolling_view_behavior">
18
19          <fragment
20              android:id="@+id/contactsFragment"
21              android:name="com.deitel.addressbook.ContactsFragment"
22              android:layout_width="0dp"
23              android:layout_height="match_parent"
24              android:layout_marginEnd="@dimen/divider_margin"
25              android:layout_weight="1"
26              tools:layout="@layout/fragment_contacts"/>
27
28          <FrameLayout
29              android:id="@+id/rightPaneContainer"
30              android:layout_width="0dp"
31              android:layout_height="match_parent"
32              android:layout_marginStart="@dimen/divider_margin"
33              android:layout_weight="2"/>
34      </LinearLayout>
```

Fig. 9.10 | `content_main.xml` used on a tablet device. (Part 2 of 2.)

9.4.8 ContactsFragment's Layout

In addition to renaming class `MainActivityFragment` as `ContactsFragment`, we renamed the corresponding layout file as `fragment_contacts.xml`. We then removed the default `TextView`, changed the default layout from a `RelativeLayout` to a `FrameLayout` and removed the layout's padding properties. Next, we added a `RecyclerView` named `recyclerView` and a `FloatingActionButton` named `addButton`. The layout's final XML is shown in Fig. 9.11. Ensure that you set the `RecyclerView` and a `FloatingActionButton` properties as shown.

```
 1  <FrameLayout
 2      xmlns:android="http://schemas.android.com/apk/res/android"
 3      android:layout_width="match_parent"
 4      android:layout_height="match_parent">
 5
 6      <android.support.v7.widget.RecyclerView
 7          android:id="@+id/recyclerView"
 8          android:layout_width="match_parent"
 9          android:layout_height="match_parent"/>
10
```

Fig. 9.11 | `fragment_contacts.xml` layout. (Part 1 of 2.)

```
11      <android.support.design.widget.FloatingActionButton
12          android:id="@+id/addButton"
13          android:layout_width="wrap_content"
14          android:layout_height="wrap_content"
15          android:layout_gravity="top|end"
16          android:layout_margin="@dimen/fab_margin"
17          android:src="@drawable/ic_add_24dp"/>
18  </FrameLayout>
```

Fig. 9.11 | fragment_contacts.xml layout. (Part 2 of 2.)

9.4.9 DetailFragment's Layout

When the user touches a contact in the MainActivity, the app displays the DetailFragment (Fig. 9.12). This Fragment's layout (fragment_details.xml) consists of a Scroll-View containing a vertical GridLayout with two columns of TextViews. A ScrollView is a ViewGroup that provides scrolling functionality for a view with content too large to display on the screen. We use a ScrollView here to ensure that the user can scroll through a contact's details if a device does not have enough vertical space to show all the TextViews in Fig. 9.12. For this fragment, create a new fragment_details.xml layout resource file and specify a ScrollView as the **Root Element**. After creating the file add a GridLayout to the ScrollView.

Fig. 9.12 | DetailFragment's GUI components labeled with their id property values.

GridLayout *Settings*

For the GridLayout, we set the layout:width to match_parent, layout:height to wrap_content, columnCount to 2 and useDefaultMargins to true. The layout:height value enables the parent ScrollView to determine the GridLayout's actual height and decide whether to provide scrolling. Add TextViews to the GridLayout as shown in Fig. 9.12.

Left Column *TextView Settings*

For each TextView in the left column set the TextView's **id** property as specified in Fig. 9.12 and set:

- layout:row to a value from 0–6 depending on the row.
- layout:column to 0.
- text to the appropriate String resource from strings.xml.
- style to @style/ContactLabelTextView—style resources are specified using the syntax @style/*styleName*.

Right Column *TextView Settings*

For each TextView in the right column set the TextView's **id** property as specified in Fig. 9.12 and set:

- layout:row to a value from 0–6 depending on the row.
- layout:column to 1.
- style to @style/ContactTextView.

9.4.10 AddEditFragment's Layout

When the user touches the ➕ FloatingActionButton in the ContactsFragment or the edit (✏) app bar item in the DetailFragment, the MainActivity displays the AddEdit-Fragment (Fig. 9.13) with the layout fragment_add_edit.xml with a root FrameLayout that contains a ScrollView and a FloatingActionButton. The ScrollView contains a vertical LinearLayout with seven TextInputLayouts.

ScrollView *Settings*

For the ScrollView, we set the layout:width and layout:height to match_parent.

LinearLayout *Settings*

For the LinearLayout, we set the layout:width to match_parent, the layout:height to wrap_content and the orientation to vertical. We then added the seven TextInputLay-outs with the ids in Fig. 9.13, each with its layout:width set to match_parent and layout:height to wrap_content.

EditText *Settings*

We placed an EditText in each TextInputLayout, then set its **hint** property to the appropriate String resource in strings.xml. We also set each EditText's **inputType** and **imeOptions** properties. For devices that display a soft keyboard, the **inputType** specifies which keyboard to display for the corresponding EditText. This enables us to *customize the keyboard* to the specific type of data the user must enter in a given EditText. To display a next button (❯) on the soft keyboards for the EditTexts in the nameTextInputLayout,

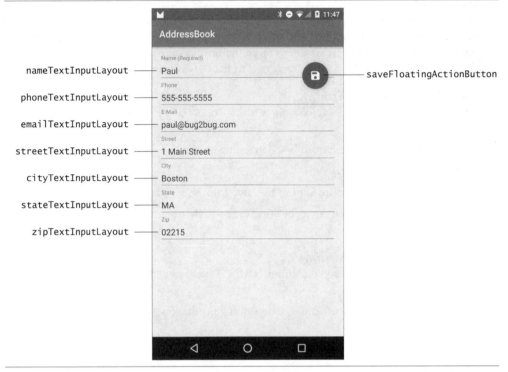

nameTextInputLayout

phoneTextInputLayout

emailTextInputLayout

streetTextInputLayout

cityTextInputLayout

stateTextInputLayout

zipTextInputLayout

saveFloatingActionButton

Fig. 9.13 | AddEditFragment's GUI components labeled with their id property values. This GUI's root component is a ScrollView that contains a vertical GridLayout.

phoneTextInputLayout, emailTextInputLayout, streetTextInputLayout, cityText-InputLayout and stateTextInputLayout, we set the **imeOptions** property to actionNext. When one of these EditTexts has the focus, touching ⊙ transfers the focus to the next EditText in the layout. If the EditText in the zipTextInputLayout has the focus, you can hide the soft keyboard by touching the keyboard's ⊘ Button—for this EditText, set the **imeOptions** property to actionDone.

Set the EditTexts' **inputType** properties to display appropriate keyboards as follows:

- nameTextInputLayout's EditText: check textPersonName and textCapWords—for entering names and starts each word with a capital letter.
- phoneTextInputLayout's EditText: check phone—for entering phone numbers.
- emailTextInputLayout's EditText: check textEmailAddress—for entering an e-mail address.
- streetTextInputLayout's EditText: check textPostalAddress and textCap-Words—for entering an address and starts each word with a capital letter.
- cityTextInputLayout's EditText: check textPostalAddress and textCapWords.
- stateTextInputLayout's EditText: check textPostalAddress and textCap-Characters—ensures that state abbreviations are displayed in capital letters.
- zipTextInputLayout's EditText: check number—for entering numbers.

9.4.11 DetailFragment's Menu

When you created the project, the IDE defined the menu resource menu_main.xml. The MainActivity in this app does not need a menu, so you can remove MainActivity's on-CreateOptionsMenu and onOptionsItemSelected methods, and rename this menu resource for use in the DetailFragment, which displays menu items on the app bar for editing an existing contact and deleting a contact. Rename the file menu_main.xml as fragment_details_menu.xml, then replace the **Settings** menu item with the menu items in Fig. 9.14. For each menu item's **android:icon** value, we specified a drawable resource that you added in Section 9.4.3.

```
1   <?xml version="1.0" encoding="utf-8"?>
2   <menu xmlns:android="http://schemas.android.com/apk/res/android"
3         xmlns:app="http://schemas.android.com/apk/res-auto">
4
5      <item
6         android:id="@+id/action_edit"
7         android:icon="@drawable/ic_mode_edit_24dp"
8         android:orderInCategory="1"
9         android:title="@string/menuitem_edit"
10        app:showAsAction="always"/>
11
12     <item
13        android:id="@+id/action_delete"
14        android:icon="@drawable/ic_delete_24dp"
15        android:orderInCategory="2"
16        android:title="@string/menuitem_delete"
17        app:showAsAction="always"/>
18  </menu>
```

Fig. 9.14 | Menu resource file fragment_details_menu.xml.

9.5 Overview of This Chapter's Classes

This app consists of nine classes in two packages. Due to the size of this app we overview the classes and their purposes here.

com.deitel.addressbook.data Package

This package contains the three classes that define this app's SQLite database access:

- DatabaseDescription (Section 9.6)—This class contains public static fields that are used with the app's ContentProvider and ContentResolver. The nested Contact class defines static fields for the name of a database table, the Uri used to access that table via the ContentProvider and the names of the database table's columns, and a static method for creating a Uri that references a specific contact in the database.

- AddressBookDatabaseHelper (Section 9.7)—A subclass of SQLiteOpenHelper. that creates the database and enables AddressBookContentProvider to access it.

- AddressBookContentProvider (Section 9.8)—A ContentProvider subclass that defines query, insert, update and delete operations on the database.

com.deitel.addressbook *Package*

This package contains the classes that define this app's MainActivity, Fragments and the adapter that's used to display database contents in a RecyclerView:

- MainActivity (Section 9.9)—This class manages the app's Fragments and implements their callback interface methods to respond when a contact is selected, a new contact is added, or an existing contact is updated or deleted.

- ContactsFragment (Section 9.10)—This class manages the contact-list RecyclerView and the FloatingActionButton for adding contacts. On a phone, this is the first Fragment presented by MainActivity. On a tablet, MainActivity always displays this Fragment. ContactsFragment's nested interface defines callback methods implemented by MainActivity so that it can respond when a contact is selected or added.

- ContactsAdapter (Section 9.11)—This subclass of RecyclerView.Adapter is used by ContactsFragment's RecyclerView to bind the sorted list of contact names to the RecyclerView. RecyclerView.Adapter was introduced in Sections 8.3.4– and 8.6, so we discuss only the database-specific operations in this class.

- AddEditFragment (Section 9.12)—This class manages the TextInputLayouts and a FloatingActionButton for adding a new contact or editing and existing one. AddEditFragment's nested interface defines a callback method implemented by MainActivity so that it can respond when a new or updated contact is saved.

- DetailFragment (Section 9.13)—This class manages the styled TextViews that display a selected contact's details and the app bar items that enable the user to edit or delete the currently displayed contact. DetailFragment's nested interface defines callback methods implemented by MainActivity so that it can respond when a contact is deleted or when the user touches the app bar item to edit a contact.

- ItemDivider—This class defines the divider that's displayed between items in the ContactsFragment's RecyclerView. We do not present the class in the chapter, because it's identical to the one presented in Section 8.7.

9.6 DatabaseDescription Class

Class DatabaseDescription contains static fields that are used with the app's ContentProvider and ContentResolver, and a nested Contact class that describes the database's only table and its columns.

9.6.1 static Fields

Class DatabaseDescription defines two static fields (Fig. 9.15; lines 12–17) that together are used to define the ContentProvider's authority—the name that's supplied to a ContentResolver to locate a ContentProvider. The authority is typically the package name of the ContentProvider subclass. Each Uri that's used to access a specific ContentProvider begins with "content://" followed by the authority—this is the ContentProvider's base Uri. Line 17 uses Uri method parse to create the base Uri.

```
 1   // DatabaseDescription.java
 2   // Describes the table name and column names for this app's database,
 3   // and other information required by the ContentProvider
 4   package com.deitel.addressbook.data;
 5
 6   import android.content.ContentUris;
 7   import android.net.Uri;
 8   import android.provider.BaseColumns;
 9
10   public class DatabaseDescription {
11      // ContentProvider's name: typically the package name
12      public static final String AUTHORITY =
13         "com.deitel.addressbook.data";
14
15      // base URI used to interact with the ContentProvider
16      private static final Uri BASE_CONTENT_URI =
17         Uri.parse("content://" + AUTHORITY);
18
```

Fig. 9.15 | DatabaseDescription class declaration and static fields.

9.6.2 Nested Class Contact

The nested class Contact (Fig. 9.16) defines the database's table name (line 21), the table's Uri for accessing the table via the ContentProvider (lines 24–25) and the table's column names (lines 28–34). The table name and column names will be used by the AddressBook-DatabaseHelper class (Section 9.7) to create the database. Method buildContactUri creates a Uri for a specific contact in the database table (lines 37–39). Class ContentUris (package android.content) contains static utility methods for manipulating "content://" Uris. Method withAppendedId appends a forward slash (/) and a record ID to the end of the Uri in its first argument. For every database table, you'd typically have a class similar to class Contact.

```
19      // nested class defines contents of the contacts table
20      public static final class Contact implements BaseColumns {
21         public static final String TABLE_NAME = "contacts"; // table's name
22
23         // Uri for the contacts table
24         public static final Uri CONTENT_URI =
25            BASE_CONTENT_URI.buildUpon().appendPath(TABLE_NAME).build();
26
27         // column names for contacts table's columns
28         public static final String COLUMN_NAME = "name";
29         public static final String COLUMN_PHONE = "phone";
30         public static final String COLUMN_EMAIL = "email";
31         public static final String COLUMN_STREET = "street";
32         public static final String COLUMN_CITY = "city";
33         public static final String COLUMN_STATE = "state";
34         public static final String COLUMN_ZIP = "zip";
35
```

Fig. 9.16 | DatabaseDescription nested class Contact. (Part 1 of 2.)

```
36          // creates a Uri for a specific contact
37          public static Uri buildContactUri(long id) {
38              return ContentUris.withAppendedId(CONTENT_URI, id);
39          }
40      }
41  }
```

Fig. 9.16 | DatabaseDescription nested class Contact. (Part 2 of 2.)

In a database table, each row typically has a primary key that uniquely identifies the row. When working with ListViews and Cursors, this column's name must be "_id"—Android also uses this for the ID column in SQLite database tables. This name is not required for RecyclerViews, but we use it here due to the similarities between ListViews and RecyclerViews, and because we're using Cursors and a SQLite database. Rather than defining this constant directly in class Contact, we implement interface BaseColumns (package android.provider; line 20), which defines the constant _ID with the value "_id".

9.7 AddressBookDatabaseHelper Class

The AddressBookDatabaseHelper class (Fig. 9.17) extends abstract class SQLiteOpenHelper, which helps apps create databases and manage database version changes.

```
1   // AddressBookDatabaseHelper.java
2   // SQLiteOpenHelper subclass that defines the app's database
3   package com.deitel.addressbook.data;
4
5   import android.content.Context;
6   import android.database.sqlite.SQLiteDatabase;
7   import android.database.sqlite.SQLiteOpenHelper;
8
9   import com.deitel.addressbook.data.DatabaseDescription.Contact;
10
11  class AddressBookDatabaseHelper extends SQLiteOpenHelper {
12      private static final String DATABASE_NAME = "AddressBook.db";
13      private static final int DATABASE_VERSION = 1;
14
15      // constructor
16      public AddressBookDatabaseHelper(Context context) {
17          super(context, DATABASE_NAME, null, DATABASE_VERSION);
18      }
19
20      // creates the contacts table when the database is created
21      @Override
22      public void onCreate(SQLiteDatabase db) {
23          // SQL for creating the contacts table
24          final String CREATE_CONTACTS_TABLE =
25              "CREATE TABLE " + Contact.TABLE_NAME + "(" +
```

Fig. 9.17 | AddressBookDatabaseHelper subclass of SQLiteOpenHelper defines the app's database. (Part 1 of 2.)

```
26              Contact._ID + " integer primary key, " +
27              Contact.COLUMN_NAME + " TEXT, " +
28              Contact.COLUMN_PHONE + " TEXT, " +
29              Contact.COLUMN_EMAIL + " TEXT, " +
30              Contact.COLUMN_STREET + " TEXT, " +
31              Contact.COLUMN_CITY + " TEXT, " +
32              Contact.COLUMN_STATE + " TEXT, " +
33              Contact.COLUMN_ZIP + " TEXT);";
34          db.execSQL(CREATE_CONTACTS_TABLE); // create the contacts table
35       }
36
37       // normally defines how to upgrade the database when the schema changes
38       @Override
39       public void onUpgrade(SQLiteDatabase db, int oldVersion,
40          int newVersion) { }
41    }
```

Fig. 9.17 | AddressBookDatabaseHelper subclass of SQLiteOpenHelper defines the app's database. (Part 2 of 2.)

Constructor

The constructor (lines 16–18) simply calls the superclass constructor, which requires four arguments:

- the Context in which the database is being created or opened,
- the database name—this can be null if you wish to use an in-memory database,
- the CursorFactory to use—null indicates that you wish to use the default SQLite CursorFactory (typically for most apps) and
- the database version number (starting from 1).

Overridden Methods

You must override this class's abstract methods onCreate and onUpgrade. If the database does not yet exist, the DatabaseOpenHelper's onCreate method will be called to create it. If you supply a newer version number than the database version currently stored on the device, the DatabaseOpenHelper's onUpgrade method will be called to upgrade the database to the new version (perhaps to add tables or to add columns to an existing table).

The onCreate method (lines 22–35) specifies the table to create with the SQL CREATE TABLE command, which is defined as a String (lines 24–33) that's constructed using constants from class Contact (Section 9.6.2). In this case, the contacts table contains an integer primary key field (Contact._ID), and text fields for all the other columns. Line 34 uses SQLiteDatabase's execSQL method to execute the CREATE TABLE command.

Since we don't need to upgrade the database, we simply override method onUpgrade with an empty body. Class SQLiteOpenHelper also provides the onDowngrade method that can be used to downgrade a database when the currently stored version has a higher version number than the one requested in the call to class SQLiteOpenHelper's constructor. Downgrading might be used to revert the database back to a prior version with fewer columns in a table or fewer tables in the database—perhaps to fix a bug in the app.

9.8 AddressBookContentProvider Class

The AddressBookContentProvider subclass of ContentProvider defines how to perform query, insert, update and delete operations on this app's database.

> **Error-Prevention Tip 9.1**
>
> *ContentProviders can be invoked from multiple threads in one process and multiple processes, so it's important to note that ContentProviders do not provide any synchronization by default. However, SQLite does synchronize access to the database, so in this app it's unnecessary to provide your own synchronization mechanisms.*

9.8.1 AddressBookContentProvider Fields

Class AddressBookContentProvider (Fig. 9.18) defines several fields:

- Instance variable dbHelper (line 17) is a reference to an AddressBookDatabaseHelper object that creates the database and enables this ContentProvider to get readable and writable access to the database.

- Class variable uriMatcher (lines 20–21) is an object of class UriMatcher (package android.content). A ContentProvider uses a UriMatcher to help determine which operation to perform in its query, insert, update and delete methods.

- The UriMatcher returns the integer constants ONE_CONTACT and CONTACTS (lines 24–25)—the ContentProvider uses these constants in switch statements in its query, insert, update and delete methods.

```
1   // AddressBookContentProvider.java
2   // ContentProvider subclass for manipulating the app's database
3   package com.deitel.addressbook.data;
4
5   import android.content.ContentProvider;
6   import android.content.ContentValues;
7   import android.content.UriMatcher;
8   import android.database.Cursor;
9   import android.database.SQLException;
10  import android.database.sqlite.SQLiteQueryBuilder;
11  import android.net.Uri;
12
13  import com.deitel.addressbook.data.DatabaseDescription.Contact;
14
15  public class AddressBookContentProvider extends ContentProvider {
16     // used to access the database
17     private AddressBookDatabaseHelper dbHelper;
18
19     // UriMatcher helps ContentProvider determine operation to perform
20     private static final UriMatcher uriMatcher =
21        new UriMatcher(UriMatcher.NO_MATCH);
22
23     // constants used with UriMatcher to determine operation to perform
24     private static final int ONE_CONTACT = 1; // manipulate one contact
25     private static final int CONTACTS = 2; // manipulate contacts table
```

Fig. 9.18 | AddressBookContentProvider fields. (Part 1 of 2.)

```
26
27     // static block to configure this ContentProvider's UriMatcher
28     static {
29       // Uri for Contact with the specified id (#)
30       uriMatcher.addURI(DatabaseDescription.AUTHORITY,
31         Contact.TABLE_NAME + "/#", ONE_CONTACT);
32
33       // Uri for Contacts table
34       uriMatcher.addURI(DatabaseDescription.AUTHORITY,
35         Contact.TABLE_NAME, CONTACTS);
36     }
37
```

Fig. 9.18 | AddressBookContentProvider fields. (Part 2 of 2.)

Lines 28–36 define a static block that adds Uris to the static UriMatcher—this block executes once when class AddressBookContentProvider is loaded into memory. UriMatcher method addUri takes three arguments:

- a String representing the ContentProvider's authority (DatabaseDescription.AUTHORITY in this app)

- a String representing a path—each Uri used to invoke the ContentProvider contains "content://" followed by the authority and a path that the ContentProvider uses to determine the task to perform

- an int code that the UriMatcher returns when a Uri supplied to to the ContentProvider matches a Uri stored in the UriMatcher.

Lines 30–31 add a Uri of the form:

```
content://com.deitel.addressbook.data/contacts/#
```

where # is a wildcard that matches a string of numeric characters—in this case, the unique primary-key value for one contact in the contacts table. There is also a * wildcard that matches any number of characters. When a Uri matches this format, the UriMatcher returns the constant ONE_CONTACT.

Lines 34–35 add a Uri of the form:

```
content://com.deitel.addressbook.data/contacts
```

which represents the entire contacts table. When a Uri matches this format, the UriMatcher returns the constant CONTACTS. As we discuss the rest of class AddressBookContentProvider, you'll see how the UriMatcher and the constants ONE_CONTACT and CONTACTS are used.

9.8.2 Overridden Methods onCreate and getType

As you'll see, you use a ContentResolver to invoke a ContentProvider's methods. When Android receives a request from a ContentResolver, it automatically creates the corresponding ContentProvider object—or uses an existing one, if it was created previously. When a ContentProvider is created, Android calls its **onCreate** method to configure the ContentProvider (Fig. 9.19, lines 39–44). Line 42 creates the AddressBookDatabase-

Helper object that enables the provider to access the database. The first time the provider is invoked to write to the database, the AddressBookDatabaseHelper object's onCreate method will be called to create the database (Fig. 9.17, lines 22–35).

```
38     // called when the AddressBookContentProvider is created
39     @Override
40     public boolean onCreate() {
41         // create the AddressBookDatabaseHelper
42         dbHelper = new AddressBookDatabaseHelper(getContext());
43         return true; // ContentProvider successfully created
44     }
45
46     // required method: Not used in this app, so we return null
47     @Override
48     public String getType(Uri uri) {
49         return null;
50     }
51
```

Fig. 9.19 | Overridden ContentProvider methods onCreate and getType.

Method getType (Fig. 9.19, lines 47–50) is a required ContentProvider method that simply returns null in this app. This method typically is used when creating and starting Intents for Uris with specific MIME types. Android can use MIME types to determine appropriate activities to handle the Intents.

9.8.3 Overridden Method query

The overridden ContentProvider method query (Fig. 9.20) retrieves data from the provider's data source—in this case, the database. The method returns a Cursor that's used to interact with the results. Method query receives five arguments:

- uri—A Uri representing the data to retrieve.
- projection—A String array representing the specific columns to retrieve. If this argument is null, all columns will be included in the result.
- selection—A String containing the selection criteria. This is the SQL WHERE clause, specified *without* the WHERE keyword. If this argument is null, all rows will be included in the result.
- selectionArgs—A String array containing the arguments used to replace any argument placeholders (?) in the selection String.
- sortOrder—A String representing the sort order. This is the SQL ORDER BY clause, specified *without* the ORDER BY keywords. If this argument is null, the provider determines this sort order—the order in which results are returned to the app is not guaranteed unless you provide an appropriate sort order.

SQLiteQueryBuilder
Line 58 creates a SQLiteQueryBuilder (package android.database.sqlite) for building SQL queries that are submitted to a SQLite database. Line 59 uses method setTables to specify that the query will select data from the database's contacts table. This method's

```
52     // query the database
53     @Override
54     public Cursor query(Uri uri, String[] projection,
55         String selection, String[] selectionArgs, String sortOrder) {
56
57         // create SQLiteQueryBuilder for querying contacts table
58         SQLiteQueryBuilder queryBuilder = new SQLiteQueryBuilder();
59         queryBuilder.setTables(Contact.TABLE_NAME);
60
61         switch (uriMatcher.match(uri)) {
62             case ONE_CONTACT: // contact with specified id will be selected
63                 queryBuilder.appendWhere(
64                     Contact._ID + "=" + uri.getLastPathSegment());
65                 break;
66             case CONTACTS: // all contacts will be selected
67                 break;
68             default:
69                 throw new UnsupportedOperationException(
70                     getContext().getString(R.string.invalid_query_uri) + uri);
71         }
72
73         // execute the query to select one or all contacts
74         Cursor cursor = queryBuilder.query(dbHelper.getReadableDatabase(),
75             projection, selection, selectionArgs, null, null, sortOrder);
76
77         // configure to watch for content changes
78         cursor.setNotificationUri(getContext().getContentResolver(), uri);
79         return cursor;
80     }
81
```

Fig. 9.20 | Overridden ContentProvider method query.

String argument can be used to perform table join operations by specifying multiple tables in a comma separated list or as an appropriate SQL JOIN clause.

Using the UriMatcher to Determine the Operation to Perform

In this app, there are two queries:

- select a specific contact from the database to display or edit its details, and

- select all contacts in the database to display their names in the ContactsFragment's RecyclerView.

Lines 61–71 use UriMatcher method match to determine which query operation to perform. This method returns one of the constants that was registered with the UriMatcher (Section 9.8.1). If the constant returned is ONE_CONTACT, only the contact with the ID specified in the Uri should be selected. In this case, lines 63–64 use the SQLiteQueryBuilder's appendWhere method to add a WHERE clause containing the contact's ID to the query. Uri method getLastPathSegment returns the last segment in the Uri—for example, the contact ID 5 in the following Uri

```
content://com.deitel.addressbook.data/contacts/5
```

If the constant returned is CONTACTS, the switch terminates without adding anything to the query—in this case, all contacts will be selected because there is no WHERE clause. For any Uri that is not a match, lines 69–70 throw an UnsupportedOperationException indicating that the Uri was invalid.

Querying the Database

Lines 74–75 use the SQLiteQueryBuilder's query method to perform the database query and get a Cursor representing the results. The method's arguments are similar to those received by the ContentProvider's query method:

- A SQLiteDatabase to query—the AddressBookDatabaseHelper's getReadable-Database method returns a read-only SQLiteDatabase object.
- projection—A String array representing the specific columns to retrieve. If this argument is null, all columns will be included in the result.
- selection—A String containing the selection criteria. This is the SQL WHERE clause, specified *without* the WHERE keyword. If this argument is null, all rows will be included in the result.
- selectionArgs—A String array containing the arguments used to replace any argument placeholders (?) in the selection String.
- groupBy—A String containing the grouping criteria. This is the SQL GROUP BY clause, specified *without* the GROUP BY keywords. If this argument is null, no grouping is performed.
- having—When using groupBy, this argument is a String indicating which groups to include in the results. This is the SQL HAVING clause, specified *without* the HAVING keyword. If this argument is null, all groups specified by the groupBy argument will be included in the results.
- sortOrder—A String representing the sort order. This is the SQL ORDER BY clause, specified *without* the ORDER BY keywords. If this argument is null, the provider determines this sort order.

Registering the Cursor to Watch for Content Changes

Line 78 calls the Cursor's setNotificationUri method to indicate that the Cursor should be updated if the data it refers to changes. This first argument is the ContentResolver that invoked the ContentProvider and the second is the Uri used to invoke the ContentProvider. Line 79 returns the Cursor containing the query results.

9.8.4 Overridden Method insert

The overridden ContentProvider method insert (Fig. 9.21) adds a new record to the contacts table. Method insert receives two arguments:

- uri—A Uri representing the table in which the data will be inserted.
- values—A ContentValues object containing key–value pairs in which the column names are the keys and each key's value is the data to insert in that column.

Lines 87–108 check whether the Uri is for the contacts table—if not, the Uri is invalid for the insert operation and lines 106–107 throw an UnsupportedOperation-

```
82      // insert a new contact in the database
83      @Override
84      public Uri insert(Uri uri, ContentValues values) {
85         Uri newContactUri = null;
86
87         switch (uriMatcher.match(uri)) {
88            case CONTACTS:
89               // insert the new contact--success yields new contact's row id
90               long rowId = dbHelper.getWritableDatabase().insert(
91                  Contact.TABLE_NAME, null, values);
92
93               // if the contact was inserted, create an appropriate Uri;
94               // otherwise, throw an exception
95               if (rowId > 0) { // SQLite row IDs start at 1
96                  newContactUri = Contact.buildContactUri(rowId);
97
98                  // notify observers that the database changed
99                  getContext().getContentResolver().notifyChange(uri, null);
100              }
101              else
102                 throw new SQLException(
103                    getContext().getString(R.string.insert_failed) + uri);
104              break;
105           default:
106              throw new UnsupportedOperationException(
107                 getContext().getString(R.string.invalid_insert_uri) + uri);
108        }
109
110        return newContactUri;
111     }
112
```

Fig. 9.21 | Overridden ContentProvider method insert.

Exception. If the Uri is a match, lines 90–91 insert the new contact in the database. First, we use the AddressBookDatabaseHelper's **getWritableDatabase** method to get a SQLite-DatabaseObject for modifying data in the database.

SQLiteDatabase's **insert** method (lines 90–91) inserts the values from the third argument's ContentValues object into the table specified as the first argument—the contacts table in this case. The second parameter of this method, which is not used in this app, is named nullColumnHack and is needed because *SQLite does not support inserting a completely empty row into a table*—this would be the equivalent of passing an empty ContentValues object to insert. Instead of making it illegal to pass an empty ContentValues to the method, the nullColumnHack parameter is used to identify a column that accepts NULL values.

Method insert returns the new contact's unique ID if the insert operation is successful or -1 otherwise. Line 95 checks whether the rowID is greater than 0 (rows are indexed from 1 in SQLite). If so, line 96 creates a Uri representing the new contact and line 99 notifies the ContentResolver that the database changed, so the ContentResolver's client code can respond to the database changes. If the rowID is not greater than 0, the database operation failed and lines 102–103 throws a SQLException.

9.8.5 Overridden Method update

The overridden ContentProvider method update (Fig. 9.22) updates an existing record. Method update receives four arguments:

- uri—A Uri representing the rows to update.

- values—A ContentValues object containig the columns to update and their corresponding values.

- selection—A String containing the selection criteria. This is the SQL WHERE clause, specified *without* the WHERE keyword. If this argument is null, all rows will be included in the result.

- selectionArgs—A String array containing the arguments used to replace any argument placeholders (?) in the selection String.

```
113    // update an existing contact in the database
114    @Override
115    public int update(Uri uri, ContentValues values,
116       String selection, String[] selectionArgs) {
117       int numberOfRowsUpdated; // 1 if update successful; 0 otherwise
118
119       switch (uriMatcher.match(uri)) {
120          case ONE_CONTACT:
121             // get from the uri the id of contact to update
122             String id = uri.getLastPathSegment();
123
124             // update the contact
125             numberOfRowsUpdated = dbHelper.getWritableDatabase().update(
126                Contact.TABLE_NAME, values, Contact._ID + "=" + id,
127                selectionArgs);
128             break;
129          default:
130             throw new UnsupportedOperationException(
131                getContext().getString(R.string.invalid_update_uri) + uri);
132       }
133
134       // if changes were made, notify observers that the database changed
135       if (numberOfRowsUpdated != 0) {
136          getContext().getContentResolver().notifyChange(uri, null);
137       }
138
139       return numberOfRowsUpdated;
140    }
141
```

Fig. 9.22 | Overridden ContentProvider method update.

Updates in this app are performed only on a specific contact, so lines 119–132 check only for a ONE_CONTACT Uri. Line 122 gets the Uri argument's last path segement, which is the contact's unique ID. Lines 125–127 get a writeable SQLiteDatabase object then call its **update method** to update the specified contact with the values from the Content-Values argument. The update method's arguments are:

- the String name of the table to update
- the ContentValues object containing the columns to update and their new values
- the String representing the SQL WHERE clause that specifies the rows to update
- a String array containing any arguments that should replace ? placeholders in the WHERE clause.

If the operation is successful, method update returns an integer indicating the number of modified rows; otherwise, update returns 0. Line 136 notifies the ContentResolver that the database changed, so the ContentResolver's client code can respond to the changes. Line 139 returns the number of modified rows.

9.8.6 Overridden Method delete

The overridden ContentProvider method delete (Fig. 9.23) removes an existing record. Method delete receives three arguments:

- uri—A Uri representing the row(s) to delete.
- selection—A String containing the WHERE clause specifying the rows to delete.
- selectionArgs—A String array containing the arguments used to replace any argument placeholders (?) in the selection String.

```
142    // delete an existing contact from the database
143    @Override
144    public int delete(Uri uri, String selection, String[] selectionArgs) {
145        int numberOfRowsDeleted;
146
147        switch (uriMatcher.match(uri)) {
148            case ONE_CONTACT:
149                // get from the uri the id of contact to update
150                String id = uri.getLastPathSegment();
151
152                // delete the contact
153                numberOfRowsDeleted = dbHelper.getWritableDatabase().delete(
154                    Contact.TABLE_NAME, Contact._ID + "=" + id, selectionArgs);
155                break;
156            default:
157                throw new UnsupportedOperationException(
158                    getContext().getString(R.string.invalid_delete_uri) + uri);
159        }
160
161        // notify observers that the database changed
162        if (numberOfRowsDeleted != 0) {
163            getContext().getContentResolver().notifyChange(uri, null);
164        }
165
166        return numberOfRowsDeleted;
167    }
168 }
```

Fig. 9.23 | Overridden ContentProvider method delete.

Deletions in this app are performed only on a specific contact, so lines 147–159 check for a ONE_CONTACT Uri—any other Uri represents an unsupported operation. Line 150 gets the Uri argument's last path segment, which is the contact's unique ID. Lines 153–154 get a writeable SQLiteDatabase object then call its **delete method** to remove the specified contact. The three arguments are the database table from which to delete the record, the WHERE clause and, if the WHERE clause has arguments, a String array of values to substitute into the WHERE clause. The method returns the number of rows deleted. Line 163 notifies the ContentResolver that the database changed, so the ContentResolver's client code can respond to the changes. Line 166 returns the number of deleted rows.

9.9 MainActivity Class

Class MainActivity manages the app's fragments and coordinates the interactions between them. On phones, MainActivity displays one Fragment at a time, starting with the ContactsFragment. On tablets, MainActivity always displays the ContactsFragment at the left of the layout and, depending on the context, displays either the DetailFragment or the AddEditFragment in the right two-thirds of the layout.

9.9.1 Superclass, Implemented Interfaces and Fields

Class MainActivity (Fig. 9.24) uses class FragmentTransaction from the v4 support library to add and remove the app's Fragments. MainActivity implements three interfaces:

- ContactsFragment.ContactsFragmentListener (Section 9.10.2) contains callback methods that the ContactsFragment uses to tell the MainActivity when the user selects a contact in the contact list or adds a new contact.

- DetailFragment.DetailFragmentListener (Section 9.13.2) contains callback methods that the DetailFragment uses to tell the MainActivity when the user deletes a contact or wishes to edit an existing contact.

- AddEditFragment.AddEditFragmentListener (Section 9.12.2) contains a callback method that the AddEditFragment uses to tell the MainActivity when the user saves a new contact or saves changes to an existing contact.

The constant CONTACT_URI (line 17) is used as a key in a key–value pair that's passed between the MainActivity and its Fragments. The instance variable ContactsFragment (line 19) is used to tell the ContactsFragment to update the displayed list of contacts after a contact is added or deleted.

```
1   // MainActivity.java
2   // Hosts the app's fragments and handles communication between them
3   package com.deitel.addressbook;
4
5   import android.net.Uri;
6   import android.os.Bundle;
7   import android.support.v4.app.FragmentTransaction;
8   import android.support.v7.app.AppCompatActivity;
9   import android.support.v7.widget.Toolbar;
```

Fig. 9.24 | MainActivity's superclass, implemented interfaces and fields. (Part 1 of 2.)

```
10
11   public class MainActivity extends AppCompatActivity
12      implements ContactsFragment.ContactsFragmentListener,
13      DetailFragment.DetailFragmentListener,
14      AddEditFragment.AddEditFragmentListener {
15
16      // key for storing a contact's Uri in a Bundle passed to a fragment
17      public static final String CONTACT_URI = "contact_uri";
18
19      private ContactsFragment contactsFragment; // displays contact list
20
```

Fig. 9.24 | MainActivity's superclass, implemented interfaces and fields, (Part 2 of 2.)

9.9.2 Overridden Method onCreate

Overridden Activity method onCreate (Fig. 9.25) inflates MainActivity's GUI and, if the app is running on a phone-sized device, creates and displays a ContactsFragment. If the Activity is being restored after being shut down or recreated from a configuration change, savedInstanceState will not be null. In this case, lines 43–45 simply get a reference to the existing ContactsFragment—on a phone, it would have been saved by Android and on a tablet, it's part of the MainActivity's layout that was inflated in line 25.

```
21      // display ContactsFragment when MainActivity first loads
22      @Override
23      protected void onCreate(Bundle savedInstanceState) {
24          super.onCreate(savedInstanceState);
25          setContentView(R.layout.activity_main);
26          Toolbar toolbar = (Toolbar) findViewById(R.id.toolbar);
27          setSupportActionBar(toolbar);
28
29          // if layout contains fragmentContainer, the phone layout is in use;
30          // create and display a ContactsFragment
31          if (savedInstanceState != null &&
32              findViewById(R.id.fragmentContainer) != null) {
33              // create ContactsFragment
34              contactsFragment = new ContactsFragment();
35
36              // add the fragment to the FrameLayout
37              FragmentTransaction transaction =
38                  getSupportFragmentManager().beginTransaction();
39              transaction.add(R.id.fragmentContainer, contactsFragment);
40              transaction.commit(); // display ContactsFragment
41          }
42          else {
43              contactsFragment =
44                  (ContactsFragment) getSupportFragmentManager().
45                      findFragmentById(R.id.contactsFragment);
46          }
47      }
48
```

Fig. 9.25 | Overridden Activity method onCreate.

If the R.id.fragmentContainer exists in MainActivity's layout (line 32), then the app is running on a phone. In this case, line 34 creates the ContactsFragment, then lines 37–40 use a FragmentTransaction to add the ContactsFragment to the user interface. Lines 37–38 call FragmentManager's **beginTransaction** method to obtain a FragmentTransaction. Next, line 39 calls FragmentTransaction method **add** to specify that, when the FragmentTransaction completes, the ContactsFragment should be attached to the View with the ID specified as the first argument. Finally, line 40 uses FragmentTransaction method **commit** to finalize the transaction and display the ContactsFragment.

9.9.3 ContactsFragment.ContactsFragmentListener Methods

Figure 9.26 contains MainActivity's implementations of the callback methods in the interface ContactsFragment.ContactsFragmentListener. Method onContactSelected (lines 50–60) is called by the ContactsFragment to notify the MainActivity when the user selects a contact to display. If the app is running on a phone (line 52), line 53 calls method displayContact (Section 9.9.4), which replaces the ContactsFragment in the fragmentContainer (defined in Section 9.4.7) with the DetailFragment that shows the contact's information. On a tablet, line 56 calls the FragmentManager's **popBackStack** method to *pop* (remove) the top Fragment on the back stack (if there is one), then line 58 calls displayContact, which replaces the contents of the rightPaneContainer (defined in Section 9.4.7) with the DetailFragment that shows the contact's information.

```
49      // display DetailFragment for selected contact
50      @Override
51      public void onContactSelected(Uri contactUri) {
52         if (findViewById(R.id.fragmentContainer) != null) // phone
53            displayContact(contactUri, R.id.fragmentContainer);
54         else { // tablet
55            // removes top of back stack
56            getSupportFragmentManager().popBackStack();
57
58            displayContact(contactUri, R.id.rightPaneContainer);
59         }
60      }
61
62      // display AddEditFragment to add a new contact
63      @Override
64      public void onAddContact() {
65         if (findViewById(R.id.fragmentContainer) != null) // phone
66            displayAddEditFragment(R.id.fragmentContainer, null);
67         else // tablet
68            displayAddEditFragment(R.id.rightPaneContainer, null);
69      }
70
```

Fig. 9.26 | ContactsFragment.ContactsFragmentListener methods.

Method onAddContact (lines 63–69) is called by the ContactsFragment to notify the MainActivity when the user chooses to add a new contact. If the layout contains the fragmentContainer, line 66 calls displayAddEditFragment (Section 9.9.5) to display the Add-

EditFragment in the fragmentContainer; otherwise, line 68 displays the Fragment in the rightPaneContainer. The second argument to displayAddEditFragment is a Bundle that the AddEditFragment uses to determine whether a new contact is being added or an existing contact is being edited—null indicates that a new contact is being added; otherwise, the bundle includes the existing contact's Uri.

9.9.4 Method displayContact

Method displayContact (Fig. 9.27) creates the DetailFragment that displays the selected contact. You can pass arguments to a Fragment by placing them in a Bundle of key–value pairs—we do this to pass the selected contact's Uri so that the DetailFragment knows which contact to get from the ContentProvider. Line 76 creates the Bundle. Line 77 calls its **putParcelable** method to store a key–value pair containing the CONTACT_URI (a String) as the key and the contactUri (a Uri) as the value. Class Uri implements the Parcelable interface, so a Uri can be stored in a Bundle as a Parcel object. Line 78 passes the Bundle to the Fragment's **setArguments** method—the Fragment can then extract the information from the Bundle (as you'll see in Section 9.13).

```
71    // display a contact
72    private void displayContact(Uri contactUri, int viewID) {
73       DetailFragment detailFragment = new DetailFragment();
74
75       // specify contact's Uri as an argument to the DetailFragment
76       Bundle arguments = new Bundle();
77       arguments.putParcelable(CONTACT_URI, contactUri);
78       detailFragment.setArguments(arguments);
79
80       // use a FragmentTransaction to display the DetailFragment
81       FragmentTransaction transaction =
82          getSupportFragmentManager().beginTransaction();
83       transaction.replace(viewID, detailFragment);
84       transaction.addToBackStack(null);
85       transaction.commit(); // causes DetailFragment to display
86    }
87
```

Fig. 9.27 | Method displayContact.

Lines 81–82 get a FragmentTransaction, then line 83 calls FragmentTransaction method **replace** to specify that, when the FragmentTransaction completes, the DetailFragment should replace the contents of the View with the ID specified as the first argument. Line 84 calls FragmentTransaction method **addToBackStack** to *push* (add) the DetailFragment onto the back stack. This allows the user to touch the back button to pop the Fragment from the back stack and allows MainActivity to programmatically pop the Fragment from the back stack. Method addToBackStack's argument is an optional name for a *back state*. This can be used to pop multiple Fragments from the back stack to return to a prior state after multiple Fragments have been added to the back stack. By default, only the topmost Fragment is popped.

9.9.5 Method `displayAddEditFragment`

Method `displayAddEditFragment` (Fig. 9.28) receives a `View`'s resource ID specifying where to attach the `AddEditFragment` and a `Uri` representing a contact to edit. If the second argument is `null`, a new contact is being added. Line 90 creates the `AddEditFragment`. If the `contactUri` argument is not `null`, line 95 puts it into the `Bundle` that's used to supply the `Fragment`'s arguments. Lines 100–104 then create the `FragmentTransaction`, replace the contents of the `View` with the specified resource ID, add the `Fragment` to the back stack and commit the transaction.

```
88    // display fragment for adding a new or editing an existing contact
89    private void displayAddEditFragment(int viewID, Uri contactUri) {
90       AddEditFragment addEditFragment = new AddEditFragment();
91
92       // if editing existing contact, provide contactUri as an argument
93       if (contactUri != null) {
94          Bundle arguments = new Bundle();
95          arguments.putParcelable(CONTACT_URI, contactUri);
96          addEditFragment.setArguments(arguments);
97       }
98
99       // use a FragmentTransaction to display the AddEditFragment
100      FragmentTransaction transaction =
101         getSupportFragmentManager().beginTransaction();
102      transaction.replace(viewID, addEditFragment);
103      transaction.addToBackStack(null);
104      transaction.commit(); // causes AddEditFragment to display
105   }
106
```

Fig. 9.28 | Method `displayAddEditFragment`.

9.9.6 `DetailFragment.DetailFragmentListener` Methods

Figure 9.29 contains `MainActivity`'s implementations of the callback methods in the interface `DetailFragment.DetailFragmentListener`. Method `onContactDeleted` (lines 108–113) is called by the `DetailFragment` to notify the `MainActivity` when the user deletes a contact. In this case, line 111 pops the `DetailFragment` from the back stack so that the now deleted contact's information is no longer displayed. Line 112 calls the `Contacts-Fragment`'s `updateContactList` method to refresh the contacts list.

```
107   // return to contact list when displayed contact deleted
108   @Override
109   public void onContactDeleted() {
110      // removes top of back stack
111      getSupportFragmentManager().popBackStack();
112      contactsFragment.updateContactList(); // refresh contacts
113   }
114
```

Fig. 9.29 | `DetailFragment.DetailFragmentListener` methods. (Part 1 of 2.)

```
115    // display the AddEditFragment to edit an existing contact
116    @Override
117    public void onEditContact(Uri contactUri) {
118       if (findViewById(R.id.fragmentContainer) != null) // phone
119          displayAddEditFragment(R.id.fragmentContainer, contactUri);
120       else // tablet
121          displayAddEditFragment(R.id.rightPaneContainer, contactUri);
122    }
123
```

Fig. 9.29 | DetailFragment.DetailFragmentListener methods. (Part 2 of 2.)

Method onEditContact (lines 116–122) is called by the DetailFragment to notify the MainActivity when the user touches the app bar item to edit a contact. The Detail-Fragment passes a Uri representing the contact to edit so that it can be displayed in the AddEditFragment's EditTexts for editing. If the layout contains the fragmentContainer, line 119 calls displayAddEditFragment (Section 9.9.5) to display the AddEditFragment in the fragmentContainer; otherwise, line 121 displays the AddEditFragment in the rightPaneContainer.

9.9.7 AddEditFragment.AddEditFragmentListener Method

Method onAddEditCompleted (Fig. 9.30) from the AddEditFragment.AddEditFragment-Listener interface is called by the AddEditFragment to notify the MainActivity when the user saves a new contact or saves changes to an existing one. Line 128 pops the AddEdit-Fragment from the back stack and line 129 updates the ContactsFragment's contact list. If the app is running on a tablet (line 131), line 133 pops the back stack again to remove the DetailFragment (if there is one). Then line 136 displays the new or updated contact's details in the rightPaneContainer.

```
124    // update GUI after new contact or updated contact saved
125    @Override
126    public void onAddEditCompleted(Uri contactUri) {
127       // removes top of back stack
128       getSupportFragmentManager().popBackStack();
129       contactsFragment.updateContactList(); // refresh contacts
130
131       if (findViewById(R.id.fragmentContainer) == null) { // tablet
132          // removes top of back stack
133          getSupportFragmentManager().popBackStack();
134
135          // on tablet, display contact that was just added or edited
136          displayContact(contactUri, R.id.rightPaneContainer);
137       }
138    }
139 }
```

Fig. 9.30 | AddEditFragment.AddEditFragmentListener method.

9.10 ContactsFragment Class

Class ContactsFragment displays the contact list in a RecyclerView and provides a FloatingActionButton that the user can touch to add a new contact.

9.10.1 Superclass and Implemented Interface

Figure 9.31 lists ContactsFragment's package statement and import statements and the beginning of its class definition. The ContactsFragment uses a LoaderManager and a Loader to query the AddressBookContentProvider and receive a Cursor that the ContactsAdapter (Section 9.11) uses to supply data to the RecyclerView. ContactsFragment implements interface LoaderManager.LoaderCallbacks<Cursor> (line 23) so that it can respond to method calls from the LoaderManager to create the Loader and process the results returned by the AddressBookContentProvider.

```java
1   // ContactsFragment.java
2   // Fragment subclass that displays the alphabetical list of contact names
3   package com.deitel.addressbook;
4
5   import android.content.Context;
6   import android.database.Cursor;
7   import android.net.Uri;
8   import android.os.Bundle;
9   import android.support.design.widget.FloatingActionButton;
10  import android.support.v4.app.Fragment;
11  import android.support.v4.app.LoaderManager;
12  import android.support.v4.content.CursorLoader;
13  import android.support.v4.content.Loader;
14  import android.support.v7.widget.LinearLayoutManager;
15  import android.support.v7.widget.RecyclerView;
16  import android.view.LayoutInflater;
17  import android.view.View;
18  import android.view.ViewGroup;
19
20  import com.deitel.addressbook.data.DatabaseDescription.Contact;
21
22  public class ContactsFragment extends Fragment
23     implements LoaderManager.LoaderCallbacks<Cursor> {
24
```

Fig. 9.31 | ContactsFragment superclass and implemented interface.

9.10.2 ContactsFragmentListener

Figure 9.32 defines the nested interface ContactsFragmentListener, which contains the callback methods that MainActivity implements to be notified when the user selects a contact (line 28) and when the user touches the FloatingActionButton to add a new contact (line 31).

```
25        // callback method implemented by MainActivity
26        public interface ContactsFragmentListener {
27           // called when contact selected
28           void onContactSelected(Uri contactUri);
29
30           // called when add button is pressed
31           void onAddContact();
32        }
33
```

Fig. 9.32 | Nested interface ContactsFragmentListener.

9.10.3 Fields

Figure 9.33 shows class ContactsFragment's fields. Line 34 declares a constant that's used to identify the Loader when processing the results returned from the AddressBookContentProvider. In this case, we have only one Loader—if a class uses more than one Loader, each should have a constant with a unique integer value so that you can identify which Loader to manipulate in the LoaderManager.LoaderCallbacks<Cursor> callback methods. The instance variable listener (line 37) will refer to the object that implements the interface (MainActivity). Instance variable contactsAdapter (line 39) will refer to the ContactsAdapter that binds data to the RecyclerView.

```
34        private static final int CONTACTS_LOADER = 0; // identifies Loader
35
36        // used to inform the MainActivity when a contact is selected
37        private ContactsFragmentListener listener;
38
39        private ContactsAdapter contactsAdapter; // adapter for recyclerView
40
```

Fig. 9.33 | ContactsFragment fields.

9.10.4 Overridden Fragment Method onCreateView

Overridden Fragment method onCreateView (Fig. 9.34) inflates and configures the Fragment's GUI. Most of this method's code has been presented in prior chapters, so we focus only on the new features here. Line 47 indicates that the ContactsFragment has menu items that should be displayed on the Activity's app bar (or in its options menu). Lines 56–74 configure the RecyclerView. Lines 60–67 create the ContactsAdapter that populates the RecyclerView. The argument to the constructor is an implementation of the ContactsAdapter.ContactClickListener interface (Section 9.11) specifying that when the user touches a contact, the ContactsFragmentListener's onContactSelected should be called with the Uri of the contact to display in a DetailFragment.

```
41    // configures this fragment's GUI
42    @Override
43    public View onCreateView(
44       LayoutInflater inflater, ViewGroup container,
45       Bundle savedInstanceState) {
46       super.onCreateView(inflater, container, savedInstanceState);
47       setHasOptionsMenu(true); // fragment has menu items to display
48
49       // inflate GUI and get reference to the RecyclerView
50       View view = inflater.inflate(
51          R.layout.fragment_contacts, container, false);
52       RecyclerView recyclerView =
53          (RecyclerView) view.findViewById(R.id.recyclerView);
54
55       // recyclerView should display items in a vertical list
56       recyclerView.setLayoutManager(
57          new LinearLayoutManager(getActivity().getBaseContext()));
58
59       // create recyclerView's adapter and item click listener
60       contactsAdapter = new ContactsAdapter(
61          new ContactsAdapter.ContactClickListener() {
62             @Override
63             public void onClick(Uri contactUri) {
64                listener.onContactSelected(contactUri);
65             }
66          }
67       );
68       recyclerView.setAdapter(contactsAdapter); // set the adapter
69
70       // attach a custom ItemDecorator to draw dividers between list items
71       recyclerView.addItemDecoration(new ItemDivider(getContext()));
72
73       // improves performance if RecyclerView's layout size never changes
74       recyclerView.setHasFixedSize(true);
75
76       // get the FloatingActionButton and configure its listener
77       FloatingActionButton addButton =
78          (FloatingActionButton) view.findViewById(R.id.addButton);
79       addButton.setOnClickListener(
80          new View.OnClickListener() {
81             // displays the AddEditFragment when FAB is touched
82             @Override
83             public void onClick(View view) {
84                listener.onAddContact();
85             }
86          }
87       );
88
89       return view;
90    }
91
```

Fig. 9.34 | Overridden Fragment method onCreateView.

9.10.5 Overridden Fragment Methods onAttach and onDetach

Class ContactsFragment overrides Fragment lifecycle methods onAttach and onDetach (Fig. 9.35) to set instance variable listener. In this app, listener refers to the host Activity (line 96) when the ContactsFragment is attached and is set to null (line 103) when the ContactsFragment is detached.

```
92      // set ContactsFragmentListener when fragment attached
93      @Override
94      public void onAttach(Context context) {
95          super.onAttach(context);
96          listener = (ContactsFragmentListener) context;
97      }
98
99      // remove ContactsFragmentListener when Fragment detached
100     @Override
101     public void onDetach() {
102         super.onDetach();
103         listener = null;
104     }
105
```

Fig. 9.35 | Overridden Fragment methods onAttach and onDetach.

9.10.6 Overridden Fragment Method onActivityCreated

Fragment lifecycle method **onActivityCreated** (Fig. 9.36) is called after a Fragment's host Activity has been created and the Fragment's onCreateView method completes execution—at this point, the Fragment's GUI is part of the Activity's view hierarchy. We use this method to tell the LoaderManager to initialize a Loader—doing this after the view hierarchy exists is important because the RecyclerView must exist before we can display the loaded data. Line 110 uses Fragment method **getLoaderManager** to obtain the Fragment's LoaderManager object. Next we call LoaderManager's initLoader method, which receives three arguments:

- the integer ID used to identify the Loader

- a Bundle containing arguments for the Loader's constructor, or null if there are no arguments

- a reference to the implementation of the interface LoaderManager.LoaderCallbacks<Cursor> (this represents the ContactsAdapter)—you'll see the implementations of this interface's methods onCreateLoader, onLoadFinished and onLoaderReset in Section 9.10.8.

If there is not already an active Loader with the specified ID, the initLoader method asynchronously calls the onCreateLoader method to create and start a Loader for that ID. If there is an active Loader, the initLoader method immediately calls the onLoadFinished method.

```
106     // initialize a Loader when this fragment's activity is created
107     @Override
108     public void onActivityCreated(Bundle savedInstanceState) {
109        super.onActivityCreated(savedInstanceState);
110        getLoaderManager().initLoader(CONTACTS_LOADER, null, this);
111     }
112
```

Fig. 9.36 | Overridden Fragment method onActivityCreated.

9.10.7 Method updateContactList

ContactsFragment method updateContactList (Fig. 9.37) simply notifies the Contacts-Adapter when the data changes. This method is called when new contacts are added and when existing contacts are updated or deleted.

```
113     // called from MainActivity when other Fragment's update database
114     public void updateContactList() {
115        contactsAdapter.notifyDataSetChanged();
116     }
117
```

Fig. 9.37 | ContactsFragment method updateContactList.

9.10.8 LoaderManager.LoaderCallbacks<Cursor> Methods

Figure 9.38 presents class ContactsFragment's implementations of the callback methods in interface LoaderManager.LoaderCallbacks<Cursor>.

```
118     // called by LoaderManager to create a Loader
119     @Override
120     public Loader<Cursor> onCreateLoader(int id, Bundle args) {
121        // create an appropriate CursorLoader based on the id argument;
122        // only one Loader in this fragment, so the switch is unnecessary
123        switch (id) {
124           case CONTACTS_LOADER:
125              return new CursorLoader(getActivity(),
126                 Contact.CONTENT_URI, // Uri of contacts table
127                 null, // null projection returns all columns
128                 null, // null selection returns all rows
129                 null, // no selection arguments
130                 Contact.COLUMN_NAME + " COLLATE NOCASE ASC"); // sort order
131           default:
132              return null;
133        }
134     }
135
```

Fig. 9.38 | LoaderManager.LoaderCallbacks<Cursor> methods. (Part 1 of 2.)

```
136    // called by LoaderManager when loading completes
137    @Override
138    public void onLoadFinished(Loader<Cursor> loader, Cursor data) {
139        contactsAdapter.swapCursor(data);
140    }
141
142    // called by LoaderManager when the Loader is being reset
143    @Override
144    public void onLoaderReset(Loader<Cursor> loader) {
145        contactsAdapter.swapCursor(null);
146    }
147 }
```

Fig. 9.38 | LoaderManager.LoaderCallbacks<Cursor> methods. (Part 2 of 2.)

Method onCreateLoader

The LoaderManager calls method onCreateLoader (lines 119–134) to create and return a new Loader for the specified ID, which the LoaderManager manages in the context of the Fragment's or Activity's lifecycle. Lines 123–133 determine the Loader to create, based on the ID received as onCreateLoader's first argument.

 Good Programming Practice 9.1

For the ContactsFragment, we need only one Loader, so the switch statement is unnecessary, but we included it here as a good practice.

Lines 125–130 create and return a CursorLoader that queries the AddressBookContentProvider to get the list of contacts, then makes the results available as a Cursor. The CursorLoader constructor receives the Context in which the Loader's lifecycle is managed and uri, projection, selection, selectionArgs and sortOrder arguments that have the same meaning as those in the ContentProvider's query method (Section 9.8.3). In this case, we specified null for the projection, selection and selectionArgs arguments and indicated that the contacts should be sorted by name in a case insensitive manner.

Method onLoadFinished

Method onLoadFinished (lines 137–140) is called by the LoaderManager after a Loader finishes loading its data, so you can process the results in the Cursor argument. In this case, we call the ContactsAdapter's swapCursor method with the Cursor as an argument, so the ContactsAdapter can refresh the RecyclerView based on the new Cursor contents.

Method onLoaderReset

Method onLoaderReset (lines 143–146) is called by the LoaderManager when a Loader is reset and its data is no longer available. At this point, the app should immediately disconnect from the data. In this case, we call the ContactsAdapter's swapCursor method with the argument null to indicate that there is no data to bind to the RecyclerView.

9.11 ContactsAdapter Class

In Section 8.6, we discussed how to create a RecyclerView.Adapter that's used to bind data to a RecyclerView. Here we highlight only the new code that helps the ContactsAdapter (Fig. 9.39) to populate the RecyclerView with contact names from a Cursor.

```
1    // ContactsAdapter.java
2    // Subclass of RecyclerView.Adapter that binds contacts to RecyclerView
3    package com.deitel.addressbook;
4
5    import android.database.Cursor;
6    import android.net.Uri;
7    import android.support.v7.widget.RecyclerView;
8    import android.view.LayoutInflater;
9    import android.view.View;
10   import android.view.ViewGroup;
11   import android.widget.TextView;
12
13   import com.deitel.addressbook.data.DatabaseDescription.Contact;
14
15   public class ContactsAdapter
16      extends RecyclerView.Adapter<ContactsAdapter.ViewHolder> {
17
18      // interface implemented by ContactsFragment to respond
19      // when the user touches an item in the RecyclerView
20      public interface ContactClickListener {
21         void onClick(Uri contactUri);
22      }
23
24      // nested subclass of RecyclerView.ViewHolder used to implement
25      // the view-holder pattern in the context of a RecyclerView
26      public class ViewHolder extends RecyclerView.ViewHolder {
27         public final TextView textView;
28         private long rowID;
29
30         // configures a RecyclerView item's ViewHolder
31         public ViewHolder(View itemView) {
32            super(itemView);
33            textView = (TextView) itemView.findViewById(android.R.id.text1);
34
35            // attach listener to itemView
36            itemView.setOnClickListener(
37               new View.OnClickListener() {
38                  // executes when the contact in this ViewHolder is clicked
39                  @Override
40                  public void onClick(View view) {
41                     clickListener.onClick(Contact.buildContactUri(rowID));
42                  }
43               }
44            );
45         }
46
47         // set the database row ID for the contact in this ViewHolder
48         public void setRowID(long rowID) {
49            this.rowID = rowID;
50         }
51      }
```

Fig. 9.39 | Subclass of RecyclerView.Adapter that binds contacts to RecyclerView. (Part 1 of 2.)

```
52
53    // ContactsAdapter instance variables
54    private Cursor cursor = null;
55    private final ContactClickListener clickListener;
56
57    // constructor
58    public ContactsAdapter(ContactClickListener clickListener) {
59       this.clickListener = clickListener;
60    }
61
62    // sets up new list item and its ViewHolder
63    @Override
64    public ViewHolder onCreateViewHolder(ViewGroup parent, int viewType) {
65       // inflate the android.R.layout.simple_list_item_1 layout
66       View view = LayoutInflater.from(parent.getContext()).inflate(
67          android.R.layout.simple_list_item_1, parent, false);
68       return new ViewHolder(view); // return current item's ViewHolder
69    }
70
71    // sets the text of the list item to display the search tag
72    @Override
73    public void onBindViewHolder(ViewHolder holder, int position) {
74       cursor.moveToPosition(position);
75       holder.setRowID(cursor.getLong(cursor.getColumnIndex(Contact._ID)));
76       holder.textView.setText(cursor.getString(cursor.getColumnIndex(
77          Contact.COLUMN_NAME)));
78    }
79
80    // returns the number of items that adapter binds
81    @Override
82    public int getItemCount() {
83       return (cursor != null) ? cursor.getCount() : 0;
84    }
85
86    // swap this adapter's current Cursor for a new one
87    public void swapCursor(Cursor cursor) {
88       this.cursor = cursor;
89       notifyDataSetChanged();
90    }
91 }
```

Fig. 9.39 | Subclass of RecyclerView.Adapter that binds contacts to RecyclerView. (Part 2 of 2.)

Nested Interface *ContactClickListener*

Lines 20–22 define the nested interface ContactClickListener that class ContactsFragment implements to be notified when the user touches a contact in the RecyclerView. Each item in the RecyclerView has a click listener that calls the ContactClickListener's onClick method and passes the selected contact's Uri. The ContactsFragment then notifies the MainActivity that a contact was selected, so the MainActivity can display the contact in a DetailFragment.

Nested Class *ViewHolder*

Class ViewHolder (lines 26–51) maintains a reference to a RecyclerView item's TextView and the database's rowID for the corresponding contact. The rowID is necessary because we sort the contacts before displaying them, so each contact's position number in the RecyclerView most likely does not match the contact's row ID in the database. ViewHolder's constructor stores a reference to the RecyclerView item's TextView and sets its View.OnClickListener, which passes the contact's URI to the adapter's ContactClickListener.

Overridden *RecyclerView.Adapter* Method *onCreateViewHolder*

Method onCreateViewHolder (lines 63–69) inflates the GUI for a ViewHolder object. In this case we used the predefined layout android.R.layout.simple_list_item_1, which defines a layout containing one TextView named text1.

Overridden *RecyclerView.Adapter* Method *onBindViewHolder*

Method onBindViewHolder (lines 72–78) uses Cursor method moveToPosition to move to the contact that corresponds to the current RecyclerView item's position. Line 75 sets the ViewHolder's rowID. To get this value, we use Cursor method getColumnIndex to look up the column number of the Contact._ID column. We then pass that number to Cursor method getLong to get the contact's row ID. Lines 76–77 set the text for the ViewHolder's textView, using a similar process—in this case, look up the column number for the Contact.COLUMN_NAME column, then call Cursor method getString to get the contact's name.

Overridden *RecyclerView.Adapter* Method *getItemCount*

Method getItemCount (lines 81–84) returns the total number of rows in the Cursor or 0 if Cursor is null.

Method *swapCursor*

Method swapCursor (lines 87–90) replaces the adapter's current Cursor and notifies the adapter that its data changed. This method is called from the ContactsFragment's onLoadFinished and onLoaderReset methods.

9.12 AddEditFragment Class

The AddEditFragment class provides a GUI for adding new contacts or editing existing ones. Many of the programming concepts used in this class have been presented earlier in this chapter or in prior chapters, so we focus here only on the new features.

9.12.1 Superclass and Implemented Interface

Figure 9.40 lists the package statement, import statements and the beginning of the AddEditFragment class definition. The class extends Fragment and implements the LoaderManager.LoaderCallbacks<Cursor> interface to respond to LoaderManager events.

```
1   // AddEditFragment.java
2   // Fragment for adding a new contact or editing an existing one
3   package com.deitel.addressbook;
```

Fig. 9.40 | AddEditFragment package statement and import statements. (Part 1 of 2.)

```
4
5    import android.content.ContentValues;
6    import android.content.Context;
7    import android.database.Cursor;
8    import android.net.Uri;
9    import android.os.Bundle;
10   import android.support.design.widget.CoordinatorLayout;
11   import android.support.design.widget.FloatingActionButton;
12   import android.support.design.widget.Snackbar;
13   import android.support.design.widget.TextInputLayout;
14   import android.support.v4.app.Fragment;
15   import android.support.v4.app.LoaderManager;
16   import android.support.v4.content.CursorLoader;
17   import android.support.v4.content.Loader;
18   import android.text.Editable;
19   import android.text.TextWatcher;
20   import android.view.LayoutInflater;
21   import android.view.View;
22   import android.view.ViewGroup;
23   import android.view.inputmethod.InputMethodManager;
24
25   import com.deitel.addressbook.data.DatabaseDescription.Contact;
26
27   public class AddEditFragment extends Fragment
28      implements LoaderManager.LoaderCallbacks<Cursor> {
29
```

Fig. 9.40 | AddEditFragment package statement and import statements. (Part 2 of 2.)

9.12.2 AddEditFragmentListener

Figure 9.41 declares the nested interface AddEditFragmentListener containing the callback method onAddEditCompleted. MainActivity implements this interface to be notified when the user saves a new contact or saves changes to an existing one.

```
30      // defines callback method implemented by MainActivity
31      public interface AddEditFragmentListener {
32         // called when contact is saved
33         void onAddEditCompleted(Uri contactUri);
34      }
35
```

Fig. 9.41 | Nested interface AddEditFragmentListener.

9.12.3 Fields

Figure 9.42 lists the class's fields:

- The constant CONTACT_LOADER (line 37) identifies the Loader that queries the AddressBookContentProvider to retrieve one contact for editing.

- The instance variable listener (line 39) refers to the AddEditFragmentListener (MainActivity) that's notified when the user saves a new or updated contact.

- The instance variable `contactUri` (line 40) represents the contact to edit.

- The instance variable `addingNewContact` (line 41) specifies whether a new contact is being added (`true`) or an existing contact is being edited (`false`).

- The instance variables at lines 44–53 refer to the Fragment's `TextInputLayouts`, `FloatingActionButton` and `CoordinatorLayout`.

```
36    // constant used to identify the Loader
37    private static final int CONTACT_LOADER = 0;
38
39    private AddEditFragmentListener listener; // MainActivity
40    private Uri contactUri; // Uri of selected contact
41    private boolean addingNewContact = true; // adding (true) or editing
42
43    // EditTexts for contact information
44    private TextInputLayout nameTextInputLayout;
45    private TextInputLayout phoneTextInputLayout;
46    private TextInputLayout emailTextInputLayout;
47    private TextInputLayout streetTextInputLayout;
48    private TextInputLayout cityTextInputLayout;
49    private TextInputLayout stateTextInputLayout;
50    private TextInputLayout zipTextInputLayout;
51    private FloatingActionButton saveContactFAB;
52
53    private CoordinatorLayout coordinatorLayout; // used with SnackBars
54
```

Fig. 9.42 | `AddEditFragment` fields.

9.12.4 Overridden Fragment Methods onAttach, onDetach and onCreateView

Figure 9.43 contains the overridden Fragment methods `onAttach`, `onDetach` and `onCreateView`. Methods `onAttach` and `onDetach` set instance variable `listener` to refer to the host `Activity` when the `AddEditFragment` is attached and to set `listener` to `null` when the `AddEditFragment` is detached.

```
55    // set AddEditFragmentListener when Fragment attached
56    @Override
57    public void onAttach(Context context) {
58       super.onAttach(context);
59       listener = (AddEditFragmentListener) context;
60    }
61
62    // remove AddEditFragmentListener when Fragment detached
63    @Override
64    public void onDetach() {
65       super.onDetach();
66       listener = null;
67    }
```

Fig. 9.43 | Overridden Fragment Methods onAttach, onDetach and onCreateView. (Part I of 2.)

```
68
69     // called when Fragment's view needs to be created
70     @Override
71     public View onCreateView(
72        LayoutInflater inflater, ViewGroup container,
73        Bundle savedInstanceState) {
74        super.onCreateView(inflater, container, savedInstanceState);
75        setHasOptionsMenu(true); // fragment has menu items to display
76
77        // inflate GUI and get references to EditTexts
78        View view =
79           inflater.inflate(R.layout.fragment_add_edit, container, false);
80        nameTextInputLayout =
81           (TextInputLayout) view.findViewById(R.id.nameTextInputLayout);
82        nameTextInputLayout.getEditText().addTextChangedListener(
83           nameChangedListener);
84        phoneTextInputLayout =
85           (TextInputLayout) view.findViewById(R.id.phoneTextInputLayout);
86        emailTextInputLayout =
87           (TextInputLayout) view.findViewById(R.id.emailTextInputLayout);
88        streetTextInputLayout =
89           (TextInputLayout) view.findViewById(R.id.streetTextInputLayout);
90        cityTextInputLayout =
91           (TextInputLayout) view.findViewById(R.id.cityTextInputLayout);
92        stateTextInputLayout =
93           (TextInputLayout) view.findViewById(R.id.stateTextInputLayout);
94        zipTextInputLayout =
95           (TextInputLayout) view.findViewById(R.id.zipTextInputLayout);
96
97        // set FloatingActionButton's event listener
98        saveContactFAB = (FloatingActionButton) view.findViewById(
99           R.id.saveFloatingActionButton);
100       saveContactFAB.setOnClickListener(saveContactButtonClicked);
101       updateSaveButtonFAB();
102
103       // used to display SnackBars with brief messages
104       coordinatorLayout = (CoordinatorLayout) getActivity().findViewById(
105          R.id.coordinatorLayout);
106
107       Bundle arguments = getArguments(); // null if creating new contact
108
109       if (arguments != null) {
110          addingNewContact = false;
111          contactUri = arguments.getParcelable(MainActivity.CONTACT_URI);
112       }
113
114       // if editing an existing contact, create Loader to get the contact
115       if (contactUri != null)
116          getLoaderManager().initLoader(CONTACT_LOADER, null, this);
117
118       return view;
119    }
120
```

Fig. 9.43 | Overridden Fragment Methods onAttach, onDetach and onCreateView. (Part 2 of 2.)

Method onCreateView inflates the GUI and gets references to the Fragment's Text-InputLayouts and configures the FloatingActionButton. Next, we use Fragment method getArguments to get the Bundle of arguments (line 107). When we launch the AddEdit-Fragment from the MainActivity, we pass null for the Bundle argument, because the user is adding a new contact's information. In this case, getArguments returns null. If getArguments returns a Bundle (line 109), then the user is editing an existing contact. Line 111 reads the contact's Uri from the Bundle by calling method getParcelable. If contactUri is not null, line 116 uses the Fragment's LoaderManager to initialize a Loader that the AddEditFragment will use to get the data for the contact being edited.

9.12.5 TextWatcher nameChangedListener and Method updateSaveButtonFAB

Figure 9.44 shows the TextWatcher nameChangedListener and method updatedSave-ButtonFAB. The listener calls method updatedSaveButtonFAB when the user edits the text in the nameTextInputLayout's EditText. The name must be non-empty in this app, so method updateSaveButtonFAB displays the FloatingActionButton only when the nameTextInputLayout's EditText is not empty.

```
121    // detects when the text in the nameTextInputLayout's EditText changes
122    // to hide or show saveButtonFAB
123    private final TextWatcher nameChangedListener = new TextWatcher() {
124       @Override
125       public void beforeTextChanged(CharSequence s, int start, int count,
126          int after) {}
127
128       // called when the text in nameTextInputLayout changes
129       @Override
130       public void onTextChanged(CharSequence s, int start, int before,
131          int count) {
132          updateSaveButtonFAB();
133       }
134
135       @Override
136       public void afterTextChanged(Editable s) { }
137    };
138
139    // shows saveButtonFAB only if the name is not empty
140    private void updateSaveButtonFAB() {
141       String input =
142          nameTextInputLayout.getEditText().getText().toString();
143
144       // if there is a name for the contact, show the FloatingActionButton
145       if (input.trim().length() != 0)
146          saveContactFAB.show();
147       else
148          saveContactFAB.hide();
149    }
150
```

Fig. 9.44 | TextWatcher nameChangedListener and method updateSaveButtonFAB.

9.12.6 View.OnClickListener saveContactButtonClicked and Method saveContact

When the user touches this Fragment's FloatingActionButton, the saveContactButton-Clicked listener (Fig. 9.45, lines 152–162) executes. Method onClick hides the keyboard (lines 157–159), then calls method saveContact.

```
151     // responds to event generated when user saves a contact
152     private final View.OnClickListener saveContactButtonClicked =
153        new View.OnClickListener() {
154           @Override
155           public void onClick(View v) {
156              // hide the virtual keyboard
157              ((InputMethodManager) getActivity().getSystemService(
158                 Context.INPUT_METHOD_SERVICE)).hideSoftInputFromWindow(
159                 getView().getWindowToken(), 0);
160              saveContact(); // save contact to the database
161           }
162        };
163
164     // saves contact information to the database
165     private void saveContact() {
166        // create ContentValues object containing contact's key-value pairs
167        ContentValues contentValues = new ContentValues();
168        contentValues.put(Contact.COLUMN_NAME,
169           nameTextInputLayout.getEditText().getText().toString());
170        contentValues.put(Contact.COLUMN_PHONE,
171           phoneTextInputLayout.getEditText().getText().toString());
172        contentValues.put(Contact.COLUMN_EMAIL,
173           emailTextInputLayout.getEditText().getText().toString());
174        contentValues.put(Contact.COLUMN_STREET,
175           streetTextInputLayout.getEditText().getText().toString());
176        contentValues.put(Contact.COLUMN_CITY,
177           cityTextInputLayout.getEditText().getText().toString());
178        contentValues.put(Contact.COLUMN_STATE,
179           stateTextInputLayout.getEditText().getText().toString());
180        contentValues.put(Contact.COLUMN_ZIP,
181           zipTextInputLayout.getEditText().getText().toString());
182
183        if (addingNewContact) {
184           // use Activity's ContentResolver to invoke
185           // insert on the AddressBookContentProvider
186           Uri newContactUri = getActivity().getContentResolver().insert(
187              Contact.CONTENT_URI, contentValues);
188
189           if (newContactUri != null) {
190              Snackbar.make(coordinatorLayout,
191                 R.string.contact_added, Snackbar.LENGTH_LONG).show();
192              listener.onAddEditCompleted(newContactUri);
193           }
```

Fig. 9.45 | View.OnClickListener saveContactButtonClicked and method saveContact. (Part 1 of 2.)

```
194                 else {
195                     Snackbar.make(coordinatorLayout,
196                         R.string.contact_not_added, Snackbar.LENGTH_LONG).show();
197                 }
198             }
199         else {
200             // use Activity's ContentResolver to invoke
201             // insert on the AddressBookContentProvider
202             int updatedRows = getActivity().getContentResolver().update(
203                 contactUri, contentValues, null, null);
204
205             if (updatedRows > 0) {
206                 listener.onAddEditCompleted(contactUri);
207                 Snackbar.make(coordinatorLayout,
208                     R.string.contact_updated, Snackbar.LENGTH_LONG).show();
209             }
210             else {
211                 Snackbar.make(coordinatorLayout,
212                     R.string.contact_not_updated, Snackbar.LENGTH_LONG).show();
213             }
214         }
215     }
216
```

Fig. 9.45 | View.OnClickListener saveContactButtonClicked and method
saveContact. (Part 2 of 2.)

The saveContact method (lines 165–215) creates a ContentValues object (line 167)
and adds to it key–value pairs representing the column names and values to be inserted
into or updated in the database (lines 168–181). If the user is adding a new contact (lines
183–198), lines 186–187 use ContentResolver method **insert** to invoke insert on the
AddressBookContentProvider and place the new contact into the database. If the insert
is successful, the returned Uri is non-null and lines 190–192 display a SnackBar indicating that the contact was added, then notify the AddEditFragmentListener with the
contact that was added. Recall that when the app is running on a tablet, this results in the
contact's data being displayed in a DetailFragment next to the ContactsFragment. If the
insert is not successful, lines 195–196 display an appropriate SnackBar.

If the user is editing an existing contact (lines 199–214), lines 202–203 use Content-
Resolver method **update** to invoke update on the AddressBookContentProvider and
store the edited contact's data. If the update is successful, the returned integer is greater
than 0 (indicating the specific number of rows updated) and lines 206–208 notify the Add-
EditFragmentListener with the contact that was edited, then display an appropriate message. If the updated is not successful, lines 211–212 display an appropriate SnackBar.

9.12.7 LoaderManager.LoaderCallbacks<Cursor> Methods

Figure 9.46 presents the AddEditFragment's implementations of the methods in interface
LoaderManager.LoaderCallbacks<Cursor>. These methods are used in class AddEdit-
Fragment only when the user is editing an existing contact. Method onCreateLoader
(lines 219–233) creates a CursorLoader for the specific contact being edited. Method on-

LoadFinished (lines 236–267) checks whether the cursor is non-null and, if so, calls cursor method moveToFirst. If this method returns true, then a contact matching the contactUri was found in the database and lines 241–263 get the contact's information from the Cursor and display it in the GUI. Method onLoaderReset is not needed in AddEditFragment, so it does nothing.

```
217    // called by LoaderManager to create a Loader
218    @Override
219    public Loader<Cursor> onCreateLoader(int id, Bundle args) {
220       // create an appropriate CursorLoader based on the id argument;
221       // only one Loader in this fragment, so the switch is unnecessary
222       switch (id) {
223          case CONTACT_LOADER:
224             return new CursorLoader(getActivity(),
225                contactUri, // Uri of contact to display
226                null, // null projection returns all columns
227                null, // null selection returns all rows
228                null, // no selection arguments
229                null); // sort order
230          default:
231             return null;
232       }
233    }
234
235    // called by LoaderManager when loading completes
236    @Override
237    public void onLoadFinished(Loader<Cursor> loader, Cursor data) {
238       // if the contact exists in the database, display its data
239       if (data != null && data.moveToFirst()) {
240          // get the column index for each data item
241          int nameIndex = data.getColumnIndex(Contact.COLUMN_NAME);
242          int phoneIndex = data.getColumnIndex(Contact.COLUMN_PHONE);
243          int emailIndex = data.getColumnIndex(Contact.COLUMN_EMAIL);
244          int streetIndex = data.getColumnIndex(Contact.COLUMN_STREET);
245          int cityIndex = data.getColumnIndex(Contact.COLUMN_CITY);
246          int stateIndex = data.getColumnIndex(Contact.COLUMN_STATE);
247          int zipIndex = data.getColumnIndex(Contact.COLUMN_ZIP);
248
249          // fill EditTexts with the retrieved data
250          nameTextInputLayout.getEditText().setText(
251             data.getString(nameIndex));
252          phoneTextInputLayout.getEditText().setText(
253             data.getString(phoneIndex));
254          emailTextInputLayout.getEditText().setText(
255             data.getString(emailIndex));
256          streetTextInputLayout.getEditText().setText(
257             data.getString(streetIndex));
258          cityTextInputLayout.getEditText().setText(
259             data.getString(cityIndex));
260          stateTextInputLayout.getEditText().setText(
261             data.getString(stateIndex));
```

Fig. 9.46 | LoaderManager.LoaderCallbacks<Cursor> methods. (Part 1 of 2.)

```
262          zipTextInputLayout.getEditText().setText(
263             data.getString(zipIndex));
264
265          updateSaveButtonFAB();
266       }
267    }
268
269    // called by LoaderManager when the Loader is being reset
270    @Override
271    public void onLoaderReset(Loader<Cursor> loader) { }
272 }
```

Fig. 9.46 | `LoaderManager.LoaderCallbacks<Cursor>` methods. (Part 2 of 2.)

9.13 DetailFragment Class

The `DetailFragment` class displays one contact's information and provides menu items on the app bar that enable the user to edit or delete that contact.

9.13.1 Superclass and Implemented Interface

Figure 9.47 lists the package statement, `import` statements and the beginning of the `DetailFragment` class definition. The class extends `Fragment` and implements the `LoaderManager.LoaderCallbacks<Cursor>` interface to respond to `LoaderManager` events.

```
1  // DetailFragment.java
2  // Fragment subclass that displays one contact's details
3  package com.deitel.addressbook;
4
5  import android.app.AlertDialog;
6  import android.app.Dialog;
7  import android.content.Context;
8  import android.content.DialogInterface;
9  import android.database.Cursor;
10 import android.net.Uri;
11 import android.os.Bundle;
12 import android.support.v4.app.DialogFragment;
13 import android.support.v4.app.Fragment;
14 import android.support.v4.app.LoaderManager;
15 import android.support.v4.content.CursorLoader;
16 import android.support.v4.content.Loader;
17 import android.view.LayoutInflater;
18 import android.view.Menu;
19 import android.view.MenuInflater;
20 import android.view.MenuItem;
21 import android.view.View;
22 import android.view.ViewGroup;
23 import android.widget.TextView;
24
```

Fig. 9.47 | package statement, `import` statements, superclass and implemented interface.
(Part 1 of 2.)

```
25    import com.deitel.addressbook.data.DatabaseDescription.Contact;
26
27    public class DetailFragment extends Fragment
28        implements LoaderManager.LoaderCallbacks<Cursor> {
29
```

Fig. 9.47 | package statement, import statements, superclass and implemented interface. (Part 2 of 2.)

9.13.2 DetailFragmentListener

Figure 9.48 declares the nested interface DetailFragmentListener containing the callback methods that MainActivity implements to be notified when the user deletes a contact (line 32) and when the user touches the edit menu item to edit a contact (line 35).

```
30        // callback methods implemented by MainActivity
31        public interface DetailFragmentListener {
32            void onContactDeleted(); // called when a contact is deleted
33
34            // pass Uri of contact to edit to the DetailFragmentListener
35            void onEditContact(Uri contactUri);
36        }
37
```

Fig. 9.48 | Nested interface DetailFragmentListener.

9.13.3 Fields

Figure 9.49 shows the class's fields:

- The constant CONTACT_LOADER (line 38) identifies the Loader that queries the AddressBookContentProvider to retrieve one contact to display.

- The instance variable listener (line 40) refers to the DetailFragmentListener (MainActivity) that's notified when the user deletes a contact or initiates editing of a contact.

- The instance variable contactUri (line 41) represents the contact to display.

- The instance variables at lines 43–49 refer to the Fragment's TextViews.

```
38        private static final int CONTACT_LOADER = 0; // identifies the Loader
39
40        private DetailFragmentListener listener; // MainActivity
41        private Uri contactUri; // Uri of selected contact
42
43        private TextView nameTextView; // displays contact's name
44        private TextView phoneTextView; // displays contact's phone
45        private TextView emailTextView; // displays contact's email
46        private TextView streetTextView; // displays contact's street
47        private TextView cityTextView; // displays contact's city
```

Fig. 9.49 | DetailFragment fields. (Part 1 of 2.)

```
48    private TextView stateTextView; // displays contact's state
49    private TextView zipTextView; // displays contact's zip
50
```

Fig. 9.49 | DetailFragment fields. (Part 2 of 2.)

9.13.4 Overridden Methods onAttach, onDetach and onCreateView

Figure 9.50 contains overridden Fragment methods onAttach, onDetach and onCreate-View. Methods onAttach and onDetach set instance variable listener to refer to the host Activity when the DetailFragment is attached and to set listener to null when the DetailFragment is detached. The onCreateView method (lines 66–95) obtains the selected contact's Uri (lines 74–77). Lines 80–90 inflate the GUI and get references to the TextViews. Line 93 uses the Fragment's LoaderManager to initialize a Loader that the DetailFragment will use to get the data for the contact to display.

```
51    // set DetailFragmentListener when fragment attached
52    @Override
53    public void onAttach(Context context) {
54       super.onAttach(context);
55       listener = (DetailFragmentListener) context;
56    }
57
58    // remove DetailFragmentListener when fragment detached
59    @Override
60    public void onDetach() {
61       super.onDetach();
62       listener = null;
63    }
64
65    // called when DetailFragmentListener's view needs to be created
66    @Override
67    public View onCreateView(
68       LayoutInflater inflater, ViewGroup container,
69       Bundle savedInstanceState) {
70       super.onCreateView(inflater, container, savedInstanceState);
71       setHasOptionsMenu(true); // this fragment has menu items to display
72
73       // get Bundle of arguments then extract the contact's Uri
74       Bundle arguments = getArguments();
75
76       if (arguments != null)
77          contactUri = arguments.getParcelable(MainActivity.CONTACT_URI);
78
79       // inflate DetailFragment's layout
80       View view =
81          inflater.inflate(R.layout.fragment_detail, container, false);
82
83       // get the EditTexts
84       nameTextView = (TextView) view.findViewById(R.id.nameTextView);
```

Fig. 9.50 | Overridden methods onAttach, onDetach and onCreateView. (Part 1 of 2.)

```
85          phoneTextView = (TextView) view.findViewById(R.id.phoneTextView);
86          emailTextView = (TextView) view.findViewById(R.id.emailTextView);
87          streetTextView = (TextView) view.findViewById(R.id.streetTextView);
88          cityTextView = (TextView) view.findViewById(R.id.cityTextView);
89          stateTextView = (TextView) view.findViewById(R.id.stateTextView);
90          zipTextView = (TextView) view.findViewById(R.id.zipTextView);
91
92          // load the contact
93          getLoaderManager().initLoader(CONTACT_LOADER, null, this);
94          return view;
95       }
96
```

Fig. 9.50 | Overridden methods onAttach, onDetach and onCreateView. (Part 2 of 2.)

9.13.5 Overridden Methods onCreateOptionsMenu and onOptionsItemSelected

The DetailFragment displays in the app bar options for editing the current contact and for deleting it. Method onCreateOptionsMenu (Fig. 9.51, lines 98–102) inflates the menu resource file fragment_details_menu.xml. Method onOptionsItemSelected (lines 105–117) uses the selected MenuItem's resource ID to determine which one was selected. If the user touched the edit option (✏), line 109 calls the DetailFragmentListener's onEdit-Contact method with the contactUri—MainActivity passes this to the AddEditFragment. If the user touched the delete option (🗑), line 112 calls method deleteContact (Fig. 9.52).

```
97       // display this fragment's menu items
98       @Override
99       public void onCreateOptionsMenu(Menu menu, MenuInflater inflater) {
100          super.onCreateOptionsMenu(menu, inflater);
101          inflater.inflate(R.menu.fragment_details_menu, menu);
102       }
103
104      // handle menu item selections
105      @Override
106      public boolean onOptionsItemSelected(MenuItem item) {
107         switch (item.getItemId()) {
108            case R.id.action_edit:
109               listener.onEditContact(contactUri); // pass Uri to listener
110               return true;
111            case R.id.action_delete:
112               deleteContact();
113               return true;
114         }
115
116         return super.onOptionsItemSelected(item);
117      }
118
```

Fig. 9.51 | Overridden methods onCreateOptionsMenu and onOptionsItemSelected.

9.13.6 Method deleteContact and DialogFragment confirmDelete

Method deleteContact (Fig. 9.52, lines 120–123) displays a DialogFragment (lines 126–157) asking the user to confirm that the currently displayed contact should be deleted. If the user touches **DELETE** in the dialog, lines 147–148 call ContentResolver method delete (lines 147–148) to invoke the AddressBookContentProvider's delete method and remove the contact from the database. Method delete receives the Uri of the content to delete, a String representing the WHERE clause that determines what to delete and a String array of arguments to insert in the WHERE clause. In this case, the last two arguments are null, because the row ID of the contact to delete is embedded in the Uri—this row ID is extracted from the Uri by the AddressBookContentProvider's delete method. Line 149 calls the listener's onContactDeleted method so that MainActivity can remove the DetailFragment from the screen.

```
119    // delete a contact
120    private void deleteContact() {
121       // use FragmentManager to display the confirmDelete DialogFragment
122       confirmDelete.show(getFragmentManager(), "confirm delete");
123    }
124
125    // DialogFragment to confirm deletion of contact
126    private final DialogFragment confirmDelete =
127       new DialogFragment() {
128          // create an AlertDialog and return it
129          @Override
130          public Dialog onCreateDialog(Bundle bundle) {
131             // create a new AlertDialog Builder
132             AlertDialog.Builder builder =
133                new AlertDialog.Builder(getActivity());
134
135             builder.setTitle(R.string.confirm_title);
136             builder.setMessage(R.string.confirm_message);
137
138             // provide an OK button that simply dismisses the dialog
139             builder.setPositiveButton(R.string.button_delete,
140                new DialogInterface.OnClickListener() {
141                   @Override
142                   public void onClick(
143                      DialogInterface dialog, int button) {
144
145                      // use Activity's ContentResolver to invoke
146                      // delete on the AddressBookContentProvider
147                      getActivity().getContentResolver().delete(
148                         contactUri, null, null);
149                      listener.onContactDeleted(); // notify listener
150                   }
151                }
152             );
153
```

Fig. 9.52 | Method deleteContact and DialogFragment confirmDelete. (Part I of 2.)

```
154                builder.setNegativeButton(R.string.button_cancel, null);
155                return builder.create(); // return the AlertDialog
156            }
157        };
158
```

Fig. 9.52 | Method deleteContact and DialogFragment confirmDelete. (Part 2 of 2.)

9.13.7 LoaderManager.LoaderCallback<Cursor> Methods

Figure 9.53 presents the DetailFragment's implementations of the methods in interface LoaderManager.LoaderCallbacks<Cursor>. Method onCreateLoader (lines 160–181) creates a CursorLoader for the specific contact being displayed. Method onLoadFinished (lines 184–206) checks whether the cursor is non-null and, if so, calls cursor method moveToFirst. If this method returns true, then a contact matching the contactUri was found in the database and lines 189–204 get the contact's information from the Cursor and display it in the GUI. Method onLoaderReset is not needed in DetailFragment, so it does nothing.

```
159        // called by LoaderManager to create a Loader
160        @Override
161        public Loader<Cursor> onCreateLoader(int id, Bundle args) {
162            // create an appropriate CursorLoader based on the id argument;
163            // only one Loader in this fragment, so the switch is unnecessary
164            CursorLoader cursorLoader;
165
166            switch (id) {
167                case CONTACT_LOADER:
168                    cursorLoader = new CursorLoader(getActivity(),
169                        contactUri, // Uri of contact to display
170                        null, // null projection returns all columns
171                        null, // null selection returns all rows
172                        null, // no selection arguments
173                        null); // sort order
174                    break;
175                default:
176                    cursorLoader = null;
177                    break;
178            }
179
180            return cursorLoader;
181        }
182
183        // called by LoaderManager when loading completes
184        @Override
185        public void onLoadFinished(Loader<Cursor> loader, Cursor data) {
186            // if the contact exists in the database, display its data
187            if (data != null && data.moveToFirst()) {
188                // get the column index for each data item
189                int nameIndex = data.getColumnIndex(Contact.COLUMN_NAME);
```

Fig. 9.53 | LoaderManager.LoaderCallback<Cursor> methods. (Part 1 of 2.)

```
190          int phoneIndex = data.getColumnIndex(Contact.COLUMN_PHONE);
191          int emailIndex = data.getColumnIndex(Contact.COLUMN_EMAIL);
192          int streetIndex = data.getColumnIndex(Contact.COLUMN_STREET);
193          int cityIndex = data.getColumnIndex(Contact.COLUMN_CITY);
194          int stateIndex = data.getColumnIndex(Contact.COLUMN_STATE);
195          int zipIndex = data.getColumnIndex(Contact.COLUMN_ZIP);
196
197          // fill TextViews with the retrieved data
198          nameTextView.setText(data.getString(nameIndex));
199          phoneTextView.setText(data.getString(phoneIndex));
200          emailTextView.setText(data.getString(emailIndex));
201          streetTextView.setText(data.getString(streetIndex));
202          cityTextView.setText(data.getString(cityIndex));
203          stateTextView.setText(data.getString(stateIndex));
204          zipTextView.setText(data.getString(zipIndex));
205       }
206    }
207
208    // called by LoaderManager when the Loader is being reset
209    @Override
210    public void onLoaderReset(Loader<Cursor> loader) { }
211 }
```

Fig. 9.53 | LoaderManager.LoaderCallback<Cursor> methods. (Part 2 of 2.)

9.14 Wrap-Up

In this chapter, you created an **Address Book** app for adding, viewing, editing and deleting contact information that's stored in a SQLite database.

You used one activity to host all of the app's Fragments. On a phone-sized device, you displayed one Fragment at a time. On a tablet, the activity displayed the Fragment containing the contact list, and you replaced that with Fragments for viewing, adding and editing contacts as necessary. You used the FragmentManager and FragmentTransactions to dynamically display Fragments. You used Android's Fragment back stack to provide automatic support for Android's back button. To communicate data between Fragments and the host activity, you defined in each Fragment subclass a nested interface of callback methods that the host activity implemented.

You used a subclass of SQLiteOpenHelper to simplify creating the database and to obtain a SQLiteDatabase object for manipulating the database's contents. You also managed database query results via a Cursor (package android.database).

To access the database asynchronously outside the GUI thread, you defined a subclass of ContentProvider that specified how to query, insert, update and delete data. When changes were made to the SQLite database, the ContentProvider notified listeners so data could be updated in the GUI. The ContentProvider defined Uris that it used to determine the tasks to perform.

To invoke the ContentProvider's query, insert, update and delete capabilities, we invoked the corresponding methods of the activity's built-in ContentResolver. You saw that the ContentProvider and ContentResolver handle communication for you. The ContentResolver's methods received as their first argument a Uri that specified the ContentProvider to access. Each ContentResolver method invoked the corresponding method of the ContentProvider, which in turn used the Uri to help determine the task to perform.

As we've stated previously, long-running operations or operations that block execution until they complete (e.g., file and database access) should be performed outside the GUI thread. You used a CursorLoader to perform asynchronous data access. You learned that Loaders are created and managed by an Activity's or Fragment's LoaderManager, which ties each Loader's lifecycle to that of its Activity or Fragment. You implmeneted interface LoaderManager.LoaderCallbacks to respond to Loader events indicating when a Loader should be created, finishes loading its data, or is reset and the data is no longer available.

You defined common GUI component attribute–value pairs as a style resource, then applied the style to the TextViews that display a contact's information. You also defined a border for a TextView by specifying a Drawable for the TextView's background. The Drawable could be an image, but in this app you defined the Drawable as a shape in a resource file.

In Chapter 10, we discuss the business side of Android app development. You'll see how to prepare your app for submission to Google Play, including making icons. We'll discuss how to test your apps on devices and publish them on Google Play. We discuss the characteristics of great apps and the Android design guidelines to follow. We provide tips for pricing and marketing your app. We also review the benefits of offering your app for free to drive sales of other products, such as a more feature-rich version of the app or premium content. We show how to use Google Play to track app sales, payments and more.

10

Google Play and App Business Issues

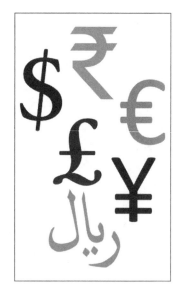

10.1 Introduction

In Chapters 2–9, we developed a variety of complete working Android apps. Once you've developed and tested your own apps, both in the emulator and on Android devices, the next step is to submit them to Google Play—and/or other app marketplaces—for distribution to a worldwide audience. In this chapter, we'll discuss

- registering for Google Play and setting up a Google Payments merchant account so that you can sell your apps

- preparing your apps for publication and

- uploading them to Google Play.

In a few cases, we'll refer you to the Android documentation instead of showing the steps in the book, because the steps are likely to change. We'll tell you about additional Android app marketplaces where you can distribute your apps. We'll discuss whether you should offer your apps for free or for a fee, and mention key means for monetizing apps, including in-app advertising, in-app billing and selling virtual goods. We'll provide resources for marketing your apps, and mention other app platforms to which you may port your Android apps to broaden your marketplace.

10.2 Preparing Your Apps for Publication

Google provides various documents to help you get ready to release your app. The *Preparing for Release* document

```
http://developer.android.com/tools/publishing/preparing.html
```

summarizes what you need to do, including:

- getting a *cryptographic key* for *digitally signing* your app

- creating an application *icon*
- including an *End User License Agreement* with your app (optional)
- *versioning* your app (e.g., 1.0, 1.1, 2.0, 2.3, 3.0)
- *compiling* your app for release and
- *testing* the release version of your app on Android devices

```
http://developer.android.com/tools/testing/what_to_test.html
```

Before publishing your app, you should also read the *Core App Quality* document

```
http://developer.android.com/distribute/essentials/quality/
    core.html
```

which provides quality guidelines for all apps, the *Tablet App Quality* document

```
http://developer.android.com/distribute/essentials/quality/
    tablets.html
```

which provides guidelines specifically for tablet apps, the *Launch Checklist* for publishing apps on the Google Play store

```
http://developer.android.com/distribute/tools/launch-checklist.html
```

and the *Localization Checklist* for apps that will be sold in various worldwide markets

```
http://developer.android.com/distribute/tools/localization-
    checklist.html
```

The remainder of this section discusses in more detail some of the items you'll need and other considerations before you publish an app.

10.2.1 Testing Your App

You should test your app thoroughly on a variety of devices. The app might work perfectly using the emulator on your computer, but problems could arise when running it on particular Android devices. Google's Cloud Test Lab[1]

```
https://developers.google.com/cloud-test-lab
```

helps you test your app across a wide range of devices.

10.2.2 End User License Agreement

You have the option to include an End User License Agreement (EULA) with your app. An EULA is an agreement through which you license your software to the user. It typically stipulates terms of use, limitations on redistribution and reverse engineering, product liability, compliance with applicable laws and more. You might want to consult an attorney when drafting an EULA for your app. To view a sample EULA, see

```
http://www.rocketlawyer.com/document/end-user-license-agreement.rl
```

---

1. Not yet available at the time of this writing.

10.2.3 Icons and Labels

Design an icon for your app and provide a text label (a name) that will appear in Google Play and on the user's device. The icon could be your company logo, an image from the app or a custom image. Google's material design documentation provides all the details to consider for your app icons:

```
https://www.google.com/design/spec/style/icons.html
```

Product icons should be 48-by-48 dp with a 1-dp border. Android scales this to the required size for various screen sizes and densities. For this reason, the guidelines recommend that you design the icon at 192-by-192 dp with a 4-dp edge—larger images that are scaled down to smaller sizes look better than smaller images scaled to larger sizes.

Google Play also displays a high-resolution app icon. This icon should be:

- 512-by-512 pixels

- 32-bit PNG

- 1 MB maximum

Since the app icon is the most important brand asset, having one that's high quality is important. Consider hiring an experienced graphic designer to help you create a compelling, professional icon. Figure 10.1 lists some design sites and firms that offer free, professionally designed icons and paid custom icon design services. Once you've created the icon, you can add it to your project using Android Studio's **Asset Studio** (as you did in Section 4.4.9), which will produce icons at various scaled sizes based on your original icon.

Company	URL	Services
glyphlab	`http://www.glyphlab.com/icon_design/`	Designs custom icons.
Iconiza	`http://www.iconiza.com`	Designs custom icons for a flat fee and sells stock icons.
The Iconfactory	`http://iconfactory.com/home`	Custom and stock icons.
Rosetta®	`http://icondesign.rosetta.com/`	Designs custom icons for a fee.
The Noun Project	`https://thenounproject.com/`	Thousands of icons from many artists.
Elance®	`http://www.elance.com`	Search for freelance icon designers.

Fig. 10.1 | Some custom app icon design firms.

10.2.4 Versioning Your App

It's important to include a *version name* (shown to the users) and a *version code* (an integer version number used internally by Google Play) for your app, and to consider your strategy for numbering updates. For example, the first version name of your app might be 1.0, minor updates might be 1.1 and 1.2, and the next major update might be 2.0. The version code is an integer that typically starts at 1 and is incremented by 1 for each new version of your app that you post. For additional guidelines, see *Versioning Your Applications* at

```
http://developer.android.com/tools/publishing/versioning.html
```

10.2.5 Licensing to Control Access to Paid Apps

The Google Play *licensing service* allows you to create licensing policies to control access to your paid apps. For example, you might use a licensing policy to limit how many simultaneous device installs are allowed. To learn more about the licensing service, visit

```
http://developer.android.com/google/play/licensing/index.html
```

10.2.6 Obfuscating Your Code

You should "obfuscate" any apps you upload to Google Play to discourage reverse engineering of your code and further protect your apps. The free ProGuard tool—which runs when you build your app in *release mode*—shrinks the size of your .apk file (the Android app package file that contains your app for installation) and optimizes and obfuscates the code "by removing unused code and renaming classes, fields, and methods with semantically obscure names."[2] To learn how to set up and use the ProGuard tool, go to

```
http://developer.android.com/tools/help/proguard.html
```

10.2.7 Getting a Private Key for Digitally Signing Your App

Before uploading your app to a device, Google Play or other app marketplaces, you must *digitally sign* the .apk file using a digital certificate that identifies you as the app's author. A digital certificate includes your name or company name, contact information, and more. It can be self-signed using a private key (i.e., a secure password used to *encrypt* the certificate); you do not need to purchase a certificate from a third-party certificate authority (though it's an option). Android Studio automatically digitally signs your app when you execute it in an emulator or on a device for *debugging* purposes. That digital certificate is *not* valid for use with Google Play. For detailed instructions on digitally signing your apps, see *Signing Your Applications* at

```
http://developer.android.com/tools/publishing/app-signing.html
```

10.2.8 Featured Image and Screenshots

The Google Play store shows promotional graphics and screenshots in your app listing—these provide potential buyers with their first impressions of your app.

Featured Image
The featured image is used by Google Play to promote an app on phones, tablets and via the Google Play website. The following Android Developers Blog post discusses the featured image's importance and its requirements:

```
http://android-developers.blogspot.com/2011/10/android-market-
    featured-image.html
```

Screenshots and Using the Android Device Manager's Screen Capture Tool
You may upload a maximum of eight screenshots for each device on which your app runs—smartphone, small tablet, large tablet, Android TV and Android Wear. These

---

2. `http://developer.android.com/tools/help/proguard.html`.

screenshots provide a preview of your app, since users can't test it before downloading it—although they can return an app for a refund within two hours after purchasing it. Choose attractive screenshots that show the app's functionality. Figure 10.2 describes the image requirements.

Specification	Description
Size	Minimum width or height of 320 pixels and maximum of 3,840 pixels—the maximum dimension may not be more than twice the minimum.
Format	24-bit PNG or JPEG format with no alpha (transparency) effects.

Fig. 10.2 | Screenshot specifications.

You can use the Android Device Monitor to capture device screenshots—this tool is installed with Android Studio and also helps you debug your apps that are running on emulators and devices. To obtain screenshots:

1. Run your app on an emulator or device.

2. In Android Studio, select **Tools > Android > Android Device Monitor** to open the Android Device Monitor.

3. In the **Devices** tab (Fig. 10.3), select the device from which you'd like to obtain a screen capture.

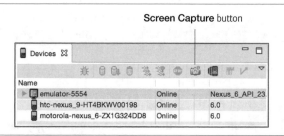

Fig. 10.3 | **Devices** window in the DDMS perspective.

4. Click the **Screen Capture** button to display the **Device Screen Capture** window.

5. After you've ensured that the screen is showing what you'd like to capture, click the **Save** button to save the image.

6. If you wish to change what's on your device's screen before saving an image, make the change on the device (or AVD), then press the **Refresh** button in the **Device Screen Capture** window to recapture the device's screen. You can also click **Rotate** to capture an image in landscape orientation.

For more information on the images you can include with your app listing, visit

```
https://support.google.com/googleplay/android-developer/answer/
    1078870
```

10.2.9 Promotional App Video

Google Play also allows you to include a URL for a short promotional video that's hosted on YouTube. To use this feature, you must sign up for a YouTube account and upload your video to the site. Figure 10.4 lists several promo video examples. Some videos show a person holding a device and interacting with the app. Others use screen captures. Figure 10.5 lists several video creation tools and services (some free, some paid). In additon, Android Studio provides a **Screen Record** tool in the **Android Monitor** window.

App	URL
Pac-Man 256	`https://youtu.be/RF0GfRvm-yg`
Angry Birds 2	`https://youtu.be/jOUEjknadEY`
Real Estate and Homes by Trulia®	`https://youtu.be/BJDPKBNuqzE`
Essential Anatomy 3	`https://youtu.be/xmBqxb0aZr8`

Fig. 10.4 | Examples of promotional videos for apps in Google Play.

Tools and services	URL
Animoto	`http://animoto.com`
Apptamin	`http://www.apptamin.com`
CamStudio™	`http://camstudio.org`
Jing	`http://www.techsmith.com/jing.html`
Camtasia Studio®	`http://www.techsmith.com/camtasia.html`
TurboDemo™	`http://www.turbodemo.com/eng/index.php`

Fig. 10.5 | Tools and services for creating promotional videos.

10.3 Pricing Your App: Free or Fee

You set the prices for your apps that are distributed through Google Play. Many developers offer their apps for free as a marketing, publicity and branding tool, earning revenue through increased sales of products and services, sales of more feature-rich versions of the same apps and sales of additional content through the apps using *in-app purchase* or *in-app advertising*. Figure 10.6 lists various ways to monetize your apps. The Google Play-specific ways to monetize your apps are listed at

`http://developer.android.com/distribute/monetize/index.html`

Ways to monetize an app
• Sell the app in Google Play.
• Sell the app in other Android app marketplaces.

Fig. 10.6 | Ways to monetize an app. (Part 1 of 2.)

Ways to monetize an app
• Sell paid upgrades.
• Sell virtual goods (Section 10.5).
• Sell an app to a company that brands it as their own.
• Use mobile advertising services for in-app ads (Section 10.4).
• Sell in-app advertising space directly to your customers.
• Use it to drive sales of a more feature-rich version of the app.

Fig. 10.6 | Ways to monetize an app. (Part 2 of 2.)

10.3.1 Paid Apps

The average price for apps varies widely by category. For example, according to the app discovery site AppBrain (`http://www.appbrain.com`), the average price for puzzle-game apps is $1.51 and for business apps is $8.44.[3] Although these prices may seem low, keep in mind that successful apps could sell tens of thousands, hundreds of thousands or even millions of copies.

When setting a price for your app, start by researching your competition. How much do they charge? Do their apps have similar functionality? Is yours more feature-rich? Will offering your app at a lower price than the competition attract users? Is your goal to recoup development costs and generate additional revenue?

If you change your strategy, you can eventually offer your paid app for free. However it's not currently possible to change your free apps to paid.

Financial transactions for paid apps in Google Play are handled by Google Wallet

```
http://google.com/wallet
```

though customers of some mobile carriers (such as AT&T, Sprint and T-Mobile) can opt to use carrier billing to charge paid apps to their wireless bill. Your earnings are paid to your Google Payments merchant account monthly.[4] You're responsible for paying taxes on the revenue you earn through Google Play.

10.3.2 Free Apps

More than 90% of the apps users download are free, and that percentage has been increasing for several years.[5] Given that users are more likely to download an app if it's free, consider offering a free "lite" version of your app to encourage users to try it. For example, if your app is a game, you might offer a free version with just the first few levels. When the user has finished playing the free levels, the app would offer an option to buy through Google Play your more robust app with numerous game levels. Or, your app would display a message that the user can purchase additional levels from within the app for a more

---

3. `http://www.appbrain.com/stats/android-market-app-categories.`
4. `http://support.google.com/googleplay/android-developer/answer/137997?hl=en&ref_topic=15867.`
5. `http://www.statista.com/topics/1002/mobile-app-usage/.`

seamless upgrade (see Section 10.5). Many companies use free apps to build brand awareness and drive sales of other products and services (Fig. 10.7).

Free app	Functionality
Amazon® Mobile	Browse and purchase items on Amazon.
Bank of America	Locate ATMs and bank branches in your area, check balances and pay bills.
Best Buy®	Browse and purchase items.
CNN	Get the latest world news, receive breaking news alerts and watch live video.
Epicurious Recipe	View thousands of recipes from several Condé Nast magazines, including *Gourmet* and *Bon Appetit*.
ESPN® ScoreCenter	Set up personalized scoreboards to track your favorite college and professional sports teams.
NFL Mobile	Get the latest NFL news and updates, live programming, NFL Replay and more.
UPS® Mobile	Track shipments, find drop-off locations, get estimated ship-ping costs and more.
NYTimes	Read articles from *The New York Times*, free of charge.
Pocket Agent™	State Farm Insurance's app enables you contact an agent, file claims, find local repair centers, check your State Farm bank and mutual fund accounts and more.
Progressive® Insurance	Report a claim and submit photos from the scene of a car acci-dent, find a local agent, get car safety information when you're shopping for a new car and more.
USA Today®	Read articles from *USA Today* and get the latest sports scores.
Wells Fargo® Mobile	Locate ATMs and bank branches in your area, check balances, make transfers and pay bills.
Women's Health Workouts Lite	View numerous workouts from one of the leading women's magazines.

Fig. 10.7 | Companies using free Android apps to build brand awareness.

10.4 Monetizing Apps with In-App Advertising

Many developers offer free apps monetized with in-app advertising—often banner ads
similar to those you find on websites. Mobile advertising networks such as AdMob

```
http://www.google.com/admob/
```

and Google AdSense for Mobile

```
http://www.google.com/adsense/start/
```

aggregate advertisers for you and serve relevant ads to your app (see Section 10.13). You
earn advertising revenue based on the number of click-throughs. The top 100 free apps
might earn a few hundred dollars to a few thousand dollars per day. In-app advertising

does not generate significant revenue for most apps, so if your goal is to recoup development costs and generate profits, you should consider charging a fee for your app.

10.5 Monetizing Apps: Using In-App Billing to Sell Virtual Goods

Google Play's in-app billing service

```
http://developer.android.com/google/play/billing/index.html
```

enables you to sell virtual goods (e.g., digital content) through apps on devices running Android 2.3 or higher (Fig. 10.8). The in-app billing service is available only for apps purchased through Google Play; it may *not* be used in apps sold through third-party app stores. To use in-app billing, you'll need a Google Play publisher account (see Section 10.6) and a Google Payments merchant account (see Section 10.7). Google pays you 70% of the revenue for all in-app purchases made through your apps.

Virtual goods		
Magazine e-subscriptions	Localized guides	Avatars
Virtual apparel	Additional game levels	Game scenery
Add-on features	Ringtones	Icons
E-cards	E-gifts	Virtual currency
Wallpapers	Images	Virtual pets
Audios	Videos	E-books and more

Fig. 10.8 | Virtual goods.

Selling virtual goods can generate higher revenue *per user* than in-app advertising.[6] Some apps that have been particularly successful selling virtual goods include Angry Birds, DragonVale, Zynga Poker, Bejeweled Blitz, NYTimes and Candy Crush Saga. Virtual goods are particularly popular in mobile games.

To implement in-app billing, follow the steps at

```
http://developer.android.com/google/play/billing/
    billing_integrate.html
```

For additional information about in-app billing, including subscriptions, sample apps, security best practices, testing and more, visit

```
http://developer.android.com/google/play/billing/
    billing_overview.html
```

You also can take the free *Selling In-app Products* training class at

```
http://developer.android.com/training/in-app-billing/index.html
```

---

6. `http://www.businessinsider.com/its-morning-in-venture-capital-2012-5?utm_source=readme&utm_medium=rightrail&utm_term=&utm_content=6&utm_campaign=recirc.`

In-App Purchase for Apps Sold Through Other App Marketplaces
If you choose to sell your apps through other marketplaces (see Section 10.11), several third-party mobile payment providers can enable you to build *in-app purchase* into your apps using APIs from mobile payment providers (Fig. 10.9)—you cannot use Google Play's in-app billing. Start by building the additional *locked functionality* (e.g., game levels, avatars) into your app. When the user opts to make a purchase, the in-app purchasing tool handles the financial transaction and returns a message to the app verifying payment. The app then unlocks the additional functionality.

Provider	URL	Description
PayPal Mobile Payments Library	`https://developer.paypal.com/webapps/developer/docs/classic/mobile/gs_MPL/`	Users click the **Pay with PayPal** button, log into their PayPal account, then click **Pay.**
Amazon In-App Purchasing	`https://developer.amazon.com/appsandservices/apis/earn/in-app-purchasing`	In-app purchase for apps sold through the Amazon App Store for Android.
Samsung In-App Purchase	`http://developer.samsung.com/in-app-purchase`	In-app purchase for apps designed specifically for Samsung devices.
Boku	`http://www.boku.com`	Users click **Pay by Mobile**, enter their mobile phone number, then complete the transaction by replying to a text message sent to their phone.

Fig. 10.9 | Mobile payment providers for in-app purchase.

10.6 Registering at Google Play

To publish your apps on Google Play, you must register for an account at

`http://play.google.com/apps/publish`

There's a one-time $25 registration fee. Unlike other popular mobile platforms, *Google Play has no approval process for uploading apps*, though there is some automated malware testing. You must, however, adhere to the *Google Play Developer Program Policies*. If your app is in violation of these policies, it can be removed at any time; serious or repeated violations may result in account termination (Fig. 10.10).

Violations of the *Google Play Content Policy for Developers*

- Infringing on others' intellectual property rights (e.g., trademarks, patents and copyrights).
- Illegal activities.

- Invading personal privacy.
- Interfering with the services of other parties.
- Harming the user's device or personal data.
- Gambling.

Fig. 10.10 | Some violations of the *Google Play Content Policy for Developers* (`http://play.google.com/about/developer-content-policy.html#showlanguages`). (Part 1 of 2.)

> **Violations of the *Google Play Content Policy for Developers***
>
> - Creating a "spammy" user experience (e.g., misleading the user about the app's purpose).
> - Adversely impacting a user's service charges or a wireless carrier's network.
> - Impersonation or deception.
> - Promoting hate or violence.
> - Providing pornographic or obscene content, or anything unsuitable for children under age 18.
> - Ads in system-level notifications and widgets.

Fig. 10.10 | Some violations of the *Google Play Content Policy for Developers* (`http://play.google.com/about/developer-content-policy.html#showlanguages`). (Part 2 of 2.)

10.7 Setting Up a Google Payments Merchant Account

To sell your apps on Google Play, you'll need a Google Payments merchant account, available to Google Play developers in over 150 countries.[7] Once you've registered and logged into Google Play at

```
http://play.google.com/apps/publish/
```

click the **set up a merchant account** link and provide

- information by which Google can contact you and
- customer-support contact information where users can contact you.

10.8 Uploading Your Apps to Google Play

Once you've prepared your files and you're ready to upload your app, review the steps in the *Launch Checklist* at:

```
http://developer.android.com/distribute/tools/launch-checklist.html
```

Then log into Google Play at `http://play.google.com/apps/publish` (Section 10.6) and click the **Publish an Android App on Google Play** button to begin the upload process. You will be asked to upload the following assets:

1. *App .apk file* that includes the app's code files, assets, resources and the manifest file.
2. At least *two screenshots* of your app to be included in Google Play. You may include screenshots for an Android phone, 7" tablet, 10" tablet, Android TV and Android Wear.
3. *High-resolution app icon* (512-by-512 pixels) to be included in Google Play.
4. *Feature graphic* is used by the Google Play Editorial team to promote apps and on your app's product page. This image must be 1024 pixels wide by 500 pixels tall in JPEG format or 24-bit PNG format with no alpha (transparency).
5. *Promotional graphic* (optional) for Google Play to be used by Google if they decide to promote your app (for examples, check out some of the graphics for fea-

---

7. `http://support.google.com/googleplay/android-developer/answer/150324?hl=en&ref_topic=15867`.

tured apps on Google Play). The graphic must be 180 pixels wide by 120 pixels tall in JPEG format or 24-bit PNG format with no alpha (transparency).

6. *Promotional video* (optional) to be included in Google Play. You may include a URL for a promotional video for your app (e.g., a YouTube link to a video that demonstrates how your app works).

In addition to app assets, you will be asked to provide the following additional listing details for Google Play:

1. *Language.* By default, your app will be listed in English. If you'd like to list it in additional languages, select them from the list provided (Fig. 10.11).

Language			
Afrikaans	English (UK)	Khmer	Romansh
Amharic	Estonian	Korean (South)	Russian
Arabic	Filipino	Kyrgyz	Serbian
Armenian	Finnish	Lao	Sinhala
Azerbaijani	French	Latvian	Slovak
Basque	French (Canada)	Lithuanian	Slovenian
Belarusian	Galician	Macedonian	Spanish (Latin America)
Bengali	Georgian	Malay	Spanish (Spain)
Bulgarian	German	Malayalam	Spanish (US)
Burmese	Greek	Marathi	Swahili
Catalan	Hebrew	Mongolian	Swedish
Chinese (Simplified)	Hindi	Nepali	Tamil
Chinese (Traditional)	Hungarian	Norwegian	Telugu
Croatian	Icelandic	Persian	Thai
Czech	Indonesian	Polish	Turkish
Danish	Italian	Portuguese (Brazil)	Ukrainian
Dutch	Japanese	Portuguese (Portugal)	Vietnamese
English	Kannada	Romanian	Zulu

Fig. 10.11 | Languages for listing apps in Google Play.

2. *Title.* The title of your app as it will appear in Google Play (30 characters maximum). It does *not* need to be unique among all Android apps.

3. *Short description.* A short description of your app (80 characters maximum).

4. *Description.* A description of your app and its features (4,000 characters maximum). It's recommended that you use the last portion of the description to explain why the app requires each permission and how it's used.

5. *Recent changes.* A walkthrough of any changes specific to the latest version of your app (500 characters maximum).

6. *Promo text.* The promotional text for marketing your app (80 characters max).

7. *Application type.* Choose **Applications** or **Games**.

8. *Category.* Select the category that best suits your game or app.

9. *Price.* To sell your app for a fee, you'll need to set up a merchant account.

10. *Content rating.* You may select **High Maturity**, **Medium Maturity**, **Low Maturity** or **Everyone**. For more information, see *Rating your application content for Google Play* at

```
http://support.google.com/googleplay/android-developer/answer/
      188189
```

11. *Locations.* By default, the app will be listed in all current and future Google Play countries. If you do not want your app to be available in all these countries, you may pick and choose specific ones where you'd like your app to be listed.

12. *Website.* A **Visit Developer's Website** link will be included in your app's listing in Google Play. Provide a direct link to the page on your website where users interested in downloading your app can find more information, including marketing copy, feature listings, additional screenshots, instructions, etc.

13. *E-mail.* Your e-mail address will also be included in Google Play, so that customers can contact you with questions, report errors, etc.

14. *Phone number.* Sometimes your phone number is included in Google Play. Therefore it's recommended that you leave this field blank unless you provide phone support. You may want to provide a customer-service phone number on your website.

15. *Privacy policy.* A link to your privacy policy.

In addition, if you sell in-app products or use any Google services, you must add your in-app products and specify the services you use. For information on adding in-app products, visit

```
http://developer.android.com/google/play/billing/billing_admin.html
```

10.9 Launching **Play Store** from Within Your App

To drive additional sales of your apps, you can launch the **Play Store** app (Google Play) from within your app (typically by including a button) so that the user can download other apps you've published or purchase a related app with functionality beyond that of the previously downloaded "lite" version. You also can launch the **Play Store** app to enable users to download the latest updates.

There are two ways to launch the **Play Store** app. First, you can bring up Google Play search results for apps with a specific developer name, package name or string of characters. For example, if you want to encourage users to download other apps you've published, you could include a button in your app that, when touched, launches the **Play Store** app and initiates a search for apps containing your name or company name. The second option is to bring the user to the details page in the **Play Store** app for a specific app. To learn about launching **Play Store** from within an app, see *Linking Your Products* at

```
http://developer.android.com/distribute/tools/promote/linking.html
```

10.10 Managing Your Apps in Google Play

The *Google Play Developer Console* allows you to manage your account and your apps, check users' star ratings for your apps (1 to 5 stars), respond to users' comments, track the overall number of installs of each app and the number of active installs (installs minus uninstalls). You can view installation trends and the distribution of app downloads across Android versions, devices, and more. Crash reports list any crash and freeze information from users. If you've made upgrades to your app, you can easily publish the new version. You can remove the app from Google Play, but users who downloaded it previously may keep it on their devices. Users who uninstalled the app will be able to reinstall it even after it's been removed (it will remain on Google's servers unless it's removed for violating the Terms of Service).

10.11 Other Android App Marketplaces

You may choose to make your apps available through other Android app marketplaces (Fig. 10.12), or through your own website using services such as AndroidLicenser (http://www.androidlicenser.com). To learn more about releasing your app through a website see

```
http://developer.android.com/tools/publishing/
    publishing_overview.html
```

Marketplace	URL
Amazon Appstore	`https://developer.amazon.com/public/solutions/platforms/android`
Opera Mobile Store	`http://android.oms.apps.opera.com/en_us/`
Moborobo	`http://www.moborobo.com`
Appitalism®	`http://www.appitalism.com/index.html`
GetJar	`http://www.getjar.com`
SlideMe	`http://www.slideme.org`
AndroidPIT	`http://www.androidpit.com`

Fig. 10.12 | Other Android app marketplaces.

10.12 Other Mobile App Platforms and Porting Your Apps

According to statista.com, users will download approximately 225 billion apps in 2016 and almost 270 billion in 2017.[8] By porting your Android apps to other mobile app platforms (Fig. 10.13), especially to iOS (for iPhone, iPad and iPod Touch devices), you could reach an even bigger audience. There are various tools to help you port your apps. For example, Microsoft provides tools that iOS and Android developers can use to port apps to Windows, and similar tools exist for porting Android apps to iOS and vice versa.[9] Various cross-platform app-development tools are also available (Fig. 10.14).

---

8. `http://www.statista.com/statistics/266488/forecast-of-mobile-app-downloads/`.
9. `http://www.wired.com/2015/04/microsoft-unveils-tools-moving-android-ios-apps-onto-windows/`.

Platform	URL
Android	`http://developer.android.com`
iOS (Apple)	`http://developer.apple.com/ios`
Windows	`https://dev.windows.com/en-us/windows-apps`

Fig. 10.13 | Popular mobile app platforms.

Tool	Website
Appcelerator Titanium	`http://www.appcelerator.com/product/`
PhoneGap	`http://phonegap.com/`
Sencha	`https://www.sencha.com/`
Visual Studio	`https://www.visualstudio.com/en-us/features/mobile-app-development-vs.aspx`
Xamarin	`https://xamarin.com/`

Fig. 10.14 | Several tools for developing cross-platform mobile apps—there are many more.

10.13 Marketing Your Apps

Once your app has been published, you'll want to market it to your audience.[10] *Viral marketing* through social media sites such as Facebook, Twitter, Google+ and YouTube can help you get your message out. These sites have tremendous visibility. According to a Pew Research Center study, 71% of adults on the Internet use social networks.[11] Figure 10.15 lists some of the most popular social media sites. Also, e-mail and electronic newsletters are still effective and often inexpensive marketing tools.

Name	URL	Description
Facebook	`http://www.facebook.com`	Social networking
Instagram	`https://instagram.com/`	Photo and video sharing
Twitter	`http://www.twitter.com`	Microblogging, social networking
Google+	`http://plus.google.com`	Social networking
Vine	`http://vine.co`	Social video sharing
Tumblr	`http://www.tumblr.com`	Blogging
Groupon	`http://www.groupon.com`	Daily deals

Fig. 10.15 | Popular social media sites. (Part 1 of 2.)

---

10. There are many books about mobile app marketing. Check out the latest ones at `http://amzn.to/1ZgpYxZ`.

11. `http://bits.blogs.nytimes.com/2015/01/09/americans-use-more-online-social-networks/?_r=0`.

Name	URL	Description
Foursquare	`http://www.foursquare.com`	Check-in
Snapchat	`http://www.snapchat.com`	Video messaging
Pinterest	`http://www.pinterest.com`	Online pinboard
YouTube	`http://www.youtube.com`	Video sharing
LinkedIn	`http://www.linkedin.com`	Social networking for business
Flickr	`http://www.flickr.com`	Photo sharing

Fig. 10.15 | Popular social media sites. (Part 2 of 2.)

Facebook

Facebook, the premier social networking site, has nearly 1.5 billion active users[12] with almost one billion active daily.[13] It's an excellent resource for *viral marketing*. Start by setting up an official Facebook page for your app or business. Use the page to post app information, news, updates, reviews, tips, videos, screenshots, high scores for games, user feedback and links to Google Play, where users can download your app. For example, we post news and updates about Deitel publications on our Facebook page at `http://www.facebook.com/DeitelFan`.

Next, you need to spread the word. Encourage your co-workers and friends to "like" your Facebook page and ask their friends to do so as well. As people interact with your page, stories will appear in their friends' news feeds, building awareness to a growing audience.

Twitter

Twitter is a microblogging, social networking site with approximately 1 billion users and 316 million monthly active users.[14] You post tweets—messages of 140 characters or less. Twitter then distributes your tweets to all of your followers (at the time of this writing, one famous pop star had over 40 million followers). Many people use Twitter to track news and trends. Tweet about your app—include announcements about new releases, tips, facts, comments from users, etc. Also, encourage your colleagues and friends to tweet about your app. Use a *hashtag* (#) to reference your app. For example, when tweeting about *Android 6 for Programmers* on our `@deitel` Twitter feed, we use the hashtag `#AndroidFP3`. Others may use this hashtag as well to write comments about the book. This enables you to easily search tweets for related messages.

Viral Video

Viral video—shared on video sites (e.g., YouTube), on social networking sites (e.g., Facebook, Instagram, Twitter, Google+), through e-mail, etc.—is another great way to spread the word about your app. If you create a compelling video, perhaps one that's humorous or even outrageous, it may quickly rise in popularity and may be tagged by users across multiple social networks.

---

12. `http://www.statista.com/statistics/272014/global-social-networks-ranked-by-number-of-users/`.
13. `http://expandedramblings.com/index.php/by-the-numbers-17-amazing-facebook-stats/`.
14. `http://www.statisticbrain.com/twitter-statistics/`.

E-Mail Newsletters
If you have an e-mail newsletter, use it to promote your app. Include links to Google Play, where users can download the app. Also include links to your social networking pages, where users can stay up-to-date with the latest news about your app.

App Reviews
Contact influential bloggers and app review sites (Fig. 10.16) and tell them about your app. Provide them with a promotional code to download your app for free (see Section 10.3). Influential bloggers and reviewers receive many requests, so keep yours concise and informative. Many app reviewers post video app reviews on YouTube and other sites (Fig. 10.17).

Android app review site	URL
Appolicious™	http://www.androidapps.com
AppBrain	http://www.appbrain.com
AppZoom	http://www.appzoom.com
Appstorm	http://android.appstorm.net
Best Android Apps Review	http://www.bestandroidappsreview.com
Android App Review Source	http://www.androidappreviewsource.com
Androinica	http://www.androinica.com
AndroidLib	http://www.androlib.com
Android and Me	http://www.androidandme.com
AndroidGuys	http://www.androidguys.com/category/reviews
Android Police	http://www.androidpolice.com
AndroidPIT	http://www.androidpit.com
Phandroid	http://phandroid.com

Fig. 10.16 | Android app review sites.

Android app review video site	URL
State of Tech	http://http://stateoftech.net/
Crazy Mike's Apps	http://crazymikesapps.com
Appolicious™	http://www.appvee.com/?device_filter=android
Life of Android™	http://www.lifeofandroid.com/video/

Fig. 10.17 | Android app review video sites.

Internet Public Relations
The public relations industry uses media outlets to help companies get their message out to consumers. Public relations practitioners incorporate blogs, tweets, podcasts, RSS feeds

and social media into their PR campaigns. Figure 10.18 lists some free and fee-based Internet public relations resources, including press-release distribution sites, press-release writing services and more.

Internet public relations resource	URL	Description
Free Services		
PRWeb®	http://www.prweb.com	Online press-release distribution service with *free* and *fee-based* services.
ClickPress™	http://www.clickpress.com	Submit news stories for approval (*free* of charge). If approved, they'll be available on the ClickPress site and to news search engines. For a *fee*, ClickPress will distribute your press releases globally to top financial newswires.
PRLog	http://www.prlog.org/pub/	*Free* press-release submission and distribution.
Newswire	http://www.newswire.com	*Free* and *fee-based* press-release submission and distribution.
openPR®	http://www.openpr.com	*Free* press-release publication.
Fee-Based Services		
PR Leap	http://www.prleap.com	Online press-release distribution service.
Marketwired	http://www.marketwired.com	Press-release distribution service allows you to target your audience by geography, industry, etc.
Mobility PR	http://www.mobilitypr.com	Public relations services for companies in the mobile industry.
eReleases	http://www.ereleases.com	Press-release distribution and services including press-release writing, proofreading and editing. Check out the tips for writing effective press releases.

Fig. 10.18 | Internet public relations resources.

Mobile Advertising Networks

Purchasing advertising spots (e.g., in other apps, online, in newspapers and magazines or on radio and television) is another way to market your app. Mobile advertising networks (Fig. 10.19) specialize in advertising Android (and other) mobile apps on mobile platforms. Many of these networks can target audiences by location, wireless carrier, platform (e.g., Android, iOS, Windows, BlackBerry) and more. Most apps don't make much money, so be careful how much you spend on advertising.

Mobile ad networks	URL
AdMob (by Google)	http://www.google.com/admob/
Medialets	http://www.medialets.com
Tapjoy®	http://www.tapjoy.com
Millennial Media®	http://www.millennialmedia.com/
Smaato®	http://www.smaato.com
mMedia™	http://mmedia.com
InMobi™	http://www.inmobi.com

Fig. 10.19 | Mobile advertising networks.

You also can use mobile advertising networks to monetize your free apps by including ads (e.g., banners, videos) in your apps. The average eCPM (effective cost per 1,000 impressions) for ads in Android apps varies by network, device, world region, etc. Most ads on Android pay are based on the *click-through rate* (*CTR*) of the ads rather than the number of impressions generated. Like eCPM, CTRs vary based on the app, the device, targeting of the ads by the ad network and more. If your app has a lot of users and the CTRs of the ads in your apps are high, you may earn substantial advertising revenue. Also, your ad network may serve you higher-paying ads, thus increasing your earnings.

10.14 Wrap-Up

In this chapter, we walked through the process of registering for Google Play and setting up a Google Wallet account so you can sell your apps. We discussed how to prepare apps for submission to Google Play, including testing them on the emulator and on Android devices, and the various resources you'll need to submit your app to Google Play. We walked through the steps for uploading your apps to Google Play. We showed you alternative Android app marketplaces. We provided tips for pricing your apps, and resources for monetizing them with in-app advertising and in-app sales of virtual goods. And we included resources for marketing your apps, once they're available through Google Play.

Staying in Contact with the Authors and Deitel & Associates, Inc.

We hope you enjoyed reading *Android 6 for Programmers* as much as we enjoyed writing it. We'd appreciate your feedback. Please send your questions, comments and suggestions to deitel@deitel.com. To stay up-to-date with the latest news about *Android 6 for Programmers*, and Deitel publications and corporate training, sign up for the *Deitel® Buzz Online* e-mail newsletter at

> http://www.deitel.com/newsletter/subscribe.html

and follow us on social media at

- Facebook—http://facebook.com/DeitelFan
- Twitter—http://twitter.com/deitel
- Google+—http://google.com/+DeitelFan

- YouTube—`http://youtube.com/DeitelTV`
- LinkedIn—`http://bit.ly/DeitelLinkedIn`

To learn more about Deitel & Associates' worldwide on-site programming training for your company or organization, visit

`http://www.deitel.com/training`

or e-mail `deitel@deitel.com`. Good luck!

Index

LiveLessons Video Training from Paul Deitel

Andriod™ 6 App-Development Fundamentals LiveLessons, Third Edition, presents the Deitels' app-driven approach to Android app development with many hours of expert video training! Watch, listen, and learn as Paul Deitel guides you through building and coding complete, working Android apps.

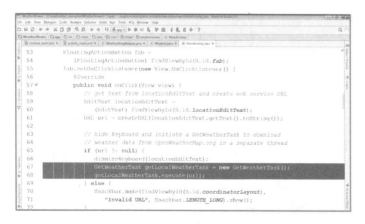

This and other Paul Deitel LiveLessons videos are available in Safari Books Online (www.safaribooksonline.com) and as individual downloads at mylivelessons.com.